Means, Motives, and Opportunities

Means, Motives, and Opportunities illuminates how states spend public money through the lens of governmental structure, executive power, and interest group competition. Christian Breunig and Chris Koski argue that policymaking is a function of not only policymakers' means (powers) but also of their motives (issues) and opportunities (interest group competition) for change. Using over twenty-five years of data across all fifty US states, four in-depth case studies, and multiple examples of budget battles, the book describes a budget-making environment in which governors must balance the preferences of interest groups with their own, all while attempting to build a budget that roughly balances. While governors are uniquely powerful, the range of changes they can make is largely impacted by interest group competition. By showing how means, motives, and opportunities matter, the book illuminates how spending decisions at the state level influence nearly every aspect of American life.

Christian Breunig is Professor of Comparative Politics at the University of Konstanz and Director of the German Policy Agendas project. He has received three awards from the American Political Science Association and was a policy fellow at the Center for Advanced Study in the Behavioral Sciences at Stanford University in 2022–2023.

Chris Koski is Professor of Political Science and Daniel B. Greenberg Chair of Environmental Studies at Reed College in Portland, Oregon. He chaired the Public Policy (2022–2023) and Science, Technology, and Environmental Policy (2020–2023) sections of the American Political Science Association and is the coauthor of *The Real World of American Politics: A Documentary Introduction* (2022).

Means, Motives, and Opportunities

How Executives and Interest Groups Set Public Policy

CHRISTIAN BREUNIG
University of Konstanz

CHRIS KOSKI
Reed College

Shaftesbury Road, Cambridge CB2 8EA, United Kingdom

One Liberty Plaza, 20th Floor, New York, NY 10006, USA

477 Williamstown Road, Port Melbourne, VIC 3207, Australia

314–321, 3rd Floor, Plot 3, Splendor Forum, Jasola District Centre,
New Delhi – 110025, India

103 Penang Road, #05–06/07, Visioncrest Commercial, Singapore 238467

Cambridge University Press is part of Cambridge University Press & Assessment,
a department of the University of Cambridge.

We share the University's mission to contribute to society through the pursuit of
education, learning and research at the highest international levels of excellence.

www.cambridge.org
Information on this title: www.cambridge.org/9781009428590

DOI: 10.1017/9781009428583

First published 2024

A catalogue record for this publication is available from the British Library

Library of Congress Cataloging-in-Publication Data
NAMES: Breunig, Christian, 1974– author. | Koski, Chris, author.
TITLE: Means, motives, and opportunities : how executives and interest
groups set public policy / Christian Breunig, Chris Koski.
DESCRIPTION: Cambridge ; New York, NY : Cambridge University Press, 2024. |
Includes bibliographical references and index.
IDENTIFIERS: LCCN 2023037160 | ISBN 9781009428590 (hardback) |
ISBN 9781009428606 (paperback) | ISBN 9781009428583 (ebook)
SUBJECTS: LCSH: Governors – United States – States. | Governors – Powers and duties. |
Pressure groups – United States – States. | Political planning – United States – States. |
U.S. states – Appropriations and expenditures.
CLASSIFICATION: LCC JK2447 .B677 2024 | DDC 320.60973–dc23/eng/20231120
LC record available at https://lccn.loc.gov/2023037160

ISBN 978-1-009-42859-0 Hardback
ISBN 978-1-009-42860-6 Paperback

Cambridge University Press & Assessment has no responsibility for the persistence
or accuracy of URLs for external or third-party internet websites referred to in this
publication and does not guarantee that any content on such websites is, or will
remain, accurate or appropriate.

For Onnie, Mio, & Felix
For Amy, Damien, & Mikko

Contents

Contents

Figures

Tables

Acknowledgments

This work began in our first quarter of the PhD program at the University of Washington in the fall of 2001 – where we met in Bryan Jones' "Theories of Decision-Making" class. The resulting book represents the culmination of our decades-long study of the policy process and state budgets. Along the way we got married, started families, finished our PhDs, took our first jobs, and then took our second jobs.

Most of this book, despite advances in technology, has been written side by side. At a kitchen table in a Seattle basement apartment, a lobby in a Chicago hotel, a home office in Portland, and university offices at the University of Konstanz, Reed College, and finally at Stanford University. Often in the academy, we measure progress in chairs – in our case, tables have proved far more valuable.

We did not complete this task without a lot of help from graduate school colleagues, mentors, discussants at conferences, referees, colleagues at our own various institutions, participants in a book workshop, and resources from multiple institutions. And while the list is long, it is also the case that over these twenty years, we may not remember all those that have helped us.

We have been incredibly fortunate to benefit from the mentorship of Bryan Jones and Frank Baumgartner, who both have read drafts of this book and other work that preceded it. They have been our advocates over these many long years.

We also held a book workshop at Reed College which Frank and Bryan attended, along with Thad Kousser, Graeme Boushey, and Ellen Seljan, who all took two days out of their lives to discuss our initial manuscript. It is safe to say this book would not have been possible without the critical and constructive input we received there. Special thanks to Emily Hebbron at Reed College for organizing this invaluable conference.

Along the way, we have had a number of faculty across North America and Europe offer us helpful comments, including (in no particular order):

Chris Wlezien, Derek Epp, David Lowery, Chris Adolph, John Wilkerson, Tim LaPira, Christoph Knill, Shana Rose, James True, Peter May, Mark Smith, Joachim Wehner, Christoffer Green-Petersen, Heike Klüver, and Peter John.

Unlike many academic products, no grad students contributed to this project. Nat Rubin helped research and cowrote Chapter 6 as well as provided research on state budget stories throughout while an undergraduate at Reed. We owe Nat a great deal of thanks and look forward to seeing them succeed as a PhD student at Columbia University.

We were blessed with an incredibly supportive cohort of graduate students while at the University of Washington. They helped us in jump-starting and developing our research agenda. Graeme Boushey, Rose Ernst, Peter Mortensen, and Sam Workman have been intimately involved in this project and offered us extensive feedback.

We have also benefited from numerous conference discussants at the Comparative Agendas Project, Midwest Political Science Association, American Political Science Association, and we extend a specific shout-out to the unnamed Hawaiian budget officer who was the only person (not just in the audience – all other panelists had dropped out) at our first conference ever. Thank you, sir, for hearing us out.

Two anonymous reviewers for Cambridge University Press greatly improved the book. And, of course, this publication would literally not have been possible without the support of Rachel Blaifeder, our editor at Cambridge University Press, who has been encouraging, efficient, and an incredible help along the way.

Our work was funded by a number of different institutions. From Reed College, this work was partially supported by the Bernard Goldhammer Summer Collaborative Research Grant Program, the Goldschmidt Fellowship, the Ducey Fund, and the Department of Political Science. This work was additionally supported by funds from the University of Konstanz. The Center for Advanced Studies in the Behavioral Sciences at Stanford University provided the final table for us to finish the job.

PART I

SETTING PUBLIC POLICY

Explaining One Million Policy Stories

On March 25, 2020, Democratic Governor of Minnesota Tim Walz announced that his state would be short of the hospital beds needed to cope with the impending demand from the COVID-19 pandemic. Governor Walz was not alone. Governors across the United States struggled to cope with a national health crisis for which the federal government offered little in the way of coordinated assistance. Hospital policy watchers in Minnesota must have looked on with some bemusement, given that Minnesota state code has had a standing moratorium on hospital construction since the mid-1980s specifically to avoid the *oversupply* of hospital beds.

Walz may have been even shorter of hospital beds were it not for a 2005 exception that allowed the construction of Maple Grove Hospital in the eponymous suburb of Minneapolis in 2009 (Yee, 2009). Hospital consolidations and massive suburban growth since the 1990s led legislators and the then-governor, Republican Tim Pawlenty, to reconsider the long-standing hospital construction moratorium. Maple Grove was one of the fastest-growing suburbs in the state and represented a logical choice for a new 300-bed hospital. The challenge for this and any project at the state level was that, while certainly a significant change to hospital policies, the relatively small matter of Maple Grove hospital had to compete with much larger issues. In this moment, hospital expansion competed for attention with headline-grabbing debates over broader health-care funding and perennial challenges associated with education funding. Pawlenty ultimately created an exception for Maple Grove, but it was not as certain as the obvious problem definition might suggest.

Pawlenty, Walz, and governors from other states have significant means at their disposal to affect public policy outcomes – particularly budget outcomes. Governors, by design, instigate the budget-making process and have powerful tools to alter legislative outputs. Nearly all governors in the United States have the power to veto legislation and most, like Pawlenty, have the power to veto particular parts of legislation using a line-item veto. Issues – such as hospital

expansion, medical payment reform, or education funding – motivate particular governors to intervene in policymaking. Governors' attempts to change
policies in issue areas is framed by the interest group environment. Given that
gubernatorial attention is ultimately limited, governors must choose when to
use their powers based not just on a desire to change policy, but also on the
opportunities interest groups provide them.

Pawlenty saw his primary political opportunity in the form of a budget designed to cut spending, particularly the "welfare health costs" found
in the state's MinnesotaCare Medicaid program (Scheck, 2005c). A political
firestorm resulted and engulfed the entire agenda, prompting each chamber of
the Minnesota legislature (the Senate controlled by the Democratic–Farmer–
Labor (DFL) Party and the House controlled by Republicans) to respond with
their own changes. As the two sides failed to agree on a budget, a special
session lasted nearly two months. Disagreement continued, causing a partial
government shutdown on July 1, 2005 (Scheck, 2005a). Back at work, after
a marathon session on July 13 – apparently working so hard that they blew a
transformer, resulting in a power outage for an hour – DFLers and Republicans agreed to a larger budget than Pawlenty proposed. This budget entailed
a MinnesotaCare expansion (Scheck, 2005b) and a significant increase in the
education budget. Maple Grove hospital, however, was tabled during the regular session in finance committees and never made it to the agenda of the 2005
special session. Pawlenty's policy agenda of a smaller budget, cuts to MinnesotaCare, and the expansion of Maple Grove appeared to not go as planned –
even though Pawlenty could have vetoed items from the budget. Despite being
highly motivated by issues and possessing the means to change policy, Pawlenty
ultimately did not see the right opportunity in 2005.

The Minnesota budget story is ubiquitous in states across America, and the
common explanation typically describes governors and legislators grappling
with competing priorities exacerbated by partisan differences. Less apparent in
the telling of these stories, however, is the role of interest groups in shaping the
environment in which budget battles are fought – what we describe as providing opportunities for policy change. In the 2005 Minnesota case, both health
care and education are large portions of the budget but have different interest group environments. Groups involved in education tend to be relatively
few: teachers' associations and often localities, who may be asked to shoulder
more of the fiscal burden of education. Education Minnesota, as a major labor
union, attempted to pull incremental increases from the budget. Minnesota
legislators and governors, regardless of party, know that Education Minnesota
dominates the interest group environment surrounding education policy. The
passage of the 2005 budget provided opportunities for all branches and all parties to claim some credit for adding a modest increase to the education budget,
while education cuts would come at significant political expense.

The health-care budget environment, in contrast, was framed by many stable interests, including: the Children's Defense Fund, the Minnesota Hospital

Association, the Minnesota Medical Association, the Minnesota chapter of the National Alliance for the Mentally Ill, and the Minnesota Citizens Concerned for Life (Scheck, 2005b). The interests in each budget area seek what funding they can from the budget in a zero-sum game with each other. Minnesota State Human Services Commissioner Kevin Goodno characterized the conflict in this sector: "The money isn't being taken out of the health care access fund to solve road problems; it's being taken out of the health care access fund to solve health care cost problems. And so it is being spent on health care" (McCallum 2005, para 14; Scheck 2005b). Republican Senator Brian LeClair disagreed: "If you believe that that is our number one priority, even at the expense of K-12 education, even at the expense of higher education and public safety, if you believe that welfare health care is the number one priority in state government, well this bill is great for you" (Scheck, 2005d, para. 9). Governors and other policymakers know that these interests will be around next year and will remember if their funds are cut so another interest's funds can be increased or spared.

The hospital sector in Minnesota does not benefit from a large hegemonic group like Education Minnesota. And, unlike MinnesotaCare advocates, hospital politics are not fought by multiple strong interest groups. Instead, the few groups who supported the new hospital were also competing to be the entity that built it. The interest group environment, in other words, was less clear for hospitals than it was for education and health care. In the fog of the 2005 budget battle, the governor and the legislature had simply less reliable pressure in pursuing an exception to the hospital moratorium than they did for other issues. Pawlenty was clearly motivated to pursue the exception and possessed the means to do so – even considering a second legislative session – but the opportunities provided by the interest group environment were not there given other agenda items. Later, in 2006, the legislature met and rapidly passed what appeared to be a minor bill for one hospital but resulted in a major shift in policy: an exception to a twenty-year moratorium on hospital construction resulting in the 2009 completion of Maple Grove. The next major shift in hospital policy would come fourteen years later when, on March 31, 2020 (six days after announcing a shortage), Governor Walz announced that he would identify space for 2,750 beds – double the state's pre-COVID supply.

1.1 FROM ONE TO ONE MILLION POLICY STORIES

The tale of Maple Grove hospital is illustrative of the myriad stories that emerge from the politics of public budgets. Long-time budget expert James True is known among colleagues and friends to marvel that a single public budget contains a million policy stories. Potentially seen as a ruse to tempt students to study what might otherwise be considered a dry, technical field, policy scholars understand that the choice to allocate resources is fundamentally a political act. Given that all policy represents governmental commitment and that governments create, destroy, or, in most cases, continue myriad policies in any given budget cycle, it would be difficult to count the number of policy stories contained within one budget.

In the United States, the number of budget stories is compounded by a litany of subgovernments. State governments, in particular, are granted formal authority to engage in independent revenue generation, expenditure, and, by the transitive property, policymaking. All governments make budgeting decisions in environments of changing problem definitions, newly emergent issues, varying degrees of political will, and some level of fiscal constraint. Policymakers understand that spending decisions are fundamentally no different from policy choices. Dye (1984, p. 2) famously notes that "public policy is whatever governments choose to do or not to do"; a modified version might include "and how much governments pay for it."

Public budgets represent a unique form of policymaking. Budgeting processes are peculiar, technical, and largely overlooked in the broader discourse of policy making. To the extent that budgets are discussed beyond technocrats and elites, reporting on public budgets is less about process and more about who gets what and how much they get.

A general approach to understanding public policy via budget decisions is to attempt to understand one, a handful, or a group of these policy stories. The challenge with this approach is that many policy decisions are described by many policy scholars and many policy theories. Because there are a million different policy stories, the literature is fragmented. Understanding one public budgeting decision may not necessarily help us understand another.

One way to escape this fragmented literature is to examine fiscal policy focused on the fiscal health of a state, rather than that focused on individual categorical spending. This logic meets a political reality in which most people – citizens and politicians – care far less about the fiscal health of governments and care far more about getting what they want. Policymakers, interest groups, and citizens attempt to move budgets to create centrifugal forces that allocate changes in budgeting decisions (either cuts or increases) toward extreme points beyond the current equilibrium.

Most of the time, these centripetal forces win the day, as budgets simply may not change dramatically from one year to another. Of course, many examples show this is not always the case. The National Aeronautical Space Administration's (NASA) budget has swung wildly over the years, spiking in the 1960s and plummeting in the 2000s. NASA's story is far from unique, however, not just because other areas of the budget experience large or erratic changes, but because these erratic changes are tied to constituents or political actors' desires. In NASA's case, it was obvious: The policy goal of putting a person on the moon mandated massive funding, while phasing out crewed space flight was also a reflection of priorities that resulted in real budget consequences. In the policy literature, this type of fluctuation is a "punctuation," a relativistic term requiring a holistic understanding of a budget. Budget changes are frequently incremental; when change occurs, however, it is sweeping and extraordinary.

When thinking about changes in public budgets, the politics of the past and present dominate the spending of the future. Public budget choices must be explicitly interdependent, given the relatively fixed pie of available resources. While such is the norm for any policymaking process, budgeting decisions draw otherwise disconnected parties into the decision-making process. Decisions to fund special needs education compete with choices to expand winter elk habitat, and each of these may be dependent on a debate regarding the definition of chewing gum as "food" for purposes of taxation. Annual and biannual struggles over budgeting decisions are both embedded in and affect the long-term trajectory of budget changes. The politics associated with the distribution of budget changes in a category varies beyond simple trends. Steady rises and declines are a function of a markedly different political environment than budgets that swing from steep annual increases to significant retrenchment. Moreover, the political environment resulting from a volatile budgeting environment is one that is uncertain for policymakers, interest groups, and, most importantly, citizens who depend on government programs.

In Section 1.2, we lay out the foundational elements of our argument, which is summarized here: Skilled and powerful governors respond to the interest group environment when allocating public monies. Interest groups operate around different policy issues that provide distinct long- and short-term gains. The interaction of issues, interest groups, and institutional powers of governors determines the dynamics of short-term budget changes and long-term growth. Public policy in the American states is driven by governors, whose opportunities are defined by interest groups that are responding to issues.

1.2 MOTIVES, MEANS, AND OPPORTUNITIES

Well-intended attempts to understand a budget as the sum of individual budget item choices produces a cacophonous explanation. The impulse to focus on individual decisions, such as special needs education, winter elk range, or NASA funding, is primarily born from necessity rather than desire. Public budgets are large and intricate documents. While we might like to understand the entirety of the budgetary process to explain one particular choice, the reality is that there are too many stories to tell.

Though public budgets are important in and of themselves, they also help explain broad patterns of policy change. Along with other scholars (Epp, 2018; Jacoby and Schneider, 2001), we start from the position that public budgets are policy aggregates, in that they consist of bundles of interdependent decision-making. Decisions that determine the composition of budgets originate from particularistic interests. Interests represent themselves and are represented by policymakers who have varying institutional power to intervene in the budgeting process. In short, budgets are decisions (a) made within issue domains (b) by governors who must contend with (c) a political environment framed by interest groups.

In this section, we use this background to build a theory of public policy and budgeting. Budgeting is not just about how much money is allocated to one budget item in a year; budgeting *is* about how money is distributed across different spending items over longer periods of time. Our task in this book is to offer a framework that characterizes a policymaking environment in which institutions and issues interact to explain (a) how governments prioritize spending and (b) the long-term impacts of these priorities. In the next few pages, we provide the three elements of our theory: motives, means, and opportunities. Motives represent the politics of issue domains, opportunities emerge from interest group competition within issue domains, and governors possess the means to formally affect budget change in issue domains.

1.2.1 Motives

Budgets are a compilation of figures that correspond to issues. Issues and authoritative decision-making on them are the principal object of politics. Concerns over the well-being of children, clean air, possession of firearms, and access to affordable health care motivate people and groups to enter the political arena.

Decision-making models in the policy process literature show that policymakers do not treat all issues equally. Some issue areas generate collective attention, which is finite and zero-sum for the entire policymaking system. Thus, attention to a few items absorbs attention that could be given to the whole. Once an item receives attention from a decision-maker, dramatic change can occur, while ignored issues change incrementally. The fundamental expectation is that a typical budget function will be ignored; it is, therefore, exceptional when budget categories are politicized and widely deliberated. The fundamental model expects policy change to be punctuated but says little about the location of that change and the long-term consequences of this change.

In Chapter 3, we delineate the contours of spending on individual functions and connect them to policy processes. In its simplest form, budgeting is a decision-making problem. Public monies must be allocated to a fixed number of activities. Punctuated equilibrium theory and its underlying decision-making model (Padgett, 1981) supply us with a theory of the policy process (Baumgartner and Jones, 1993; Jones and Baumgartner, 2005; Jones et al., 2003). One of the attractive features of punctuated equilibrium theory for our analysis of state spending on particular policy issues is that it assumes that politics revolves around individual policies. The works of Baumgartner, Jones, and many others (e.g., Baumgartner et al., 2009c) show that policy change occurs when decision-makers focus on a particular issue. Collective attention to a policy problem erodes institutional barriers to policy change. This dynamic creates a policymaking environment where small changes in policy transpire in institutionally contained domains. When this equilibrium is disturbed by collective attention, however, the resulting policy change on an issue is massive.

A path to understanding the location of policy change requires examining actors who attempt to draw attention to issues. Issue politics is interest group politics. Issues and interests can be placed within clearly demarcated policy domains that correspond with items in a budget. Thus, the sum of issue politics is the budget, essentially a bundle of interests; therefore, to know a budget, we must understand the environment in which interests operate.

Political conflicts start in particular domains but then spill over into the broader political agenda. The combination of localized policymaking interacting with collective consequences is akin to budgeting. In budgeting, individual budget items need to be processed and then condensed into a single document, which is then approved by the legislative and executive branch. In short, the process of budgeting directly corresponds with a process model of policymaking (Jones et al., 2003; True, 1999). Both begin in individual policy domains, and both end with decision-makers collectively agreeing on a bundle of policy changes.

We leverage the basic model of political decision-making found in the policy literature and contend that some issues are more likely than others to display patterns of temporary, transformative change. However, it is exactly these categories within a budget that will not experience significant growth in the long run. When a particular policy concern motivates all political actors, policy domains offer distinct rewards and display a short-term versus long-term trade-off. Political interests operating within a policy domain must be aware of this trade-off and adjust their strategies accordingly. Likewise, governors responding to group interests realize that only short-term gains are possible on some issues, while other areas offer long-term rewards.

1.2.2 Means

Governors possess the means – the legal authority – to propose and pass a budget, potentially comprising myriad policy changes. Executives – particularly independently elected executives – have responsibilities that force them to consider all government decision-making jointly across issues (Dometrius and Wright, 2010; Kousser and Phillips, 2012). Executives are, in most cases, the only offices to consider the entirety of preferences within a jurisdiction. Other actors in the policymaking process are incentivized to attend to issue-specific (in the case of interest groups) or sub-jurisdictional (in terms of legislators) concerns. The executive is also tasked with managing and responding to requests from the bureaucracy regarding rule-making and agency expenditure (Abney and Lauth, 1983; Barrilleaux, 2000). The bureaucracy's preferences overlap with the executive's preferences insofar as bureaucracies "work" for the executive; overlap with legislators' preferences given the role of oversight in the policy process; and overlap with interest groups' preferences given the role of constituents as clients of bureaucratic agencies (Goodman, 2008; Goodman and Clynch, 2004). Thus, the executive is not only tasked with a wider, more diverse preference set, but also tasked with negotiating between particularistic preferences within their jurisdiction (Wildavsky, 1986).

The negotiation among preferences is political and administrative. Executives are (typically) responsible for producing fiscally responsible budget documents in an environment where individual interests attempt to maximize their gains (or reduce their losses) from government (Baumgartner et al., 2009a). In many subnational cases where revenue streams are relatively fixed, and the capacity to borrow is very low, executives must process information from a variety of sources (constituents, the bureaucracy, interest groups, and legislators) to compile a spending package that fulfills a variety of needs but also is fiscally sound.

Not all governors are created equal, however. Perhaps, a better way of saying this is, not all offices of the governor are created institutionally equal. State-level public budgeting is sufficiently important for subnational governance to manifest not only particular taxing and spending rules but also role-specific rules for actors. Governors have powers peculiar to the budgeting process in the form of setting the budgetary agenda, powers that shape the influence governors can have on state spending in one year and beyond. For example, many states submit agency requests to public hearings prior to their placement in a state budget; however, the budgeting process in Washington skips that step, giving the governor more control over the budget. Governors who write up a budget with their own staff and little outside influence have a dramatically different impact on state spending than a governor that sits in a room with the legislature to hammer out a proposal.

In addition to budget-specific rules, there are other features of the executive which tip the scales of power toward executives in all interactions with legislatures. Governors are unitary actors who suffer less from coordination problems than their counterparts in the legislature and are also afforded the ability to veto legislation; most governors are given the opportunity to veto-specific pieces of legislation or, in the case of Wisconsin, specific letters or numbers within legislation. Legislatures can override these decisions to varying degrees; however, the same collective action problem that positions governors as a singularly effective actor in negotiations with legislatures also makes veto overrides challenging.

While these powers are strong when examined individually, it is the joint power of setting the agenda and possessing the tools to defend it that truly sets governors apart as institutional actors. For example, the governor of New Jersey not only shut down funding to state beaches in the summer of 2017, but then gave himself access to them (Mullany, 2017). Governors can modify legislative requests to change the budget they have proposed by threatening a veto; in most states, this includes a veto of particular features legislatures might add (or subtract). Essentially, the governor has the *potential* to shape the budget every year and dictate the long-term financial story of a state. When do governors wield this power?

Executives have political preferences that may be specific to positions taken during elections, that may respond to particular rather than general problems, or that may, in fact, be simply personal convictions. Executives can often respond to these preferences by introducing legislation; in the case of budgets, executives are often responsible for producing the budget in the first place (Kousser and Phillips, 2009, 2012). Thus, executives can not only negotiate between competing interests on behalf of the whole but can also pick which battles to fight.

Executives' desires incorporate negotiating between various interests and working toward a broader whole while maintaining some control over the process, so that the executives' preferences are also expressed. This negotiating environment not only affords the executive some advantages over other actors in the policy process but also creates limitations. In a relative sense, an executive is a unitary actor in making policy decisions (Bowman et al., 2010; Breunig and Koski, 2009; McCarty, 2000b). This autonomy allows for fewer transaction costs in comparison to other institutions (as long as the executive effectively "agrees" with itself). Budgeting theory suggests that executives ought to get their way in bargaining, in part, because they have to build fewer coalitions – this coordination advantage increases as the executive becomes more powerful (Ryu et al., 2007). Thus, stronger executives ought to be able to hold sway over policy decisions.

This institutional advantage comes at an informational cost. Because executives must serve an expanded domain of preferences, they also require a greater capacity to process information. While executives may rely on staff to mitigate the flood of information, they must make trade-offs between attending to holistic issues (e.g., the entire budget) and individual preferences (e.g., the education budget), including their own preferences. This limitation in information processing capacity, coupled with the amount of information, means that executives are also likely to rely on strategic considerations when making policy decisions. Like other cognitively strapped individuals and institutions, executives rely upon preference aggregators – interest groups – to distill information. Interest group information is biased, but that is ultimately the point.

While they may provide biased information, consulting interest groups and other actors attached to a policy domain can give executives a sense of the type of issue environment in which political conflict, or lack thereof, occurs. Is the interest environment stable? Are there many groups or a few groups? Have previous policy outcomes been consistent over time? The answers to these questions assist executives in a strategy of attention, which ultimately explains why governors engage in particularistic policymaking or why they focus on composing the whole budget. Executives attend to issues when the political climate is favorable to intervention – this intervention might be significant, or it might be minor. Answering these questions helps in explaining in which contexts executive powers are capable of influencing policymaking.

1.2.3 Opportunities

While all political actors are passionate about particular policy issues, actual policy change requires political opportunities. We argue that these favorable circumstances arise out of the structure of the interest group environment on an issue. Interest groups inherently serve a narrower purpose than executives. Groups are aware of their impact on the totality of the policy agenda, but are ultimately concerned with maximizing returns to their constituents (Austen-Smith, 1993; Baumgartner and Leech, 1998; Grossmann, 2006, 2012) within a particular policy domain. To gain their (perceived) fair share of the budgets, groups could theoretically attempt to increase the overall size of the budgetary pie. But, this rarely happens. Even when it does, new revenue sources are subject to similar types of conflict as existing revenue sources.

The institutional context of policymaking inhibits the ability to broaden the pie. Though the agenda might be flexible in its size, the agenda space is empirically finite, and policymakers have a limited capacity to consider most of the issues of the day (Baumgartner and Jones, 1993; Jones, 1994). Attention limitations prevent full consideration of most issues, leaving groups who advocate stability in a stronger position than rivals who call for change. Consequently, expanding the attention horizon or the budget frontier is unlikely, and zero-sum interactions among interest groups prevail most of the time. To the extent this ambition translates into a zero-sum game, interest groups compete to receive benefits from the government.

Thus, where executives attempt balance, interest groups push imbalance. Interest groups can consistently focus attention on specific issues, while executives must be nimble and attentive to a broad range of considerations. Interest groups, at the same time, face varying competition with other groups for agenda space within policy domains.

Different constellations of interest groups provide different opportunities for group interactions within a policy domain, but ultimately also offer some level of certainty regarding interest group strategies for agenda control. Challengers within a policy domain seek to expand the conflict in order to wrest control away from dominant groups who seek to maintain the status quo with little variation (Baumgartner and Leech, 2001; Boehmke et al., 2013; Constantelos, 2010; Pralle, 2003). In a domain with many interest groups, interests are at once rivals with established groups and dominant over groups that seek to enter the conflict with clear strategies in line with Lindblom's (1959, 1965) "partisan mutual adjustment." The fluctuations of interest group populations in some policy domains create dilemmas for group strategies: In some cases, groups might want to move to uncertainty if they are certain always to lose, while in other cases, groups might favor stability over the potential for greater favorable change.

The main takeaway from this discussion is that the political environment created by interest group competition dictates lobbying strategies and the prospect of policy change. These strategies rely on keeping policy domains off the agenda, maintaining attention to specific issues, or changing attention to issues for the purpose of major shifts at the expense of stability. In short, the domain-specific interest group politics of policy issues are not in direct conflict with other policy issues. However, the aggregate of issue politics engages a holistic budget that simply cannot fund all the preferences of all interest groups. Thus, individual policy issues dominate attention to themselves and, by consuming different amounts of a finite agenda, each other. In Chapter 2, we identify three interest group environments based on the density of groups and their interactions within a policy domain. Each of these three interest group environments demarcate distinct political opportunities for policymakers.

The first interest group environment, **capture**, refers to issue areas with few associated groups. This low density of interest groups could stem from a variety of reasons but, generally following a pluralistic understanding of interest group formation around issues, low-density interest group environments generally attract less attention from policymakers. Broadly, less attention produces greater stability. Groups in a "captured" interest group environment, thus, do not want to draw attention to issues. Instead of raising issue attention to *potentially* receive greater benefits, groups are happy to take their consistent share (which they have positioned themselves to receive) of the budget related to their issue. Because groups have asked for just a fair share and because groups maintain a low profile, they can speak in a more or less unified voice and can lobby against cutbacks. Groups' preferred outcome in a capture scenario is slow, smooth, and steady growth. Likewise, this approach offers a steady and reliable supportive environment for governors.

The second interest group environment, **deadlock**, results in a similarly stable outcome as capture, but for a different reason. A high density of interest groups yields consistent competition over issues. There are many groups, and each group wants more from the budget. In these deadlock environments, the stakes are high, and the space occupied by these budget items is vast. Stability is maintained because groups consistently work to maintain an issue's presence on policymakers' agenda. Groups' preferred outcome in a deadlock scenario is that their item continues to occupy a large share of the budget, but one that gets larger over time at a relatively slow rate. Given the large share of the budget that deadlock issues occupy, all policymakers are attentive to deadlock categories. Governors are particularly attentive to deadlock categories as part of their general concern regarding the overall budget, but also the lobbying efforts of a multitude of groups that are hard to ignore collectively.

The third environment, **instability**, results when interest group density is high enough that issues motivating these groups are not mute, but not sufficiently high enough to generate continuous policymaker attention to a policy domain. Interest group density in the instability environment is between capture and deadlock. In this transitional state, group composition and competition change over time. Because competition and composition change over time, it is difficult for policymakers to build long-term relationships with groups. In one year, Group A could be dominant, while in another year, it could be Group B. Politicians are uncertain who will provide rewards for actions related to budgetary items; thus, not only is the agenda in these interest group environments ephemeral, but political support for issues from state policymakers within these environments is fickle. Groups within this domain compete for attention, and therefore, instability offers the greatest opportunity for rapid budgetary change. The potential outcomes of the instability scenario are volatile changes from continued shifts in attention and less long-term growth in budget share because of a lack of cohesive leadership from groups.

1.3 COMMITTING A PUBLIC BUDGET

The existing literature describes budgeting as a decision-making model, a model we envision as an investigator reconstructing a crime: What are the motives, means, and opportunities? Regarding motivation, several budgeting process actors desire policy change: governors, legislators, and interest groups. In practical terms, these preferences result in an executive cobbling together a budget that fits her preferences. However, governors cannot always get what they want because they have finite time and resources to attend to all their preferences. These limitations mean governors must pick and choose which motives on which to act. A policy model of decision-making tells us that attention and institutions influence the severity of budget changes. We show in Chapters 3–6 that the abstract policy model is empirically valid, but we provide a policy process theory of how this prioritization of spending preferences occurs.

We arrive now at the means to commit a budget: A governor's agency in the choice of intervening in the budgeting process is constrained not just by attention, but, the means by which they can make policy change. The distribution of political power varies across institutions; yet, the ability to use this power also varies within a budget across different issues. Veto threats are simply less credible in the face of powerful groups with must-pass legislation than they are for issues with ephemeral group representation.

The same gubernatorial power displays different effects on different domains within the same budget because of the opportunities provided by interest groups, the third element of investigation. Inspired by the decision-making literature's findings that budgeting starts within policy domains, we show how individual policy domains are subject to subsystem-specific policy dynamics – in particular, the composition of interest groups attached to each domain. While interest groups are certainly aware of the happenings in other domains, they have much narrower and well-defined preferences. Interest group politics and strategy depend heavily on competition: Groups with little competition in a policy domain attempt to shield attention from their issues, whereas groups with great competition naturally have attention focused upon them. Interest groups are focused on spending in their policy domain, with little consideration for the budget as a whole. Executives must consider an entire range of policy domains while simultaneously being engaged in setting their own priorities for spending. How much executives are able to realize these priorities in the final budget is a function of institutional powers. Stronger executives can use their agenda-setting and veto powers to shape the budget to a greater extent than weaker governors.

Executives are responsible for making choices that drive changes in public budgets, but interest groups are responsible for shaping the options from which executives choose. We are not referring to individual interest groups in this context, but rather interest group interactions in the form of competition, collusion, or coexistence. Even a single interest group in a field offers rewards to an executive to maintain the status quo and thereby stable or incremental spending. Many competing groups in a policy domain offer executives opportunities to make changes, but also present a great difficulty in doing so given the presence of established groups. The scenario in which executives can influence the budget most is also the riskiest – where interest group competition is variable, issues emerge and then fall off the agenda with periodicity, and winners and losers shift regularly. Executives are uncertain of the future, uncertain whether they will be on the side of next year's dominant or rival group, and uncertain about the potential benefits of intervention.

Thus, while executive power plays a key role in the capacity to influence policymaking, the choice of which policy to influence is determined by interest groups. Where the executive steps away – or is weak – interest group politics dominate. Indeed, the reverse is a truer statement: Executive power matters when interest groups do not have a clear pattern of interaction such that executives can make strategic choices to intervene based upon much more certain payoffs.

1.3.1 Executives and Interest Groups Meet on the Margins

Despite their institutional strength, governors are still subject to decision-making limitations that hamstring other policymakers. In addition, the utility of these powers is not limited to budget battles; thus, governors are wise to be somewhat reserved in their application of these powerful tools. Gubernatorial action is most likely to occur at the vertex of attention and rewards. Governors decide feast for some budget categories and famine for others. Interest groups are well aware of the powers of the governor, the value of attention in policymaking, and the role of attention in the issue environment in which they operate. Interest groups need to decide whether it is advantageous to their interests to draw attention to a domain; governors need to determine how interest group competition offers rewards to themselves. This interest group–governor interaction can play out in three ways.

First, policy domains with few interest groups produce stable policy outcomes, in part, because of a lack of general attention to these issues. A governor's safest option is to simply maintain the status quo–groups maintain their share of the budget, and change occurs slowly. From interest groups' perspectives, governors translate the wishful outcome of the groups into reality. The riskier option for an executive is to initiate significant change in these interest group environments. Executives draw attention to themselves, and the under-attended policy area will upset the dynamic that previously produced stable change. An executive's cost of entry in our *capture* scenario is relatively high, as they must act entrepreneurially to raise attention to issues. Increased issue attention creates opportunities for otherwise weak interest group rivals to upset the existing equilibrium. In other words, the executive must expand the conflict to rupture the captured scenario. This is generally unlikely, and capture categories are thus positioned for steady long-term growth.

Second, policy domains can also be stable because of significant interest group competition. We labeled this scenario *deadlock*. Here again, the safest option for the executive is the status quo, but for different reasons than the *capture* scenario. In a deadlock scenario, a large group of actors currently benefit from the outputs of the status quo, and the potential rewards for governors are significant. The extant share of the budget deadlock categories occupy is large, and the number of groups these categories serve is many. The governor's choice to maintain the status quo benefits involved groups, even those in competition, given that the outcome is the maintenance of a large share of the budget for all. For governors wishing to wade into conflict, attention cuts both ways: While governors may make a political statement in attending to an issue followed by many, executives risk angering a known constituency if they initiate change. In a deadlock scenario, an executive's role in policy change is less in heightening attention to an issue (given that the current policy definition is already contested) than attempting to tip the scales in favor of one group versus another. Therefore, the cost of entry into the conflict is low, as attention is already high, but the cost of producing change is relatively high: Aligning with any side immediately pits the executive against a strong rival. We argue that governors are interested in maintaining the status quo, but will use every opportunity to change policy to satisfy a large constituency. Thus, in the long run, budgets for policies with heavily populated issue environments are going to be very large.

Third, in cases of *instability* in interest group participation, policy outcomes are likewise volatile. Executives face a difficult political choice in unstable interest group environments. On the one hand, in scenarios with volatile interest group membership, the governor takes a long-term risk in backing this year's victory at the expense of next year's dominant group. On the other hand, executives might find themselves afforded an opportunity to make a policy change in an interest group environment for which there is no rival because the issues for which policy is being made are worthy of neither capture nor deadlock. The reward structure for the governor is somewhat risky as it is unclear that stability provides any rewards in the long run – there are no dominant groups to service, and the item is a small share of the budget. The same risks apply to interest groups in this situation. If groups draw attention to themselves and lose, then the domain is captured by a rival. If groups are successful in drawing attention, they still need to generate attention and rewards for the following year – a feat that had previously proved elusive. However, there is one scenario where significant executive action can pay off: to generate attention for their own actions and to produce a policy monopoly. Such actions are, of course, rare. Given this uncertain scenario, we expect that there will be very small annual changes, but over time, we expect there to be dramatic changes – a similar distribution as predicted by PET. Because of the ephemeral nature of the groups in this interest group environment, we also expect long-term growth to be low.

1.3.2 How We Study Budgeting in the American States

We consider states as laboratories of democracy, though perhaps not in the traditional sense of this term (Morehouse and Jewell, 2004): We do not necessarily believe one state's budgeting ought to be mimicked by other states, and we are not mining state political institutions for solutions to federal budget problems. Lowery et al. (2010) show that state agendas often substitute for lack of federal government attention to issues, rather than creating feedforward effects from which the federal government can learn. States as laboratories help us understand broad variation in attention to policy issues, as well as in competitive and institutional settings.

Public budgets at the state level offer multiple layers of analysis to researchers. Researchers can focus on budgets as a whole, individual budget categories, or drill down deeper into subcategories. We examine categorical state budget data from the US Census over a period of twenty-six years (1984–2010). These data cover multiple gubernatorial and legislative elections; waves of partisan turnover at the state and federal level; exogenous shocks; changes in the federal relationship with state governments; and the modernization of the budget process. Our data cover southern states' shift from one-party Democratic rule to one-party Republican rule. Our time period includes a fundamental restructuring of welfare financing in the mid-1990s, which led to significant changes in revenue flows to states, but also in how they could allocate existing monies. The two-and-a-half decade data series also covers the significant internal movement of the U.S. population to southern and western regions. Our data series captures these historical shifts and others to understand the roles that institutional gubernatorial strength and interest group concentration play in the general distribution of expenditures given the inherently changing political environment of state politics.

The dependent variable in the study is variation in public budgets; our two primary independent variables are gubernatorial strength and interest group composition. We collect measures of gubernatorial power over the same twenty-six-year period using Beyle's (2003) index. In all cases, governors have some capability to influence the budget that emerges from states; we are able to concentrate this institutional influence into these two measures to test theories of agenda-setting and budgeting. We are specifically interested in governors' institutional strength to set the agenda and veto legislation. Variation in veto strength is rather minimal, but agenda-setting power differs. Our analysis assesses these powers individually and collectively.

State interest group data are a challenge to collect, given variation in state disclosure rules and the relatively opaque political environment in which interest groups operate. The fifty states have varying rules concerning interest group registration and lobbying restrictions, so it is difficult to track interest group numbers and what the actions they take. We use Gray and Lowery's multidecadal data on interest group concentration to assess the relative density of interest group types within a state (Lowery et al., 2015). We then match interest group data with categories in the budget, giving us a relative measure of the interest group environment at the categorical level across all states for twenty-six years.

We collect other state and federal characteristics that feature in the crucible of public budgeting, in addition to gubernatorial power and interest group concentration. Legislatures have a constitutionally prescribed role in budgeting, but their capacity to offset the influence of the governor is a function of resources at their disposal. The state politics literature refers to the capacity and presence of state legislatures as "professionalism." States also face differing rules regarding the budget process intended to constrain the ability of governments to deviate from financial commitments. Finally, changes in party control likely dictate the preferences of governments, though party shifts may not dictate the extent of changes in budgets. We include these other important structural and contextual features of states in our data analysis.

State data provide unique opportunities to test theoretical expectations associated with policy theory across a range of similar institutions. However, there are methodological challenges associated with pooling expenditure data across all states over long periods of time for budgets that are inherently sums of interdependent parts. Thus, we leverage sophisticated quantitative methods to test our arguments. Rather than determining specific expenditures within state budgets, we use quantitative analyses that understand variations in how state budgets change over time. Our theory intends to explain the role of executives and interest groups in producing patterns of change and particular kinds of change. Within these models, we can also identify where in the overall distribution of budget changes individual determinants are influential and in what way. For example, traditional quantitative analysis might tell us that, on average, stronger governors get what they want; however, these analyses would say little about whether a governor's strength produced a more volatile budget, a budget that was more punctuated, or whether a governor's strength has the same magnitude of influence across a range of changes. Our analysis addresses deficiencies that single traditional modeling techniques present when attempting to understand policy change.

By using statistical profiles of states, we identify four states as case studies to add context to our findings: New York, North Carolina, West Virginia, and Vermont. Two states (New York and North Carolina) have relatively large budgets, while two states (West Virginia and Vermont) have small budgets. For each budget size, we choose a state that has a strong and a weak governor for the purpose of understanding the budget stories that accompany the shifts in budgeting we identify in our quantitative analysis. These cases call upon specific budgeting issues as reported in local media regarding preferences of governors and relevant interest groups. Our focus concentrates on corrections, hospitals, and welfare. These policy issues are populated with particular compositions of interest groups. The diversity of composition enables us to portray how governors are identifying different opportunities during the making of an annual budget. The cases also highlight the importance of having the institutional means available so that astute governors actually convert these opportunities into actual policy changes in keeping with their motives. Thus, our empirical work explains the aggregation of millions of budget stories as well as a disaggregated few.

1.3.3 Implications of Our Theory

Given the interest group–governor dynamic we describe, our theory allows us to generate several testable propositions. In general, we expect the pattern of interest group involvement to be the dominant force in leading to the prioritization of particular spending items. Because of the trade-offs within a constrained agenda space, we also expect that particular budget items undergo more rapid budget changes than others.

All things equal, executives are wise to avoid staying out of particularistic policy dilemmas. Executives, as we have stated, are important actors in composing the whole budget, actors who have the means to create large-scale change as a function of their power. Executives who attempt to break up policy monopolies or galvanize attention around issues for which there are no consistent champions are only able to do so because of their institutional strength. Weak executives are less likely to intervene in policy domains, in part because they do not have the institutional strength to credibly threaten existing groups.

We argue that the interest group–governor interaction assists in understanding variation within particular policy domains over time. Specific public policy domains have emerged as consistently more volatile than other domains over long periods of time, which contrasts with the general theoretical expectation that policies achieve equilibrium. Our expectation is that policy domains remain unstable because of a weak interest group environment and the lack of a strong executive. Even a strong executive will be hard-pressed to shift the pattern of change in policy domains populated by stability-inducing interest group concentrations. It is certainly true that governors are a part of all discussions in each policy domain, but their individual capacity to create change is induced by interest group opportunities.

The extent to which governors can take advantage of interest group opportunities is a function of their official means. Variation in spending priorities across states, we argue, is a function of the strength of governors to engage in the policy process. Executives, unlike interest groups, see the entire policy landscape and are perfectly aware that creating winners in one domain will create losers not just in that domain, but in other domains, too. In reality, this may be the exact strategy of the executive, regardless if they are weak or strong. Variation in spending priorities within states results in cascading effects, given the finite capacity of governments to consider issues. Individual domains are largely influenced by interest group politics of capture, instability, and deadlock – particularly when governors are weak. Thus, we argue interest groups generate attention, and governors decide how to react.

1.4 CONTRIBUTIONS OF OUR RESEARCH

This book is an ambitious effort to understand governmental decision-making, specifically how governments spend public money. We bring together three vast literatures: policy process, interest groups, and state politics. Our motives, means, and opportunities model of public policymaking and budgeting, in particular, draws on and enriches these distinct theoretical approaches by offering four primary contributions to the politics of public policy and public budgeting.

The first contribution is to understand that issue-based politics provide motives for action. While it is true that the fifty states have idiosyncratic problems, solutions to those problems, and methods to pay for them; we show that patterns of policymaking vary by issue rather than by state or, crucially, by party. Within these issue-based politics, policymakers make choices between policy changes that fit with the hitherto incremental pattern of budget-making and occasional large changes. The analysis of budget functions that correspond to key policy domains shows how state governments determine the share of budgets devoted to specific categories, what causes variation in the magnitude of change within categories, and the impacts that patterns of change have on long-term growth within spending areas. Some budget functions are enormous because there is long-term steady growth. These items reflect policy issues, such as welfare, that are always on a government's agenda. Small budget items oscillate wildly, but do not grow substantially over the long run. These small budget items are policy issues that compete for political attention and, from time to time, make it to the top of the political agenda.

Second, we argue that governors are powerful actors in their ability to affect policy outcomes within particular issue areas. All governors possess some means to influence expenditures within policy areas; however, governors with sufficient means (e.g., institutional power) are able to shape expenditures more to their liking. Governors are bound by several features of state governments, including budget rules, but also the inertia of issue areas. Thus, we find that rather than making major changes to public policy, governors are able to make large changes even larger, especially in the case of institutionally strong governors. Our contribution is to offer a nuanced impression of the institutional strength of governors: All have the means to affect policy, but the range of potential policy change is bound by the politics of issue areas.

Third, issue area politics – and, thus, opportunities for governors to intervene – are determined, in large part, by interest group competition. Governors may compose a budget, but they choose from a menu prepared by interest groups. Most interest groups are unconcerned with the extent to which their individual victories might affect the budget as a whole (except groups who focus specifically on government spending). The literature on spending for particular purposes, such as welfare, speaks to the types of findings we might expect, which is, that groups pursue their own goals. These independent battles for spending – the forte of interest groups – aggregate into a budget as a whole.

Finally, our work reinvigorates interest group literature's interest in policy outcomes, as the majority of the literature focuses on tools, campaigns, and so on. Though everyone knows interest groups matter in public policy, policy and political science literatures are often challenged in demonstrating it. While we do not link specific interest groups with particular spending, we show how the interest group environment influences the broad contours of public policy and shapes the opportunities for political actors to influence policy.

In summary, our project understands interdependent decision-making patterns of change across fifty institutions (i.e., states). We offer a theoretical approach for investigating macro decision-making that attends to the realities of budgeting as an exercise in balancing politically unrelated goals and groups in a single policy document. We build a theoretical model of how the institutional and political landscape of subnational governments interacts to understand how governments prioritize programs. Empirical testing of our theory suggests that this approach to understanding state policymaking could be expanded to other subnational and national governments, in comparative or single case studies, for budgeting or other policy decision-making.

1.5 OVERVIEW OF THE BOOK

Overall, we find that, first, policy domains, rather than states, motivate variations in patterns of spending. Second, policy domain-specific forces–interest groups, in particular–influence when and how governors are willing to change policy. Third, gubernatorial power manifests at the margins of policy change. Governors are not indiscriminate in their use of power – they apply it to change policy in particular policy domains.

We illustrate these patterns using budget data on different spending categories, measures of interest group populations, and institutional powers of governors for all fifty American states between 1984 and 2010. The chapters of the book are organized around a further explication of our theoretical argument (Chapter 2); a description of the underlying motives (Chapter 3); empirical testing of interest group opportunities (Chapter 4) and gubernatorial powers (Chapter 5); case studies to bear out these relationships (Chapter 6); and thoughts on how this relationship between governors, interest groups, and expenditures can influence future institutional design choices (Chapter 7).

In Chapter 2, we explicate our theoretical argument by first reviewing and synthesizing literature in policy process theory, executive politics, interest group politics to produce a general theory of public policy as a function of the motive governors have to intervene in policymaking and the opportunity they are afforded by interest group competition to intervene. We argue that this process occurs in three steps, informed by the three literatures we engage. In step one, preferences are relatively fixed, that problems are constant, but that attention to policy issues shifts over time. In step two, interest groups champion particular political issues and that the competition between these groups creates different risks and rewards for policymakers to engage in attempts to change policy. In step three, governors as individuals have individual policy preferences and collective responsibility to the budget. All else equal, interest group competition sets the stage for governors to intervene, but governors are not equal when it comes to assembling and passing a budget. We then derive theoretical implications from this model for three particular budget features: budget distributions, budget changes, and long-term budget growth. We situate the model within the contextual features of state politics, specifically legislatures and political parties.

In Chapters 3–6, we test specific features of the model we describe in Chapter 2. In Chapter 3, we create a typology of state spending based on our theory of public budgeting. A starting point for the typology is a detailed description of our data–state expenditures over time and across ten budget functions. We begin by assessing the distributions of public budgets across states to empirically verify the assumption that state budgets are subject to similar policymaking forces as other forms of policymaking, thereby empirically verifying the conditions of step one of our theoretical argument in Chapter 2. We find that budgets are punctuated across space (states) and, more importantly, across budgetary functions. These punctuations have long-term consequences: Spending on policy issues that are punctuated grows little in the long run. Hence, the trade-off on policy issues is between short-term rewards (in terms of substantial increases at one point in time) and long-term steady growth. We then map this trade-off onto particular spending domains and their issue politics. The chapter yields of four types of policymaking: *majoritarian politics*, *runaway issue expansion*, *normal politics*, and *interest group politics*. We use these policy types to understand governor and interest group motives in policymaking.

In Chapter 4, we examine the empirical relationship between interests and budget outcomes. We specifically examine step two of the theoretical argument in Chapter 2, where the interest group environment determines the direction of policy change. We show the empirical curvilinear relationship between interest group density and budget change, where small and large concentrations of groups generally produce positive budget outcomes, but negative changes occur in between. By showing how different interest group scenarios, which we call capture, instability, and deadlock, contribute to changes in spending, we characterize opportunities for policymaking.

Chapter 5 shows how institutional means affect policy outcomes. We examine step three of the theoretical argument in Chapter 2 where we test the relationship between gubernatorial power and budgeting. Our argument describes governors as contending with distinct challenges associated with the office. We consider these forces throughout the book as related to their tasks of balancing budgets but also getting what they want: There is variation in the extent to which governors can dictate the terms of the budget to the legislature. Stronger governors are better able to mold balanced budgets that also allow for individual preference expression; weaker governors are still required to balance budgets, but are less likely to secure their desired changes. We term this process *bottoming-out* and *topping-off*.

Chapter 6 combines the quantitative findings of Chapters 4 and 5 in four state case studies. We choose states based on their size and variation in gubernatorial strength; issues that span each of the interest group categories of capture, instability, and deadlock; and categories that fit our *interest group politics* typology outlined in Chapter 3. Our examination of New York, West Virginia, North Carolina, and Vermont in the areas of welfare, corrections, and hospital spending suggests that all governors are engaged in conflict with interest groups to create a budget, but that stronger governors are more successful in intervening when interest group competition is less stable. The chapter also dissects how motives, opportunities, and means offer an understanding of the annual budgeting process in the American states.

Chapter 7 explores the implications of our findings. Theoretically, we both affirm and extend policy process theories that examine the role that institutions play in determining patterns of policy outcomes. Our theory makes bold claims about the role that interest groups play at the state level – notably, that interest group environments essentially create the menu of options from which governors choose. Thus, policies that influence interest group presence, composition, and competition also have the potential to influence the power of governors to shape budgets. As the composition of group dynamics shifts in American politics in response to reductions in funding transparency for some groups and explicit attempts to weaken organization among others, the opportunities to secure budgetary victories for groups with an uncertain future are less than those who can maintain a consistent presence.

2

Meeting at the Margins

Interests and Governors in Public Budgeting

In this book, we apply a policy process view to public budgeting. We make assumptions about the logic of decision-making in the policy process, identify political arrangements that encourage or discourage deviation from the status quo, and locate the political institutions that structure decision-making. Our argument draws on three well-established fields of study within political science: (1) policy process theory to understand budget processes and motives, (2) interest group literature to understand opportunities for political action, and (3) institutionalist theory to understand constraints on and empowerment of political actors.

Our argument answers several important and thorny questions about the comparative study of budgeting processes. Budgeting processes across governments contain structural and political idiosyncrasies that lead to significant institutional variation. Given this institutional variation, which policy issues are attended to and translated to spending decisions? How do interest groups engage in agenda-setting in budgeting? How do executive powers influence governors' abilities to compose budgets in the face of interest group pressure? More broadly, what are the conditions for policymaking in the American states?

The budget process is ultimately a compromise (or a clash) between the interests of the many and the interests of the few. In state budgets, governors are the single representative of the many, as they are responsible for producing a document that considers a broad range of interests and attached some values to them. At the same time, governors must also represent their own individual preferences. Interest groups pursue a narrow agenda focusing on their constituency, which sometimes is in opposition to the whole. As the ostensible stalwart servant of the many, the desire to create budgets as holistic documents and to express individual preferences leaves governors in a bind. To the extent that governors wish to mold budgets to their own liking, they must navigate the political environment created by interest groups' pursuit of their interests – be it budgetary change or in some cases simply the protection of the status quo. We argue that governors create public budgets as a function of the political opportunities interest groups create. Our theory of public budgeting accounts for process theories of public policy, interest groups in aggregating preferences, and the structure of institutions in shaping preference expression.

Our model engages the relationship between executive power and interest group environments that empirically takes place in the American states. Our literature review also considers other political factors – notably legislatures and parties – to contextualize the particular relationship between interest groups and governors across the U.S. sub-national governmental landscape. As with any study of public policy, we begin by developing a decision-making model for policymakers.

2.1 FROM POLICY PROCESSES TO GOVERNING THE BUDGET

2.1.1 Policy Processes

In democratic societies, the creation of public budgets may vary across institutional contexts, but budgets are compiled via a specified process. Budget processes reflect a larger concern about how societies agree on collective solutions. How these agreements emerge is the core interest of policy processes theories. Though the policy process theory literature is vast, it can be categorized by level of analysis. Some theories examine micro-level interactions of individuals and institutions (e.g., the Institutional Analysis and Development framework of Ostrom (1990, 2009)), while others explore meso-level policy processes through the lens of beliefs and group activities (Sabatier and Jenkins-Smith (1993); Sabatier and Weible (2007) working on the advocacy coalition framework). We leverage punctuated equilibrium theory (PET) as a macro-level understanding of policy outputs. PET offers a foundation on which to trace and understand policy change over long periods of time.

Punctuated equilibrium theory is an institutionally focused theory that views policymaking as a function of agenda-setting. The short version of PET is that agenda change is a necessary precursor to policy change, but a singularly insufficient explanation of policy change. To employ PET as an analytical tool, thus, researchers generally try to understand two phenomena: the issue environment in which problems emerge and how institutions influence policy change. At the heart of PET is an understanding of information processing. While other theories of public policy and political science may focus on changes in beliefs as a source of policy change, PET assumes that preferences are generally fixed. Policy change occurs not because of new information updates or contrasts with prior beliefs, but because new information results in an attention shift. This is the "Obi-Wan Kenobi" understanding of policy change, where information is less important than attention. Or, rather, that information is important, but less in changing beliefs and more in activating existing beliefs.[1]

The mechanics of PET can be found in Baumgartner and Jones' early work, *Agendas and Instability* (1993) and in subsequent works such as *The Politics of Attention* (2005). PET views the information processing capacity of institutions as important, finite, and variable. Baumgartner and Jones build on Kingdon's (1984) conceptualization of a policy process that does not proceed in the mold of classical rational analytic thinking. The professionalization of writing on policy analysis in the 1970s gave structure to a policymaking process that was previously ad hoc; however, it could also be said that this process also produced an idealized theoretical version of problem-solving at the institutional level. This theoretical development did not suggest that institutions are inherently rational, but that institutions enable policymakers to make better decisions if they could only acquire sufficient information. Thus, inefficient problem-solving could be viewed as a function of an inadequate information search; that with perfect information, policymakers could make the right choices.

Baumgartner and Jones[2] suggest that information *is* a problem for institutions, but not in the way that rational choice scholars might envision. The greatest challenge for institutions is not a dearth of information, but a deluge. Baumgartner and Jones (2015) highlight another dimension of the information problem in that even when institutions have access to information, they may not have access to the *right kind* of information. Policymaking institutions face two information processing problems: seeking the right type of information to solve problems, but also sorting through information both sought and offered to institutions.

Policymakers and the institutions they comprise face limitations in attention (Jones and Baumgartner, 2005), which is zero-sum and finite (Workman, 2015). Whether governments choose to address new problems or adopt new solutions for existing problems is inherently a function of governmental capacity to attend to these problems. In general, governments cannot attend to all problems at all times: They are limited by the cognitive capacity of the humans that inhabit them.

Through institutional design, governments develop coping mechanisms associated with the challenges of processing information with finite attention. Governments delegate authority to subgovernments as a means of concentrating policy expertise, which results in a delegation of attention. While such actions expand the attention span for governments, subgovernments themselves face limits in attention and their own biases in seeking and sorting information. Subgovernments are faced with more problems than they can solve and more information than they can sort. The pattern of policymaking

---

[1] "So what I told you was true, from a certain point of view" – Star Wars Episode VI.
[2] Preceded by Kingdon (1984), preceded by Cohen, March, and Olson (1972).

that emerges is one that incrementally updates policies based on similar sets of actors within subgovernments applying similar sets of filters for new and old information that overtakes institutions. If one wants to know what policy outputs will be this year, last year is a good guide.

But even the best guides are wrong from time to time. Institutions continually update their information from sources that fit with their extant problem definition, referred to in the PET literature as the "policy image." Subgovernments are structured specifically so that governments need not constantly attend to particular issues because subgovernments have been delegated to do so. Over time, the dilemma of delegation becomes that subgovernments maintain an increasingly idiosyncratic problem definition that drifts away from alternative conceptualizations of the policy area over which they govern, or even drifts away from a new reality. Subgovernments maintain the status quo long after quo has lost its status.

The devolution of information processing to subgovernments is essentially a delegation of attention. Governments can initially process information in parallel with the help of subgovernments, but decisions ultimately proceed in serial. Governments shift their macro-attention to different issues as a function of a combination of entrepreneurs, events, and other broader political forces. While governmental attention is not specifically focused on a subgovernment (which is most of the time), the policy agenda of that subgovernment is a function of the attention of the actors within that subgovernment – actors that typically wish to provide a narrow set of rents to established interests.

Therefore, the primary motivation for policy change is an increase in attention to an issue beyond the attention within a subgovernment. Some policy images are also continually contested by competing interests. Competition over issues eventually begets shifts in attention and upsets the equilibrium associated with current problem definitions. Typically, scholars consider policy change as a function of increases in attention: More attention attracts new actors, which brings in alternative sources of information and problem definitions. Existing gatekeepers in subgovernments, contend with the current definition of problem and its solution, attempt to stop the expansion of an issue beyond their realm. If they are successful, the policy image stays the same, and macro-attention subsides. However, if the existing arrangement of actors – termed an "issue monopoly" – is unable to maintain control of the existing policy image, then new actors with different preferences and different focal points for attention change the issue monopoly (Baumgartner and Jones, 1993).

Shifts in macro-attention have many causal factors, but the point of PET is less about identifying these factors and more about understanding that attention shifts frequently occur as governments attempt to solve the myriad problems that face them. When attention shifts, new actors occupy policy-making systems, and new information floods a policy area. Governments compensate for years of disconnect between the evolved versus initial problem

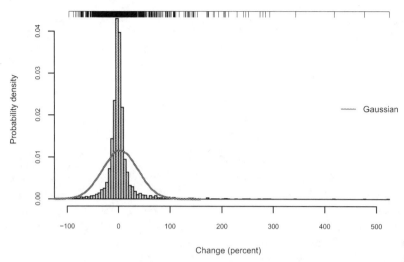

FIGURE 2.1 Histogram of the percentage changes in the shares of budget appropriations in the United Kingdom, Germany, Denmark, and the United States, 1964–1999. Adapted from Breunig (1063, 2011).

definition, and the subsequent change is large – the "punctuation." New institutions form to make policy in the new image: the new "equilibrium."

Institutional arrangements channel information flows, but in contrast to expectations from original theories of policymaking, the outputs from this information are not distributed incrementally. While the world is not normal, as Bryan Jones is fond of saying (e.g., in Jones, 1994), a rational analytic mode of policymaking would expect (Padgett, 1980) the outputs of political systems to be. This normal distribution is demonstrably not the case. Instead, a foundational empirical finding for PET scholars is patterns of policymaking that produce many small changes punctuated by large changes with little moderate updating in between (Baumgartner et al., 2009c; Jones and Baumgartner, 2005; Jones et al., 2009). Figure 2.1 provides a simple inspection of this "general pattern." Though the histogram is from Breunig's (2011) analysis of budgeting in four advanced democracies, similar findings have been made in budgets at local, state, national, and supra-national level, as we delineate in Section 2.1.2.

Variations in institutional design are important for understanding policy outputs in PET, given the impact of institutions on information processing and attention. While PET was initially based on US federal governmental policy, the theory has been expanded to many democracies across the world (Baumgartner et al., 2006b, 2009c; Breunig, 2006; Brouard et al., 2009; John and Jennings, 2010; Jones et al., 2009). Comparative research indicates that the pattern of policymaking predicted by and observed in the early PET investigations is found in other democratic systems. The world is not only not normal but produces even less normal results. However common the general pattern of policy punctuations across democratic systems, the aggregate of these multiple studies suggests that the extent to which policymaking systems are punctuated varies. There is less discussion in PET literature regarding the specific features of institutional design that lead to more or less punctuated policy distributions, but we know such variation exists, and PET suggests the variation is a function of institutional design.

PET focuses on macro-politics rather than specific relationships for specific policies. Though there are some exceptions to this rule (Givel, 2006; Jennings et al., 2020; Park and Sapotichne, 2020), PET attempts to understand policymaking in the aggregate as part of a system rather than linkages between specific groups, actors, and policies. For the policy process, then, the takeaway for our research is that we understand policy change to be a function of the issue environment in which political information emerges and the structure of the institutions that make decisions.

As a general framework, we connect PET to particular mechanisms of how budget decisions are made. In order to do so, we first describe budgeting from a policy processes perspective. Next, we show how literature on interest groups offers insights into how political systems provide and process information. The work of interest group scholars provides an acute understanding of how policymaking environments and subsystems provide structure in the context of budgeting. Finally, we marshal a vast institutionalist literature on fiscal policy and inter-branch bargaining to tease out how particular institutional features of decision-making make it easier or harder for governors to assemble and pass a budget.

2.1.2 Public Budgeting and Punctuated Equilibrium Theory

Since foundational work by Wildavsky (1964), public policy scholars and political scientists have understood that budgeting is a political process. Subsequent scholarship therefore concentrated less on the administrative structures and economic consequences of budgeting and more on the politics of budgeting and the policy process that lead to a particular set of spending decisions. Since the 1990s, works on punctuated equilibrium rejuvenated this classical focus on budgets and budget outcomes because budgeting presents a political process leading to policy outcomes.

Since PET literature is central to our argument and distinct from political economy literature that focuses on fiscal policy and debt, we delineate how PET scholarship that utilized budgetary data moved from uncovering broad empirical regularities to more nuanced research designs, aimed at isolating particular causal features of the budget process. This progress has been accomplished, in part, by broadening the scope of inquiry from the US federal budget to state and local political units, as well as cross-national studies of budgeting. Collectively, the PET literature highlights that spending items within a given budget clearly map onto policymaking and government commitments to specific policy domains. To varying degrees, these works also foreshadow the importance of institutional features and attention to budgetary outcomes.

The first forays of PET into budgetary data focused on single country studies that explored general patterns of policy change, namely the distribution of budgetary change exhibiting the visual pattern displayed in the figure shown earlier in the chapter (see Figure 2.1). One important prerequisite for all works mentioned below is the availability spending data that follow consistent functional definitions over long periods of time. Soroka et al. (2006) show that obtaining budget data that fulfill these requirements is challenging, even in advanced democracies, such as the United Kingdom.

The two core features of the model – (1) institutional friction and attention, and (2) their influence on budgetary changes – have been examined using various research designs. One approach considers how budgeting had changed since the 1800s by classifying federal budgeting according to different epochs. The first of these studies, by Jones et al. (1998), identified three epochs of budgeting in the post-World War II era. Each of these epochs was interrupted by large-scale punctuations in the budget in 1956 and 1974. Along this line, Robinson et al. (2007) argue that the dispersal of power and accompanying weakening of potential veto points in Congress during the early 1970s led to fewer punctuated budgets. Alternatively, Jones et al. (1997) contend that gridlock in the form of divided government, which became the typical pattern of governing in the United States beginning in the 1970s, contributed to more volatility in budgeting. Even long-term analyses stretching back to 1800, such as Jones and Breunig (2007), identify a structural break in the mid-1970s for domestic spending. Jones and Breunig attribute this change to the Congressional Budget and Impoundment Control Act of 1974, which institutionalized a regular budgeting process. Besides these various institutional changes, long periods of slow growth in particular budget items are disrupted by wars and economic collapse (Jones et al., 2014a), exemplified by the turbulent interwar period.

Arguments about how information and attention shape budgetary outcomes have typically examined changes in particular functions of government. A classic study in this vein is Schulman (1975), who leverages the dramatic rise and decline of spending on space exploration as a case against incrementalism (Davis et al., 1966). Schulman alluded to the importance of public opinion and the notion of urgency as a necessity for budget increases. Likewise, governmental spending commitments to renewable energy (Liang and Fiorino, 2013) or to social security (True, 1999) experience disruptive periods but also depend on (long-term) political consensus. Hegelich et al. (2015) even go so far as to argue that attention is central in identifying budget change, and that they could use measures of attention for making point predictions about large-scale budget change. Finally, Mortensen (2009) is interested in how American legislators navigate between voters' budgetary demands and vested interests' demands for particular spending items. His analysis of twelve budget items indicates that "attention effects are expected to be strongest when the trade-off between reelection incentives and intensive group interests is low, which is the case when attention peaks for popular issues and attention to unpopular issues declines" (Mortensen, 2009, 44).

Research on punctuated equilibrium in budgets of the American states and spending at the municipal level takes advantage of the substantial variation of political entities. The payoffs of this comparative focus are a more specific understanding of certain institutional and administrative features contributing to PET and budgeting. The literature first showed that state (Breunig and Koski, 2006) and local (Jordan, 2003; Mortensen, 2005) budgets are punctuated. One line of scholarship, including our own work, focused on how a state-level institution (e.g., Breunig and Koski, 2009, 2018) affects dramatic budget changes. Other works concentrated on budgetary differences across policy sectors and administrative difference among those sectors (Flink, 2017; Jordan, 2003; Mortensen, 2005; Robinson, 2004; Robinson et al., 2007, 2014; Ryu, 2009).

Heeding a broader call for comparative work on agenda-setting (Baumgartner et al., 2006a), scholars interested in PET explored how well their core concepts and empirical findings traveled outside the United States. Researchers discovered that punctuated budgets exist in several advanced democracies, including the United Kingdom (John and Margetts, 2003), France (Baumgartner et al., 2006b), Germany and Denmark (Breunig, 2006), and Hungary (Sebók and Berki, 2017). Once this general pattern of punctuation had been established (Jones et al., 2009), institutional features and their contribution to more or less smooth budgeting were explored further. The clear design advantage of these comparative works is their ability to leverage institutional variation within and across countries to discriminate among several rules and their potential impact.

Three institutional features are particularly important for punctuations. First on the level of political systems, more veto players lead to more volatile (Franzese, 2010) and punctuated (Breunig, 2011) budgets. Second, on a policy level, less centralized budgeting procedures lead to more punctuated budgets (Breunig, 2011). Each of these institutions increases decision-making and transaction costs, and thereby increases the threshold for decision-making to adapt to a changing environment. The third institution is federalism. Fagan et al. (2017) use budget changes in twenty-four countries from 1996 to 2011 to highlight how budgets in federal systems are more punctuated than those of their unitary counterparts. They argue more generally that "institutional factors that impede democratic responsiveness lead to inefficiencies that cause policy changes to become more punctuated" (Fagan et al., 2017, 809) because dispersion of power weakens public demands for policy change.

In addition to these institutional insights, comparative work also illuminates how ideological shifts in government have little impact on large-scale changes in spending patterns. Neither Breunig's (2006) study of four countries nor Baumgartner et al. (2009b) of French budgeting found partisan effects, measured as government ideology or polarization in the legislative branch. Instead, Breunig (2011) suggests that attention shifts to particular policy issues lead to contractions and expansions of budgetary items and thereby eliminating potential partisan changes. Indeed, comparative scholars (Jensen, 2009; Martin and Streams, 2015; Mortensen, 2007), like their counterparts who study state and local government, identified differences in program type and specific features within a policy domain as crucial components in creating punctuations. In a most-different system design comparing Denmark to the United States, Breunig et al. (2009, 2010) conclude that similar features for particular spending items have a stronger effect on budgets than cross-national institutional differences.

2.2 INTEREST GROUPS

Policy process theories, particularly PET, treat interest groups as preference aggregators and arbiters of the status quo bias in public policy. While interest groups are broadly considered to be an integral part of public policymaking, scholars seldom have explored the particular role these groups play in the construction of public budgets. Budgetary policymaking shares much in common with non-budgetary policymaking, particularly from the perspective of interest groups. If politics is the study of who gets what and why, then public budgets are the principal canvas for interest group dynamics. Public budgets represent the aggregation of multiple interest group efforts across individual budget priorities.

Interest group organization has a similar effect on budgetary negotiations as other areas of policy: (1) Interest groups have the same motivations to pursue resources on behalf of their constituents in the budget as they do for public policy, (2) interest groups employ similar tools in budgetary negotiations as they would in any other policy negotiation, and (3) interest groups compete with other groups for the distribution of scarce resources in budgets as they do in securing other benefits. Given the similarities between policymaking and budget preparation, we draw on the literature on interest groups and public policy in building a model of interest group influence over budgetary policymaking.

The vast interest group literature has no shortage of theories of "basic interest" group behaviors (Baumgartner and Leech, 1998). Since 2000, this literature has moved from simple cross-sectional studies of mobilization (Baumgartner and Leech, 1998, 176) toward empirical studies and rigorous theories of behavior (Baumgartner et al., 2009a; Hojnacki et al., 2012; Lowery, 2013). Truman's (1951) notion of pluralism – while much engaged and disputed in the literature – still stands one general theoretical expectation regarding the explanation of interest group formation. According to Truman, groups form to defend or advocate for their interests; to the extent that institutional impediments allow, opposition interests have the opportunity to form to blunt or stop significant changes to the status quo. The general theory of pluralism has severe detractors – most notably that interest formation is expensive for diffuse populations, access for groups is unequal in political systems, concentrated interests often form around issues about which little knowledge is held outside this community (Schlozman et al., 2012; Wilson, 1989), and opposition groups may simply allow for change so long as they are appeased via other rents (Mitchell and Munger, 1991).

Interest groups compete with one another to extract different types of benefits from governments (Baumgartner et al., 2009a). Often, interest group competition is seen as a game in which groups descend upon legislatures and executive agencies en masse and compete for the precious time and attention of these policymakers. The literature on lobbying focuses much of its attention on the capacities and strategies of groups to gain access to policymakers (Holyoke, 2003, 2009; Kollman, 1998; Rosenthal, 2001). To the extent that groups gain access, attention becomes a zero-sum game for potential policy space. Thus, groups compete with one another in a grander sense than even pluralism would suggest: Competition is not determined by common interests jockeying for alternative policy specifications within the same policy area, but across the range of policy areas considered by the policymaking body which the groups intend to lobby. However, this is only part of the story, as strong groups can actively keep issues off the agenda that might be of concern to the broader public (LaPira, 2015).

Interest groups and public policy form a long-standing, long-studied relationship for many instrumental and logical reasons. Public policies generally define which populations stand to benefit from government intervention and which are burdened with funding the intervention. Interest groups naturally fill the roles as advocates for each group. In its most positive form, the concept of interest group activity in public policy fulfills the promise and prophecy of pluralism (Truman, 1951); at its most nefarious, interest groups consolidate benefits for the powerful and distribute burdens to the weak (Schneider and Ingram, 1993, 1997).

Interest group behavior in the policy process is largely motivated by current gains and future relationships with members of the legislative and executive branches. Interest groups can provide information, link voters to politicians, and pursue preferences for represented groups. Even in cases where policymaking is easily observable, interest groups are at their most influential when they are viewed as the authority on a particular policy. Mitchell and Munger (1991) argue that interest groups tend to be most effective when voters are less informed. Baumgartner and Leech (1998) show that the vast majority of policies that interest groups pursue have very little competition and interest groups intend to keep it this way, even if victory is assured (see Hojnacki and Kimball (1998), too).

Interest groups have many arenas in which they can influence policy and many tools to use in these arenas. They can have the capacity to affect nearly every stage of the policy process; the literature on interest groups and public policy focuses on the role of interest groups in lobbying for policies that increase benefits to the members they represent (or to mitigate burdens). Groups are also active in agenda-setting prior to legislative action and in "post-legislative" policymaking, such as rule-making (Furlong, 1997; Furlong and Kerwin, 2004; Haeder and Yackee, 2015; Yackee, 2006; You, 2017), implementation (Koski and May, 2006), and learning (Koski, 2010). Interest groups can be active in one or a few venues of the policy process, many, or all, depending on which venue offers the greatest possibility of success (Baumgartner and Leech, 1998; Boehmke et al., 2013; Holyoke, 2003). Interest groups can affect these stages by way of discourse, information provision, enforcement via monitoring or the use of the legal system, lobbying, and, in the case of the legislative part of policymaking, by helping candidates win reelection by way of monetary contributions or mobilizing a constituency (Nownes and Freeman, 1998).

Just who, or what, interest groups represent presents challenges to a pluralist model of democracy. Presumably, groups emerge to represent individual opinions of the public, firms, or governments and the combination of these individual interests approximates the national interest. However, political scientists have long noted that the representation of public opinion in the United States does not match the distribution of income and many other traits, such as gender and race (Bartels, 2016; Gilens, 2012; Schattschneider, 1960). Insofar as interest groups influence public policy, a logical conclusion might be that interest groups representing the interests of broader or poorer publics are simply not as effective at obtaining concessions from governments. Another logical conclusion might be that there is an inequitable distribution of groups representing interests. Both of these conclusions are correct.

While gains from lobbying are far from certain (Drutman, 2015), suffice it to say that groups that spend more money lobbying are more likely to get what they seek. The distribution of lobbying resources is profoundly skewed toward groups that represent particularly wealthy entities (LaPira and Thomas, 2017) and, while each dollar spent might not translate into public policy, dollars do translate into opportunities for policy change. Schlozman et al.'s (2012) voluminous study of American interest groups show that interest group participation and influence is largely limited to an increasingly small share of the population. The result of this concentration has been an unequal distribution of resources to established groups at the expense of majoritarian politics (Gilens and Page, 2014). Paraphrasing Schlozman et al. (2012), interest group policymaking is biased toward the status quo with an incrementally increasing upper-class accent. Studies of public budgeting we have previously enumerated also describe a pattern of public budgeting that conforms to the status quo bias reinforced by interest groups. But these studies have not explicitly spelled out the linkage between interest group competition and budget outcomes.

Interest group dynamics help us understand stability and change in public policy outcomes. Interests mobilize to maintain existing programs, and that mobilization is enhanced by access to resources. In some cases, policy changes because existing interests' preferences match shifts in public opinion or, in rarer cases, public opinion overwhelms organized interest opposition. Interest groups deal with finite attention from policymakers and finite resources in budgets. Thus, in their quest to capture rents from governments for their members, interest groups influence the distribution of policy attention and resources from governments. The aggregate result of individual interest group behavior, coupled with other political factors, produces the overall distribution of resources from governments.

Scholarship on state-level interest groups has begun to examine the proliferation of well-organized groups found in America's state legislatures and governor's offices. In the broad scheme of venue-shopping, states represent a prime arena in which interest groups can pursue their policy goals, particularly for interests that are concentrated in states or in areas over which states have primary jurisdiction. Regardless, as power has (albeit involuntarily) devolved from the federal government to states, public policy at the subnational level in the United States has increased in importance, which transitively means that interest groups continue to become more important in shaping policy. Virginia Gray and David Lowery have been at the forefront in researching the landscape of state interest groups (Gray and Lowery, 1996, 2000; Lowery and Gray, 1995; Lowery et al., 2015), undertaking the monumental task of categorizing all interest groups registered to lobby in all states. Their efforts have yielded numerous research studies that identify the concentration of varied interests in different states and, along with Nownes and Freeman's (1998) study of state interest group activity, have served to identify the mechanisms by which groups have influenced policy.

In their now-classic work on interest group systems at the state level, Gray and Lowery (Gray and Lowery, 1996, 2000; Lowery and Gray, 1995) use fluctuations in rabbit populations in Australia and Great Britain as an example of species behavior in different environments. One (the United States) experiences runaway growth and then a crash; while the other (Great Britain), experiences a more stable environment given existing predators, parasites, and other pressures. This is a common ecological model: cyclical patterns of population growth and decline that approach equilibrium over time. Some populations are large (rabbits breed like, well, rabbits) and subject to wild swings, others are large and subject to more moderate swings; while smaller populations have less security in their variability. According to Lowery and Gray (1995), the "ecology" of the interest group system is one that finds variability in interest group influence as a function of the overall interactions of the population size and diversity of organized interests.

The important takeaway from literature on interest groups is twofold. First, interest groups engage in public policy in order to obtain benefits for their supporters in a particular policy domain. For budgeting, this means that interests concentrate their efforts on a particular government function with the goal to defend and expand resources therein. It is groups private interest in securing public monies. Second, interest groups, not just one single entity, populate around policy domains and spending functions. Instead of thinking about interests as one unified block, it is more fruitful and empirically accurate to understand interests groups as an environment in which a diverse and changing number of groups operate. Some policy domains will be sparsely populated with a unified and quiet voice; others policy issues, such as welfare, witness lots of groups that might even confront each other. The density and volume of interest groups engaged in a policy problem signals to political actors, in particular governors, that changing public policy presents a political opportunity.

Thus far, we have reviewed policy process literature suggestive of a policymaking environment that favors the status quo long after public opinion has shifted. We have also reviewed literature that describes interest groups as the key defenders of the status quo. Both policy process and interest group theories are conditioned by the institutional environment that shapes policymaking. Formal political actors, particularly the executive, have their own unique preferences and abilities to express them. We now turn to this institutional analysis.

2.3 INSTITUTIONS, PUBLIC POLICY, AND BUDGETS

2.3.1 Institutional Role of Governors

The role of governors in policymaking, and budgeting in particular, provides us with a broader lens on how political institutions bestow particular actors with power, how relations among institutions are arranged by rules and practices, and ultimately how institutions influence policy. As political institutions have been the central subject of political science for the last thirty years (Hall and Taylor, 1996; Ostrom, 2009; Rhodes et al., 2008; Weaver and Rockman, 1993), we contribute to this literature through understanding how political institutions shape policy outcomes (Lieberman, 2002; Tsebelis, 2002) and what kind of institutional tools enable particular actors within a political system to influence policy.

We focus on institutional arrangements in a particular environment: the budget. Budget institutions are "all the rules and regulations to which budgets are drafted, approved, and implemented" (Alesina and Perotti, 1996, 401). These typically include (1) numerical targets, including balanced budget requirements that need to be met when budgets are cobbled together; (2) procedural rules that specify how budgets are proposed and passed; and (3) transparency rules that guide implementation and post-hoc adjustments.

Since our focus is on the political process of budgeting and how spending commitments emerge and are legislated, our institutional focus is on the second aspect – procedural rules. The following literature review is limited to this area.

Governors are powerful, especially in the budget process (Beyle, 1996; Hedge, 1983; Sharkansky, 1967; Thurmaier and Willoughby, 2001). Governors employ two institutional tools for policymaking and budgeting: agenda-setting and veto powers. Agenda-setting enables them to offer policy solutions and forces legislatures to react to executive proposals. Veto power empowers governors to reject potential alternatives, or to signal they will reject potential alternatives discussed in the legislature. For the budgeting process, this means that governors with a greater institutional ability propose and defend their budget, and are thereby able to reorganize individual spending commitments easily.

The institutional strength that allows governors to fully exploit their position as an influential unitary actor in the budget process varies across states (Beyle, 1996; Garand, 1985; Sharkansky, 1968). State constitutions assign governors the responsibility of producing a budget with the input of the legislature, though they have three institutional advantages vis-à-vis legislators. First, governors are unitary actors. In contrast to legislatures, a governor as a unitary actor is not plagued by incompatible preferences and the need to aggregate them. Instead, a governor is the sole authority for expressing executive preferences. Governors also possess a second advantage in the ability to set the budgetary agenda by acting first and thereby defining alternatives. Governors typically start the budgeting process by submitting agency requests to the legislature. The control of agenda-setting confers governors an early advantage in enacting their spending preferences. Third, governors can reject legislative demands by relying on their extensive veto powers. In contrast to American presidents, governors have the additional advantage of a line-item veto. This tool confers governors the power to cross out individual spending items or alter spending levels (Brown, 2012; Carter and Schap, 1990). Variation in veto strength across states influences the efficacy of vetoes as a negotiating tool in shaping the budget; governors possessing line-item vetoes with significant override provisions are able to extract preferences that involve both increases and decreases in expenditures (McGrath et al., 2016).

2.3.2 Budget Institutions: Institutional Variations and Diverse Outcomes

The preceding description of institutional rules of governors can be placed within a larger institutionalist literature on budgeting and on policymaking more generally. This literature aims at capturing the policy consequences – for individual spending behavior and overall fiscal policy – of enormous institutional variation within American politics and internationally. The institutional roles of governors correspond with several strains of rational choice institutionalism. The basic premise is that political actors maximize some form of utility. To obtain this utility, which is often defined as remaining in office, politicians need to engage strategically with their constituents who demand some form of benefit in exchange for their votes. Hence, political institutions are used by politicians to create public policies and budgets that serve electoral purposes.

A canonical example of this interaction is pork-barrel politics (Weingast et al., 1981), where individual legislators prefer spending on local public goods. In this model, all politics occurs in the legislature. In order to attract a sufficient number of supporters, a bill or budget needs to contain enough "side payments" to individual constituencies. This demand need encourages legislators to "log roll" (i.e., back each other's locally targeted spending proposal). Consequently, public monies are inefficiently distributed and government spending balloons. In short, politicians have an institutional incentive – re-election – to deplete public resources. The ability to deplete public resources depends, to some extent, on the legislative rules governing the budget process, including amendment procedures and the ability to package spending requests (Baron, 1991; Ferejohn and Krehbiel, 1987). Empirical support (Stein and Bickers, 1997) for the existence of pork-barrel politics has been rather mixed.

One obvious shortcoming of early pork-barrel models was that the initial setup ignored the executive branch and inter-institutional bargaining. The premise is that the executive has an interest in providing public goods (a sound budget) and therefore incentivized to limit legislative spending. Kiewiet and McCubbins (1988) offer an early model of this executive-legislative interaction through an analysis of how presidential vetoes influence legislative decision-making on annual budgets. The authors highlight a veto's asymmetry: Vetoes can be used to constrain legislative spending requests, though the executive is unable to extract additional resources from the legislative branch for a particular purpose. Thus, vetoes are a purely defensive tool.

The dominant concern for institutionalists remains how institution can limit spending and produce sound fiscal policy. Literature in comparative political economy frames this task as a common pool resource problem (Hallerberg, 2004; Hallerberg et al., 2009; von Hagen, 2008; von Hagen and Harden, 1995) . The basic setup is the following: The common resource of public money is generated by general taxation of all citizens. How should all revenues then split among functions of government or groups within society? The simple answer is that policymakers work for their respective constituency to extract as much as possible. They are interested in spending on their specific purposes without regard to the depletion of the overall budget.

The common pool resource problem might be remedied through two institutional solutions (Hallerberg, 2004; Hallerberg et al., 2009): contracts or delegation. In the American context of checks and balances, contractual solutions are less important, since neither the executive nor the legislative branch formally rely on each other. The second solution is to give one political actor authority over the entire budget and to ensure she cares about overall fiscal well-being. This idea stretches back to Heclo and Wildavsky (1974)'s distinction between "budget guardians" and "spending advocates." In their account, the management of post-War British budgets is conceived as a secretive and reoccurring battle between the Chancellor of the Exchequer and his trusted public servants at Her Majesty's Treasury (the guardians) against the spending ministers (the advocates). The task of the Chancellor of the Exchequer is to keep the spending requests of each minister in check. Finance ministers or other policymakers who are delegated to control the budget may rely on several institutional tools: the ability to propose a budget, being chief negotiator with individual spending ministers, and being able to cut individual spending items unilaterally. von Hagen (2008, 470) pithily summarizes this solution to the budgeting problem: "a centralized budget process contains elements that induce decision-makers to internalize the common-pool externality by taking a comprehensive view of their decisions." In a scenario where institutional authority is widely distributed among political actors, how can this dilemma be resolved?

Early answers to interbranch conflicts were put forward by the social choice literature (Shepsle and Weingast, 1981) and concentrated on how institutional rules induced equilibria that privilege some policymakers over others when making collectively binding decisions. In the American setting, much of the discussion was less on budget rules and fiscal institutions per se, but more often inspired by thinking about the spatial distribution of preferences (Downs, 1957). Both McKelvey (1976) and Romer and Rosenthal (1978) show how voting on policy proposals can become possible and change significantly if one actor has the ability to set the agenda. An agenda-setter is a policymaker who can structure voting choices so that all decision-makers must decide between the status quo and an alternative. In this quasi-dictatorial role, the agenda-setter is able to confront decision-makers, be it voters or fellow legislators, with a "take it or leave it" offer. This monopoly power enables the agenda-setter to shift policy outcomes toward their preferences.

In the case of budgeting, agenda-setting often entails a formal spending proposal for the upcoming fiscal year. The current budget serves as a status quo. Across American institutions, the formal agenda-setting actually varies substantively. The US president does not have the power to make a formal spending request, instead their budget proposal to Congress is essentially a meaningless wish list. At the state level, some governors do hold formal powers. Governors formally present a budget and then the legislature has to debate and decide. If they do not create an alternative, the governor's budget becomes law.

Next to agenda-setting, Tsebelis (1995, 2002) stresses a second aspect. Some institutional rules allow some decision-makers to make it challenging to change the status quo. The power to veto – to block change – and its consequences for policymaking is a key part of the institutional debate on executive power. Much of the institutionalist work has dissected the veto powers of the president. Hammond and Miller (1987) examine presidential veto powers and its companion – the legislative override – in a broader context of how US institutions create stability. They show formally that executive vetoes create stability. In the same vein, Kiewiet and McCubbins (1988) explore a president's ability to constrain Congress in the budget process. They find that the threat of a presidential veto limits legislative requests. Kiewiet and McCubbins tell us that veto power is asymmetrical: Vetoes enable the president to constrain total spending, but it cannot be used to increase a budget.

Several works have followed these initial insights. Importantly, McCarty (2000b) models the impact of vetoes, not just on the overall budget, but also on the distribution of government spending. He shows that vetoes may prevent budget increases, but even then, distributional effects may prevail. Targeted spending on small presidential constituencies can still be accomplished when a president prefers this allocation. Hence, preferences over how a budget is split up and distributed influence the size and composition of the winning coalition. Carter and Schap (1987) expose how different veto rules and legislative override provisions interact and that these interactions have distinct consequences for budget outcomes. In particular, the president's line-item veto may be ineffective in lowering congressional requests because the legislature is willing to increase spending on presidential priorities more than they compromise on in reducing their own spending priorities.

Empirical work on vetoes at the federal level has always been hampered by the lack of variation in institutional tools for presidents. This dilemma is compounded by a few observations (forty-six presidents as of 2023). Early institutionalist scholars turned to the American states for measuring and examining veto powers of the executive empirically (Beyle, 1968; Dometrius, 1979; Fairlie, 1917; Krupnikov and Shipan, 2012; Schlesinger, 1965). In fact, Fairlie (1917) suggests that variation in governors' veto power goes back prior to the adoption of the Constitution. Colonies ruled by a governor appointed by the British Crown were vested with veto powers, following the British custom that bills required royal assent. Governors in the chartered colonies, on the other hand, lacked this tool.

Since then and across the states, Dearden and Husted (1993) identified a threefold veto typology: (1) an all-or-nothing veto, (2) a simple line-item veto, and (3) an item-reducing veto. All-or-nothing vetoes simply kill a proposal in its entirety; line-item vetoes enable the executive to cross out individual budget lines, sentences, or even just letters; and item-reducing vetoes allow governors to reduce budget numbers according to their preference. Scholars continue to debate how the relative power of vetoes and what type of spending (e.g., total or distributive) they might constrain. Dearden and Husted (1993) argue that the more bite a veto power has, the closer to governor's ideal budget (which is not necessarily the smallest budget proposal) is implemented. Their empirical analysis shows that veto power is particularly powerful under divided government. More broadly, Klarner and Karch (2008) suggest that governors' institutional resources determine veto usage: Governors with stronger formal powers use them more regularly and successfully than those with weaker tools.

More recent work examines the contextual factors of vetoes. Primo (2006) highlights that governors' ability to reduce the total budget via a veto is contingent on ideological factors and a general balanced budget requirement. McGrath et al. (2016) delve more deeply into interbranch bargaining and show that supermajoritarian legislative requirements to override a governor's veto provide a substantial advantage to governors in policymaking and budgeting. Collectively, these works show that real variation in veto power exists, that governors possess different powers, and that these differences make a difference in total spending, budget balance, and a budget's distributive consequences.

One of the less-recognized effects of executive vetoes is their indirect and anticipatory features: Powerful governors may not need to use the veto to realize their preferences. Instead, the legislature knows that their policy choices are inherently bounded by a veto threat. When legislatures anticipate a governor will veto their proposal, they are less likely to submit it in the first place. Therefore, the power to threaten a veto, and not the veto itself, matters. In the context of interbranch bargaining, Manow and Burkhart (2007) simplify Vanberg (1998)'s compromise-or-confrontation game and argue that conflict emerges not under strong ideological differences and clear majorities because parties anticipate potential losses at electoral costs; instead, narrow majorities fuel conflict and the usage of formal institutional powers.

Two lessons from the institutionalist literature shape our subsequent discussion and argument. First, there is an inherent tension about role assignment between the comparative works on common pools and the American work on institutional bargaining. In both literature, legislatures are self-interested in exploiting particular spending types to their advantage, especially for electoral survival. However, the common pool resource literature holds that one policymaker has an interest in preserving the public good – public monies – and that this actor can be located in the executive branch. This is particularly true for the delegation model where one actor, typically a finance minister, has the institutional tools to make sound budgets. Literature on agenda-setters and veto power, on the other hand, is interested in how bargaining conflicts are resolved. While the executive may be interested in limiting spending, the executive is even more interested in extracting spending to the executive's advantage.

Second, different institutional tools interact with one another (see McCarty (2000a)), and they might matter for different outcomes, for example, total budget vs spending on particular items. Governors are in a unique institutional position when it comes to budgeting, as they possess formal agenda-setting and veto powers. Anyone who works in state government will tell you that governors use many tools in their approach to governing as they deem necessary to employ.

Kousser and Phillips' (2012) *The Power of American Governors* offer perhaps the most expansive and in-depth analysis of the role that governors play in the policy process. The authors develop a grand theory of gubernatorial bargaining and offer methodologically sophisticated and qualitatively rich evidence about the behavior of American governors. Kousser and Phillips make three central claims relevant to our work. First, in contrast with traditional spatial models of legislative negotiation, they argue for a "staring match" model given the variation in characteristics of governors and variations in legislative session length. They broadly consider the power of governors to veto legislation as a kind of side payment that can be offered to legislators.

Second, governors' ability to get the spending they want from legislatures is largely conditioned on the types of requests governors make. By analyzing state-of-the-state addresses, Kousser and Phillips show that governors are far more successful in motivating legislator opinion on budgetary issues than they are non-budgetary issues. They reason this is because the budget is essentially a must-pass piece of legislation in which multiple opportunities for compromise exist, whereas individual policy priorities are necessarily narrower. The primary finding is that governors are more successful in getting what they want in budget proposals than they are in non-budget proposals.

Third and most directly related to our research, Kousser and Phillips find that governors' proposals *expand* the size of government. This effect is conditioned on legislative session length, but suffice to say that powerful governors are able to expand the government should they so choose. The gubernatorial budgeting literature is replete with folk and empirical stories regarding the power of partisanship in understanding budgetary size and preferences. Democratic governors supposedly spend more, raise more taxes, and particularly cherish social welfare programs. However, evidence for these expenditure proclivities is lacking; indeed, Kousser and Phillips find that political party is simply less relevant to gubernatorial expenditures (agreeing with a comparative literature such as Breunig (2011) and Baumgartner et al. (2006b)). The primary factor shaping budgets is the ability to offer the initial package, which fits well with the extant literature on budgeting and the policy process (Ferejohn and Krehbiel, 1987; Hallerberg et al., 2001).

In summary, governors as institutional actors have a diverse set of preferences with regard to the overall budget and for particular spending priorities. The tricky part is how governors consider which institutional tools they will use under what conditions to achieve different goals. Governors basically operate simultaneously as a spending minister and a finance minister: They want to spend in some areas more than in others, but they are also responsible for an appropriate fiscal policy. In subsequent pages of this chapter, we offer an argument that accounts for the multidimensional nature of single-issue politics and shows how a governor committed to some issues also needs to address all others. As such, institutions constrain and enable the expression of executive preferences.

Why is this important? Governors are essentially empowered to blow up budgets or at least make them incredibly unbalanced – yet they do not. While budget rules outline how flexible governors can be, the combination of powers we identify compels them to consider the consequences of their actions across domains and for the entire budget. Governors have a double-layered institutional commitment: They are responsible for the overall health of the budget and have the ability to affect the fortunes of each budget item individually. Put another way, governors must tie their own hands but still be able to move their fingers.

State budgetary politics is the single most important area through which governors can influence state policy. While we devote much of our analysis to identifying the unique features of governors in the budgeting process, the general political environment they face is similar to other executives. Executives in all governmental situations are hampered by attention limitations, are variably empowered to influence the budgetary process, and face variably organized interests. How governors make the series of individual choices that lead to the creation of the whole budget is a question we will address once we examine the limitations of the extant literature.

2.4 QUESTIONS FROM THE LITERATURE

Thus far, we have reviewed three distinct literatures that attempt to understand variations in policy outputs. The policy process literature provides a model of decision-making to explain the motivations for policymakers. The interest group literature describes the tools that interest groups can use to attempt to leverage those motivations. The institutional design literature postulates that variations in the powers given to different positions in government enable and constrain policymakers in responding to policy demands (Cohen et al., 2009).

Though the political science community is familiar with the policy process, how interest groups function and the influence of institutions on structuring choice, each of these literatures has drawbacks in explaining public policy, particularly public policies that are interdependent composites of multiple policy areas. First, the institutional literature excels at examining executive action on individual issues, but has trouble explaining the multiple policy issues executives can work on. Executives must govern the few and the whole if they are to succeed in crafting composite legislation, such as budgets. The institutional literature also needs to attend to motivations of actors – re-election is important, but it is not everything. In public budgeting, governors' ideological predilections seem to matter far less than we might think if we used an institutional lens. If an executive has institutional power to achieve their goals, then institutional theory suggests that they ought to prioritize those goals that are most important and achieve them.

Second, the policy process literature can offer some assistance in understanding the match between preferences and power. Preferences are fixed, but attention is not; thus, understanding what causes attention shifts is tantamount to understanding the causes of policy change. However, attention does not always lead to policy change, even in cases where executives are powerful.

Thus, the process literature tells us when attention matters in leading to policy change, but is challenged to tell us when attention does not.

Third, interest groups provide more diverse sets of rewards to policymakers than reelection, which helps to complete the institutionalist picture of executive action. In relation to the policy process, the interest group literature provides some ideas regarding the sources of attention; this is a less-than-clear relationship, however, as many interest groups are in the business of *not* calling attention to problems, while others are interested in raising the agenda profile of issues. Each policy area has a peculiar interest group dynamic that contributes to efforts to affect issue salience. What happens when groups agree that issues should go unnoticed? What happens when both groups want issues to have a position high on the agenda? What happens when groups do not have a set pattern of competition? Thus, the interest group literature can help us understand some deficiencies of the institutional literature (priorities) using what we know about the process literature (attention); however, the interest group literature has not considered how interest groups affect budgeting.

The ultimate question is, how do governors actually arrive at and pass a budget? Though the vast state budgeting literature has asked this question before, previous studies relied on either an institutional or process approach and, in rare cases, a combination of both. But the act of budgeting is a compositional one: How do governors make the bundle of decisions to cut and expand particular items within a budget? The answer depends on an as-yet unanswered question in the interest group literature: How does interest group competition shape the budgetary agenda for executives? Our argument, which links the strands of research together and contributes to each, is inspired by the answers to these collective questions.

2.5 THE ARGUMENT: GOVERNORS, INTERESTS, AND BUDGETS

Ours is a theory that uses literature in attention, interest groups, and institutional authority to understand how states spend money. When we say we focus on "how" states spend their (our) money, we are broadly interested in the processes by which the issue environment creates opportunities for institutional actors, specifically executives, to shape the overall distribution of policy changes in their image. While much of the previous work on government spending focused on and explained how specific combinations of these factors contribute to specific expenditures, our view is much broader. Budgeting is a policy environment in which policymakers legislate binding decisions in several domains simultaneously. Budgets contain social, health, transportation, and many other spending decisions.

How does this process work? We proceed in three steps. The first step is about how policy issues provide motives for action. The underlying political competition, taken from theories of decision-making, focuses on attention to issues as a driver for policy change. The second step is about how the formation of interest groups around issues to make those issues more or less amenable to policy change. The interest group environment surrounding issues generates opportunities for policy change. The third step is about how the institutional strength of a governor provides the means to change policy given the interest group context surrounding issues. We identify the logical foundation of each of these steps in detail in the paragraphs that follow. Each step generates a set of testable expectations.

Step 1. Issues Motivate Attention in the Policy Process In the first step, policy issues motivate political actors to intervene in public policy. Issues may emerge episodically or periodically. In an idealized setting, governors would respond to issues as they emerge with an eye to the whole budget, motivated by desires to solve problems for constituents as well as shape the final budget to maintain balance.

This basic scenario is equivalent to a *bare-attention model* in which the policymaker is unfettered by politics and only must choose which items they prefer. Before considering the relative strength policymakers have to make changes or the political context of those choices, we can imagine a random policymaker as having preferences that are activated by attention to particular issues. The only constraints for the policymaker, in this case, are their own cognitive capabilities, which will limit the issues to which they can attend and the information they can bring to bear on policy choices. The only challenge for a policymaker is set by the number of issues demanding attention and the amount of information provided for each issue.

In Figure 2.2, we present a stylized scenario of a governor faced with a menu of five issues from which to choose.[3] This executive's baseline motivation is to

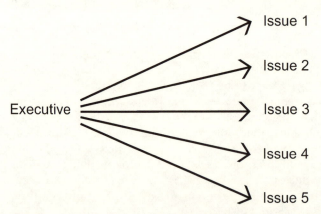

FIGURE 2.2 Basic executive decision-making for budgets. Solid lines represent attention to potential issues.

[3] Obviously, our governor is the envy of all other governors, given the relatively narrow agenda of issues with which they must contend.

reward constituencies and make good policy, often in this order, and hopefully simultaneously. The point of the simple model in Figure 2.2 is less about realistically describing the *actual* choice sets facing governors and more to show that the policymaker is driven to make decisions based on the issues presented to them.

While we present a comparatively simple case of two features that produce public policy – governors and the issues they are motivated to address – we know that the simple case is not that simple. The decision-making literature suggests that the governor attends to our five issues in serial order, which means that it is unlikely she will be able to make changes for all policy issues, and certainly not at the same time. Thus, even in the ideal world where the governor has complete control over the agenda and can legislate by fiat, we know that policymaking inevitably vacillates between incremental and large changes. This, of course, is an idealized model given that policymaking – particularly budgetary policymaking – does not occur in a vacuum.

Step 2. Interest Group Championship of Political Issues Shapes Political Opportunities If politics did occur in a vacuum, issues would not make a sound. In politics, though, issues do not exist without interest groups, which certainly strive to be heard. Policy issues emerge from political action, and political action emerges from public policy (Lowi, 1964). Interest groups form to defend existing policy arrangements and to deliver rents to their members. Pluralistic accounts of interest group actions suggest that groups form in opposition to other groups to battle for a share of the pie. For smaller issues, the interest group ecology literature (Gray and Lowery, 1993; Lowery and Gray, 1995) suggests that groups find niches with relatively little competition, in part because of lower stakes. The particular combination of issue scope and interest group competition shapes the opportunities for policy change.

Interest group literature in the aggregate suggests a policymaking environment in which groups engage in distinct agenda-setting strategies. In some cases, groups are vocal and attempt to maintain a prominent agenda position for issues they champion. In other cases, groups engage in "quiet politics" where the status quo of relative silence equates to issue dominance. These strategies create different interest group environments that complicate our bare-attention model and turn it into an *interest group model*. Issues are still motivating factors for our executive; however, as the political environment can enhance or mitigate opportunities to make decisions on political issues. In other words, our political vacuum now has sources of friction.

The source of friction varies in important ways for creating patterns of political action and the policy change that emerge from it. We have previously described three general types of interest group environments that shape opportunities for change within policy domains. The first is *capture* in which few groups are active, the stakes are low and groups avoid direct, universal attention to produce stable outputs for their members. The second is *deadlock* in

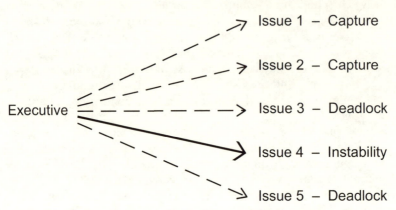

FIGURE 2.3 Executive decision-making for budgets across different interest group environments. Potential alignment of issues and interest group environments are displayed. Dashed lines represent potential attention to issues. Solid lines represent more likely choices.

which many groups are active, the stakes are high because the groups compete with one another for a large share of the budget, and groups will be vocal about their issue as a strategy to ensure they receive their piece of the budgetary pie. The commonalities between *capture* and *deadlock* are that attention is the same (stable) and outputs are the same (stable); the key difference between the two is the level of attention: low for *capture* and high for *deadlock*. The third interest group environment, *instability*, can be characterized by a shifting dynamic of inter-group conflict, no one dominant group, intermittent attention, and volatile outputs. *Instable* interest group environments offer the greatest opportunities for political change. We detail and discuss these categories in Chapter 4.

In Figure 2.3, we updated our stylized scenario of a governor faced with a menu of five issues from which to choose. Here, our governor still has to make choices regarding modifications to distinct budget categories as a function of their preferences in issue domains as well as their need to maintain a budget that balances these preferences against some kind of holistic goal. Now, the specific opportunities presented to our governor by interest group environments dictate the extent to which our governor can feasibly intervene. Deadlock and capture categories are likely to see less gubernatorial influence (though this does not mean our governor will not try), but the instability category, with less stable interest group coalitions, presents a prime opportunity for the governor to intervene. For all categories, the governor's preferences are important, but the governor's preferences have greater success in the instable interest group environment.

In addition to the opportunities presented to a governor in instable interest environments, budget decisions need to be made on all other issues. Stable interest-group, either in the form of deadlock or capture, ecosystems offer executives little opportunity for large policy change. Therefore, it is viable to think about long-term strategies. Here the choice becomes picking an interest group environment that is stable and populated by a few interests who would like to remain out of the public spotlight or taking a side in a heavy-populate, but antagonistic interest group environment that always is in the public's view. On average, governors favor captured over deadlocked interests as long-term strategy, because they do not want to and need to generate more attention for deadlock environment. When governors pick one side in heavy-populated environments, they anticipate visible and combative opposition, and they know that interest groups excel in stopping policy change. As such, the tranquil and mutually beneficial relationship to captured interests is a preferable long-term opportunity.

Stability in issue attention is, therefore, a function of interest group cooperation, collusion, or change; changes in attention result from shifts in dynamics in interest groups at the issue level. In general, interest groups and their members prefer stable, steady returns from policymaking to volatile swings. Thus, large changes in policymaking systems are indications of instability in interest group ecology.

Step 3. Governors Seize the Opportunity Through Institutional Means While interest groups may create political opportunities, opportunities by themselves do not necessarily equate to policy change. Governors are not entirely helpless in this complex environment; successful governors seize political opportunities to serve their electoral desires. Gubernatorial success in changing policy at the issue level is particularly a function of the means that governors have to create the budget. Governors are also responsible for budgets in their entirety and, thus, cannot make any one choice without considering its impact on other budget categories. Therefore, governors must thread a narrow needle of providing stable rents to policy domains that exist in interest environments with stable interest group dynamics, but also to make changes when opportunities present themselves.

All executives shop for policymaking opportunities in domains where interest group ecosystems are unstable. In those ecosystems that are inherently less stable, there may be many opportunities for governors to intervene to create policy change. The advantage for governors in this scenario is that these issue areas are amenable to more frequent policy change. The disadvantage is that the result can be volatility in policymaking, which presents challenges for long-term policymaking, long-term governance, or interest groups in the long term. However, governors may find the opportunity to change policy beguiling. Though such events are rare, powerful executives are well-positioned to seize these opportunities.

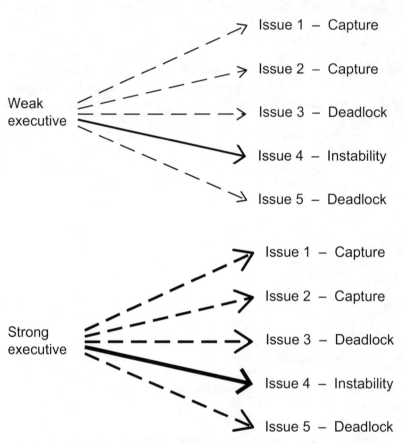

FIGURE 2.4 Executive decision-making for budgets across different interest group environments with different institutional powers. Potential alignment of issues and interest group environments are displayed. The top graph illustrates decision-making based on weak agenda-setting and veto powers. The bottom graph shows executives with strong powers. Dashed lines represent potential attention to issues. Solid lines represent more likely choices. The thickness of lines indicates the magnitude of change.

Not all governors have the same means to make policy change, regardless of the interest group environment in front of them. Figure 2.4 displays the third dimension of our policymaking model. Stronger governors – in this case, governors with the power to set the budgetary agenda and veto changes to their policy priorities – are better able to take advantage of the opportunities presented to them by interest groups. Governors exert their influence, though the impact of their powers is more muted in some interest group environments than others. Stable interest group environments produced by either the domination of a few interest groups set on conserving a small share of the budget, or by the competition of many groups competing for a larger share, will be harder for governors to move, particularly for weak governors. This insight can be detailed for each of the interest group scenarios.

All governors' choices are highly visible to interest groups. Governors across the United States spend large portions of their time in capture and deadlock scenario, despite the relative inability to make major changes there. Their choices have different implications in each scenario, though. In the case of the capture, the playing field is relatively small and governors know that there is one winner. The sector and the dominant groups are intertwined – losses to the sector mean losses to the group. Therefore, strong governors can signal their commitment to a particular policy issue and their groups more strongly than a weaker governor. Gubernatorial choices in the deadlock scenario are more politically fraught, as they involve picking a side between competing groups. Powerful governors can be more decisive in picking a side and reward it than weaker governors. Finally, in the instability scenario, the playfield is volatile. Interest groups aim for attracting attention and providing opportunities, but present an uncertain reward structure for governors. Governors' intervention thus is not bound by an obvious long-term reward structure, but by the craving for transformative change. Stronger governors can match their power with this opportunity and create particularly large changes. In all of these environments, a clear budgetary commitment by a strong governor delivers more noticeable action toward interest groups, compared to the more modest choices of weak governors. As such, institutional power becomes an exercise in its strategic usage.

In sum, executives are the most powerful individual players in policymaking. Governors know that the budgeting environment, in general, follows the pattern of punctuated equilibrium – things change a little, until they change a lot. Governors can, and certainly do, try to buck this trend; however, the fate of governors to make meaningful changes depends in part upon the relative stability of the interest group environment on s policy issue, which we argue is responsible for determining the stability of policy outputs. Interactions among interest groups within a policy domain provide governors opportunities to make noticeable contributions to policy change. In seeking these attention-induced opportunities, executives marshal their institutional weapons – agenda-setting and vetoes – to propose and defend a budget to their liking. We argue that while executives are the strongest actors in fiscal policymaking, they are dependent upon the choice opportunities presented to them by interest groups for each particular spending item.

2.5.1 Implications for Public Policy and Budgeting

Thus far, we have presented the interaction between interest groups and governors as an interaction that occurs during the budget process, in which governors want to intervene in extant subsystem politics where interest groups are active. Budget categories support interest group communities, the composition of which provides costs and benefits to intervention by policymakers. The constellation of interests engaging in policy issues provides opportunities for governors to intervene. Gubernatorial intervention is aided by institutional means, notably veto and agenda-setting powers.

The budgeting process is interdependent categorically – cuts to one category influence the availability to fund others. Categorical interdependence influences the budgeting process, which a long-term game that is interdependent and cumulative with previous budgeting process. The repeated interaction between categories, interest groups, and governors has consequences for the short-term direction of change, how changes are distributed, and the rate of growth in the long term. Depending on the means of governors and opportunities created by different types of interest group environments, we expect policy change to take different *forms*, which we discuss further in Chapter 3.

First, the number of decisions that deviate from the trends of the previous year is the *direction* of policy change. Does a policy area see a cut in one year and then an increase in the other, or, does a category see steady growth for a few years followed by years of cuts? Are changes relatively similar year in and year out? In each of these cases, policy change has real consequences for the interests lobbying the government for money, notably, for the predictability of change. As indicated in the literature review, predictable changes are, for most groups, important for the purpose of credit-claiming, member recruitment, and reputation. In most cases, interest groups are interested in predictable *positive* change.

A second form of policy change takes is in the *distribution* of the magnitude of changes over an extended period of time. Though the direction of policy change is important to identifying winners and losers one year, winning and losing may not be equally distributed within and across categories. Long-term distributions of categories provide an account of the results of the stable opportunity structures interest groups offer policymakers. Policy process literature in budgeting views the extent of budget *punctuations* as a measure of stability. Punctuated budgets offer mostly small returns punctuated by large changes; less punctuated budgets offer a more even distribution of budgetary changes. As such, punctuations signal how much policy domains are disrupted over time.

Budget changes are also associated with different long-term rates of *growth*. Long-term growth, our third form of policy change, refers to the trajectory of the share of a budget category over an extended time period. Essentially, how much bigger a piece of a pie gets. If a budget category experiences sustained periods of positive budget changes, compared to other categories, its overall share within a budget eventually increases. These sustained periods of growth are more likely to occur through continuous, incremental spending

TABLE 2.1 *Theoretical implications for policy change, punctuations, and growth.*

Governor power	Capture	Instability	Deadlock
A. Direction			
High	High-positive	Negative-high	Highest-positive
Low	Medium-positive	Negative-low	High-positive
B. Punctuation			
High	Low	Highest	Middle-high
Low	Lowest	High	Middle-low
C. Long-term growth			
High	High	Lowest	Medium-low
Low	Highest	Low	Medium-high

commitments, than they are through irregular, attention-induced, punctuations (Breunig and Koski, 2012). The distinction between punctuations and long-term growth yields two distinct motives for interest groups and governors – one-time transformations of a policy issue with a massive influx of spending or steady returns through uninterrupted spending commitment.

The implications of these three forms of budget change are summarized in Table 2.1. In unpacking Table 2.1, change, punctuations, and growth are a function of the opportunities the interest group environment presents to governors and the means by which governors navigate it. Our model generally argues that the opportunities dictate the course of public budgeting, although the means are still important at the margins in determining the magnitude of change.

In the capture scenario, there are few interest groups, so the governor's opportunities to intervene are limited. Fewer groups equate to less attention paid to a category, and those few groups generally prefer it that way. We expect captured categories will experience year-on-year increases. On the other hand, we also expect these increases will be relatively steady, leading to a less punctuated distribution. Positive changes and fewer punctuations should lead to a category's higher long-term growth in the overall *share* of the budget. Group alignments are likely to be stable, such that gubernatorial intervention that produces any particular winners and losers is likely to affect the entire interest group ecosystem. Governors are, thus, motivated to intervene to reproduce the existing distribution (i.e., status quo) of monies to the groups in the capture scenario. Gubernatorial means are limited in influencing the rate and direction of change in these categories, and weaker governors able to move the needle even less – states with weak governors ought to see the least punctuated distributions. Captured categories in states with weak governors will experience the least institutional political meddling and enjoy the highest growth rates in budget share over time.

In the instable scenario, groups' ability to maintain a steady policy image is hindered. Group dominance is in flux, the group dynamic is unstable, and attention to issues is uneven. The opportunities for policy intervention by governors are many, both in serving interests within these categories, but also in using these categories to offset budget crises that might affect categories to which there is more consistent attention. The result is that categories in an instable interest group regime are more likely to be cut than those of capture and deadlock. In such a volatile environment, it is difficult for groups to hold back the governor from making more substantial changes to categorical budgets. Governors are aware of ephemeral attention to issues and use attention to their advantage in making larger changes, understanding that the constellation of groups during the next budget cycle may be different and, thus, may not reward or punish the governor for more self-interested actions. Consistency, or more likely, cuts, lead to a scenario in which governments play catch up to re-fund labile categories. The de-fund/re-fund cycle produces punctuated budgets but also results in the lowest categorical growth over time as positive changes are justified as make-up funds rather than incremental programmatic improvements.

Deadlock interest group scenarios attract the most groups, which can be good for groups given that the government is more likely to attend to their issues, but challenging insofar as each group is seeking government revenue. Each interest has its own desires to extract rents from government coffers and the status quo is simply to reward all, if for no other reason than competition within the category is strong, but also that the deadlock chorus is much louder than either capture or instability. Deadlock categories also enjoy the most attention over time of all categories; thus, there are fairly smooth adjustments over time in the distribution of cuts and increases. However, there may be times (e.g., fiscal crisis) where cuts or boosts are necessary and the sheer volume of interests gives policymakers a way to sacrifice the interests of one or two in order to benefit the remainder. To the extent that cuts are refilled or boosts clawed back by governments, we expect to see greater punctuations than the capture scenario, but still less than the instability scenario.

Deadlock interest group environments also include several groups competing in high-attention budget categories. Therefore, policymakers' motivations to intervene are quite high. Governors are challenged to make significant changes given the inertia of multiple interests, though it can be in the governor's interest to attempt to alter expenditures given the high-profile nature of deadlock issues. When faced with budget decisions during tough times, it is possible to isolate programs that essentially punish one group to save the many. Using this logic, it is also possible for governors to benefit one or two groups above the others, akin to the logic of distributive politics. Stronger governors may be able to promote large changes when opportunities arise, leading to a more punctuated distribution than would be the case for weaker governors. As governors can alter the distribution of changes in deadlock budgets, we expect that long-term growth in these categories generally occurs somewhere between the low growth of the instability scenario and the high growth of the capture scenario.

2.6 MAKING POLICY IN THE CONTEXT OF THE AMERICAN STATES: NEGOTIATING WITH LEGISLATURES AND REPRESENTING PARTIES

We have focused the argument of this book on literatures concerning the policy process, executive power, and interest groups. However, other institutions are involved in democratic policymaking and are alternative setters of the agenda across governments. More specifically, executives must negotiate with other policymaking bodies (typically legislatures) and interest groups may dominate specific issues while competing for agenda space with other preference aggregators (typically parties).

For our book, we use state governments to understand the influence of governors and interest groups on budgetary outcomes. State politics research has evolved over time to reflect states' growing roles as sophisticated policymaking apparatuses forced to respond to an increasing share of political demands in the United States. States are not only responsible for home-grown political problems, but are also called on to implement a greater share of federal programs (Chatfield and Rocco, 2014). States are responsible for a range of federal programs that including American environmental (Clark and Whitford, 2011; Cline, 2008), welfare (Conlan, 2017; Haskins, 2007), transportation (Dilger, 1998; Gerber and Gibson, 2009), and health care policy (Béland et al., 2016; Haeder and Weimer, 2013).

Much of states' increased role in making and implementing policy appears in the form of public budgeting. In many cases, federal policies are essentially chunks (or blocks, though this has a specific fiduciary connotation) of money given to states to manage. States are granted varying degrees of flexibility regarding how to use these monies, but, managing money and, importantly, managing spending obligations that are externally and self-imposed are critical features of state budgeting. The vast amount of funds in state budgets creates opportunities for political actors, even if some of these funds are constrained. Competition for discretionary funds is particularly fierce. In the paragraphs that follow, we examine the literature on these alternative sources of power within state policymaking systems.

2.6.1 Legislatures and Budgeting

Legislatures in the American states vary in many ways (for an overview, see Squire (2012)), and a substantial literature has therefore examined the structure, capacity, role, and efficacy of state legislatures. We focus on the extent to which legislatures may compete or collude with a theory of executive

policymaking that situates executives as uniquely powerful, uniquely constrained, and uniquely concerned political actors in policymaking systems.
Theoretically, legislatures ought to offer a substantial counterweight to executive action, given their formal role in the budgeting process and the way that
district-level representation (rather than statewide representation) aggregates
preferences. In this section, we contrast the structural and representational
features of legislatures and executives.

State legislatures are broadly similar to the US Congress: All state legislatures have two chambers (except Nebraska), are generally run by political
parties (again, Nebraska is exceptional), have legislative staff to assist legislators in understanding public policy, are directly elected by the people, and
perform oversight. Despite these surface similarities, there are many differences
in the basic structure of state legislatures.

First, while state legislatures may develop systems to address coordination
problems, not all legislatures have committee systems, and those with committee systems vary in their sophistication (Hamm et al., 2006, 2014). Some of
this variation is a function of the size of the agenda associated with the legislature given the size of the overall agenda in a state; however, in some cases,
committee structures have simply not evolved to address increased problem
complexity. As discussed previously, PET indicates that systems with fewer
committees have less capacity to process information in parallel, leading to
bottlenecks of decision-making and issues that are simply not addressed in a
timely fashion. Committees serve as opportunities for legislators to both exercise and develop expertise (Battista, 2012; Richman, 2008); fewer committees
lead to fewer legislators committed to issue specialization.

Second, legislatures vary in size, which influences coordination and the
degree to which they are representative. Famously, the largest legislature is
the New Hampshire assembly with 400 members, while the smallest is the
Alaska Senate with 20 members. New Hampshire is also the most representative, with 400 legislators serving 1.335 million people, while the Texas Senate
manages to use 31 people to represent 27.86 million citizens. (Not *everything*
is bigger in Texas.) Furthermore, a key difference between state legislatures
and the Congress is that districts must be equal in population size for each
chamber. Similar to the federal model, some states apportioned their senates
based on geography – county boundaries – though the Supreme Court ruled
this unconstitutional (Webster, 2013). The impact of this distinction between
state senates and the US Senate can be seen in Ansolabehere and Snyder's
(2008) study of legislatures, which shows major policy change after states
reapportioned their senate districts.

The third, and perhaps most well-studied variation in state legislatures,
is legislative professionalism (King, 2000; Squire, 1992, 2007). Legislatures
simply have less capacity to understand wide-ranging policy problems and to
generate broad policy solutions, in contrast with their federal counterpart. This
is somewhat counterintuitive insofar as state legislatures are often seen as think

tanks for policy solutions that spread vertically or horizontally. The "laboratories of democracy" (Morehouse and Jewell, 2004) description of policymaking in state legislatures owes much to specializations of entire legislatures on state-specific policy problems. Some laboratories are better equipped than others in terms of the structures of decision-making previously described, as well as resources available to members.

Legislative Structures and Executives in Budgeting. These structural features ought to impact the activities of individual legislators and the outputs of legislatures. Though an extensive literature examines the types of individuals who become legislators (Hedge, 2018; Rosenthal, 2008; Squire and Moncrief, 2015), we are more concerned about legislature features' role in the interplay between policymaking institutions. We argue that executives are powerful in the budgeting process as a function of their institutional position and power, but we must also consider the alternative power source in state politics. These two institutions contrast in three ways: their formal role in the budgeting process, their coordination of preferences, and their capacity to seek information.

Formal Role of Legislatures in the Budgeting Process. We have already discussed executives' formal role in the budgeting process as a function of the role of legislatures. As public budgets result from negotiations between executives and legislatures, executive power in public budgeting is an inherently relativistic concept. Legislatures have attempted to claw back budgeting power from governors, but are typically unsuccessful, as governors can simply veto such attempts. In 1999, the North Dakota House introduced a measure to allow the legislature to create a pre-session budget akin to the governor's budget. Governor Ed Schafer chafed at this measure, claiming the executive had the exclusive ability to create budgets. The House Majority Leader John Dorso disagreed, arguing the legislature had authority over policy issues and that "sometimes you can't separate policy and the budget" (Serhienko, 1999). North Dakota Senate Majority Leader Gary Nelson concurred: "we want to be proactive on the budget, not reactive" (Serhienko, 1999). Governor Schafer threatened a veto that Senate Majority Leader Nelson countered with a threat to override. The game of budgetary chicken eventually ended when the legislature blinked. That the 1999 North Dakota government was a Republican triad further illustrates that institutional wrangling supersedes party.

Legislatures are a required part of the budgeting process – without them, even the strongest governor cannot enact their agenda. Recent battles between state legislatures and governors make this point clear. Illinois endured a two-year stalemate over the budget between the governor and legislature, ending in July 2017 with a legislative override of a gubernatorial veto. A similar budget battle occurred in Kansas in June 2017: The legislature voted to override the governor on revenue to produce a budget bill (which was passed by a veto-proof margin). In June 2017, the governor of North Carolina saw his budget veto overridden by the legislature. Despite their prominence, these cases are rare because governors and legislatures hammer out compromises before the brinkmanship of policymaking by veto. Such clashes are empirically rare but also expected to be rare from the literature on veto players, which would expect few vetoes in the state policymaking process since vetoes loom over budget negotiations. In short, a governor need not veto legislation to invoke veto power.

Coordination of Gubernatorial and Legislative Preferences. While legislatures are institutionally empowered to counteract gubernatorial authority, they face significant challenges in coordinating preferences in comparison with executives. Legislators represent districts as distinct as congressional districts, which can feature narrower preferences than the national legislature given size and homogeneity of state district populations. In contrast, governors represent more heterogeneous state interests. Legislators are likely to pursue distributive benefits for their districts (i.e., pork-barrel spending), similar to members of Congress (Jewell, 1982). However, legislators need to coordinate with one another to express these preferences in budgeting. An individual legislator's ability to add, subtract, or shift spending within a budget is relative to the size of the legislature, her stature within the majority party, her tenure in the legislature, and her placement with the committee structure (if one exists) of the legislature (Wu and Williams, 2015). Individual legislators simply have fewer opportunities to influence the overall budget because they are only one of many; thus, coordination of an individual's preferences with the whole is crucial to any preference expression. In contrast, state executives are formally required to coordinate with very few actors, at least when setting the budgetary agenda.

Legislative Capacity to Seek Information. So far, we have described two features of legislatures that help explain their powers relative to governors: institutional authority and coordination of preferences. Institutional authority, as we have framed it, is an inherently relative concept, such that capturing gubernatorial authority in budgeting ought to also account for legislative authority. Additionally, coordination problems for legislatures, while varying as a function of heterogeneity of preferences and perhaps legislature size, represent a more-or-less fixed challenge for legislatures across states. A feature of state legislatures that does vary significantly is legislative professionalism, which could provide critical support for classic features of policy analysis, such as problem identification and solution generation. For our purposes, professionalization might influence the scope of the agenda for legislatures.

2.6.2 Political Parties

Our budgeting story focuses on a policymaking environment in which executives navigate an agenda largely set by interest groups. The extent to which executives are successful in creating their own policy given these opportunities is a function of their institutional powers. In Section 2.6.1, we described legislatures as alternative institutional power sources to governors in state budgeting. As an alternative to interest groups as sources of agenda-setting in governments, we look to political parties. Interest groups and political parties differ significantly in how they set the agenda and in the specific resources they offer legislatures and governors. However, in both cases, each organization offers elected officials a set of signals regarding the salience of issues and resources to solve those issues.

Political parties at the state level are important for similar reasons as they are at the national level: Parties help choose candidates, aggregate mass preferences, and provide for machinery to assist like-minded candidates to achieve electoral success (Cohen et al., 2009; Grumbach, 2018; Wright and Schaffner, 2002). Nevertheless, non-partisan or third-party candidates are more likely to have electoral success in state governments than national governments. This is partially due to the ability to appeal to a narrow group of already narrow preferences and the fact that state-level political office involves lower stakes.

Parties in Government. Parties not only provide support for candidates in electoral contexts, but also in policymaking. Parties funnel mass preferences, provide policy ideas, and, importantly, serve as alternative organizational structures in legislatures (Wright and Schaffner, 2002). Parties coordinate legislators' activities in individual chambers as well as across chambers and institutions. Just as they play a central role in elections for less professional legislatures, parties serve as alternative organizational structures to provide resources to candidates who intermittently interact with the legislative system.

Parties and Polarization. Despite differences at the state level, party government in the US states has followed polarization trends (Hinchliffe and Lee, 2016; Shor and McCarty, 2011) seen at the federal level. Beyond the comparison with federal-level politics, though, party governance in US statehouses is not only polarized but also one-sided. Over time, statehouses have become dominated by single-party governance. Single-party governance has emerged as a result of a partisan sorting – the West Coast and Northeast have become more Democratic, while the South has become more Republican (Fiorina et al., 2010; Levendusky, 2009). American state legislatures are therefore the poles of a polarized political system.

Parties and Budgets. The links between budgets and party control are straightforward and well-documented (Blais et al., 1993; Bräuninger, 2005; Kittel et al., 2003). The motivation for any party's actions is a future electoral payoff; thus, parties ought to advocate spending that delivers financial rewards to constituents who can return electoral rewards to parties. Literatures in comparative politics and welfare spending have shown that left parties are rewarded for spending more government funds, while right parties are benefited when they spend less. This is particularly true in the European context, where higher social spending enables wage restraint and foster international competitiveness and economic growth (e.g., Alvarez et al., 1991).

Partisan preferences have been found to influence spending levels in some state budget areas (Besley and Case, 2003). Barrilleaux has confirmed state Democratic parties prefer spending more on welfare, health care, and education (Barrilleaux and Miller, 1988; Barrilleaux et al., 2002). Beland and Oloomi (2017) identify a similar relationship between gubernatorial partisanship and expenditure preference, with Democrats spending more on health care, education, and public safety. Curiously, Beland and Oloomi also reveal that partisanship does not influence the *overall* size of the budget – a finding that corresponds with an institutional understanding of the role and responsibility of governors in the state budgeting process. Regardless of the budget items parties prefer, partisan competition can influence the distribution of funds to particular districts for the purpose of motivating positive electoral outcomes. For example, Ansolobehere and Snyder (2006) find that the distribution of state expenditures (in their case, to counties) is less likely to be a partisan reward for previous electoral performance and more a desire to motivate future political support.

Parties as Sources of the Political Agenda. Parties act as overt sources of issues on an agenda to which members of the legislature are likely to attend given their allegiance to parties (Aldrich, 1995). The effect is somewhat endogenous, as parties not only guide legislatures but are also vehicles for legislators to set the agenda for their own preferences. While parties may focus on individual issues (e.g., affirmative action, welfare, or Medicaid expansion), any one issue is part of a party's issue bundle. The party agenda is an interdependent document, such that attention for one item means less attention for another. Interest groups are not so constrained. While groups certainly form coalitions, interest groups – by definition – need not concern themselves with the impact of their victories on the entire budget. Thus, parties and interest groups offer alternative, and sometimes overlapping, sources of policy agendas for state policymakers.

2.7 A BRIEF OVERVIEW OF THE BUDGET PROCESS IN AMERICAN STATE GOVERNMENTS

Throughout this book, we claim that public budgets provide a suitable case to test broad theories of the policy process, interest groups, and institutions. Here we offer evidence that not only are public budgets suitable, but they are *ideal* for testing these theories. Budgeting at the state level is more regimented than most other budget and policy processes in US governments. The structure of the budget process more closely approximates an ideal in which policy – in this case, budgets – must occur; the actors are known, and there are rules that privilege and constrain certain decisions (Garand et al., 2014). While regimented, the budget process across the fifty states is remarkably similar even though states have different political histories, confront different policy problems, and have vastly varying capacities to contend with those problems. To the extent that the budgeting process does differ by state, it is challenging to discern systematic reasons for such variance. State budget processes are distinct from other state policy processes given that states have rules specific to the budget process and that budgets are akin to "must-pass" legislation. The state budgeting process shares some similarities with the federal budgeting process, though there are notable differences that enhance the position of executives relative to legislatures and also greatly reduce the capacity of states to deficit spend.

The broad outline of the state budgeting process is not dissimilar to the federal government, see Table 2.2. The state budget office or equivalent organization in the executive branch issues instructions to agencies regarding a state's expected revenues and expected demands placed on agencies. Most state budget officers provide revenue forecasting (40 states out of 50) and many perform functions similar to firms, such as resolving expenditures relative to budgets, executing program reviews, and even undertaking demographic analysis (National Association of Budget Officers, 2015). Individual agencies rely on guidelines by the budget officer and undertake an analysis of their extant commitments and future needs as a function of statutory obligations. In the next step, state agencies submit budget requests to the state budget officers. State budget officers then work with the agencies' requests to arrive at an amicable (or, at least, reasonable) demand for each agency. The sum total of these requests are included in the budget proposal the governor submits to the legislature.

State budget processes have differing levels of transparency, which the state budgeting literature has shown to affect taxation and expenditures. Budget transparency scholarship has long been a focus in comparative budgeting. Alt and coauthors (2002) develop a composite index of budget process transparency for the fifty states from NASBO and NCSL publication.[4] They find that fiscal transparency leads to greater spending since players have a greater understanding of where money goes, and that more transparent governors have higher job approval. While they also show that higher transparency leads to greater taxation, such tax increases are not commensurate with expenditure increases (see also Alt and Lowry, 2010). Transparency can result from extant institutional processes, but can also come from partisan competition (Alt et al., 2006).

---

[4] The transparency index includes: "Budget is reported using generally accepted accounting principles (GAAP); Multiyear expenditure forecasts are used; Budget cycle is annual; Revenue forecasts are binding; Legislative branch has or shares responsibility for revenue forecasts; All appropriations are included in a single bill; Appropriation bills are written by non-partisan staff; Open-ended appropriations are prohibited; and Budget requires published performance measures" (Alt and Lowry, 2010).

TABLE 2.2 *Example state budget process and timeline.*

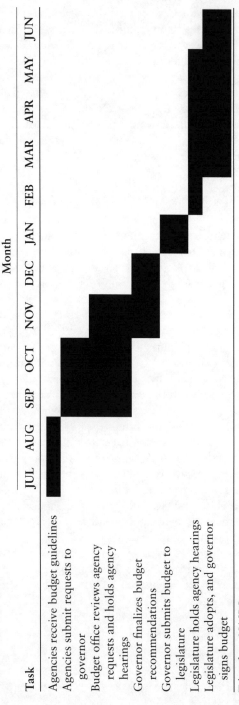

Task	JUL	AUG	SEP	OCT	NOV	DEC	JAN	FEB	MAR	APR	MAY	JUN
Agencies receive budget guidelines	■											
Agencies submit requests to governor			■	■								
Budget office reviews agency requests and holds agency hearings				■	■	■						
Governor finalizes budget recommendations						■	■					
Governor submits budget to legislature							■	■				
Legislature holds agency hearings								■	■	■	■	
Legislature adopts, and governor signs budget											■	■

Taken from NASBO 2015.

Comparing State Budget Processes to the Federal Budget Process. State budget processes, also display key differences from the federal processes pertinent to our process-based policy analysis. First, and perhaps most importantly, the governor is a much stronger actor in promoting a budget than a president. Modern presidential budgets are, to be blunt, aspirational. Presidents signify their preferences for spending both in magnitude and in program area by creating a presidential budget. Though the presidential budget begins a negotiation with Congress in setting the agenda for discussion over the next several months of budget talks, Congress is *under no formal obligation* to take any of the President's suggestions. Procedurally, the President does not introduce budget legislation, as this is Congress' role. Governors, however, introduce budgets to the legislature, and the legislature is bound to a debate that modifies a governor's proposal. This crucial difference places governors in a much stronger position relative to legislatures than the President relative to Congress. Governors drive the budgetary agenda.

Second, state budget processes are intentionally less flexible than federal processes. First, nearly all states have some balanced budget requirement. However, as state budget officers and policy scholars learned: not all balanced budget requirements are created equally. States have developed numerous ways in both statute and constitution (Hou and Smith, 2006) to constrain different points of the budget process in order to create a balanced outcome (Poterba, 1995). Most states require governors to submit a balanced budget to the legislature (Hou and Smith, 2010). In amending the budget, the legislature could pass a budget unbalanced with projected revenue; thus, some states require the legislature to pass a balanced budget. There are also variations across states in what a "budget" means for the purpose of balance – some states require the budget to be submitted in full, while other states make use of supplemental appropriations, which some states require to be balanced. Once the budget reaches the governor's desk, some states require that the governor sign a balanced budget – if the legislature has done its job of passing a balanced budget, then this is a straightforward task provided the governor is satisfied with the final document. If legislatures pass an out-of-balance budget, then governors are responsible for balancing the budget using veto powers. The item veto enables gubernatorial flexibility in bringing a budget (back) into balance or in shaping the budget to fit a governor's preferences. In vetoing features of a budget bill, governors must be conscious of their obligations to sign a balanced budget; crafty governors can be constrained and enabled by budgetary rules to intervene in public budgets with their veto pens.

Not only do balanced budget requirements limit budgeting, revenue forecasts also can be incorrect. Shifts in the economy can alter both the supply of revenue for states and the demand for services. Thus, states can and do run deficits, despite balanced budget requirements. How these deficits affect state government services and the response of the governor and legislature is also a function of budget rules. Some states have automatic triggers for both revenue shortfalls and windfalls. For example, Oregon has a "kicker" rule where all revenues collected in excess of 2 percent of revenue forecasts must be refunded to the taxpayers. Such rules, which make forecasting incredibly high-stakes and challenging, enforce balanced budget requirements on both the positive and negative ends of the distribution. A more common response to spendthrift legislatures or unanticipated revenue shortfalls is deficit and carry-over restrictions. In other words, it is conceivable that responsible legislatures and governors produce budgets that are balanced insofar as their forecasts dictate, but can still run a deficit. Most states have a carryover or deficit restriction to push the state government to deal with its fiscal obligations (Smith and Hou, 2013). States can and do deficit spend, but this is more challenging than for the federal government. State legislatures must publicly approve the issuance of bonds to service public debt. The issuance of bonds for capital spending is quite common given challenges associated with the mismatch between long-term spending priorities of infrastructure projects and the short-term political attention of elected officials.

As we discuss later, the literature is challenged to produce consistent findings of these rules on fiscal outcomes – be they categorical, general expenditure, or distributional. What the literature does find is that a handful of these rules matter depending on the question that is asked. While there are various iterations of classifying budget requirements, Smith and Hou (2013) find that balanced budget requirements in the form of gubernatorial initiation, limits on supplemental appropriations, and carryover requirements, are most likely to affect budget outcomes.

Comparing State Budget Processes to Other Policy Processes. State budget processes not only differ from federal budget processes, but also differ from other state policy processes. The first difference is organizational. State budget agencies vary in their capacity to make revenue forecasts and correctly adjust expenditure patterns to anticipate a changing state economic environment. Hence, there *is* some kind of agency whose task it is to investigate the implications of the passage of a budget. Even in the smallest states, the executive branch has qualified staff to oversee the creation of budgets. The same is true for legislative staff who specialize in broad areas of public policy (e.g., education), but not for all areas, nor for all pieces of legislation that members put forward. For much of the public law created in legislatures, there is simply less capacity to assess the need and long-term impact of these policy decisions. Budgets not only get the attention of elected officials, but also get the attention of professional staff.

Further, state budgets occur on a regular timeline. State governments budget on an annual (30 states) or biannual (20 states) basis. The regularity of the budget negotiating process displays a difference between the federal budget process as well as the state policy process. In contrast to the federal budget process, state budgets must be negotiated for a set period of time; thus, the stopgap spending in recent Congresses is an uncommon occurrence (special sessions to deal with fiscal shortfalls notwithstanding). Distinct from the state policy process, the set timeline for the budget process creates a shared window of opportunity for negotiation for elected officials from the executive and legislative branches.

2.8 CONCLUSIONS: A BUDGETING APPROACH TO THE POLICY PROCESS

Public budgeting at the state level is a process that resembles an idealized type of policymaking not found, perhaps ironically, in the actual policy process. State budgeting occurs on a specific calendar producing predictable windows of opportunity for change; it uses a relatively routine and generally well-known procedure involving the executive and legislative branches; it is fostered with the assistance of dedicated policy-specific staff to make up for variations in elected official capacity; and must conform to specific rules that constrain budgetary outcomes – rules that all parties know (if not understand). A casual perusal of the policy literature reveals scholars mightily attempting to understand the twisted, yet relatively unconstrained, path of most policymaking. While budgeting is far from simple (remember, there are millions of stories in a budget), at least the budget game *typically* follows its own rules, displays and trades excitement in uncertainty for the thrill of consistency. Public budgeting is, to paraphrase Rob Zombie, "more policy than policy."

We use state budgets to test our argument. State budgets provide the motives for political action: Every budget season, the possibility to add resources to one spending item and take it away from another exists. These changes in commitment of public monies either transpire steadily over time or materialize suddenly and transformatively. Interest groups are aware of these possibilities and rivet their attention to particular policy issues and thus spending items. As interests populate around policy issues, their competition creates policymaking opportunities for executives who are responsible for the budget. Governors then observe policy issues around which interests are captured, instable or deadlocked. Once governors identify an opportune change in a budget, they rely on their institutional means for shaping a budget accordingly. Motives, opportunities and means thus determine changes, punctuations and long-term outcomes in state budgets and public policy at large.

We are certainly not the first to use public budgets to test theories of the policy process. Our review of the policy process literature suggests that public budgeting research does much heavy lifting for academic studies intending to understand patterns of policymaking. Subnational budgeting, particularly in the United States, has served to answer several theoretical questions about agenda-setting in the policy process and substantive questions regarding the decisions governments make in particular policy domains. In the Chapter 3, we empirically describe public budgets at the state level, identify how motives for policy change appear and develop a typology for relating these moments of budgeting to interest group dynamics.

PART II

MOTIVES, OPPORTUNITIES, AND MEANS
OF POLICY CHANGE

3

Motives

Issues of the Moment(s)

Investigating university presidential leadership, Cohen and March (1974) developed an enduring metaphor for issues and the policy process in their famous "garbage can model." Issues (problems) continually pile up in multiple garbage cans (choice opportunities) along with particular solutions (policies). Participants move in and out of decision-making processes, leading to random policy outputs. Kingdon (1984) describes the processes in what is either the saddest or most exciting paragraph ever written about public policy: "Sometimes, problems are actually resolved. At least as often, problems drift away from the choice at hand to another garbage can, not being resolved in the current round at least. Or important problems are ignored altogether, possibly because there is no available solution for them" (p. 86). Since then, the garbage can model serves less as a policy analytic tool and more as a foundation for the decision-making environment of major policy process theories, such as the multiple streams approach (Kingdon, 1984) and punctuated equilibrium theory (Baumgartner and Jones, 1993).

Issues and their resolutions are the fundamental reasons why governments exist. Problem definition is the starting point for the much-maligned heuristic of "stages in policymaking" or the point of tangency for the policy cycle. Politicians and interest groups exist to address issues within the bounds of institutions. Problems are fabricated within issue domains, but, as many policy process scholars observe, few problems are ever fixed. In politics, it seems, the garbage is never really taken out.

As issues are fundamental to governments, they are also fundamental to the motivations of policymakers. Policymakers are motivated to address issues relative to their preferences, which are, in large part, a function of electoral pressures to deliver promises to constituents. The policy literature paints the policymaking environment as one where issues are constant, but attention to them is not. The extent of change policymakers attempt to make, thus, is a function of both the drive to address issues that match their preferences and the reality of exogenous changes in issue attention. In short, politicians are motivated to address both the things they want and the things they must. In either case, politicians seek to bend policy to their preferences, positioning issues as the primary motives for policymaking.

Public budgets present multiple avenues for policymakers and interest groups to influence individual issues. Budgets are comprehensive documents subject to holistic constraints, but the war over the budget is fought in successive battles over issues. While there may be partisan differences over how much money state governments spend (Adolph et al., 2018), interest groups are concerned with particular shares of the budget. Each budget category, then, provides the grounds for policymakers and interest groups to intervene in the budgeting process on behalf of specific issues.

Governors and interest groups are impelled to engage in political contests to reap short- and long-term gains. In general, established groups are motivated by long-term gains, coincident with constant attention to particular issues. Governors, too, are motivated by long-term gains in service of political legacies and stable political structures, though they are also occupied by the incremental inertia of interest groups. At the same time, governors are incentivized by short-term gains that result from desires to demonstrate efficacy within an electoral cycle and to respond to emergent problems. These short-term motivations may conflict with interest groups' long-term goals; thus, governors' motives for budgetary action are, as we argue in Chapter 2, met with the political realities of interest group competition. Governors must balance legacy concerns with instable interest group environments because these environments provide them with opportunities for using their institutional tools to their advantage.

Although interest groups and governors both can have the capacity to intervene in individual categories of budgets, their attention to issues is unequal. Interest groups constantly attend to individual issues, while executives must spread their limited attention across multiple issues and be aware of the politics of the entire budget. Because governors spread their attention, individual policy issues mostly change a little, but, when they change more than a little, they change a lot (Baumgartner et al., 2009c; Breunig and Koski, 2006; Jones et al., 2009; Mortensen, 2006; True, 1999). This is the classic expectation of the punctuated equilibrium model.

So PET applied to public budgeting tells us to expect a particular pattern of policy change across policy issues. We have argued that issues provide the motive to intervene; however, we have also argued that opportunities for politicians – in this case, governors – to act on these motives are likely to be unevenly distributed across issues. The empirical question that follows is: To what extent is the range of policy changes consistent across political issues? A logical follow-up question asks: If there are certain features of a policy domain that produce greater or less stability? If there are variations in stability that are particular to issue domains, what are the long-term impacts? Does today's policy change in a particular domain have long-term consequences, ten, or even twenty years later?

In the first part of this chapter, we address these questions by reintroducing two competing models of policy change: (1) incrementalism with its origins in rational decision-making models of the 1960s and (2) punctuated equilibrium theory stemming from Simon's (1955) bounded rationality model. Both decision-making models are attractive for our endeavor because they start with a common assumption: Political decisions are choices among distinct political issues. A decision-maker must consider and select *how much* to spend *on what*. We test both models and show that the rational model of incremental policy change does not fit the experience of the American states over the last twenty-six years. We rely on budgetary data to make our case. Budgets across America display long periods of stability interspersed with massive budget changes. This finding supplies strong evidence for the PET model.

Our finding implies that the motive of political action is a policymaker's ability to spend money on a particular policy issues, resulting in massive budgetary changes. To put it another way, in every budget cycle, there is a chance that a particular policy issue becomes a top priority and experiences a huge change in funding. This event motivates political actors. The idea that budgets are punctuated is well established (Jones et al., 2009), but we dig deeper and show that *all states* are prone to large-scale changes in budgetary policy in the second part of the chapter. The reason for this proclivity is that individual budget functions – issue politics – display punctuated behavior. Hence, regardless of state, how policy domains are decided on and legislated leads to punctuated budgets. This empirical regularity means that large gains on some budget items are occasionally a real possibility for stakeholders. Likewise, there is a rare but real threat that the financing for a particular policy might collapse. These statements hold for all fifty states.

We find that variations in patterns of budgetary change across policy issues have long-term consequences: Policy domains with more punctuated budgets display smaller growth in the long run, while small and steady changes lead to larger growth. Large, single-policy shifts cannot catch up to persistent small changes. The identified pattern suggests that a trade-off between massive one-shot budget changes and incremental long-term transformations exists. These two options present themselves as distinct motivational forces for interest groups and governors alike. Once again, we show that this relationship is due to issue-specific politics. On particular policy issues, governors and interest groups are impelled by short-term and long-term gains.

Annual policy change and long-term growth emerge from the politics of particular budget functions. In the final part of this chapter, we introduce a two-by-two typology that relates policy issues to four types of policymaking: *majoritarian politics, runaway issue expansion, normal politics,* and *interest group politics*. Each type describes a particular style of politics depending on (1) the distribution of costs and benefits, (2) the locus of policymaking and its primary actors, (3) the type of interest group competition, and (4) attention. We then test to what extent particular issues match to the four types of policymaking. For example, we show that spending on welfare or health care across the fifty states is typically part of interest group politics. For welfare, the number of issues under the purview of welfare expenditures is many, there are numerous stakeholders, and the competition for resources is fierce. Major changes to social welfare policy expenditures are few, yet this category grows steadily. As such, the driving force for governmental action on welfare is long-term growth and not punctuations.

We move from classical theories of decision-making to a novel typology of public policy in this chapter. Based on the presented evidence, we are able to infer that policy issues motive political action. In state budgets, two possibilities for both action exist: massive one-time changes (punctuations) or steady long-term growth. Both possibilities correspond to particular types of public policy, namely, *majoritarian* and *interest group politics*. Moreover, these two types of policy congeal around particular spending functions and thus policy issues. In short, the motives behind policy issues can be grouped and classified.

Going beyond motivational concerns, democratic principles are at stake in this conversation. Democratic theory suggests that institutions are developed for the explicit purpose of imposing order and stability in political systems. In the paradigmatic phrasing of American federalism, institutions check the momentary passions of the people. Perhaps part of the long-term allegiance to incrementalism was not simply a function of theories regarding budget creation and observed outcomes, but the result of a normative proclivity in democratic institutions. Have we built institutions to foster incrementalism? Moreover, democratic institutions must be responsive, and therein lies the friction found between institutional and political agendas. Thus, the phenomena described by punctuated equilibrium theory can be seen as the result of a Faustian deal that trades overall stability for periods of short-term, rapid change. The evidence presented in this chapter indicates that this trade-off also has long-term consequences. The friction of institutions is stronger than the responsiveness to attention: Some policy issues do not easily catch up despite occasional jumps in spending. Indeed, at the national level, where most punctuated equilibrium research on budgets takes place, this is merely a counterfactual given that these studies only look at one set of institutions. However, at the subnational level (see also Epp, 2018), there is an opportunity to not only assess the long-term impacts of punctuations but also to examine how different political features affect these long-term effects.

3.1 BUDGETS AND POLICY CHANGE

We begin by explaining how policy issues are identified by examining state budgets, introducing basic models of decision-making (over budgets), and delineating the contours of budget change in the American states since the mid-1980s.

Public budgeting is a reflection of expressed preferences by elected governments. As such, budget decisions represent policy "wins" at the upper levels of government (Goggin et al., 1990) for three reasons. First, budgets present us with a clear numerical assessment of a state government's collective preferences. According to John and Margetts (2003, 415), "[t]he advantage of budgets is that they reflect 'real' decisions." Second, budgets represent the final outcome of a decision-making process. Changes in government spending summarizes "the outcome of hard-won negotiations and disputes between government ministries and where increases and decreases in service heads reflect shifts in the priorities of the executive, which may have been generated by lobbying and have been influenced by experts, the media and the public" (John and Margetts, 2003, 416). The assignment of funds to a specific issue over another is an external manifestation of whether the decision-maker believes the issue is salient. Finally, Kahneman and Tversky (1979, 277) show that "our perceptual apparatus is attuned to the evaluation of changes or differences rather than to the evaluation of absolute magnitudes." In sum, budgets are a direct measure of politicians' preferences and their awareness of trade-offs in policymaking.

Most budgetary scholarship is based on examinations of a single-policy area (such as welfare spending, see Barrilleaux et al. (2002); Brown (1995), and many other domains; including corrections and education, see various chapters in Gray et al. (2017)). By utilizing budget outcomes as a proxy for policymaking, these studies examine a specific budget category and provide a detailed inquiry in how American states address social problems. While useful as measures of individual priorities, budgets are produced as holistic documents. Thus, expenditures on particular categories should be viewed in terms of government priorities for policy areas *relative to other categories*, rather than only in terms of individual preferences for spending relative to previous years. In a series of works, Schneider and Jacoby (Jacoby and Schneider, 2001, 2008; Lewis et al., 2015; Schneider and Jacoby, 2006) consistently have demonstrated budget analysis as a series of trade-offs representing of policy priorities. More importantly, budgeting is not solely an elite-level opinion, but also matches opinions held by citizens: Programs receive more money if they are more popular with the public (Schneider et al., 2011).

While expenditures in budgets may be proxies for public policy priorities, we shift this conversation to suggest that, as policy priorities are essentially proxies for issues, so are budget priorities. "Policies determine politics" (Lowi, 1972, 299), and politics is essentially a fight over issues: "who gets what and how" (Lasswell, 1936). In this classic conception, then, expenditures *are* the "what" and the politics of public budgeting are the "how."

Budget decisions are incredibly complex, challenging, and controversial. While not all members may have firm preferences regarding all pieces of legislation, it is safe to say that all politicians have firm opinions about budgets. Politicians are generally concerned less with the message of the entire budget that emerges from a negotiating process, but quite concerned about expenditures for specific items. In this way, budgetary politics represent a classic political challenge: conflicts over scarce resources and, in many cases, a zero-sum game where one person's loss is another person's gain. Some governing bodies (e.g., the US Congress) have solved this by essentially creating more flexibility in creating trade-offs (read: deficit spending); but the rise and fall of issues in a budget generally have tangible consequences for organized interests operating in those policy domains.

3.2 DECISION-MAKING MODELS OF POLICYMAKING

3.2.1 Incrementing to the Future

Incrementalism emerged in the 1960s as a way to describe the process by which budgets are produced. The logic of incrementalism rests on a beguilingly simple understanding of budgeting: To determine what a state will spend this year, look at what it spent last year. As a theory, incrementalism is a compelling starting point for those interested in holistic budget change rather than specific priorities within a budget. Incrementalism represents the theoretical realization that budgets are created as total documents, often by multiple government institutions. Early scholars (Davis et al., 1966, 1974; Lindblom, 1975) argued that governments examined their previous budget allocations and added or subtracted from these as a function of incremental developments in issues related to expenditure categories. Padgett (1980) offers a consolidated understanding: "a pattern of marginal change in final allocation outcome relative to some base, which frequently is the previous year's allocation outcome" (p. 355).

The theoretical expectation of incrementalism in budgeting is a distribution of budget changes that is normal (Padgett, 1980). Policymakers constantly update information relative to all categories within a budget. As new problems emerge, policymakers judge the existing policy response and then decide what increment of funding to add or subtract from the current budget item to make a change. In this scenario, most changes should be relatively small, moderate changes less frequent, and large changes infrequent. This process does not imply the supply of information or problems regarding issues is normally distributed, but that a rational analytic decision-making apparatus ought to forge a normal response to a nonnormal world by incrementally updating policy.

3.2.2 Punctuating the Incrementalist Equilibrium

Incrementalism represents an ideal type of the policy process rather than an accurate portrayal of it. As such, distributions of policy change rarely approximate outputs predicted by incrementalist logic. From the perspective of decision-making, institutions are challenged to both gather information associated with decision-making and to make sense of it. One empirical challenge to the incremental model is structural constraints on budgets. Budget outputs associated with differences in the form of controllable (i.e., mandatory) and uncontrollable (i.e., discretionary) spending (Berry and Lowery, 1990; Gist, 1977, 1978; Kamlet and Mowery, 1980) provide different opportunities and costs for political action. For example, Schulman's (1975) cataloged the meteoric rise and fall of National Aeronautics and Space Administration expenditures as a function of Downs' (1972) fiscal issue attention cycle rather than as incremental change.

If not incrementalism, then what? As detailed in Chapter 2, institutions are built around the ideal type of delegating information processing capacity to experts under the assumption that experts will gather and process information to make policy choices. Under the label PET, Baumgartner and Jones (Baumgartner and Jones, 1993; Jones and Baumgartner, 2005) offer an alternative theory that explains long periods of stability punctuated by short periods of rapid change. PET assumes that decision-makers and institutions intend to be rational, but even the best intentions lead to serial decision-making that is subject to limited attention. Consequently, public policymaking is punctuated: Large periods of stability are interspersed with dramatic change because of issue–attention shifts.

Figure 3.1 provides a visual account of expectations in policymaking under incrementalism and punctuated equilibrium theory. Punctuated equilibrium theory is well suited to describe budget changes owing to the defined process by which budgets are made and the ability to calculate budget changes more easily than other types of policy change (Breunig and Jones, 2011). Budgetary policymaking under PET finds an over-dispersion of small and very large changes, as well as an under-dispersion of midrange changes. Critically, the PET model predicts an over-dispersion of changes *as compared to* the normal curve. We, along with other scholars employing PET for budgeting studies, overlay a normal curve onto our distributions as a way of visually distinguishing these distributions from the outputs we might expect under incrementalism. The normal curve represents an ideal type of policymaking (though not the only one): one that theoretically responds to changing problem conditions and that considers previous responses to problems in offering current solutions.

3.2.3 Punctuated Equilibrium and Long-Term Growth

We leverage the consistent finding that budget punctuations occur in virtually every budget to theorize a relationship between processes that produce short-term punctuations and patterns of long-term growth. We offer two different lines of reasoning. Once a budget function experiences a large change, it may be harder for all the other spending items to catch up. Alternatively, the slow and steady crawl of incremental policy change might outpace the quick bursts

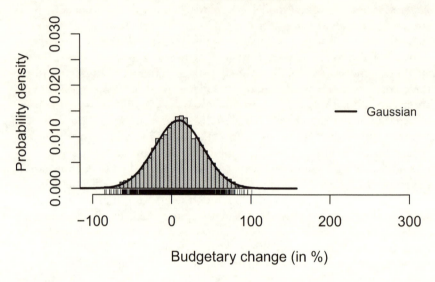

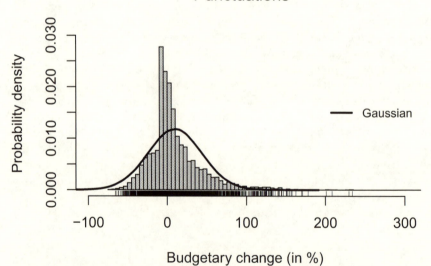

FIGURE 3.1 Incrementalist model versus punctuated equilibrium theory and their expectations about budgetary change. Both budget distributions are simulated based on model expectations.

of brief activity over the long run. Both these possibilities indicate that policy change should be examined not only on a yearly basis across all states, but also over long periods within the same set of domains. Only a combination of short-term bursts and long-term growth can offer a full picture of how consequential budgeting is in the American states.

Punctuations on a particular policy issue are related to its long-term fortunes. This assertion suggests that policy issues – budget functions in our case – are crucial for how budgets evolve. If policy issues create punctuated state budgets, they also create distinct growth patterns over time. This realization ties back to Baumgartner and Jones' (1993) argument that the organization of policy subsystems and their breakup determines public policy outcomes. Therefore, we expect the ways in which spending items and their interests are organized influence how these budget functions change and grow over time. If this is the case, what makes policy issues distinct? Do policy issues represent particular political arenas? If different policy outcomes exist in different policy domains, can we develop a domain-specific typology for policy change and growth?

In Sections 3.3–3.5, we address each of these questions using budgetary data from the American states. Our guiding principle for classifying spending is to mirror actual budget categories, which both the US Census and the International Monetary Fund identified as politically relevant categories. Throughout the chapter, we introduce several descriptive and inferential statistical tools and provide short method boxes that explain each tool succinctly. These boxes help the reader to follow the more technical aspects of studying budgetary data.

3.3 STATES AND BUDGETS

Before delving into the budgetary data analysis, we delineate why we examine the American states for the given time period, how we gathered and classified the data, and how well various functions of government are funded. The Hawaiian budget illustrates how we utilize a state budget to derive our core concepts: budgetary change, punctuations, and policy issues.

The American States. The American states provide a rich ground for our empirical study. The fifty states are roughly similar in basic processes and institutional structure; however, they offer significant variation in authority granted to executives and in specific budgeting procedures. States' varied political environments create unique cross-pressures on officials in policymaking capacities. Working with state governments offers us the opportunity to meld studies of the highly developed policy process literature with the rich literature on state politics.

American states also offer the advantage that their budgets are a simple and versatile measure of public policy. This book's empirical analysis uses annual state expenditure data from the US Census Bureau's State Government Finances publication. The US Census has long made an effort to aggregate

TABLE 3.1 *Description of state budget categories.*

Budget category	Spending falling within this category
Education	Spending on elementary, secondary, and postsecondary education; schools for the blind and vocational schools.
Welfare	Cash assistance programs (SSI, TANF); vendor payments for medical care (Medicaid); emergency relief; welfare administration costs.
Highways	Construction and maintenance of roads and highways; ferries.
Hospitals	Construction and maintenance of state hospitals, university hospitals, and mental health facilities; subsidies to private hospitals.
Health	Provision of services for the conservation and improvement of public health, other than hospital care; for example, health inspections; regulation of air and water quality; environmental cleanup.
Corrections	Construction and maintenance of prisons and jails; funding for inmate rehabilitation programs; salary for prison workers and probation officers.
Natural resources	Fish and game expenditures; state administration of forests.
Police	State police; sheriffs; state highway patrol; training academies; crime labs; vehicle inspection.
Parks	Provision and support of recreational and cultural–scientific facilities maintained for the benefit of residents and visitors; for example, parks, tennis courts, stadiums, zoos, etc.
Government	Judicial and legal expenditures; central staff services; public building costs; state legislative pay.

state expenditures into common categories, with large degrees of continuity despite drastic changes in the roles of state governments and in accounting methods. The American states are well suited to our analysis because high-quality (mutually exclusive, comparable, and backward-adjustable) budgetary data are easily available for an extended period of time and variegated institutional settings. We obtained budgetary data from all fifty states from 1984 to 2010.

The Classification Scheme. The data are classified in ten spending components delineated by the Department of the Census: education, public welfare, highways, natural resources, health, hospitals, police, corrections, parks, and administration. Table 3.1 describes each category and their content in detail. Of particular note are the *Government* categories that include several services necessary to running a state. We use these categories and their labels throughout the book. These ten budget functions, which we also call categories, allow us to identify the size of a policy domain, its growth over time, as well as the level of punctuation. Budget functions constitute therefore a straightforward and consistent measure of policy issues.

Spending totals for each budget function are hard to compare, given the different sizes of overall state budgets. In our sample, Vermont (in 1984) had the smallest total budget at $0.9 billion, whereas California's 2009 budget was $211 billion. That is a whopping 230 times larger outlay. Given these substantial differences across the American states, we compare the shares a government spends on a particular function, thereby identifying each state's policy issue priorities.

We begin with simple descriptive facts. Figure 3.2 plots the divisions of budgets across our ten categories over time. The black line represents the median share of spending. All budget items are ordered from smallest to largest. Individual dots represent the budget share of a particular state in a given year and

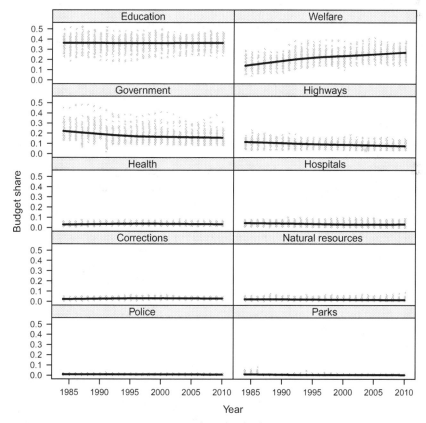

FIGURE 3.2 Variation in state spending by budget category, 1984–2010. The plot shows the mean share within an annual budget for spending by category for all states over the period. The dots are individual shares for each state and year.

item. The top two categories, welfare and education, typically accounted for more than half of all spending. The median state in 1984 spent 52 percent of its budget on these two categories. By 2010, education and welfare spending accounted for 63 percent of the budget. Health and hospital spending averaged around 7.5 percent in the examined period. The remaining four categories – corrections, natural resources, police, and parks – aggregated to just 7 percent of an average state's budget.

Over time, welfare spending increased in all states, whereas spending on government and highways experienced the biggest cutbacks as a proportion of their initial budget shares. For example, the share of highway spending dropped from around 11 percent in 1984 to less than 8 percent in 2010. As the spread of individual spending items around the median suggests, especially on big-ticket items, individual states exercise discretion in how they prioritize particular policy domains. Our task is to illustrate and then explain how this variation emerges.

Hawaii. The history of the Hawaiian budget illustrates the many moving parts of an annual budget. Figure 3.3 presents Hawaii's annual budget from different perspectives. The top graphic in the plot shows how budget shares are divided up over time. Education and government spending are typically the largest spending items, with averages above 30 percent of the budget. Education was cut in the 1980s, while spending on government operations continuously declined since the early 1990s. Similar to all other states, natural resources, corrections, police, and parks are comparatively small budget items.

The bottom half of Figure 3.3 reveals the reality of how turbulent annual budgeting is in Hawaii. The 1993 Hawaiian budget exemplifies the importance of examining individual policy issues rather than focusing only on total spending or an individual category. As we show later, the Hawaiian budget is not unique; the median change of this budget across all government functions from the previous year is a moderate increase of around 7 percent. However, if we examine the budget further across all ten spending categories, we find that some categories were cut (natural resources, parks, and government operations), some modestly increased (education, public welfare, highways, hospitals, and corrections), and two increased substantially (public health by 21 percent and police by 47 percent). The 1993 Hawaiian budget is typical for many other years, as the annual box plots show. In nearly every year, we find an outlier: Spending in at least one budget item changes dramatically, while the rest of the budget remains largely unchanged (see tight boxes with little variance and marginally positive averages). It was public health in the Hawaiian case, but what will it be in other states?

The right side of Figure 3.3 depicts all spending changes as a histogram. In the aggregate of twenty-five years, annual budget stories can be recounted numerous times. Indeed, across all years, the median budget change is 6.7 percent, just like in 1993. Half of all budget changes range between a 1 percent

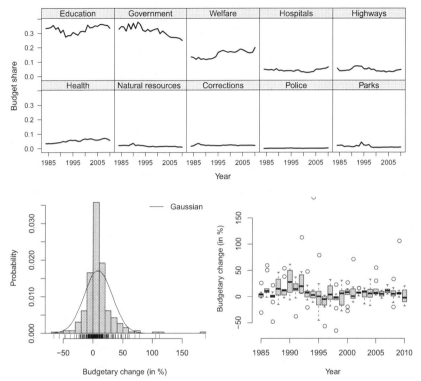

FIGURE 3.3 Budget changes in Hawaii, 1984–2010. The line plot on top displays the development of budget shares over time. The histogram (left) and the annual boxplots (right) summarize all budget changes for all years. The Hawaiian budget represents a typical case of punctuations in American state budgets (L-kurtosis ≈ 0.36).

cutback to a 14 percent increase. However, outside of this fifteen-point range, one finds budget reductions up to 65 percent as well as a few rare incidents where a particular budget item more than doubled. The Hawaiian budget is punctuated. The Hawaiian example indicates that it is crucial to think about how budget changes in categories are connected to decision-making, as well as to their long-term consequences. Since policy change on issues is budget change, Section 3.4 analyzes policy change for all states.

3.4 THE DYNAMICS OF STATE BUDGETS

The upshot of the Hawaiian example is that a simple visual accounting of budgetary change, long-term consequences, and punctuations are insufficient to fully diagnose the dynamics that lead to policy changes in spending domains across the American states. We leverage several descriptive and inferential statistics to contextualize our argument that state budgets are punctuated and that these punctuations vary systematically across policy domains.

Our approach is structured to take a more complex look at state budgets using techniques that treat budgets as discrete components of broad policy domains and as the aggregate of these policy domains. The purpose of this analysis is to verify the punctuated nature of public budgets, but also to show that punctuations are a function of policy domains and not a feature of particular states. Individual states should not, prima facie, be associated with punctuations – that is, Michigan ought not to be inherently more volatile in its public budgeting than Montana. Michigan may have more punctuated distributions of budget change than Montana, but this would be a function of institutional variations, such as its decision-making authority, rather than some idiosyncratic nature. We can expect, though, that certain categories of state budgets would be more volatile (e.g., parks) than others (e.g., education) because of the consistency in attention that one (e.g., education) has over the other (e.g., parks).

Our domain-level analysis of punctuations grounds our understanding of the difference between actors that cross issues, aka governors, versus issue-specific actors, aka interest groups. Accounting for variation within subsystems thereby ties back to discussions of the underlying decision-making model. Methodologically important for our work is also the ability to control for an alternative form of causality in budget changes beyond macro- and micro-influences.

Method: Calculating budget changes

Two possibilities for calculation exist. First, the year-to-year percentage change for each budget function is simply

$$(budget_t - budget_{t-1})/budget_{t-1}.$$

This methods picks up large changes in budgets fairly well. Second, if one is interested in the relative changes within a budget, one can compute the change in budget shares:

$$(budgetshare_t - budgetshare_{t-1})/budgetshare_{t-1}.$$

This method does not pick up overall budget growth.

The basic building block for our inquiry is annual budget change in each policy domain for a given state. We calculate "budgetary change" by taking the budget outlays in a year, minus the budget outlays from the year before, divided by the earlier outlays for each category. This results in year-to-year percentage changes for each budget category as described in the methods box "Calculating budget changes."

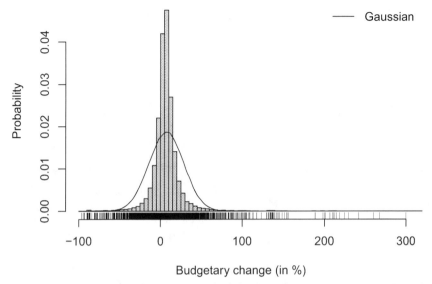

FIGURE 3.4 Budget changes for all states of the United States, 1985–2010. Seven budget changes that are larger than 300 percent point changes are not shown. The rug at the bottom indicates individual changes. The Gaussian distribution is superimposed for comparison.

3.4.1 Punctuations

We rely on budgetary change across policy domains and states over long periods as a strong comparative research design for analyzing decision-making across these three dimensions. We follow the approach outlined in the Hawaiian case and move from a visual inspection using histograms to statistical tests to examine budget changes and their probability distribution.

Histograms group budget changes into distinct categories (i.e., bins). We create these bins using a nonparametric approach that presupposes the existence of minimal density smoothness (Sheather and Jones, 1991) to compute the optimal number and size of bins. The addition of a normal curve to a histogram facilitates comparison to the incrementalist model.

Our previous research (Breunig and Koski, 2006) showed that state budgets are punctuated for a shorter time period. Adding another ten years of data does not change the canonical finding of PET. Figure 3.4 makes this clear: The distribution of budgetary changes across all budget functions displays long tails, weak shoulders, and high peaks at the center. That is, most budgets change only incrementally most of the time, but occasionally policymakers create large-scale changes. Summary statistics confirm this visualization. While the median budget change is around 6 percent, half the nearly 13,000 budget changes in our sample range between 0 and 12 percent increases. This range means that, on average, all budget functions have grown at least a small amount. Indeed, compared to a hypothetical normal distribution, little change in the budget from one year to another is at least twice as likely in reality. The rug at the bottom of the histogram also shows that a budget function is nearly completely removed from a state budget on rare occasions; likewise, a doubling or even tripling of existing budget items does occur.

Method: Measuring the shape of a distribution

In statistics, the shape of a probability distribution is measured as kurtosis. Several methods exist for computing this descriptive statistic. In the most common form, kurtosis is defined as the fourth moment around the mean. This statistic can be defined as $k = \frac{E[(X-\mu)^4]}{(E[(X-\mu)^2])^2} = \frac{\mu_4}{\sigma^4}$ where X is a random variable with a mean μ and E is the expectation operator. μ_4 is the fourth moment of the mean, and σ^4 its standard deviation. The kurtosis k provides a scale-free measure of the shape of a distribution, but it is sensitive to outliers (Groneveld, 1998).

L-moments (Hosking, 1990, 1998) provide more efficient and robust descriptions of distributions. L-moments are the expected values of linear combinations of order statistics $X_{1:n}$ multiplied by scalar constants. If $F(x)$ is a distribution function of a random variable X and $X_{1:n} \leq X_{2:n} \leq \ldots \leq X_{n:n}$ are the order statistics associated with the distribution F (or ordered values of a sample of size n), then the L-moments $L_r(F)$ are defined as $L_r(F) = \frac{1}{r} \sum_{j=0}^{r-1} (-1)^j \binom{r-1}{j} E(X_{r-j:r})$. The first L-moment $L_1 F$ is a measure of location; $L_2(F)$ measures dispersion. The fourth moment (L-kurtosis) is the ratio $\tau_4 = \frac{L_4(F)}{L_2(F)}$. The L-kurtosis of a normal distribution is about 0.12, and the L-kurtosis of an exponential is $\frac{1}{6}$.

Kurtosis measures the shape of a distribution (DeCarlo, 1997) and thereby provides us with a descriptive tool for measuring budget punctuations. One distinguishes typically between two shapes: Platykurtosis denotes light tails and flatness in the center, and leptokurtosis indicates fat tails, sharp central peaks, and "weak shoulders" (i.e., few moderate change). In methods box, "Measuring the shape of a distribution," we discuss two descriptive statistics that summarize these shapes numerically. We use L-moments (Hosking, 1998) for computing kurtosis scores. The L-kurtosis ranges from 0 to 1 where an increasing number identifies a higher level of kurtosis (i.e., more punctuations). As a reference point, the standard normal distribution has an approximate L-kurtosis score of 0.12.

A high kurtosis for all pooled budget changes confirms the visual assessment. The kurtosis is 137, and the L-kurtosis is 0.38. These numbers indicate that state budgets are leptokurtic; they are marked by large occurrence of small changes and a considerable number of extreme changes. Our visual assessment and the summary statistics indicate that state budgets display the typical over- and under-reaction of a political system (Jones and Baumgartner, 2005; Jones et al., 2009).

More importantly, we are able to reject the classical incremental model of budgeting and policy change. The overall form of a hypothetical probability distribution can be compared directly to the actual distribution for budget changes. We generate two goodness-of-fit tests (Breunig and Jones, 2011) that assess whether the given observations could have reasonably come from a normal distribution matching the incremental decision-making model. We apply two simple test statistics: Shapiro–Wilk and Kolmogorov–Smirnov. First, a Kolmogorov–Smirnov (K-S) test compares given distributions to a normal distribution. The K-S test allows for a rejection of the hypothesis that a set of frequencies is normally distributed. Second, we employ the Shapiro–Wilk (S-W) test as a more powerful test than the K-S test for assessing the normality of a distribution. The S-W test generates a W statistic, with a small W-value indicating non-normality.

Table 3.2 shows the results for all states. In all cases, we can reject that budget change can be described by a normal distribution. The test statistics and the accompanying p-values for both the K-S test and the S-W test suggest that we can reject with a high confidence ($p < 0.001$) the hypothesis that budget changes across all states and years are distributed normally.

Put simply, there is no evidence for the incremental model. This finding leads us to use PET as a starting point for further inquiry. The fact that budgets are punctuated and do not adjust incrementally is an essential feature of decision-making. If political actors are impelled by policy change, this underlying decision-making suggests that they focus on a particular issue and ignore many others. This focus of attention results in rapid and monumental policy change. Hence, the motives for policymaking on issues inadvertently lead to transformative policy change.

Marshalled with the knowledge that state budgets are not normal but punctuated, we explore whether we can detect differences in the degree of punctuations across American states and among policy issues. If we can identify variation here, we will be able to connect the general PET model to the politics of budgeting in states. As a first step, we compute the degree of punctuation for all states by pooling budget changes across all available years and functions.

Figure 3.5 shows that variation in punctuations exists across states. Darker colors on the map of the fifty states correspond to higher L-kurtosis scores. Across the American states, large variation in the degree of punctuations exists. There are states with high scores (L-kurtosis exceeds 0.5) such as New York, Kansas, or Alaska. In these states in particular, budgeting is a process with plenty of very little change interspersed by huge transformations in spending on particular items. Budgeting in North Carolina, California, and Colorado are average cases close to the mean level of L-kurtosis in the whole sample (0.38). At the other end of the scale, states such as Oregon, Massachusetts,

TABLE 3.2 *Normality tests for state budgets.*

State	KS statistic	KS p-value	SW statistic	SW p-value
Alabama	.40	0.00	.30	0.00
Alaska	.37	0.00	.80	0.00
Arizona	.41	0.00	.90	0.00
Arkansas	.40	0.00	.81	0.00
California	.39	0.00	.69	0.00
Colorado	.41	0.00	.72	0.00
Connecticut	.37	0.00	.44	0.00
Delaware	.40	0.00	.82	0.00
Florida	.39	0.00	.69	0.00
Georgia	.40	0.00	.80	0.00
Hawaii	.38	0.00	.80	0.00
Idaho	.42	0.00	.85	0.00
Illinois	.41	0.00	.84	0.00
Indiana	.39	0.00	.88	0.00
Iowa	.41	0.00	.74	0.00
Kansas	.40	0.00	.51	0.00
Kentucky	.41	0.00	.91	0.00
Louisiana	.39	0.00	.85	0.00
Maine	.42	0.00	.71	0.00
Maryland	.40	0.00	.72	0.00
Massachusetts	.39	0.00	.91	0.00
Michigan	.39	0.00	.70	0.00
Minnesota	.42	0.00	.88	0.00
Mississippi	.40	0.00	.83	0.00
Missouri	.41	0.00	.79	0.00
Montana	.39	0.00	.44	0.00
Nebraska	.42	0.00	.58	0.00
Nevada	.41	0.00	.87	0.00
New Hampshire	.40	0.00	.81	0.00
New Jersey	.41	0.00	.94	0.00
New Mexico	.41	0.00	.92	0.00
New York	.42	0.00	.13	0.00
North Carolina	.41	0.00	.79	0.00
North Dakota	.39	0.00	.59	0.00
Ohio	.42	0.00	.85	0.00
Oklahoma	.40	0.00	.57	0.00
Oregon	.40	0.00	.91	0.00
Pennsylvania	.40	0.00	.62	0.00
Rhode Island	.36	0.00	.62	0.00
South Carolina	.41	0.00	.59	0.00
South Dakota	.41	0.00	.86	0.00
Tennessee	.40	0.00	.79	0.00
Texas	.41	0.00	.43	0.00
Utah	.39	0.00	.82	0.00

TABLE 3.2 *(continued)*

State	KS statistic	KS p-value	SW statistic	SW p-value
Vermont	.38	0.00	.40	0.00
Virginia	.41	0.00	.57	0.00
Washington	.39	0.00	.80	0.00
West Virginia	.41	0.00	.90	0.00
Wisconsin	.41	0.00	.73	0.00
Wyoming	.37	0.00	.58	0.00

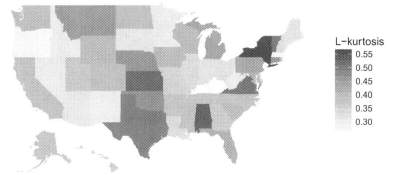

FIGURE 3.5 Budget punctuations across American states. The higher L-kurtosis scores indicate higher degree of punctuations. Based on all functional changes within a state's budget, 1985–2010.

Kentucky, and New Jersey have L-kurtosis scores of less than 0.3. While these scores are much lower than those states mentioned above, they remain far-removed from budgeting models described by incrementalism. The map indicates that budget changes transpire quite differently across the American states. No clear geographical patterns are visible. Some states change their budgets in a more orderly fashion; in others, budgeting is a "wild" and "extreme" affair.

Neither the histogram above nor the summary statistics of the 12,997 budgetary changes reveal anything about which states or budget functions are prone to stasis and which are likely to change dramatically. Breunig and Koski (2006) show that some states have more punctuated budgets than others, while Breunig et al. (2009) argue that large variation across budget functions exists irrespective of political system. We compute the degree of punctuation for each policy issue across all states.

Figure 3.6 delivers a clear verdict. State spending on health and government is much more punctuated than spending on welfare, education, and highways. Spending on health, corrections, and police falls somewhere in between. To be sure, all these different policy issues are punctuated. Table 3.3 summarizes

TABLE 3.3 *Normality tests for functions.*

Function	KS statistic	KS p-value	SW statistic	SW p-value
Education	.46	0.00	.83	0.00
Welfare	.45	0.00	.72	0.00
Highways	.40	0.00	.94	0.00
Natural resources	.40	0.00	.29	0.00
Health	.40	0.00	.64	0.00
Hospitals	.39	0.00	.44	0.00
Police	.41	0.00	.60	0.00
Corrections	.43	0.00	.69	0.00
Parks	.31	0.00	.73	0.00
Government	.36	0.00	.62	0.00

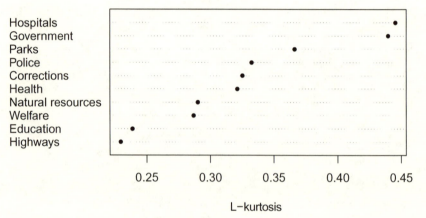

FIGURE 3.6 Punctuations across budget functions. All L-kurtosis statistics are based on budgetary changes within a function for all states of the United States, 1985–2010.

the test for a normal distribution. Rejection of normality means that changes in policy issues are not due to incremental budgeting. Instead, we find that state budgets and policy domains are punctuated. Indeed, large variation in the degree of punctuation exists among states as well as policy issues.

Can we adjudicate if budget changes are predominately driven by differences in policy issues or in differences across states? As a first assessment, we compute L-kurtosis for each function in each state. This results in 500 observed budget distributions (fifty states multiplied by ten budget categories). We rely on a two-way ANOVA test (Gelman and Hill, 2006, 45–46) using simple indicators for states and functions as independent variables. Table 3.4 summarizes the results, which suggest that differences in the degree of punctuation in policy domains across the states are due to variation across functions and not states themselves. The function variable is statistically different from zero at

TABLE 3.4 *ANOVA for regression of L-kurtosis on all states and all budget functions, N = 500.*

	Df	Sum Sq	Mean Sq	F-value	Pr(>F)
States	49	0.99	0.02	1.29	0.10
Function	9	1.81	0.20	12.81	0.00
Residuals	441	6.91	0.02		

the 0.001 level, whereas the p-value for states is about 0.1. This initial evidence directs our subsequent analysis of budgeting in the states to pay close attention to policy dynamics emanating from individual policy domains.

Overall, the preceding analyses illustrate that budgets are not monolithically punctuated. We find substantive variation in the degree of punctuation across states and, more importantly, spending categories. In support of punctuated equilibrium theory, we find that states do not produce normal budget distributions as would be expected in an incremental decision-making model. These findings are not novel, but they highlight that we should employ the variation in the degree of punctuation in order to inquire how these punctuations affect long-term changes in state spending.

Punctuations in state budgets occur because of budget changes on particular policy issues. The ANOVA results in Table 3.4 provide us with a first indicator that an underlying force for budget outcomes is a decision-making model based on issue prioritization. Making an issue a top priority within a budget motivates political actors in all states in every budget cycle for this reason. Put another way, policy advocates are unlikely to see much change in the budget if no one, especially the governor, is paying attention to their particular political issues.

3.4.2 Long-Term Growth

Annual budget decisions reverberate throughout future iterations of the budgetary process. The long-term implications of budgetary decisions are hard to overstate: bureaucratic inertia, spillovers, and trade-offs, as well as long-term substantive consequences for state citizens. First, bureaucratic inertia may accompany increased funding streams to existing programs or the creation of new programs. It is difficult to remove state employees once they are hired and attached to a particular program; thus, when programs are created, they gain an instant support network vis-a-vis bureaucratic dependence (Niskanen, 1971).

Second, government spending in one budget category is interdependent upon spending in other categories (Adolph et al., 2018; Breunig and Busemeyer, 2012; Hendrick and Garand, 1991). Budgetary decisions affect policy outcomes in one way or another because the choice to fund one category usually means not funding another. Consequently, today's budget decision not only affects a specific budget area in the future, but also spreads its influence across all other areas (Jacoby and Schneider, 2001; Schneider and Jacoby, 2006). These spillovers and trade-offs committed in one year potentially set in motion long-term trajectories of spending commitments.

Third, budgetary decisions are policy commitments made by state governments in specific policy areas (Goggin et al., 1990). High spending levels in one area of policy may produce "better" outcomes over time because of consistent support, whereas low, consistent spending in other categories may produce "deficient" policy outcomes. Ultimately, policy outcomes – such as the consumption of a good, environmental pollution, or traffic stops – have dramatic, visible, and long-term implications on the lives of citizens. For these three reasons, it is important to understand how immediate shifts in the budgets can affect the long-term outcomes of state spending.

Before we explore the relationship between long-term budget developments and punctuations, it is critical to discuss the temporal aspect of budgeting. State, national, and international agencies employ typical medium- and long-term budget planning scenarios. They commonly focus on five-to-ten-year planning scenarios. For empirical work on budgets, Jones and colleagues (Jones and Breunig, 2007; Jones et al., 1998, 2014a) constructed long time series of over 200 years for examining budget trajectories. So, administrative procedures and empirical possibility instruct us to amassed state data for assessing long-term differences. We managed to assemble data series for a twenty-five-year period.

To measure cumulative policy change, we computed the long-term growth rate by subtracting 1984 spending from 2010 spending and dividing this by the 1984 budget figure for each state and each function. These long-term changes provide us with a simple measure of how budgets evolve irrespective of their size. We computed a corresponding measure for budget shares by subtracting the budget share in 1984 from that of 2010 and dividing the difference by the 1984 share of a budget item.

We explore long-term growth in state budgets and its connection to punctuations in order to show the consequences of policy change. Figure 3.7 presents the scatter plots for both measures of long-term change. The figure essentially shows how much a budget category in a particular state grew over a twenty-five-year span in relative (top) and absolute (bottom) terms compared to their degree of punctuation. The graphs display 500 observations consisting of the 10 budget functions in each of the 50 states. We colored each observation according to three broad groups of spending items: (1) hospitals, parks, and government; (2) welfare, health, and corrections; and (3) education, highways, natural resources, and police.

In the long run, the fortunes of policy issues vary widely. Across states and budget functions, the average spending item in a state was more than triples

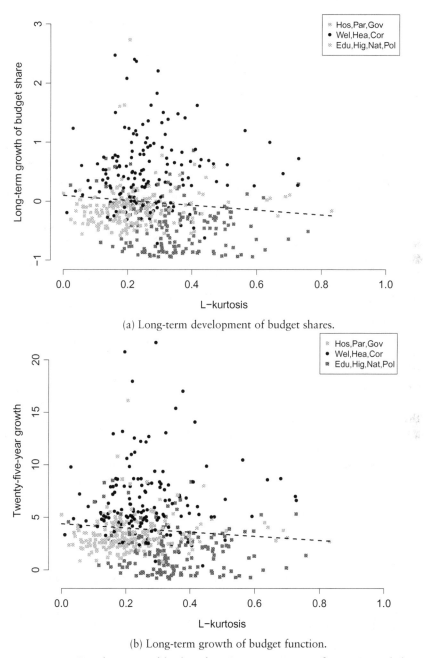

(a) Long-term development of budget shares.

(b) Long-term growth of budget function.

FIGURE 3.7 Development of budget functions over twenty-five years and degree of punctuation. For all budget function for all states of the United States, 1985–2010. Each colored dot corresponds to a budget function in a state. The dashed line is the OLS estimated relationship. $N = 500$.

between 1984 and 2010. Nevertheless, wide fluctuations among spending items are apparent. While some items even shrank over time, others increased more than tenfold. This pattern holds even when looking at spending shares. While the mean change is close to zero, a few items were reduced by more than 85 percent over the last twenty-five years, while the share of some other spending items more than doubled. Given these huge differences, it is safe to say that some policy domains offer potential gains in the long run.

In relation to punctuations, the bottom graph in Figure 3.7 shows that incremental budgets – such as corrections and welfare – grew faster than punctuated ones over time. Punctuated policy domains, such as the domain of hospitals, experience stunted growth. This graph procures two observations. First, some policy domains manage to blossom without large-scale punctuations. In these domains, political actors might be content obtaining steady returns without receiving much attention. Second, for the punctuated domains, the amount of continuous underadjustment is larger than the subsequent attentive overreaction in the long run.

The top graph in Figure 3.7 displays the relationship between punctuation and the development of budget shares. Again, a negative relationship emerges. Policy issues that dominate the budget display low levels of punctuation, while smaller items are more likely to be punctuated. Education and welfare cover, on average, nearly 60 percent of all spending, and both these domains rarely change the budget dramatically from one year to the next. The opposite is true for relatively small items, such as hospitals and parks. Small fortunes change dramatically over time.

To assess the existence of any potential relationships between punctuations and long-term development, we fit a simple least squares (OLS) regression line through the data. The estimate is superimposed as a dashed line in Figure 3.7. The negative slope indicates a negative relationship between the degree of punctuation and long-term growth: An increase in punctuations leads to less long-term growth in spending. The regression coefficients suggest that a 0.1 increase in L-kurtosis (i.e., an increase in the degree of punctuation) is associated with a roughly 20 percent point reduction in a state budget function over twenty-five years. Given that the colored observations also cluster together, we can already speculate that budgeting at the functional level might be related to the observed negative slope.

This graphical exploration suggests that the long-term growth of state budget functions is related to the extent to which their budgets are punctuated. Punctuated equilibrium theory holds that institutions (and, implicitly, the funding behind them) remain long after attention has subsided (Baumgartner and Jones, 1993). However, relative to incremental budgets, the longer-term outputs of budgets that are punctuated appear to be smaller. In other words, incremental budgets grow more than punctuated budgets over time. We (Breunig and Koski, 2012, 56) call this finding "the tortoise is faster than the hare."

Creating new monopolies around policy issues provides a stark motivating force for political action. Scholarship on PET purports that sometimes a policy area is overthrown and changes dramatically once attention is focused and institutional barriers are overcome. The negative association between punctuation and long-term growth suggests that this threshold effect is stronger than suspected in the literature. Our analysis of the long-term consequences of punctuations hints that in the long run, the amount of continuous underadjustment to new information in the political system is larger than the subsequent attentive overreaction. Adjacent literature on "political" and "policy bubbles" (Jones et al., 2014b; McCarty et al., 2006) is similarly unaware that catching up is hardly possible when compared to steady incremental policy change.

The alternative political and institutional story we explore in Chapters 4–6 is that, in the long run, constellations of political interests and political institutions, such as the means of governor's powers, are even stronger than PET hypothesizes. These constellations of political interests and political institutions not only keep a policy equilibrium in place longer than one would expect, but also create politically erected institutional roadblocks that stymie long-term growth.

As a first step in identifying why long-term growth concentrates on some policy issues more than on others, we probe whether macro (state-level) or subsystem (functional-level) features are related to long-term growth. In this first crude step, we contend that institutional friction arising out of state-level political arrangements and rules can be measured by the level of punctuation in a state. Correspondingly, the information environment can be captured by the level of punctuation in a state's budget function. With this simple assessment, we juxtapose state-wide and issue-level considerations influencing long-term growth.

The data for our long-term budget growth model include two levels. The lower level comprises the budget function i in each state, and the higher level is the j American states. Following Gelman and Hill (2006), we set up the nested model as: $y_{ij} = \alpha_{j[i]} + X_i\beta + \epsilon$, where y_{ij} are the long-term budget changes and distributed as $N(\alpha_{i[j]} + \beta x_i, \sigma_y^2)$, α_i are the varying intercepts for the fifty states distributed as $N(\mu_\alpha, \sigma_\alpha^2)$, X_i consist of the kurtosis scores for each state's budget functions (*functional L-kurtosis*) as well as the state-level kurtosis (*state L-kurtosis*), and ϵ is the error term. The estimation results for the regression on the long-term budgetary changes are shown in Table 3.5. The estimated effects of our two variables of interest on budgetary changes after twenty-five years are displayed in Figure 3.8.

Two findings are important. First, the estimates for state-level punctuations have a negative slope, indicating that an increase in state-level institutional friction leads to lower long-term budget growth, as Figure 3.8 shows. However, the Wald χ^2 test in Table 3.5 suggests that we should not be confident in our estimate of the effect of state L-kurtosis on long-term growth. The estimation

TABLE 3.5 *Multilevel regression for long-term growth rates plus χ² tests for both covariates. Data are all states and budget functions.*

	Estimate	Std. error
State L-kurtosis	−2.30	1.91
Functional L-kurtosis	−1.76	1.01
Constant	5.19	0.73
Observations	500	
Log likelihood	−1,271	
AIC	2,552	

Analysis of deviance table (type II Wald χ² tests)		
	χ²	Pr(> χ²)
State L-kurtosis	1.45	0.23
Functional L-kurtosis	3.04	0.08

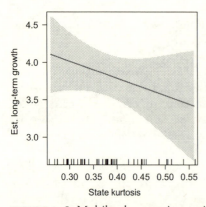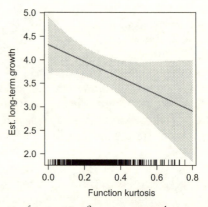

FIGURE 3.8 Multilevel regression estimates for twenty-five-year growth rates. The left plot displays the estimated effect of state-level punctuations on growth, and the right plot displays the functional-level estimates on growth for all states and budget functions. N = 500.

indicates that the degree of punctuation of a state budget as a whole has no distinguishable effect on long-term budget growth.

Second and more importantly, the estimated effect for functional-level punctuations on the right side of Figure 3.8 illustrates that increasing levels of punctuation in budget functions contribute to lower long-term budget growth. The slope for this estimate is steeper than for state punctuations. More importantly, the Wald χ² test for functional L-kurtosis is 0.08 in Table 3.5, suggesting that it might be different from zero. Substantively, we expect that an increase of the L-kurtosis from 0.2 to 0.4 for a budget function would roughly lead to a 50 percent point reduction in the function's twenty-five-year growth. These are substantial results. Put simply, differences in long-term budget growth depend on the degree of punctuation in policy issues. Budget items that are adjusted incrementally over time will grow considerably in the long run, regardless of the surrounding institutional setup of state government.

The results from this section clarify the real differences between the long-term results for punctuated and incremental budgets. The preceding analysis allows us to postulate that functional differences and not state-level punctuations alter budgetary growth over time. The scatter plots illustrate that spending categories do not necessarily behave in the same way (i.e., different subsystem politics subsist). Certain types of spending categories are more likely to be punctuated, regardless of the systemic features of a state's politics. Consequently, our analysis confirms the idea that policy issues and their accompanying subsystem politics are more likely to shape policy outcomes than state-level institutional structures. More broadly, political action originates in the desire to change policy on a particular issue. This motive appears to be much stronger than state-level features about budgeting.

When taken together, this section highlights a tremendous variation in the level of punctuation across political systems and policy domains. Much of this variation is due to how budget categories are modified over time. Large and growing budget items are less punctuated. This finding confirms the importance of subsystem politics (Baumgartner and Jones, 1993) and suggests that budget categories have varying levels of importance to policymakers and citizens. Some categories are large and encapsulate the issues to which citizens and policymakers pay attention most of the time; these categories are more likely to see conflict and receive continuous attention. Other policy domains, such as hospitals and government, rise and fall with ephemeral collective attention. As these domains also have a smaller share of the budget, political actors pushing for policy change in these domains are in a double-bind. They have to fight for attention vis-a-vis the highly contested big-ticket items, as well as compete for attention across the other small items.

Our analysis implies that working toward changing the fortunes of a particular spending item can be rewarding, regardless of the state. Budget functions and thus policy issues matter because of their consequences. All of the above analyses highlight that spending domains are more important than state institutions for motivating political action. Long-term budget developments and budget punctuations emanate from spending domains and the politics within these domains. We have demonstrated policy issues are distinct, but are there broad patterns of growth and punctuations found within groupings of functions? Can we make sense of patterns' functional association? If so, what is the underlying reason for these groupings? Are functions truly unique, or can we classify the politics within issues to provide insight into which issues present opportunities for the long term, and which offer punctuations? To the possibility of some underlying commonalities across functions we turn now.

3.5 ISSUE POLITICS AND BUDGETING MOMENTS

Broad patterns of policy dynamics and policy types are the basis of our inquiry about policy issues. More specifically, to what extent are policy typologies useful in identifying the conditions under which punctuations and long-term growth might occur? We set forth a basic model that connects four policy types to the cumulative effect of policy change. These four types depend on four features of politics: attention, interest group politics, the locus of policy-making, and the distribution of cost and benefits. The development of these four types helps us understand how and why policy issues matter, and how distinct motives of political action prevail within each domain.

In this section, we compare and contrast our typology with two classic typologies of policy domains: Lowi's four groups (1964) and Wilson's (1974) classification according to benefits and costs of particular policy alternatives. Policy typologies are universally understood by the scholarly community studying the policy process and yet, at the same time, widely criticized for their inability to explain all cases. However, Lowi's and Wilson's fundamental arguments – that certain types of policy are more likely to experience conflict than others and that this conflict determines politics – still resonate. Their logic complements PET, where institutional friction is a necessary component for policy change. Institutions are sticky; when they finally move because of some change in the internal or external conditions surrounding policy, they lurch forward in a fashion more volatile than a smoothly updating machine. Macro-political conditions, target populations, and policy types contribute to the extent to which policy subsystems are compelled to incorporate new preferences and hear challenges to the status quo. The result is a maxim for studies of policy change: Conflict creates winners and losers. Less consistency in each produces a greater opportunity for punctuations, but speaks less to the overall cumulative effect of these victories.

We theoretically derive group characteristics along the two dimensions developed in Section 3.4: the "degree" of punctuation in a budget category and its long-term trajectory. We follow Elman's (2005) idea of using typologies in an "explanatory" manner by constructing our two-by-two matrix. Statistical work on model-based clustering (Ahlquist and Breunig, 2012; Banfield and Raftery, 1993; Fraley and Raftery, 1998) offers a methodological tool for testing typologies. We use these tools and show that policy issues cluster according to our two-by-two typology. Policy issues in each group are shown to produce different types of "policy wins."

3.5.1 Issue Politics and Policy Characteristics

Thinking about PET as a theory of distributional change offers an opportunity to link PET to other conceptions of policymaking which predict patterns of policy change as a function of issue-specific structures of political competition. We create a lexicon of policy change using four indicators from the literature on policy dynamics, interest groups, and the stakes associated with policy change. Issue-specific public policy change is a function of assumptions about the type and extent of attention to a policy area; the type and extent of interest group competition; the distribution of costs and benefits to diffuse or concentrated groups; and of the structure of preferred (if any) venues of policy change. The interaction of these individual characteristics can help explain punctuations and long-term trends in broad categories of policy issues using assumptions about the general conditions under which many policy subsystems operate.

We employ these characteristics for developing four ideal-type policy arenas: *interest group politics, standard politics, majoritarian politics,* and *runway expansionary politics.* We assume that some specific subsystems within these general categories are likely to be explained by different dynamics. We empirically examine broad categories to develop a proof of concept for further investigating policy change at a subsystem-specific level, beginning a critical feature of PET: attention.

Attention. Arguably the most enduring feature of Jones and Baumgartner's work in public policy is a broad and deep focus on shifts in attention (Jones and Baumgartner, 2005). Particular issues are likely to enjoy a lasting and high agenda position, whereas other issues are likely to be inherently episodic. Both citizen awareness and institutional structure are responsible for the variation (or lack thereof) in attention to different policy areas.

High levels of attention quite possibly cut both ways. Persistently high public awareness may lead to great rewards for large-scale changes on the part of policy entrepreneurs and policymakers. But, by definition, the majority of policy areas do not enjoy continued public or institutional attention. Policy areas with little institutional attention and little public attention may simply be low stakes or issues largely of interest to experts. Or, low-salience issues might be highly important to a narrow range of groups who control the policy image. Such dominance contributes to the quintessential cause of punctuated equilibrium, wherein sudden attention to an issue can cause a larger public to realize the extent to which the extant definition of the policy image is out of step with current public opinion. Thus, attention can be viewed as a predictor for policy change in a policy area. Therefore, the important distinction is between institutionalized and episodic attention. Understanding attention begets understanding of the issue's stakes and the arrangement of interest group conflict.

Interest Group Competition. Interest group competition is a key component in understanding the distribution of policy changes in a policy area, both in influencing attention and influencing policymakers' decisions regarding solutions to problems. Classic accounts of policymaking (Lowi, 1964; Wilson, 1974) argue that, while politics is central to understanding the policy process, the structure of politics is a function of policy tools and target populations.

Politicians know that running afoul of powerful groups results in conflict and that attempting to change behaviors in fundamental ways results in conflict. Thus, a fully formed theory of policy change through the lens of distributions should also include some characterization of policy type. Conflict and cooperation manifest themselves in different levels of attention to issues, but ultimately in the types of and variation in policies that emerge from subsystems. High levels of conflict can lead to rapid change if the conflict is over the fundamental goals of what government does, but high conflict might also lead to relatively incremental updating insofar as the conflict is constrained to finer issues of policymaking. At a minimum, we need to draw a clear distinction between interest group competition and interest group dominance over policy issues.

Distribution of Policy Costs and Benefits. Perhaps the most enduring feature of Lowi's work is that policy determines politics, specifically the distribution of benefits and burdens associated with policy. The critiques of the Lowi typology are well known, but the fundamental relationship between coercion (in the case of Lowi), the concentration of costs versus benefits (in the case of Wilson), and politics is quite useful when attempting to assess the cumulative changes we might see in otherwise punctuated distributions. Schneider and Ingram's (1993) contribution of "burdens" and "benefits" better defines the policy typology canon, but also expands the canon to better include social regulatory policies.

Benefits and burdens raise or lower the payoffs and risks associated with pursuing policy change. Policies with diffuse benefits and diffuse costs are likely to see fewer consistent entrepreneurs interested in pursuing policy change. One might expect to find these policy areas dominated by events, but the overall policy direction associated with change is relatively minor (attention giveth and taketh away). Policies with concentrated benefits are likely to elicit a great deal of attention from interest groups, but the extent to which this affects policy change and its direction is associated with factors such as attention, interest group competition, and the opportunity for change afforded by the policymaking venue. Ultimately, the key distinction is between concentrated and diffuse distributions of costs and benefits.

Locus of Policymaking. A fourth element in understanding policy change according to virtually any model of public policy is the role of institutions in structuring information flows and in shaping the structures through which interested actors can express preferences. One of the early contributions of *Agendas and Instability* (Baumgartner and Jones, 1993) is the sense that issue expansion is aided by a political system with a wider array of venues for policymaking and entrepreneurs who seek out favorable institutions for policy change. Pralle's (2006a) work on environmental issues honed the concept of venue-shopping to help explain the mechanisms behind policy disruption. Thus, we expect that policy areas more amenable to change in a variety of policy venues produce a different pattern of punctuations and long-term change than those that are more constrained.

Venue availability is only part of the locus of policymaking story. Grossmann (2013) suggests that some policy areas are likely to experience policy change in particular venues; for example, most environmental policy change occurs via rule-making and court decisions rather than the legislature. Pralle's work (2006b) and the work of other scholars (Mintrom and Norman, 2009; Weissert, 1991) are instructive in that entrepreneurs are aware of the most successful locus of policy change for a particular policy. This awareness does not automatically prevent interest group conflict across a broad spectrum of policymaking arenas, however. Entrepreneurs may still pursue policy change in less successful venues to appeal to interest group constituencies (Pralle, 2003). Specific venues could be imagined to produce different patterns of policy change as a result of institutional structure; thus, patterns of change for a policy area may well be a function of the "preferred" loci of policy change.

3.5.2 A Typology of Issue Politics

Using these four elements, we develop a series of expectations regarding policy change on particular policy issues. Issue subsystems are a function of (a) the degree of punctuation derived from PET and (b) the politics that emerge from the distribution of burdens and benefits of a policy. Our two-by-two typology is summarized in Table 3.6. In it, particular policy issues are associated with particular types of policy change. Political actors engage in policymaking strategies that understand the short- and long-term dynamics on individual issues. The politics of these issue domains drive policymakers' behavior.

A short review of empirical classifications of policy domains is necessary before we detail each quadrant. In an exhaustive meta-analysis of the literature on policy change, Grossmann (2013) found that political scientists assign different explanatory concepts to each major policy domain, such as health care, defense, or environmental concerns. This finding suggests that policy change has distinct sources in each domain, and that generalizations across policy domains are challenging. However, quantitative work on public budgeting finds that some spending categories are more malleable than others. For example, in Section 3.4 and in Breunig and Koski (2012), and Breunig et al. (2009), we find that some budget functions, particularly education and

TABLE 3.6 *Typology of issue politics.*

		Degree of punctuation	
		Small	Large
Long-term growth	Large	*Interest group politics*	*Runaway expansionary politics*
	Small	*Standard politics*	*Majoritarian politics*

health, are less punctuated than others, such as agriculture and general government spending, regardless of institutional setting at the subnational and
national level. Epp and Baumgartner (2017) also find some spending domains
to be more prone to punctuations than others. Mortensen (2005) moves a step
further in our direction by distinguishing four policy domains according to
growth and punctuation. Unfortunately, he does not develop theoretical expectations about each domain based on these distinctions. The takeaway is that,
according to existing literature on spending, different policy outcomes exist in
different policy domains. Developing a typology around policy issues is still a
worthwhile endeavor. We start with the lower left quadrant in Table 3.6.

Standard Politics. In our conception of *standard politics*, policymaking is characterized by a low degree of punctuation and accompanied by small long-term
change. Standard politics plays out in subsystems that engage in less coercion,
where benefits are reaped by small groups and costs are diffuse. In these cases,
we expect that low coercion and an oversubscription of benefits produce less
extreme distributions of change. In standard politics, we also expect that policymaking occurs through multibranch interaction, but neither the executive
nor the legislative branch continuously takes a leading role. Hence, multiple
venues for policymaking are available, at least in theory.

The style of policymaking between both branches is characterized by focus
on problem-solving based on a mutually agreed-upon policy image. This stability is enhanced even further by one-sided interest group mobilization. The
dominance of a well-organized and enduring interest group on one side and
weak opposition on the other contributes to a stable, incremental policymaking environment. Taken together, we would expect that the desire for these
subsystems to remain off the radar would contain the overall long-term growth
for a given policy issue. In a "standard politics" scenario, we still expect to
find punctuations, but these punctuations would be more constrained relative
to other scenarios.

In standard politics, interest group competition is one-sided and dominated
by a given interest group environment. The locus of policymaking remains
among different branches of government. Given concentrated costs and diffuse
benefits of policy, political actors' motivations when operating in this scenario
are steady long-term gains.

Interest Group Politics. Policy issues displaying a low degree of punctuation,
but large long-term growth can be distinguished as *interest group politics*.
Wilson (1974) notes that, while not coercive, the distribution of resources
is a zero-sum game. Even within a subsystem that largely engages in policymaking that can be framed as distributive politics, there are often not enough
resources to be distributed among all actors. In some of these cases, the conflict over scarce resources can provide great political opportunities to both
reward and punish political actors. We expect the politics associated with this

policymaking to be akin to Wilson's "interest group politics" model. While groups win and lose over time, the ultimate value of the policy subsystem is not in question, just some of the lower-order policy decisions (to use Cashore and Howlett's 2007, 2009 terms) within that subsystem are contested. Thus, we expect that the overall subsystem ought to have a similarly low degree of punctuation as our *standard politics* model. The difference here is that the constant attention from groups as an endorsement of the overall value of the subsystem would produce a greater cumulative effect on policy change. Long-term growth in budgets is the consequence.

More importantly, subsystems that deal with a predominately regulatory agenda are familiar with conflict associated with policies that advocate governmental coercion. Such subsystems are typically populated by representatives of both those in favor of regulation and regulated groups themselves. The primary actors and locus of policymaking are legislative committees and their heads. These policymakers champion their respective policy field and use their position to extract policy concessions through bargaining and log-rolling. These policy areas should be fairly volatile, with a great deal of push and pull from both sides in terms of average annual changes, but the long-term accumulation of policy change is likely to be in the same direction.

The difference might come in the form of Schneider and Ingram's Schneider and Ingram's (1993) critique of Lowi's original idea that all government coercion is to be met with resistance. That is, in some regulatory subsystems, questions about coercive policies pertain to the magnitude of such efforts rather than more fundamental questions about whether the government should take a coercive role per se. In these cases and similar to policy domains with distributive benefits, we are likely to see the long-term growth as well as low levels of conflict. Interest group politics are, therefore, characterized by episodic and event-driven attention. As interest groups, legislatures, and governors engage with the prevalent issue at any given time, short-term gains within a policy domain might occur, but long-term growth is the dominant motive for political action.

Majoritarian Politics. In policy domains with a high degree of punctuation and little long-term growth, we expect *majoritarian politics* is a driving force. In this context, low long-term change occurs in two distinct cases related to an overall distribution that is punctuated. First, groups have varying degrees of interest in majoritarian political issues. Some groups have narrow interests particular to the policy domain and, thus, are likely to maintain more constant attention. Majoritarian policy domains are also influenced by groups that have episodic stakes in these issues. Such groups may be small or large; regardless, the group populations within majoritarian politics are dynamic. Dedicated groups might keep attention on an issue during slow news days, but be easily overwhelmed by larger groups during times of heightened attention to the issue. The fluidity of groups means that policies that emerge from majoritarian politics may have trouble maintaining the same coalition of groups that converged to make them. Wins and losses are distributed unequally across time, groups, and other policy domains.

Interest groups in majoritarian politics are dependent not simply on attention, but also on how other interest groups and policymakers react to attention to majoritarian policy domains. Given the constant battle among interest groups over policy, policymaking occurs through multibranch interaction as groups and their institutional advocates try to claim authority over the given policy issue. Yet, such institutional advocacy can be swept away by heightened attention.

In many ways, this description mirrors the quintessential long-term expectation of punctuated equilibrium theory: Many tiny changes occur over time, and occasional ruptures of the policy equilibrium produce enormous changes for a short period. This process leads to a long period of stability via new institutions carrying out the new policy regime. However, this institutionally induced stability creates the opportunity for massive changes, because the status quo remains relatively constant, thereby providing an incremental baseline against which to compare future changes. In our conception of majoritarian politics, the new policy monopoly created by the institutional setup will maintain a status quo position that does not marginally update according to macro-political preferences. In this case, we expect a highly punctuated distribution, but low degrees of long-term growth.

The second case through which to predict low long-term change with interstitial high punctuation is through the types of policies most susceptible to swings in public opinion, specifically those policies for which there are neither many opponents nor many advocates. The types of policy that produce politics with few supporters are akin to Wilson's "majoritarian" politics, where there are few groups and advocacy is ad hoc. Ad hoc advocacy should produce wide swings with very little specific sustained strategy toward a particular direction of policy. May's "policies without publics" (1991) – policies that have moderate benefits widely distributed with dispersed costs – are likely examples in this area, when policies are not championed by experts. In Schneider and Ingram (1993) terms, one might expect policies that distribute benefits to deviant or dependent groups to emerge in greater numbers because of a wave of public opinion, only to be pushed back years later.

In summary, the following features are central to *majoritarian politics*: Attention is institutionalized by steady interest group competition, and politics occurs across all branches of government. In this crowded scenario, political actors are motivated to secure short-term gains, given that the competitive environment constrains long-term growth.

Runaway Expansionary Politics. The category in which we expected the most fundamental policy changes to occur – in degree of punctuations and long-term change – is called *runaway expansionary politics arena*. From the perspective of PET, the combination of high conflict and large cumulative changes is the least likely combination of conflict and change. Policy areas with sustained conflict over time are unlikely to produce fundamental winners and losers in perpetuity. For cumulative policy outputs to persist in the same direction over time, winning coalitions would have to remain constant and receive significant gains despite vigorous opposition. This category would be representative of a perpetual positive feedback cycle over the long term, where issues would constantly expand with previous victories.

While constant issue expansion is theoretically possible, it seems unlikely that such continued gains would produce continued vigorous opposition. At some point, the opposition would likely become overpowered, and the punctuated nature of the distribution in this area would settle into a new equilibrium. A continued positive feedback cycle is akin to a runaway greenhouse effect in climate modeling; we term it "runaway expansionary politics." Examples of runaway issue expansion might include the Department of Homeland Security from 2003 until 2008.

Runaway issue expansion occurs in policy domains with less formalized structures of governance, such as policy areas spanning multiple domains, which therefore have no policy monopoly to guide growth. A simultaneous feature is that opposition, while occasionally strong, is equally fragmented, leading to little retrenchment. The result is a policy area with high volatility, but this volatility is largely a function of the variation between incremental and large positive change. Of the four typologies we advocate, this is the least likely to occur, given the difficulty in sustaining frequent large changes with few losses. The type of change described in *runaway expansionary politics arena* mirrors the mechanisms of change found in issue expansion within the PET framework, which is itself intended to be short-lived. Fragmentation of issues across many domains is not a necessary and sufficient condition to lead to runaway issue expansion; indeed, undefined problems can have very few political upsides for interest groups, leading to anemic "policy regimes" (May and Jochim, 2013; May et al., 2011). Anemic policy regimes have less of an ability to control their policy destiny, which can produce continuous large policy change.

Given these characteristics of one-sided interest group dominance with a stable policy image as well as concentrated benefits, we expect that political actors in this scenario are motivated to reap repeated and large short-term gains. In the unlikely event where political actors are able to repeat this feat multiple times, long-term growth is a real possibility.

3.5.3 Assessing Policy Typologies with Model-Based Clustering

We assess the placement of particular policy issues (budget functions in our case) in distinct quadrants of policymaking using cluster analysis. The formation of typologies and classification of cases into groups remains a core tool in social science research (Collier et al., 2012; Elman, 2005). These authors highlight that typologies are not only useful for generating case groupings inductively, but also for classification and testing of an explicitly stated theory.

The most common quantitative tool for assessing typologies and placement of individual observations is cluster analysis. Cluster analysis strives to identify some overarching structure in the data and to place individual observations into clusters based on some defined metric. Unfortunately, researchers regularly employ hierarchical cluster analysis as an inferential tool and consequently may overinterpret their results. Hierarchical cluster analysis possesses several threats to careful analysis of the underlying data: It offers several measures of similarity, no statistical basis for picking a specific solution, no uncertainties about individual cluster assignments, and severely restricts the geometrical arrangements of the studied objects. Thus, traditional cluster methods only should serve exploratory purposes.

Recent applications of mixture models to clustering problems provide an appropriate methodology for testing typological explanations. Model-based clustering (MBC) using a mixture of probability distributions (Ahlquist and Breunig, 2012; Banfield and Raftery, 1993; Fraley and Raftery, 2002) formulates the clustering problem as a problem of model choice. This formulation allows researchers to rely on statistical methods for model evaluation and selection (using the Bayesian information criterion) and to provide measures of uncertainty about cluster placement.

The identification of clusters and the placement of individual observations is driven by models. In our analysis, we assumed that the number of clusters is between one and four. A one-cluster solution indicates that clustering policy issues are not possible or even futile. We set four clusters as the upper limit because our typology identifies four groups of issue politics. Throughout the next empirical section, the estimated results are presented visually. Two-dimensional classification plots contain the labeled observations as well as the estimated mixture component. We rely on model comparisons using BIC for each estimated model and their cluster geometries. When several models perform within the suggested cutoff point of 10 points lower than the BIC of the best fitting model, we use the model with the lowest number of clusters.

3.5.4 Connecting Budgeting Moments and Policy Issues

The goal of the empirical analysis is to detect a match between our typology and individual spending domains (policy issues). First, we pool long-term growth rates and L-kurtosis scores across all states to focus on functional differences only. Doing so results in an analysis with very sparse data: the ten budget functions. We use the median growth rates across all fifty states for a basic picture. With this first analysis in mind, we employ all 500 observations (i.e., state–functional-level growth and L-kurtosis scores) to verify the more

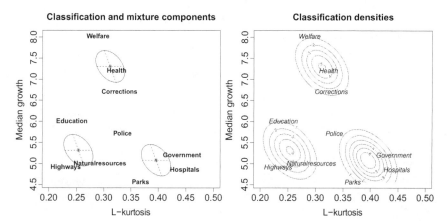

FIGURE 3.9 Classification of median long-term growth rate and degree of punctuation at functional level for all fifty states over twenty-five years. The left plot displays the median growth rate and the L-kurtosis of each budget function. The three ellipses are the identified mixture components and their form. The right plot displays the mixture model's density.

narrow analysis in a second step. As a precautionary step, we examined if long-term growth rates and L-kurtosis scores could be clustered by states. The MBC algorithm identified a one-cluster solution as the best model. This result means that one cannot group American states meaningfully along these two dimensions. Indirectly, one might also speculate that, therefore, institutional and political variation alone cannot provide us with a clear picture of public policymaking.

A comparison of median long-term growth rates and L-kurtosis scores shows that three types of policymaking prevail. The MBC algorithm suggests that the best fitting model contains three clusters. Figure 3.9 displays the results. The right plot shows that the upper-left quadrant – high long-term growth combined with a low degree of punctuations – is occupied by the domains of welfare, corrections, and health. These domains represent *interest group politics*. The lower-right corner of the right plots holds four budget functions: education, police, natural resources, and highways. These four categories are characterized by *standard politics*, which result in a low degree of punctuation and small long-term changes. The third cluster entails government, parks, and hospital spending. These three domains are highly punctuated but lack large cumulative changes. We labeled this type of policymaking as *majoritarian politics*. The cluster algorithm is a bit uncertain (less than 2 percent) in placing police and parks spending in a particular category. We do not find *runaway expansionary politics* in our data. The absence of this type of politics is likely due to the fact that most state governments are required to produce a balanced budget.

The model suggests a very high degree of certainty ($p > 0.99$) about the placement of each function, and the density contours (see right plot of Figure 3.9) identify three high-density regions. However, the overall model fit is less promising. The left plot indicates that a three-cluster solution provides the best overall fit. But one-, two-, or even four-cluster solutions are a possibility. The various BIC values close to the best fitting model indicate that any one solution is not substantively superior. Obviously, the uncertainty about the number of clusters might be due to the low number of cases (ten budget functions).

We provide more substantive evidence by expanding the analysis to each budget function for each state. Figure 3.10 summarizes our findings. In both plots of the figure, we color the observations according to the categorization scheme that we just identified. This way, we can visually assess if certain policy domains are placed predominantly within one of the four quadrants across all states. The MBC algorithm finds that a four-cluster solution is the most suitable for the given data, but a solution with three clusters performs marginally poorer. The BIC is a mere three points lower.

The left plot of Figure 3.10 displays the four mixture component and their placements. Apparently, the best fitting mixture model distinguishes between a category characterized by a fairly low degree of punctuation and medium long-term growth and a very small group of observations with huge growth rates and low punctuations. The model suggests it might be worthwhile to distinguish among observations within the *interest group politics* group between those policy issues that grow in the long run and those that grow phenomenally, such as welfare spending in the western states of Nevada, New Mexico, and Arizona.

Due to the four-cluster solution, it is apparent in the right plot that all types of budget functions are to some extent akin to *standard politics* type. The clustering algorithm indicates some uncertainty about placing particular observations in this cluster. For example, there is a 53 percent chance that correction spending in Michigan should be included here; but it is also likely that this observation belongs to *interest group politics* with a 31 percent chance and even to a third cluster with a 0.16 probability. MBC will not force cases in particular clusters; instead, we can use the method to acknowledge that some tough cases are hard to classify. This difficulty might arise given that the politics of a particular domain changes over time.

As is visually apparent, placement in three of the clusters closely matches our previous findings. Hospital, parks, and government spending from various American states is placed in the low-growth–high-punctuation domain of *majoritarian politics*. This assessment is conveyed by the large amount of green dots in the lower-right quadrant. Welfare and health spending (orange dots) in the fifty states predominately are classified together and located in the *interest group politics* quadrant of low levels of punctuation and large long-term changes. Finally, spending on highways, natural resources, and police

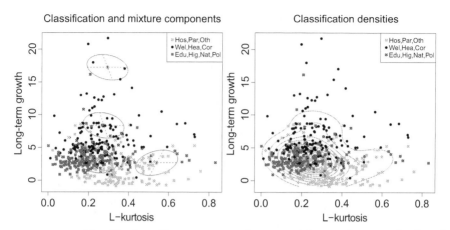

FIGURE 3.10 Classification of long-term growth rates and degree of punctuation for all fifty states and each function over twenty-five years. The left plot displays the long-term growth and the L-kurtosis of each budget function. The four ellipses are the identified mixture components. The right plot displays the mixture model's density. The colored dots indicate the three groups of budget functions that are identified in Figure 3.9.

is *standard politics* in many states (purple dots). In this group, states do not change the budget much over time and make adjustments in a rather incremental fashion. About one-third (150 out of the 500) of the observations are placed in this type of policymaking.

3.6 MOTIVES: THE CENTRALITY OF POLICY ISSUES

This chapter gave a representation of how policy issues constitute motives for political action. Spending items in state budgets epitomize policy issues. First, we delineate the theoretical distinction between incrementalism, punctuated equilibrium theory, and broader theoretical debates on policy change. These theories show that policy change does not transpire as isolated, independent events: policy issues influence each other over time and across policy domains.

Second, we describe how spending on different functions of government has evolved across the American states since 1984. Illustrating broad spending patterns allows us to connect spending data to core concepts of the book: punctuations in budgets and long-term spending growth. We find that (1) some policy domains are more likely to be punctuated than others, and (2) large and growing budget items are less punctuated. Indeed, a negative relationship between punctuations and long-term growth is manifest in our data. This empirical pattern signifies that two types of opportunities coexist in state budgets, and that political actors often have to choose one of them. The trade-off is between one-time transformative policy change or long-term incremental growth.

Third, we show that policy issues play an important but largely underappreciated role in theories of policy change. Our various analyses of spending functions illustrate their substance. Differences among policy issues suggest that budget categories have varying levels of importance to policymakers and citizens. Some categories are large and encapsulate the issues to which citizens and policymakers pay attention; these categories are likely to see more conflict and receive continuous attention. Other items rise and fall ephemerally, without much long-term growth. This set of findings refocuses the discussion back on the issue of attention and subsystem politics, where motivations of governors and interest groups are exposed. Strategically, interest groups and governors can seek short-term gains in particular categories, which generally stultify the long-term trajectory of categories. Long-term motivations evince incremental changes that build on existing gains from stable subsystem politics. While there are some exceptions to this rule – exceptions where one or two major changes result in permanent disruption – the path to stable long-term growth is generally paved by many small changes. Political actors, particularly governors, are motivated to make legacy-building long-term changes working with the equilibrium created by the dynamics of existing subsystem actors.

Fourth, at first sight, the centrality of policy issues echoes Baumgartner and Jones's (1993) argument about the importance of subsystem politics. We advance the notion that subsystems matter further by connecting policy issues to the classic typologies of public policy. This connection demonstrates that different types of politics prevail across policy issues. Distinct subsystem politics have consequences for the degree of punctuation and long-term policy change. We pieced together disparate literature and developed four types of policymaking: majoritarian politics, runaway expansionary politics, interest group politics, and standard politics. These four types can be distinguished along four characteristics: (1) the distribution of costs and benefits, (2) the locus of policymaking and its primary actors, (3) the type of interest group competition, and (4) attention.

In this last section of the chapter, we empirically identified which policy issues correspond to the four hypothesized types of policymaking. When we examined budget functions across all states, we found a similar pattern. No budget function in the American states can be classified as *runaway expansionary politics*. For keepers of the purse, this absence is a good thing. The policy domains of hospitals and government are identified as *majoritarian politics*. This type produces large punctuations, but these punctuations do not translate to large long-term policy changes. Spending on highways, police, and natural resources corresponds to *standard politics*. In these spending domains, punctuations are comparatively rare, and budgets grow comparatively little over time. Welfare, corrections, and health spending are classified as *interest group politics*. Here, continuously positive incremental increases in spending over time aid long-term growth. Our applied methodology also revealed that some spending domains in some states are difficult to classify and do not correspond well to ideal types.

Policy issues and budget categories alone cannot encapsulate all the politics of policymaking. The purpose of the chapter is to show how budget functions and their interests are organized influences the way public policy changes over time. Policy issues matter, and they can be grouped and classified. Their grouping signifies distinct motives of political action. We therefore are able to assess policy outcomes according to the developed "ideal types." In particular, governors and interest groups cannot envisage *runaway expansionary politics* and want to obviate *standard politics*. Their motives are crystallized around *majoritarian* and *interest group politics*. The question is how governors and interest groups settle among these options. The Chapter 4 focuses on interest group relations within each policy domain and probes more deeply into their specific attributes and budgetary consequences.

4

Opportunities

Interest Groups and Their Budgetary Issues

Interest groups are motivated to deliver rents to their constituents in the form of public policy (Austen-Smith, 1993; Hansen, 1991; Mitchell and Munger, 1991). A large proportion of the rents that groups seek to obtain is incremental rather than large-scale change. Interest group activity is often associated with landmark legislation, and, while certainly critical to these efforts, the majority of interest group activity concerns working within policy subsystems to maintain existing subsystem dynamics. As such, interest groups not only attempt to set the agenda but also attempt to structure political opportunities for policymakers to intervene.

In 2014, Vermont and Oregon joined several states and localities in considering different policies to address so-called genetically modified (GM) foods. Unlike Vermont, which created a GM law via the legislature (Assembly Bill 120) to label foods produced with "genetic engineering," Oregon's GM law was contested via the ballot initiative process in Measure 92. This was not the first time Oregon voters had been asked to create a labeling regime for genetically engineered foods. In 2002, Oregonians overwhelmingly rejected an initiative petition, Measure 27, by a two-to-one ratio. Opponents, including local and multinational agricultural interests, outspent proponents of Measure 27. The contest for Measure 92 saw the same amount of opposition from large firms, who outspent proponents by a two-to-one ratio; however, the national mood regarding GM labeling had shifted. Whereas Measure 27 was a relatively sleepy contest, the passage of Vermont's AB 120 in May 2014 provoked agricultural firms and GM activists alike to focus their efforts on November ballot contests. In 2014, two high-profile initiatives regarding GM foods worked their way through electorates in Colorado and Oregon. The Colorado initiative (Proposition 105) had less support from the start; however, Oregon initially showed Measure 92 cruising to a resounding victory.

The interests involved in GM politics do not fall along traditional party lines, though Democrats favor labeling more than Republicans. While the policy issue is certainly agricultural, GM politics also split agricultural interests.

In the summer of 2013, GM wheat was discovered in eastern Oregon fields, despite having not yet been approved for market by the USDA. Monsanto, a large multinational agricultural firm, denied any involvement even though they owned the patent on the escaped wheat, which had not been planted in Oregon since 2005. Later, after the Measure 92 election, Monsanto settled with several aggrieved parties for $2.5 million. The Oregon wheat market is heavily dependent upon wheat exports to Japan and South Korea that ban GM products. The immediate effect of the discovered GM wheat was a temporary ban on shipments from the United States to Japan and South Korea, which harmed eastern Oregon farmers in particular, a traditionally conservative group. Activists in four Oregon counties (Benton, Lane, Josephine, and Jackson) attempted to ban GM crops altogether. In each case, proponents were local grassroots organizations, while multinational corporations largely funded opponents. Multinational corporations, fearful that successful GM bans at the county level would lead to further county actions, additionally sought to halt local GM bans at the state level via the legislature.

The 2013 Oregon legislative session featured several major issues regarding the budget. Three-term Democratic Governor John Kitzhaber, like all governors, faced other higher-priority issues than GM food labeling. The most prominent issue during this phase of his administration was how to manage pension debt. Oregon had been (and still is) facing a significant budget hole in the form of pension obligations to public employees under the Public Employees Retirement System (PERS) with unfunded liabilities equivalent to two years of the state's general fund. Oregon Democratic governors (in power since 1987) face a twofold challenge in attempting to reform PERS: (1) Public employees unions form a significant base of support, and (2) they must operate in a state with no sales tax and a penchant for ballot initiatives that restrict revenue.

After Jackson County had passed its ban and while organizers were gathering signatures from Benton, Lane, and Josephine counties, Kitzhaber called a special session to address PERS reform in the fall of 2013. Only five bills were on the docket: Four addressed pension reform through benefit cuts and revenue increases, and one (SB 863) proclaimed the state – not local government – had the ultimate authority to regulate food labeling.

Before the session began, Kitzhaber declared he would not sign any bill unless he signed *all* the bills. For four days, the house and the senate deliberated but finally gave Kitzhaber his pension reform, as well as state primacy in GM product labeling regulation for any new GM bans after the session. Kitzhaber later noted the oddity of SB 863 as a part of pension reform: "The random factor, the free radical, was the GMO bill, which I would be the first to acknowledge has nothing to do with the purposes for which I originally called the session. I wish I could tell you there was a rational reason for it to be in there, but there isn't – except apparently the Republicans needed it to get enough votes" (Esteve, 2013, para. 8). Kitzhaber signed all five special session bills that later invalidated Josephine County's successful initiative campaign since the county voted after the legislature had passed SB 863, though Jackson County's ban still stands. Perhaps somewhat ironically, the Oregon Supreme Court's invalidation of key parts of the pension reform all but killed the deal, but the GM labeling bill remained unscathed.

In this instance, interest groups, particularly agricultural groups, shaped the governor's opportunity to intervene. Large farming interests – notably alfalfa, corn, and sugar beets in Oregon – as well as large food processors viewed the special session as an opportunity to put their interests in a must-pass bill. Senate Bill 863 essentially dictated that any labeling in Oregon would occur at the state level, thus setting up Measure 92 as a major battle. Interest groups had created opportunities for the governor in the special session and then picked the battlefield for labeling: the state rather than county level.

The subsequent Measure 92 campaign featured pressure from groups across the state. Large agricultural companies, buoyed by interventions that success-fully stopped California (2012) and Washington (2013) initiatives to label GM crops, poured $20 million into the Oregon campaign. Opponents also included the Oregon Farm Bureau, the trade group Oregonians for Food & Shelter, and the editorial boards of the major newspapers, including *The Oregonian* and the *Statesman-Journal*. The initiative's primary proponents included the newly formed Oregon GMO Right to Know, Dr. Bronner's soap company, the Oregon League of Conservation Voters, OSPIRG, and other consumer safety advocates. While significantly outspent by opponents, proponents amassed a healthy war chest of $10 million.

Agricultural issues such as these fall in the natural resources policy subsys-tem; however, the very public consumer dynamic resulted in a distinct and ephemeral interest group arrangement. During the Measure 92 campaign, Democratic Governor John Kitzhaber was also running for reelection to his fourth term against Republican Dennis Richardson. The uncertain nature (what we call "instability") of the interest group environment is telling: Both candidates endorsed Measure 92. In one of the most expensive initiative cam-paigns in Oregon's history, Measure 92 ultimately failed by 837 votes out of 1,506,311 votes cast.[1]

The efforts to control GMO labeling in Oregon, Vermont, and other states show the power of interest groups to set the agenda for policymakers to inter-vene. In initiative states, it is particularly noticeable given that interest groups are, in most cases, authoring policies (this happens in legislatures, too, but there at least is the veneer of legislative authorship in bill introduction). In the

---

[1] The Oregon case later played out nationally at the federal level in what must have felt like cruel irony for GM regulation proponents. When faced with a patchwork of state-level GM laws, a bipartisan bill to create a national standard and disallow state standards was signed by President Obama on July 29, 2016, and took effect on January 1, 2020. Instead of local and state laws serving as model policies for GM regulation at the federal level, opponents' efforts to *preempt* GM legislation in states like Oregon served as the model for federal GM policy.

case of Oregon, anti-labeling groups shifted the political discourse to a venue where they could better consolidate their message. Governor Kitzhaber was presented with an opportunity to position himself on the side of anti-labeling groups in 2013 with SB 863, but then turned around and advocated for the pro-labeling Measure 92 in 2014. Clearly, the interest group arrangement for GM labeling was in flux, which is precisely what our theory would predict leading to incentives to intervene, even if those interventions were not entirely consistent.

In this chapter, we investigate interest groups' role in shaping budget dynamics. In Chapter 3, we showed that certain budget categories have distinct spending profiles in terms of direction, magnitude, and long-term trajectory. This is an empirical phenomenon that leads to specific patterns of change. A policy issue fuels political actors' motivation to intervene; we argue here that interest group dynamics produce opportunities for policymakers to alter public budgets. Interest groups have a direct impact through their tactics, but act as an intermediary force on the primary budget-makers: governors. This chapter shows, in line with the in-depth analysis found in Chapter 5, that governors have influence over changes in budget category expenditures. Stronger governors are responsible for larger changes in the budget. More importantly, interest groups have a stronger yet nonlinear effect on budget changes. We show that governors seek opportunities to increase budget categories and that particular interest group dynamics provide opportunities to make cuts.

Opportunities for budgetary cuts arise in instable interest group environments (see Chapter 2). *Instability* of interest groups refers to a situation in which the composition of groups is readily changed. In these situations, it is unclear how many interest groups populate a policy field for longer periods and how the interest group preferences are distributed. In contrast to an instable interest group environment, the dominance of a few groups (*capture*) and competition among many groups (*deadlock*) appear to be more predictable and offer opportunities for long-term cooperation. Governors may face distinct interest group environments over time and across states. As such, our first task in this chapter is to delineate interest group populations. Using data collected by Gray and Lowery and their collaborators (Gray and Lowery, 2000; Lowery and Gray, 1995), we match their data to our ten individual budget domains to show that the range of interest group environments is considerable. Some policy domains, especially in small states in the 1980s, are comprised of a few groups, whereas by 2010 we can find over 2,500 groups in states such as Texas and Florida. Group size also varies among policy domains. For example, corrections and police typically encompass a few groups, while the welfare domain holds about a quarter of all interest groups in a state.

We then map our three interest group environments – capture, instability, and deadlock – to opportunities to change the budget within each populated domain. Building on the interest group and public policy literature, we contend that interest groups provide political opportunities for themselves and for others to make policy change. At the state level, interest groups engage with the executive branch headed by the governor and the state's core agencies. A stable and lasting relationship between both parties is a desirable outcome. Stability offers not only predictable and steady returns for groups, but also predictable opportunities for intervention-minded politicians. Less stable relationships hold divergent opportunities for governors; shifting policy images and changing interest group membership turn policymaking in a fickle endeavor.

Our regression analysis shows that the proposed convex relationship between spending on a policy issue and its interest group environment holds true in our state data. The same applies to long-term budget issues. Long-term budgetary growth is more pronounced in policy domains with a small share *and* with a high share of interest groups. Policy domains that maintained a stable share of interest groups, on average across state budgets, increased fivefold between 1984 and 2010. Contrariwise, interest group environments in flux over time are likely to be accompanied by budget cuts and thwarted long-term growth. Budget categories in unstable environments barely doubled during the same twenty-five-year period. Once again, we can see how annual changes in budget composition have huge consequences for aggregate spending in the long run.

The chapter closes with a discussion of how interest group competition is related to opportunities for policy change. We respond to Anzia's (2019) call for a policy-focused approach for studying interest groups and leveraging the American states as a broad sample of interest group environments. Anzia (2019, 347) contends "if interest groups care about public policy, then to assess whether interest groups have influence, naturally we should be focused on the extent to which they get policy to reflect their interests." Throughout this chapter, we stress the importance of groups in demarcating opportunities for change for governors. Interest groups rely on state government responsiveness to accomplish policy change. We establish that powerful governors are the conduit for budgetary change. In Chapter 5, we discuss how powerful governors are able to do so and detect their unique ability to "augment" budgetary change.

4.1 INTEREST GROUPS IN THE AMERICAN STATES

As the policy process literature argues convincingly, interest groups and their interactions are the attention-getters in a political system. Interest groups can concentrate on a particular policy domain and then decide if it is possible to arrange a cozy capture scenario (akin to iron-triangle subsystem politics) or to flourish in a more pluralist setting with many other groups, resulting in mutual adjustment policymaking. The uncertain world for interest groups and governors lies in between these two scenarios. We expect that policy domains with a modest number of groups experience fluctuation in the interest group population over time and contribute to unstable policymaking that does not produce clear winners and losers. In this volatile environment, the executive must consider whether policy change will produce the next policy monopoly or if the domain will be elevated to a more pluralist setting with open competition.

The interest group environment across the American states is varied and particular to each state (Gray and Lowery, 1996; Holyoke, 2019). This makes sense, given the variety of institutional structures, industries, and interests contained within fifty different democracies. While federal politics and, importantly, federal dollars are influential, states have peculiar concentrations of groups that vary across space and time. We rely on the reclassified interest group density data, ending in 2007, from Gray et al. (2004) and Lowery et al. (2015), and summarize interest groups across the states along several dimensions.

The interest group landscape changes substantially between 1980 and 2010. As the maps in Figure 4.1 show, regional variation in the number of interest

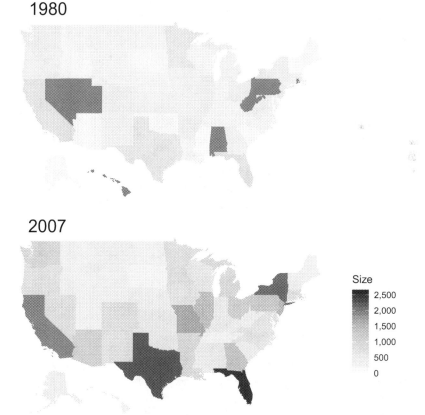

1980

2007

Size

2,500
2,000
1,500
1,000
500
0

FIGURE 4.1 Total number of interest groups per state in 1980 (top) and 2007 (bottom). Grayed areas are no data.

TABLE 4.1 *Interest group concentration in the American states.*

Policy issue	Median share of interest group density	Mean change in interest group density	SD of change in interest group density
Welfare	25.5	0.04	0.3
Health	16.3	0.4	0.8
Natural resources	15.7	−0.1	0.2
Hospitals	15.6	0.5	1.0
Government	12.3	0.01	0.5
Highways	8.6	−0.1	0.3
Parks	7.0	0.1	0.6
Education	6.9	0.3	0.7
Police	5.0	0.3	0.8
Corrections	2.5	0.4	1.3

groups is large in 1980 and even more so in 2007. Around 10,000 interest groups are found in the American states in 1980. Among them, just over 100 are active in states such as Mississippi, while over 700 are located in Florida. By 2007, the total number of groups increased by a factor of four and ranged from just over 200 in South Dakota to over 2,000 groups in states like Texas, New York, and Florida. Table 4.1 also shows that the mean number of groups changed by at least 60 percent between 1980 and 2007. Clearly, the data show a flourishing landscape of interest groups in the American states.

These trends are corroborated by a survey from Holyoke (2019). He documents interest groups in the American states from 2005 to 2015 and compares his findings with Gray and Lowery's data as well as Strickland (2019). His database makes clear that interest group growth began leveling off in the 2010s. Geographical differences increasingly widened between highly populated states, such as Florida, California, and New York, and sparsely represented states, such as Wyoming, North Dakota, Hawaii, and Maine. Typically, interest group populations often doubled in small states and quadrupled in larger states. Texas is a prime example of this trend: The Texan interest group population was among the largest in the country by 2010.

In addition to variation across space and time, interest group density varies by policy issue. Figure 4.2 aggregates interest groups by budget categories to show the relative share of interest groups by policy issue. The patterns revealed in Figure 4.2 are suggestive of an interest group environment where no one group entirely dominates a budget – this can also be seen in Table 4.1. The mean share of interest groups in a policy domain is about 10 percent with a range from close to 0 up to 37 percent.

Visually and statistically, even the most crowded policy domains rarely made up more than 30 percent of the entire interest group ecosystem in a state. As Table 4.1 illustrates, categories such as police, corrections, and education

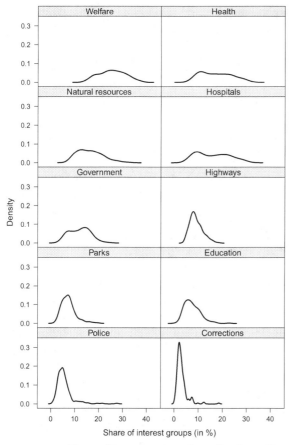

FIGURE 4.2 Share of interest groups by policy issue. Data are from all American states, 1980–2007. Shares are ordered by median share of categories.

find small concentrations of groups; categories such as welfare and health find the largest concentrations; and natural resources and highways are somewhere in between. The second and third columns of Table 4.1 hint at issue-specific differences. Over the nearly thirty-year period, most large interest group domains remain large and most small ones small.

Nevertheless, the standard deviation of these changes suggests that large fluctuations accompany the increase. There is plenty of variation over time within some domains, such as hospitals, health, and corrections. Welfare, on the other hand, remains a rather crowed policy domain across states and time. Thus, while there are variations in interest group concentrations that are specific to policy issues, there are also variations *within* categories to determine the opportunity structure associated with interest group competition.

The type of interest groups prevalent in a state is also becoming more diverse. Existing surveys of interest groups in the American states (Gray and Lowery, 1996; Holyoke, 2019) show that business interests dominate, while social service nonprofits remain small. However, interest groups are not just organized as membership organizations, but corporations, universities, and even local governments are lobbying in the states (Holyoke, 2019). Previous studies found that more membership organizations are active in the North than in the South. As Strickland (2019) makes clear, an increase in the number of interest groups as a measure of interest representation is accompanied by a rise in lobbyists in statehouses.

4.2 BEHAVIORAL ASSUMPTIONS OF INTEREST GROUP INTERACTIONS IN THE POLICY PROCESS

Interest groups create political opportunities for themselves and for others to make policy change. The literature on interest group behavior suggests individual motivations aggregate to the particular kinds of opportunities we discuss in this book. Pluralists, such as Truman (1951), linked interest groups to political outcomes. Schattschneider (1960) and Olson (1965) followed with a more critical perspective on how and what kind of groups are influential. Extant scholarship investigates interest group influence over policymaking by focusing on tactics, strategy, resources, and other political activities (Baumgartner et al., 2009a). The literature fundamentally agrees that interest groups influence policy; however, findings that systematically relate interest groups to policy outputs are thin at best (Baumgartner and Leech, 1998; Burstein and Linton, 2002). Studies focus on particular policies, particular time periods, or visible strategies in a political environment where much of interest group activity occurs outside traditional political channels. Lowery (2013) has provided for a thorough review of this issue.

Group motivations and strategies are well articulated in political science, beginning with Olson's (1965) basic assumption that groups form to pursue rents from governments and Mayhew's (1974) argument that politicians are inclined to listen to what interest groups say if it assists policymakers' reelection goals. Insofar as groups are useful to reelection-minded politicians, they exchange information with policymakers regarding issues related to policy and offer financial resources to candidates (Nownes and Freeman, 1998). Interest groups can be active in one venue of the policy process, many, or all, depending which offers the greatest possibility of success (Baumgartner and Leech, 1998; Boehmke et al., 2013; Holyoke, 2003). Groups are active in problem definition (Kingdon, 1995), agenda-setting (Austen-Smith, 1993; Cobb, 1983), law-making (Baumgartner et al., 2009a), rule-making (Furlong and Kerwin, 2004; Yackee, 2006), implementation (Koski and May, 2006), and learning (Koski, 2010).

In addition to understanding the general assumptions regarding individual group motivations, interest group literature also considers interactions with other groups in setting the policymaking agenda (Baumgartner and Jones, 1993; Baumgartner et al., 2009a; Gilens and Page, 2014; LaPira, 2015). Membership motivates much of individual groups' behaviors in shaping and responding to policy (Ahlquist and Levi, 2013; Holyoke, 2009), but this behavior is conditioned by the presence of other groups with which groups may choose to cooperate or compete (Heinz et al., 1993). A group's decision to cooperate or compete with other groups is often dependent on its desire to lobby for change (Leifeld and Schneider, 2012). At the same time, motivations to lobby for change are influenced greatly by the number and positions of groups active in the same policy domain. Interest groups compete and collaborate based on the opportunities they see to deliver rents (Holyoke, 2003). Often, the safest strategy for groups to consistently deliver rents is to maintain the status quo (Baumgartner and Leech, 1998).

It is politically risky for a group to oppose the status quo if there is little hope of policy change. Ultimately, groups that fail in their efforts to change policy have trouble demonstrating their value to the members that empower them, though there are cases (e.g., interest groups connected to social movements) where groups make decisions based less on the likelihood of success and more based on the strategic desires of members (Pralle, 2003). Depending on the constellation of other groups in the subsystem, interest group competition occurs (Axelrod, 1967; Salisbury, 1992), but less often than cooperation (Holyoke, 2009). Gray and Lowery (1998) suggest that a high density of interest groups in a policy domain leads to cooperation among interest groups. Moreover, competition does not necessarily lead to policy change; rather, competition can stem from a desire to defend the status quo. The end result is an interest group system that generally forms stable relationships between groups, even those that may compete with one another. Stable relationships offer not only stable returns for groups, but also predictable opportunities for intervention-minded politicians (in our case, governors). Less stable relationships offer different types of opportunities to politicians who are less invested in a repetition of the status quo.

4.3 INTEREST GROUP DYNAMICS AND POLICY CHANGE

Interest group dynamics emerge depending upon an individual group's capacity to influence policy, the institutional characteristics of the policymaking environment, and the presence of other groups. Status quo groups generally prefer low-conflict scenarios to maintain their position, while challenger groups seek to expand conflict (Schattschneider, 1960). Economic theories of interest group mobilization suggest that more groups will flock to policy areas that produce greater rewards (Mitchell and Munger, 1991; Moe, 1988; Olson, 1965). Neopluralism (McFarland, 2004) and interest group ecology (Gray and Lowery, 1996, 2000; Lowery and Gray, 1995) inform our expectations of group behaviors in influencing public policy. This literature suggests that memberships of interest groups and their relations (competition and cooperation) to other groups within a policy domain influence policy outcomes.

The policy process literature contends that the relationship between interest groups and policy outcomes is determined by two features: policy image and attention (Baumgartner and Jones, 1993; Jones and Baumgartner, 2005). Policy entrepreneurs wanting to change the status quo direct attention to stable policy images to expand the number of actors involved in a policy domain. Policy images offer factual information and emotional appeals (Robinson, 2016); this information focuses attention on particular policy problems. Increased attention facilitates issue expansion which can destroy the existing policy image, introduce new participants, and otherwise unlock the policy monopoly. This breakdown results in policy change. Thus, in addition to the characteristics of the interest group population, the policy process literature argues interest groups compete for attention and contest policy images. These battles affect policy outcomes.

We assume interest groups are concerned with maintaining or increasing their share of resources from governments. Government resources are allocated across different policy domains, which mobilizes groups that represent interests in those domains to "protect themselves against losses and to seek additional resources" (Strickland, 2019, 358). Strickland (2019, 358) argues "not only will the groups become active, but they will also seek to secure their gains through sustained increased lobbying activity." In general, this is a reasonably attainable goal, as state budgets almost always increase in size. Thus, groups wishing to maintain their current share of the budget must at least increase categories at the same rate as the overall budget. Groups merely able to maintain current expenditures will lose ground relative to other groups; groups who see their budgets cut see more dramatic decreases in budget share.

As in Chapter 2, we argue that policy outcomes are related to the dynamism of the interest group context and the policy process. We suggest three scenarios – capture, deadlock, instability – that map onto a curvilinear relationship between interest group density and policy change. Interest group environments create capture, instability, and deadlock experience policy change and distributional outcomes equivalent to standard politics, majoritarian politics, and interest group politics in our typology. We further develop and test the influence of these scenarios on policy change.

Capture. The capture scenario includes two features: comparatively few interest groups and a stable policy image resulting from low attention to the policy domain. Some policy domains are populated by a small number of groups that have long-lasting, stable memberships that interact in an environment of mutual understanding and trust. Legislators can more easily create coalitions of smaller groups or allow one or more to dominate policymaking (Olson,

1965). Long-term stability of in-group dominance dissuades rival groups from contributing to a political environment. The same conditions that contribute to low levels of participation from rival groups also contribute to less attention to the policy domain itself. A stable policy image in this scenario is as much a function of in-group dominance as a lack of attention.

The terminology of "capture" is evocative of (a) purposeful action on the part of groups to actively control a policy domain and (b) normative connotations regarding the particularistic benefits of policy outputs from a domain at the expense of the public interest. While this is a possible mechanism associated with the low interest group scenario, Culpepper's (2011) "quiet politics" in which policy stability is a function of a lack of attention highlights how a small number of groups may determine policy. In either case – active capture or quiet politics – we expect steady and positive returns. Following interest group theory, there are simply fewer defined interests bringing fractionalized perspectives to policy debates in the capture scenario than in either the "instability" or "deadlock" scenarios. While it is it true that singular groups may have multiple interests, interest group ecology theory suggests that more populated issue areas are likely to contain groups that represent narrow unique interests ("niches") that may differ from collective interests contained within one dominant group. Thus, lesser populated policy areas may not be formally captured in the classic sense. However, interest group representation in the subsystem may be similar: fewer, more concentrated interests weighing in on the policymaking process. Capture dynamics features are akin to the "interest group politics" scenario, in which one or two groups dominate a small policy area to reproduce a stable policy image.

A stable policy image has three proximate consequences. First, the groups in the policy monopoly are linked to a clearly defined constituency and serve that constituency's interest. Second, because of stable membership, groups are better able to maintain a strong link to the bureaucracy that serves the policy domain. Third, this stability allows groups to consider their long-term interests. Long-term thinking results in groups lobbying less for larger immediate change and lobbying more for steady changes that build toward broader group goals (Hojnacki et al., 2012). There is little demand for open interest group pressure; instead, a "quiet politics" prevails (Baumgartner and Leech, 1998; Culpepper, 2011). Together, these consequences generate behavioral patterns by interest groups that are attuned to the long-term well-being of the policy domain.

Policymaking under "interest group" politics manifests in steady increases to budgetary share that results in significant long-term growth. The reward structure for policymakers is clear in providing more benefits, and the costs of cutting benefits are equally clear. With so few groups, the winners and losers are obvious; thus, major cuts are unlikely. Because of consistent inattention and consistent increases, massive gains are also less likely. Interest groups aim at maximizing rents to a degree that allows them to maintain a low profile. Low-profile groups pursue enough government resources to satisfy constituents, but not so much that rivals are attracted to the policy domain. Additionally, low-profile groups seek to avoid attention beyond the subsystem. In the long run, this adherence to the status quo produces more increases with fewer punctuations.

Deadlock. The deadlock scenario is characterized by two features: many interest groups competing for resources and sustained attention to a policy domain. Gray and Lowery's 1993 and 1996 energy–stability–area model argues that many groups populate some policy domains because of a large potential constituency, presence of available resources, and great policy uncertainty. A high level of interest group presence prevents the formation of a cozy policy monopoly. In contrast to less crowded policy domains, groups may be hyper-competitive in these established fields because gridlock creates conditions for lobbyists to push positions closer to groups' ideal points (Holyoke, 2009). Legislators are likely to be punished as much as rewarded for change (Bowling and Ferguson, 2001; Gray and Lowery, 1996). However, the lack of a policy monopoly does not mean the domain is unstable; rather, stability results from sustained competition and cooperation across rival dominant groups.

If interest group density is an indicator of attention, as neopluralist logic would suggest, then policy domains with many groups ought to be macropolitically "important" or at least worthy of many policymakers' attention. Just as exchange theory (e.g., Hanegraaff et al., 2019; Hansen, 1991) suggests, environments with a high density of groups result in "encompassing policy-making," while low density in capture scenarios leads to exclusive access. At the same time, issue areas served by many interest groups, what Baumgartner and Leech (1998) refer to as the "noisy end," are likely to be contentious with groups often taking positions for the sake of their own members or in opposition to other groups. Policy domains that experience constant interest group competition are unable to remain independent of the broader political agenda (Baumgartner and Jones, 1993, 175). Therefore, political competition within the wider political system creates constant attention.

With political competition, the macro-political environment, rather than subsystem politics, induces changes in a policy domain. Policy outcomes follow a pattern set in our conception of "standard politics." The result of a diverse set of interests can be *deadlock*, where groups have difficulty establishing dominance. Consistent attention to these issues results in a policy process more heavily monitored by groups and constituents, such that major deviations are anticipated to be politically controversial. Moreover, in the case of budgets, issues that enjoy a high agenda position are also likely to occupy significant portions of the overall distribution of dollars within a budget. Similar to Jones et al.'s (2014b) findings, even incremental changes can be large in real terms if the base of the category is large, too. Thus, incremental changes can be major victories for interest groups.

To the extent that groups actively participate in policy creation, the net result of significant interactions between advocacy coalitions is most often an incremental updating of previous policy, especially as groups are often repeat players in this exchange and sometimes cooperate with one another. Hanegraaff et al. (2019) show that increasing density means more competition for policymakers' attention. Consequently, any given interest group is less likely to interact with policymakers, but the overall attention to a "crowded" policy domain remains persistent. Indeed, this is the hope of the original conception of pluralism: Loud groups representing multiple interests offset one another and allow for consistent updating by relevant policymakers. However, a competition-based equilibrium is one that occasionally produces multiple losses for groups across the category, which makes for large categorical cuts – at least in the short term. In the long term, large categorical cuts require some catching up in future budget cycles, resulting in a budget distribution a bit more punctuated than the capture scenario. Our "standard politics" typology asserts that deadlock scenarios should see positive increases over time, but because of occasional punctuations, long-term growth lags behind capture categories.

Instability. In the instability scenario, the number of interest groups operating in a policy domain is too many for an issue to stay low profile, but too few to generate constant attention from outside the subsystem. In addition to a medium-sized presence of interest groups, different interest groups populate these policy domains over time. The development of a policy monopoly under such unstable interest constellations is challenging. Variegated interest group presence stunts the growth of linkages both among interest groups and between the bureaucracies that serve the domain.

In this scenario, the interaction among interest groups and policymakers is complex. Group preferences are diverse enough to discourage a large coalition of actors and strong enough to prevent a small coalition from dominating the entire issue. Interest group density is low enough that groups still have some opportunity to form coalitions with other groups, a process that leads to compromise. Additionally, issues may not be as polarizing, or legislators' positions may be flexible so that compromise is a legitimate possibility. Under these conditions, lobbyists do not have the cover of gridlock to assume interest group ideal points without some real risk of being excluded from a winning coalition. However, group density is high enough to produce variation in preferences that prevent capture-induced stability.

Groups' abilities to influence the policy that emerges in these moderate cases are heightened because they can offer information to policymakers, and policymakers are rewarded for making changes in these areas by rival groups (Austen-Smith, 1993). The institutions in which the conflict occurs are more responsive to demand and are not locked into a particular pattern of lobbying, such as subtle agenda control (capture) or open tactical battles (deadlock). The instability scenario is akin to situations described by Holyoke and Brown

(2019, 3) as "reactions to political pressures in an environment fraught with uncertainty." Policymakers are in a tough spot because they must either consult with groups who advocated policy change (but might not have accomplished all their goals) or return to consult interest groups that were once prominent and influential (but have not completely vanished).

Volatile membership profiles hinder the generation and maintenance of a stable policy image. With no stable policy image, groups are challenged to provide factual and emotive information to current and potential constituents. Instead, groups in this position are more heavily dependent upon shifts in attention to achieve their policy goals in a given domain. Interest groups attempting to pursue policy goals in the instability scenario must be flexible strategically. Groups must be able to focus attention when pursuing gains; however, they must also shift tactics to suppress attention from rivals once those gains are achieved. The types of issues that attract a moderate range of interest groups rise and fall with cascades of attention (Halpin, 2011; Jones and Baumgartner, 2005), rather than staying consistently off (capture) or on (deadlock) the policy radar.

This is a scenario that most groups would like to avoid. All groups are in a similarly unstable position: Policy gains and losses alternate regularly, and often not because of their volition. Groups are uncertain about which other groups will comprise a policy domain over time, making it difficult to identify potential rivals and allies when lobbying for policy change. Actors in this scenario can rely upon neither the stability of a dominant policy image nor constant attention to their cause. Thus, swings in political attention drive policy outcomes in a moderately populated policy domain. Attention is temporary and unstable; thus, policymaking alternates between over-reaction and under-reaction (Jones and Baumgartner, 2005).

The first obvious casualty of the pitch and yaw of groups in this scenario is that there is a greater likelihood for affiliated budget categories to be cut. The equilibrium scenarios we have described in capture and deadlock assume a relatively stable agenda presence, which leads to fewer opportunities for policymakers to upset this equilibrium through budget cuts. The second casualty is that policy change is prone to be punctuated as policymakers attempt to compensate for cuts with corrective increases in future budgets. Further, policymakers have opportunities to make a larger impact in budget categories represented by instability scenarios and, under the right conditions, will take advantage of these opportunities. Third, because of negative changes and a punctuated distribution, it is likely that instability budget categories will grow the least.

Our argument conceives of the association of interest group densities and policy change as a continuum of outcomes rather than a discrete set. Interest group density is a relative concept, such that characterizing a "few" groups means understanding the "many." The range of hypotheses we offer is inherently nonlinear: We argue that both high- and low-interest group density

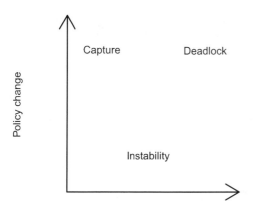

FIGURE 4.3 Visual display of the relationship between policy change and interest group density.

scenarios produce positive changes, but that the area between high and low will produce negative changes. We summarize our argument in Figure 4.3.

4.4 METHODOLOGY: BUDGETARY CHANGE IN THE AMERICAN STATES

We expand on Chapter 3 in the following analysis and move from exploratory analyses of budget functions to identifying interest group constellations within each policy domain. Relating interest groups to particular policy domains recognizes that fiscal resources are the lifeblood of programs, the agencies responsible for their implementation, and the citizens and businesses they serve. With so much at stake for existing and new programs, it makes sense that the conflict over budgeting is the workhorse of policy outcomes rather than the "show horse" of agenda-setting and law-making. It also makes sense that interest groups exert great efforts in obtaining favorable budgetary outcomes.

As we have previously stated, a state-level budget process involves a host of actors who are variably empowered across states and have various rules to follow regarding the point at which they are influential in the process (Alt and Lowry, 1994, 2003; Bowling and Ferguson, 2001; Crain, 2003; Kousser and Phillips, 2012; Lowry et al., 1998). Most studies identify the governor as the focal point in state budgeting, particularly if a governor has both agenda-setting and veto powers. We examine the specific relationship between governors and budgets in Chapter 5. Our task in this chapter is to assess the role of interest groups in the context of gubernatorial power. Other important state features, such as partisan composition and competition, as well as institutional features, are also introduced and discussed briefly.

4.4.1 Core Quantities of Interest: Interest Groups and Budget Change

Our dependent variable choice speaks to the general goals of budgeting research: We seek to understand factors that affect how policy is made. Budgeting does not occur in a vacuum. Interest groups pursue their share of a budget in a specific policy domain, while policymakers operate within institutional and economic constraints across spending items. It is in this context that we investigate changes in American state budgets.

Again, we analyze the same annual state expenditure data from State Government Finances (United States Government Census Bureau) available for all fifty states from 1984 to 2010, according to the ten functional categories we identify in Table 3.1: corrections, education, health, highways, hospitals, natural resources, parks and recreation, police and law enforcement, welfare, and government administration (which also includes other minor spending). We described the basic contours of the data in Chapter 3. Because interest groups are surveyed only in four waves (Gray and Lowery, 1996) between 1980 and 2010, we are limited in our analysis of budgetary change. With this limitation and our focus on how interest groups affect spending on budget functions in mind, we employed a research design that concentrates on changes across states and policy issues. As such, our dependent variable measures the median budget change in a given state and function. We show the results for mean changes later in the chapter as a robustness check. Using the median budgetary change is a conservative approach, given the many massive budgetary changes we uncover in Chapter 3. In our sample, the largest budget cut is around three percentage points, the median is around six, and the maximum is around fourteen percentage points.

We expect a curvilinear relationship between interest group density and budget change. Interest group density is based on four surveys (conducted in 1980, 1990, 1997, 2007) by Gray and Lowery (1993, 2000, 2001, 2015). We assigned interest groups-specific budget functions and then compute their share of all interest groups for each functional area across the surveys. In most cases, doing so was a straightforward exercise (e.g., education groups belong to education spending, or highways spending includes interest groups concerned with construction and transportation). Some groups are matched with two budget categories, such as health-related groups, which are matched to health and hospital spending, or interest groups about legal issues are matched to both policy and corrections spending. This matching remained consistent across all survey waves. The four survey waves are consistently carried out by Gray and Lowery and categorize all interest groups in a state at regular intervals. Gray and Lowery have used these data in both pooled and longitudinal form, so we follow their lead here.

We already described the interest group population, their growth, and their spread earlier this chapter, but it is worth noting that two descriptive features corroborate the face validity of the measure and prove the stability of interest group constellations within policy domains over time. First, there is a general growth of interest groups across states over time. Lowery and Gray (1995) also identify this proliferation: Interest group density in a policy area increases over time. Relying on the percentages of interest groups per domain (rather than raw values), we safeguarded ourselves against this overall time trend. Second, the distribution of groups is fairly stable over time. In our sample, the median standard deviation change in the share of interest groups in a particular state and policy domain is just 2.8 percentage points. Most growth occurs in the hospital and health domains across all states. These domains were often the most crowded policy fields at the outset and became even bigger over time. Hence, they started in our *deadlock* scenario and remained there. Several of the domains with fluctuations in interest group shares also turned out to be identified as outliers in the regression model (e.g., the hospitals category in Vermont). We therefore safeguard our analysis by rerunning the model without these outliers.

As a first descriptive step for our analysis, Figure 4.4 presents the basic relationship between interest group density and budgetary change for our sample. Each dot in the scatter plot represents an observation of a particular state and budget functions. The color of each dot signifies a particular policy issue, and the line is a loess regression line. The line suggests that budget functions grow more when interest group density is either low or high. Medium interest group densities correspond to lower levels of budgetary change. The obvious question is whether this pattern can be explored in a multivariate setting.

4.4.2 Other Covariates and Descriptive Statistics

We consider the following institutional, political, and economic covariates to be systemically related to budget changes. We focus on interest groups in the analysis and discussion here; we turn to a related empirical analysis focusing on governors in Chapter 5. The basic descriptive statistics for all variables operationalized and used in the subsequent analysis are given in Table 4.2.

First, we examine gubernatorial powers based on the two Beyle indices measuring budget agenda-setting and veto powers (see Chapter 5 for a fuller description of these data). The combined scores are each state average and can range from 0 to 10 with stronger governors scoring higher. An alternative operationalization with Krupnikov and Shipan's (2012) measure does not alter the results, as our analysis shows (see the *Robustness* section).

Second, budgets are likely to grow at a functional level when there is regular partisan turnover of the governor because each turnover enables the legislation of a different preference set. Governor turnover counts how many times the partisan affiliation of the governor changes over time. We also suspect that the

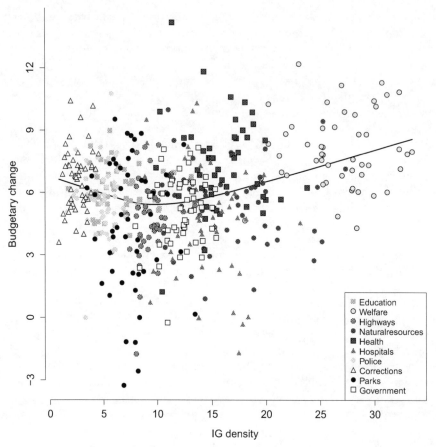

FIGURE 4.4 Budgetary change (in %) and interest group shares (in %), 1985–2010. Colors represent individual policy issues.

longer a state is ruled by divided government with its ongoing conflict over the budget, the smaller its budget changes will be. Divided government is similarly operationalized as in Chapter 5, as the percent of years a state has elected a governor who is of a different party than at least one legislative chamber. The possibility to instill policy change outside of the typical legislative process via referenda is another potential source of budgetary change. A simple dummy variable indicates whether a state has a referendum process in place.

Third, we account for two institutional features of the budgeting process. States vary in their propensity to submit a balanced budget, as discussed in Chapter 2. We expect that increasing budget stringency leads to lower budget growth because these institutional rules limit the budgeter's room to make large-scale changes (we use the ACIR score here and elsewhere in the book).

TABLE 4.2 *Descriptive statistics for regressions with interest groups: American states, 1983–2010.*

Variable	Min	Pctl(25)	Median	Pctl(75)	Max	Mean	St dev
Budget change	−3.26	4.53	5.94	7.22	14.20	5.83	2.31
Interest group density	1.18	6.73	10.52	16.41	32.79	11.89	6.89
Governor power	4.52	7.68	8.68	8.68	10.00	8.09	1.19
Governor turnover	0	1	2	3	6	2.26	1.33
Divided government	0.05	0.41	0.64	0.77	1.00	0.58	0.23
Referendum	0	0	0	1	1	0.47	0.49
Budget stringency	0	6	10	10	10	8.08	2.60
Supermajority req.	0	0	0	0	1	0.10	0.30
Business cycle	2.14	3.44	4.29	5.53	9.60	4.64	1.63

Similarly, supermajority requirements in the legislative arena also stymie budgetary change – we use the same dichotomous classification where states with supermajority requirements are scored as a one, as we do elsewhere.

Fourth, we account for a state's economic fortunes through a measure of the business cycle. Wider swings in the business cycle induce budget changes. The business cycle measure is based on the Federal Reserve Bank of Philadelphia's monthly coincident index (Crone and Clayton-Matthews, 2005). We constructed a business cycle volatility measure by computing the standard deviation of the growth rates of monthly coincident indices multiplied by the square root of the total time period.

Finally, we test several additional expectations, including measures of partisanship, partisan competition, and polarization. We subjected two more ideas to empirical scrutiny: (1) that more professional legislatures produce less budgetary growth and (2) that flows of federal funds affect spending on a particular policy domain. We explain our sources and measurement of these concepts in Section 4.4.3.

4.4.3 Model Estimation and Specification

Our theoretical expectations point to the use of flexible nonlinear modeling. Most social science theories express relationships are simple linear (positive or negative) form (Beck and Jackman, 1998). We posited a U-shaped relationship between policy change and interest group density. This means that we expect that our relationship varies locally over the range of interest group density (and not globally, as in "budget change increases with interest group density"). Additive regression models (GAMs) (Beck and Jackman, 1998; Hastie, 2017; Keele, 2008) allow researchers to pick up and assess the local features of the data; in our case, this is how interest group density varies along budget change. In addition to this flexibility, GAMS can incorporate the typical parametric expectations for the remaining adjustment variables (such as governor power or partisanship). As such, GAMs are a compromise between the extreme flexibility of a purely nonparametric approach and the simplicity of the linear model. Specifically, we use the following semi-parametric additive regression model in order to examine specific political factors of policy volatility:

$$y = \alpha + \sum_{j=1}^{m} \beta_j X_j + \sum_{k=1}^{p} s_k(Z_k) + \epsilon$$

where y is a vector for median budget change in each state and budget function, s is the function of a penalized regression spline, and X and Z are vectors of covariates. The function s is responsible for identifying the local features in the data and called "smoothing" (for a technical overview, see Hastie (2017)). Several ways (e.g., *loess*) exist for estimating s and solving the optimization problem of picking up just enough local features of the data and avoiding overfitting. In our case, the model is solved by penalized iteratively reweighted least squares, while s is numerically optimized using the generalized cross-validation criterion (see Wood, 2011). Z is our interest group density measure. Z does not possess a to-be-estimated coefficient. Instead, it is easiest to interpret the estimated smoothing spline by plotting Z_k versus $s_k(Z_k)$, thereby showing the estimated nonlinearities and the accompanying confidence bands in the relationship between Z_k and the dependent variable. Beyond the nonparametric estimates, X_j contains institutional and economic variables specific to states.

In our analysis, we discuss two model specifications to ensure the robustness of the results. First, we only smooth interest group density and estimate a linear effect for the business cycle. The second model adds the following covariates: governor power, government turnover, divided government, referendum, ACIR, and supermajority, including state fixed effects.

We conducted several diagnostic analyses after obtaining our baseline results. We removed potential outliers and influential observations from the sample and found minute differences in the results. Additional robustness tests included checking for the optimal number of splines and selecting different smoothing methods. We also checked for omitted variables by including measures of legislative professionalism, legislative and executive partisanship, partisan polarization, and federal block grants. As a final robustness check, we computed budget change using the mean instead of the median and then reestimated the full model. We display the estimated effects for these additional tests in Table 4.4. In all model estimations, our core finding on the association between budget change and interest group remains substantively unchanged.

For some of the more interesting findings, such as the missing evidence for partisanship, we offer our interpretations in Section 4.4.4.

4.4.4 Results

Table 4.3 displays the results of the two estimated models. Our primary interest in this chapter is the relationship between interest group density and budgetary change. Our three-part hypothesis understands this relationship to be nonlinear. The estimation results presented in Table 4.3 do not allow us to reject this argument. To assess our individual hypotheses, we present the estimates for interest group density graphically in Figure 4.5. The plots present the local marginal relationship between interest group density and budget change and the 95 percent confidence band in a gray shade. While keeping all other covariates constant, the graph indicates the estimated effect of interest groups

TABLE 4.3 *Semiparametric additive regression estimates of budgetary change.*[†]

Independent variables	Model 1	Model 2
Governor power		0.272***
		(0.058)
Governor turnover		−0.002
		(0.121)
Divided government		1.068**
		(0.485)
Referendum		−0.078
		(0.275)
Budget stringency		0.160***
		(0.056)
Supermajority req.		−0.049
		(0.306)
Business cycle	−0.311***	−0.167
	(0.059)	(0.127)
Constant	7.272***	2.571***
	(0.289)	(0.337)
S (interest group density)	3.78***	3.88***
	(4.70)	(4.82)
Observations	500	490
Log likelihood	−1,091.36	−1,092.46
UBRE	4.59	5.10
State fixed effects	No	Yes

Note: $^*p < 0.1$; $^{**}p < 0.05$; $^{***}p < 0.01$
[†] The estimated effect plots for interpreting the spline on interest group density are presented in Figure 4.5.

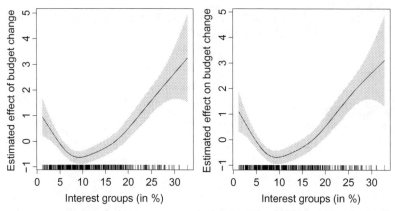

FIGURE 4.5 Spline fit for interest group density. The solid black line is the fitted spline function, and the shaded region is the 95 percent pointwise confidence band. The rug on the x-axis represents the individual observations of interest group density. Estimate for Model 1 is on the left and Model 2 is on the right.

is curvilinear and not constant. At low and at high levels of interest group density, we find an increase in budgetary change. However, a medium (in relative terms) level of interest group density contributes to a reduction in budget change. An F-test (F = 16.08 and p < 0.001) shows the generalized additive model is a more appropriate estimator than an OLS regression. While the confidence bands cross 0 in the transition between low, medium, and high levels of interest group density, most of the nonlinear estimates are statistically significant at 95 percent. Substantively, the size of these local effects is quite large, too, covering nearly 25 percent of the range of budget change. Overall, the nonlinear influence of interest group density on policy change is therefore considerable and statistically significant.

Table 4.3 summarizes the estimates for the linear covariates in the model. Governor power is the most pertinent for the purposes of this book. As outlined in Chapter 2 institutionally strong governors – that is, those who possess sufficient agenda-setting and veto powers – are able to mold spending to their liking. Therefore, we expect that an increase in institutional powers leads to positive changes in budgets and, indeed, that is what we find. The estimates show that a 1-unit increase in governor power leads to a 0.27-point increase in spending on a particular budgeting item, ceteris paribus. Substantively, this estimate means that the difference between the institutionally weakest to stronger governor is the addition of a roughly 1.6 percent point increase in spending in a policy domain. In short, states with institutionally strong governors are beset by targeted budget increases.

There are few other notable results from the remaining covariates included in the models. Our model includes governor turnover to assess if frequent changes in the executive lead to smaller spending items. The estimated coefficient is negative, but does not reach conventional levels of statistical significance. The same is not true for divided government, where one might expect that a partisan division between the executive and legislative branch would induce smaller changes in a budget. We find no evidence for this assertion in our models. Instead, the positive and statistically significant estimate suggests that partisan log-rolling may occur: Spending on a particular budget item increases when government is divided. The role of referenda on spending is not distinguishable from zero. We also considered the role of budget rules, particularly stringency and supermajority requirements.

While supermajority requirements do not display statistically meaningful effects, budget stringency is, against expectations, positive and significant. Finally, there is a negative association between business cycle volatility and budget change, suggesting that fluctuations in a state's economic well-being translate into decreases in spending. However, the estimate fails to reach conventional levels of statistical significance in the full model.

Alternative Explanations. We have explored several alternative explanations, though none change the curvilinear association between interest group density and budgetary change. When there are few (*capture*) and many (*deadlock*) interest groups in a policy domain, budgets increase. When the interest group environment is instable, budgets decrease. Models (1) to (3) in Table 4.4 display the estimated effects for four political and one economic source of budgetary change.

In the first model, we consider the role of partisan competition over state spending. A baseline expectation in political science and political economy is that leftist parties increase government spending (Downs, 1957; Hibbs, 1977). Garand (1985) offers an early examination for this in the American states. We measure partisanship as the share of Democratic house seats using data from the *Book of the States*. The estimated coefficient is positive and not statistically significant. We thereby add to the long list of null findings for the plausible effect of partisanship on government spending. Alternative measures of competition also fail to be statistically distinguishable from zero. Our models include the number of switches in the partisanship of governors, legislative professionalism (King, 2000), and polarization in the ideological composition of statehouses (Shor, 2014). One might also hypothesize that increases in federal funds lead to more spending on the various functions of government. The data for funds come from the US Census's Consolidated Federal Funds Report (various years) and measure average federal aid to states in billions of dollars. The estimated coefficient is positive and statistically significant, but the substantive size is very small. Per our estimation, a one billion dollar increase in federal funds would lead to a 0.006 percentage point increase in spending on a budget function.

TABLE 4.4 *Regression results for robustness test on the effect of interest groups.*

Variables	(1)	(2)	(3)	(4)	(5)	(6)	(7)
Governor power	0.24*** (0.06)	0.23*** (0.06)	0.22*** (0.06)		0.28*** (0.06)	0.27*** (0.06)	0.39*** (0.09)
Governor power (KS)				1.58*** (0.17)			
Governor turnover	−0.01 (0.09)	−0.01 (0.13)	−0.01 (0.12)	−0.04 (0.12)	−0.02 (0.12)	−0.003 (0.12)	0.09 (0.13)
Divided government	0.96** (0.45)	1.00* (0.53)	1.00** (0.50)	0.32 (0.45)	1.10** (0.48)	1.07** (0.48)	0.42 (0.55)
Referendum	0.11 (0.21)	−0.24 (0.21)	−0.09 (0.27)	0.09 (0.28)	−0.13 (0.27)	−0.08 (0.28)	−0.89** (0.38)
Budget stringency	0.14*** (0.04)	0.18*** (0.05)	0.18*** (0.05)	0.08 (0.05)	0.15*** (0.05)	0.16*** (0.06)	0.06 (0.07)
Supermajority req.	−0.15 (0.36)	−0.02 (0.31)	−0.23 (0.30)	−0.29 (0.31)	−0.06 (0.30)	−0.05 (0.31)	0.13 (0.48)
Business cycle	−0.19** (0.09)	−0.17 (0.12)	−0.13 (0.13)	−0.25* (0.14)	−0.16 (0.12)	−0.17 (0.13)	−0.45** (0.19)
Democratic house	0.96 (0.74)						
Governing party switch	0.51 (0.57)						
Legislative professionalism	−0.04 (0.46)						

	(1)	(2)	(3)	(4)	(5)	(6)	(7)
Polarization house		0.41					
		(0.36)					
Federal funds			0.01*				
			(0.00)				
Constant	2.28***	2.43***	2.49***	0.77***	2.55***	2.57***	5.11***
	(0.30)	(0.39)	(0.34)	(0.17)	(0.33)	(0.34)	(0.91)
S (interest group density)	3.98***	3.98***	3.98***	3.98***	3.74***	4.13***	7.43***
	(0.00)	(0.00)	(0.00)	(0.00)	(0.00)	(0.00)	(0.00)
Observations	490	490	490	490	487	490	490
Log likelihood	−1,092.46	−1,092.46	−1,092.46	−1,092.46	−1,077.64	−1,092.43	−1,335.42
UBRE	5.10	5.10	5.10	5.10	4.93	5.10	13.76
State fixed effects	Yes	Yes	Yes	Yes	Yes	Yes	Yes

Note: $^*p < 0.1$; $^{**}p < 0.05$; $^{***}p < 0.01$

Robustness. The robustness of our results is corroborated in the various regressions summarized in Table 4.4. The curvilinear relationship between interest group density and policy change remains statistically significant across all model specifications. Likewise, the estimate for governor power is also positive and statistically significant in all models. This relationship also holds if we substitute the governor power measure of Beyle (1968, 2003) with a more recent measure by Krupnikov and Shipan (2012) based on National Association of State Budget Officer (NASBO) surveys. Employing the Krupnikov and Shipan measure does alter the results (see Model (4)). The new estimates for governor power remain positive and statistically significant. The size of the estimates is similar, too. The same is true if we remove three potential outliers (Model 5), estimated the splines using restricted maximum likelihood (Model 6), and operationalized our dependent variable as mean budgetary change (Model 7). Nothing changes substantively across these models: Interest group density leads to distinct types of budgetary change.

Overall, the estimated models indicate that specific politics within a policy domain contribute to budgetary change rather than macroeconomic and political features that affect all domains equally. The density of interest groups for specific budget functions has a crucial but varied effect: Low and high levels of interest group density result in increases within a budget, while medium levels lead to budgetary cuts. An important finding here for our discussion on a governor's means to influence a budget in Chapter 5 is that powerful governors are able to raise the average spending on a budget function. Greater ability to set and defend the budgetary agenda translates into greater spending within particular domains.

4.5 HOW INTEREST GROUPS MATTER FOR BUDGETING AND PUBLIC POLICY

Analyzing how interest groups "matter" in American state politics allows us to offer some provocative new insights into the power of interest groups to supersede institutional structure in determining public policy. Our theoretical model and the empirical research indicate that (1) budgetary change and policy change are not the result of institutional rules, and (2) interest groups have a nonlinear relationship with policy change. This nonlinear relationship is related to the opportunities political actors encounter in making public policy.

First, most institutions specifically designed to induce policy stability have no effect in the models we test. This null finding is particularly surprising in the case of budgets because budgeting has even more rules that explicitly aim to create stability than most other aspects of the policy process that explicitly aim to create stability. Certainly, institutions influence policy in *some* way; however, our study adds to the mixed findings regarding institutional attempts to induce policy stability (Breunig and Koski, 2009; Crain, 2003; Crain and Miller, 1990). It is simply difficult to assess the impact of institutions on all facets of policymaking when considering institutional design. Our findings suggest there are no "silver bullets" in solving commonly identified problems in explaining policy change.

Among all institutions, only the agenda-setting and veto powers of governors affect budgets. Strong governors are able to induce growth in budgets by shifting resources from one policy issue to another. We will explore the power of governors in making budgets and inducing policy change in Chapter 5.

Second, whereas institutions exhibit an inconclusive influence, interest groups produce a consistent and strong convex relationship with budget change. We can connect the role of interest groups back to particular policy domains we explored in Chapter 3. The easiest and most obvious way is to do so visually. The coloring in Figures 4.2 and 4.4 indicates that the density of interest groups within a policy domain is fairly limited. Across states, interests representing police are rather small, while other issues, such as welfare, attract many groups. The same is true for budgetary change, to some extent. Police, corrections, and education exhibit very low interest group densities across states and also, generally speaking, historically positive spending rates. Parks and, to a lesser extent, hospitals, have a comparatively moderate amount of interest group presence and are often subject to budget cuts. Welfare experiences budget increases regularly and has high levels of interest group involvement.

Our analysis speaks to broad theories on interest groups and public policy. Common and empirically verified wisdom on interest groups typically stems from theories related to interest group capture and pluralism. Our findings allude to scenarios in which each of these theories is supported. When interest groups are few, as is the case in police and education, the conditions for capture are better, which means less change in existing arrangements. Captured policy domains can better defend against losses and take on little new turf, necessitating significant policy gains. In addition, our findings that show crowded policy domains experiencing growth support pluralist conceptions of interest group competition. The typical arguments raised against pluralism stem from a lack of competition leading to capture (Bardhan and Mookherjee, 2000); curiously, our research shows pluralism leading to similar outcomes as capture. Even in crowded policy domains, interest groups may secure policy wins. Perhaps the most interesting finding regarding interest group presence, however, is that the middle ground between capture and pluralism experiences budgetary cuts. In a policy domain in which no one group dominates, but competition is variegated, winners and losers are subject to losses and scarcely any gains. Our research provides nuance to the vast middle ground of interest group theory between capture and deadlock.

The regression results of interest group density on budgetary changes are also important because of their long-term consequences on public budgets. Figure 4.6 relates interest group density to long-term growth. Figure 4.6 displays a U-shaped relationship indicating that low- as well as high-density policy

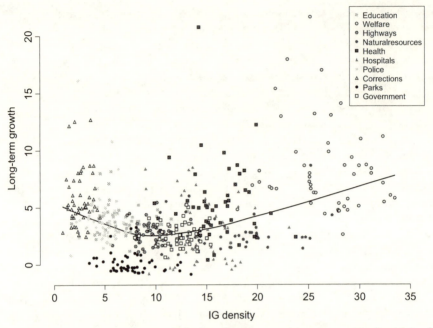

FIGURE 4.6 Long-term changes in budget functions and interest group density in the same function. Each dot represents a policy issue in an American state.

domains experience more long-term growth. The colored dots suggest that it is the domains of welfare and corrections that do well. These policy domains have either few groups and stable outputs – indicative of *capture* – or they have many groups and stable outputs, signifying *deadlock*. What is clear is that there are two possible scenarios for interest group success in the long run. Both low and high interest group densities lead to positive policy changes and long-run cumulative growth.

In contrast, budgets of policy domains with a moderate number of groups barely grow in the long run. These domains are characterized by changes in the number of groups over time and fairly limited ability to grow in the long run. Instead, policymaking is punctuated – occasionally large-scale changes occur, but these policy wins are not substantiated over several budget rounds. One interpretation of the occurrence of punctuated but low long-term policy change is that in cases of instability in interest group participation, executives evaluate their strategic options differently over time. In some years, they are willing to appease this year's rival group with the hope that the same group is next year's dominant group. Hence, executives employ their powers in cases where they believe they can produce the next policy monopoly. However, at other times, executives may also be most tempted to ignore potential rivals and domain-level conflict because they realize this particular domain will not fall back into capture and does not offer sufficient resources for attracting sustained interest group activity (deadlock).

4.6 INTEREST GROUP COMPETITION AND OPPORTUNITIES FOR POLICY CHANGE

In this chapter, we have theoretically expanded and empirically tested the relationship between interest group competition and public budgeting. We verify that the relationship between interest group density and budget change depends upon the relative concentration of groups in budget categories. These findings not only provide evidence for our theoretical expectations we offer in Chapter 2, but also correspond to findings presented in Chapter 3, which suggest that variation within public budgets occurs at the issue level. Insofar as they are entities organized around policy issues rather than the whole budget, interest groups drive the shape of a budget as a sum of its parts.

The findings from this chapter enable us to connect motives with opportunities. Policy issues are what citizens care about and what motivates policy actors. The currency of policy issues is the gains and losses in budgets. Decision-making models of budgeting, such as Wildavsky (1964) or Padgett (1980), hardly ever specify which policy issues are going to experience policy and budgetary change. In contrast, we argue that the desire to obtain gains depends on the opportunities provided to decision-makers. Our analysis highlights that opportunities are generated in stable interest group environments. The description of interest group environments has shown that interest groups and their constellations are variegated. Tremendous growth occurred in many states and in several policy domains in the last thirty years: This expansion and diversification of groups lead to the three distinct patterns of politics within policy domains we describe in this chapter. Capture and deadlock scenarios are predictable and reoccurring. Instability is, per definition, a state of disequilibrium and hence suffers from cuts. Governors who scan the political landscape for opportunities notice and take advantage of these different interest group environments. In short, subsystem dynamics defined by policy issues and the accompanying interest group environment structure policy change.

There are two implications of this research. First, our nonlinear findings suggest a subtle relationship between political competition and policymaking. How groups navigate the transition phases between each of our model's three scenarios is crucial to understanding interest group strategy and policy outcomes. If a policy domain becomes more populated, the domain moves from stable, certain gains (capture) to an uncertain policymaking environment in which rare gains and more likely losses occur (lability). At this critical phase, the question becomes whether the policy domain reverts back to capture or advances to open competition (deadlock). In a moderately dense environment, interest groups might consider two strategies: purge rival groups to move back to a stable subsystem or add allies in order to compete in a more open political environment.

The strategic choices of interest groups in the instability scenario provide a new dimension of agenda-setting. The previous literature on issue expansion, most prominently Baumgartner and Jones (1993), largely describes a pattern of capture–instability–capture as a function of feedback mechanisms. Our study describes an alternative scenario in which groups move between instability and deadlock and may not have the opportunity to move to a capture scenario. If groups want to achieve stable policy returns, the extant literature on the policy process suggests pursuing a capture strategy. However, our findings indicate that groups may also achieve policy stability and a steady flow of resources by engaging in ally expansion. Ally expansion allows groups in an instability scenario to move to a high-attention, stable-returns policymaking environment. In a dense interest group domain, groups face a risky decision in attempting to move to a low-attention, stable-returns policy environment because they must pass through a period of volatility and cut-backs between deadlock and capture. Contrary to conventional wisdom about policy monopolies, groups may prefer the certainty of constant competition to the treacherous voyage to capture.

Second, our research affirms advice from deliberative democracy scholars (Fishkin, 2011; Page, 2008). Greater opportunities for diverse participation might enhance policy stability and thereby reduce uncertainty in future policymaking. Our conclusions reaffirm the functional utility of iron triangles to their members: Agency heads, members of legislatures, and client groups benefit from low interest group competition in the form of stable policy returns. That said, a more democratic path by which governments achieve policy stability (if this is the value they wish to maximize) could be through public and intense interest group competition rather than through cozy, quiet subsystem arrangements. This logic follows Baumgartner and Jones' (2015) call for more complex information sources in public policymaking: Our results suggest a dynamic interest group environment can actually produce good governance.

The research we present here characterizes patterns of policymaking from interest group dynamics as they exist; however, our research does not explain how these interest group dynamics emerged. The field of interest group politics identifies characteristics associated with interest group mobilization in subsystem politics as a function of government actions (Baumgartner et al., 2009a; Gray and Lowery, 1996). Our research characterizes neither the causes of policy activity on the part of interest groups nor particular policy changes they bring. However, our work builds on this theoretical foundation in displaying the pattern of policymaking that results from three states of interest group concentration.

The analysis we present in this chapter offers strong support for step two of our argument in this book (see Chapter 2): That interest group competition shapes opportunities for change. Some budget categories are ripe for political actors to swoop in and legislate changes; stable categories dictate a measured but rewarding approach. Stable interest group scenarios translate into more spending on particular policy issues. Stable interest group environments produce stable policy gains. Governors have particularly strong interests in public budgeting and have specific powers to engage; however, there is a sharp contrast in interest group's and governor's perspectives on budget construction. While interest groups are concerned with pieces of budgets, governors are concerned with the budget as a whole. We show that interest groups are responsible for budget change within spending functions, but how do governors shape the magnitude of policy change within the interest-group-created environment? We present the analysis for this third step of our argument in Chapter 5.

5

Means

How Governors Shape Budgetary Outcomes

We hope readers now understand that apolitical budgeting does not exist. Budgets – even the US federal budget, despite repeated deficit spending – are subject to finite financial resources. Additionally, budget-making processes are subject to finite attention resources on the part of policymakers. In his memoir, George A. "Bud" Sinner, Democratic Governor of North Dakota from 1984 to 1992, noted that "most people would be shocked to know the amount of time I spent on the budget. It was hundreds of hours ... " (Sinner and Jansen, 2011). In a theoretically perfect world, budgets would expand or contract to meet the needs of citizens, conditioned insofar as those needs would be preferences held by elected officials.

Of course, this is a budgeting fantasy, regardless of government type. The notion that budgets are demand-responsive assumes a kind of mind-meld between citizens and legislatures, which is simply unrealistic and, indeed, even explicitly discouraged in the philosophical structure of governments. To the extent that preferences are aggregated, they are typically distilled in interest groups or blended in parties. As we saw Chapter 4, even though the interests of citizens dissipate, interest groups' presence in issue areas defends existing financial commitments by governments.

All democratic systems must contend with a budget process constrained by governmental financial and informational capacity. Budgets are made according to deeply held value systems of legislators, groups, parties, and so on – beyond even preferences regarding specific categories of spending – that include fundamental questions regarding the idea and role of the state. As many individual policy questions can find their politics rooted in value conflicts, budgets represent multiple value conflicts.

American states' policy-specific expenditures vary in which values they choose to fund, but also because of the structure of government decision-making. The structure of budgetary decision-making in American governments contrasts with parliamentary or other systems (Hallerberg, 2004; Wehner, 2010). In typical parliamentary systems, budget negotiations occur among the governing party or party coalition. Where the executive is simply an extension of this coalition, we might expect a distinct form of budgeting. The literature on comparative budgeting suggests the *general form* of the outcomes of budgets across political entities is largely the same (Baumgartner et al., 2017; Breunig and Koski, 2006; Jones et al., 2009; Sebók and Berki, 2017). Plainly, governments' same general information-processing problems lead to the same kinds of predictable distributions of paradoxically unexpected changes: many little changes and more big changes than we would expect ((Baumgartner et al., 2009c; Breunig and Koski, 2012; Epp, 2018; Epp and Baumgartner, 2017; Jones et al., 1998) and Chapter 3).

Our point is that budget fights are not unique to state politics; however, there are features of states that lead to distinct political conflicts and outcomes (Lee, 1997; Morehouse and Jewell, 2004). It is difficult to understate the importance of the distinction between independently elected executives and legislatures. Each of these groups, as we have previously written, have their own constituencies and preferences, but also significant disparities in the powers to express them (Dometrius and Wright, 2010; Lewis et al., 2015). From an institutional design perspective, these groups have a differing breadth of agenda space to which they can attend. Yes, legislatures compile a budget, but this process is an amalgam of individual legislators' preferences and, ultimately, votes. Yes, governors' agencies submit requests for funding (it is not as if the governor simply sits at a table and selects random numbers for a budget), but the decision to submit and sign a budget is ultimately in the hands of a single person (Sharkansky, 1968): a governor.

Executive independence, coupled with the independent authority of legislatures, creates what we call *centrifugal* and *centripetal* budget dynamics in the American states. Centrifugal forces push categories of a budget toward extremes and, centripetal forces pull the budget together. Governors' preferences and obligations work to expand some expenditure decisions while reigning in others. Under *centrifugal budgeting*, governors' primary aim is to expand budget cuts or increases for the purpose of credit claiming. The interest group environment is unstable and provides little resistance to the powers of the governor. Significant interventions by the governor challenge the formation of stable interest group arrangements, which enhances volatility. Governors use their powers to propose substantial increases or cuts and back up their actions by issuing veto threats or actual vetoes. Centrifugal budgeting generally focuses on a few categories in the budget rather than the whole.

Under *centripetal budgeting*, governors advance incrementalist spending policies. The primary aim for governors in centripetal budgeting is to produce a sound budget. The interest group environment in a particular policy field is structured such that the opportunities for major change are limited. As a result, centripetal budgeting contributes to the stability of existing interest group arrangements. The governor also uses institutional powers for centripetal budgeting for the purpose of proposing marginal adjustments and employing vetoes to moderate large cuts and increases. Centripetal budgeting emphasizes the compositional nature of budgets. The torque of centrifugal and centripetal budgeting depends on gubernatorial powers, while the interest group environment provides friction. In this chapter, we investigate the variation in institutional structures that influence attention and information flows across the states themselves (Breunig and Koski, 2012; Epp and Baumgartner, 2017). We show how institutional structures influence decisions to trade-off preferred programs for programs that are less preferred, and how these decisions manifest themselves in collective outcomes. Put simply, governors cannot know everything, in part, because they cannot attend to everything. While legislatures theoretically have a greater capacity to attend to a broader range of narrow issues, the same cannot be said for governors. Although governors are designated as the most powerful actors in states to corral legislators and advance statewide interests (Kousser and Phillips, 2009, 2012), this designation paradoxically produces an even tighter bottleneck of attention compared to legislatures (Breunig and Koski, 2009). Governors can achieve their goals by dominating the agenda, but this means the agenda remains limited. We argue that gubernatorial strength exacerbates this paradox because stronger governors can better bend legislatures to their will.

We call this process *topping-off* and *bottoming-out*. Topping-off and bottoming-out emerge from three key features of the policymaking environment in which budget decisions are made: (1) a governor's institutional tools, (2) gubernatorial responsiveness to interests, and (3) their own spending preferences. Specifically, we explain institutional features that cast the executive in recurring starring roles in the budget process. We contrast these roles with the fragmented audiences to whom executives must attend. Governors want to serve their own interests, but must do so in an environment conditioned by rules, previous commitments to existing interests, and, ostensibly, the collective interest of the state (which may not match their own) (Dometrius and Wright, 2010). In short, with great power comes great responsibility.

5.1 GUBERNATORIAL TOOLS TO TORQUE THE BUDGET

Signing budgets may be the single most visible act a governor makes in setting the financial course of a state. Governors are explicitly positioned to have a unique impact on all legislation in state governments, and this is particularly true for state budgets. Governors are the single most important player in creating budget not just because they sign or veto legislation, but also because they have a particular working knowledge of budget requests as chief executive of the bureaucracy (Bernick, 2016; Krause and Melusky, 2012; Rudalevige, 2002; Saiegh, 2011). Previous studies show that, because of existing commitments to legacy programs (e.g., education or Medicaid) and the constraint of balanced budget amendments, partisanship has a lesser influence over budgetary outcomes than in other legislation (Grossmann, 2019). Instead, structural features of the budget-making process – specifically the extent to which governors have control over the budget agenda and the particular veto powers governors have – are responsible for changes in the distribution of funds in budgets.

5.1.1 Agenda-Setting

Governors are involved at the earliest stages of budgeting as managers and entrepreneurs (Ryu, 2015). Agencies submit requests related to their expenditures, but governors (as the boss) can (and often do) tell agencies how much they can increase or decrease their budgets for the year. As the initial recipient of agency requests, governors can send budget items back to agencies and again suggest increases and decreases. At the end of the process, governors aggregate budget items in a final document presented to the legislature. Thus, even if agencies are unwilling to comply with a governor's request, the governor can still override these preferences by altering their budgets in the document sent to the legislature.

Much of governors' expenditure desires are not secret. Governors take positions in campaigns that inherently involve expenditures. During the 2010 Kansas governor's race, Sam Brownback promised to freeze general fund spending while cutting taxes (Lefler, 2010) In his first State of the State address (2011), he prioritized job creation and education spending, despite cutting K-12 per child spending by $232 in his budget (Milburn, 2011). He promised to cut 2,000 state jobs and eight agencies. Doubling down on his promise to freeze spending, he declared he would reduce the following year's budget by three-quarters of a billion dollars (Brownback, 2011). In his 1998 run for governor of California, Gray Davis promised to increase per-pupil spending in public schools and set aside $3 billion over five years to purchase new textbooks (Marinucci, 1998; San Francisco Chronicle Editorial Board, 1998). In his first State of the State (1999), Davis made education his priority, promising to include $444 million for education in his budget and to call a special session of the legislature to work on school funding (Gunnison, 1999).

In these ways, governors set the pre-legislative agenda for agencies and create markers for legislatures regarding their preferences (Romer and Rosenthal, 1978; Tsebelis, 2002; Wildavsky, 1986). The ability to compile agency preferences into a single budget puts the governor in a position to start the discussion with the legislature. Kentucky governor Phil Bredeson's 2006 $25.6 billion budget cut spending by 2.6 percent, but included $232.8 million in new education spending. The budget was lean on many other items, including health care (Humphrey, 2006b). Several months later, when the state came into a $170 million budget surplus, Bredesen recommended putting the majority in a rainy day fund, while also providing some funds to higher education and raises for state employees (Humphrey, 2006d). He left the remaining $35 million to lawmakers to spend as they saw fit (Humphrey, 2006c). By that point, legislators had filed budget amendments that would add another $900 million to the budget (Humphrey, 2006d). The final budget passed by the legislature included $416 million more in spending than Bredeson's budget, drawing on even more projected growth in the state surplus. The legislature followed Bredeson's lead in putting additional money toward education, while also adding funds to health care (Humphrey, 2006a). In his 1999 budget, Rhode Island governor Lincoln Almond included $5 million in planning and construction costs for a new basketball arena at the University of Rhode Island (Rowland, 1999). This was in addition to another $7 million appropriation he tried to push through the legislature as part of the mid-year budget adjustment. Almond was initially unsuccessful in convincing the legislature to include arena funds in the adjustment, but legislators did include $5 million for the arena in the annual budget that followed (Providence Journal Editorial Board, 1999; Saltzman, 1999). These two examples highlight the advantage governors can have in setting the agenda.

5.1.2 Vetoes

While signing legislation is a powerful and visible display of the role of the executive in state policy, vetoes can be even greater displays of power (Kiewiet and McCubbins, 1988). In some cases, literally. On April 13, 2011, Democratic Governor of Montana, Brian Schweitzer, gathered the local media on the capitol steps to demonstrate his opposition to several bills passed by the Republican-dominated legislature. The bills – including a repeal of Montana's medical marijuana laws, tort liability caps, and measures to repeal environmental laws – were vetoed by the governor, one-by-one, using a branding iron. After the branding session, Governor Schweitzer told reporters: "At an actual branding party, there's some castration, but we're not doing any of that today" (Gouras, 2011, para 5).

Vetoes are powerful tools for governors to obtain their preferences from legislatures. In 1993, New Hampshire governor Steve Merrill vetoed the capital budget in its entirety (New Hampshire Union Leader, 1993). The $76 million budget was larger than the $51 million plan he had proposed earlier in the year, and included a $15 million for a library at the University of New Hampshire, which proved the state did, according to Merrill, "not have a handle on university system spending." As New Hampshire is one of the few states that does not give the governor the power of a line-item veto, Merrill chose to veto the entire plan. Both Republicans and Democrats in the legislature said they would formulate possible compromises, while also not dismissing the possibility of an override vote (DiStaso, 1993; Tibbetts, 1993b). A vote was scheduled, but leaders in the House were unsure if they would be able to secure the two-thirds majority needed to override (Tibbetts, 1993c). The day before the vote, Merrill and legislative leaders came to a compromise on a $69.5 million plan. "This veto," Merrill said, "has accomplished what it was designed to do, cut spending" (Tibbetts, 1993a, p. 1).

The item veto has a long history in the state budget process (de Figueiredo, 2003; Wells, 1924). While vetoes are a last resort for many governors, they are opportunities to shape the entire budget negotiation process. In essence, the veto represents the ability to simply walk away from a discussion. The item veto offers a last opportunity for governors to shape policy outcomes and is a unique feature allowing the governor to remove parts of budgets while maintaining the basic budget document. The item veto is a particularly important tool for a governor's managerial duties in order to reign in legislatures that might overspend (Brown, 2012; Carter and Schap, 1990; McGrath et al., 2018).

At the same time, the item veto enables governors to make explicit trade-offs within budgets to fulfill their political preferences (Holtz-Eakin, 1988). Governor Sonny Perdue used line-item vetoes to cut $130 million in "pork" projects from Georgia's $20 billion 2008 budget (McNaughton and King, 2007). It was public knowledge that Perdue cut his own party members' pet projects in retaliation for opposing him during supplemental budget talks earlier in the year (McNaughton and King, 2007; Salzer, 2007). In 2009, Arizona governor Jan Brewer used line-item vetoes to reject $464 million in welfare and education cuts from the state's budget bills (Davenport, 2009a,c). Brewer, a Republican, fought against lawmakers in her own party to advocate for raising the sales tax and maintaining property taxes in order to prevent the cuts (Davenport, 2009b). Her vetoes led to a $1 billion budget shortfall, requiring more legislation before the end of the session to balance the budget in accordance with the state constitution (Davenport, 2009a,c).

As legislatures are aware of the item veto and often of what the governor might veto (McGrath et al., 2015), it is in their interest to align budget items with the governor's preferences if they hope to see them in the final budget. The alternative is for legislatures to include they know they will be vetoed in order to take positions (Kousser and Phillips, 2012). In extreme cases, governors who overstep the legislature's preferences can be overridden, though this is a relatively rare occurrence.

The budget flows through the executive at multiple points (Ryu et al., 2007): Governors take positions on issues as candidates, offer explicit priorities before the budget process, dictate the terms of agency requests, compile the budget as a complete document, work with legislatures to set budget priorities, and have the ability (in many cases) to insert their preferences in a final document through the item veto (Dearden and Husted, 1990). Despite the illustrative cases above, not all executives are created equal (Hale, 2013). At the beginning of the process, formal agenda-setting powers matter. Veto powers are crucial at the end of the budgeting process.

As a full illustration of gubernatorial powers, we describe Beyle's index (Beyle, 1996, 2003) compiled and updated from *Book of the States* records. The maps in Figure 5.1 display existing variation across states and times. For agenda-setting, stronger governors maintain a greater degree of autonomy over

FIGURE 5.1 The four maps display the institutional powers of governors in 1984 (top) and 2010 (bottom). Agenda-setting power is mapped on the right and veto power on the left. Each of these items is scored from 0 (weak) to 5 (strong). All data are originally collected by Beyle.

the budget process and are shielded from legislative interference. In 1984, governors in most states outside the South held strong agenda-setting powers. By 2010, these powers were increasingly constrained. One exception is Texas, where the governor always had few institutional tools for setting the agenda and keeping the legislative branch at bay. The important institutional difference between strong and weak veto powers lies between governors who are able to item-veto with a supermajority requirement for overrides and those governors who must use the blunt tool to veto the entire budget but can be overridden by a simple majority of the legislature. In 1984, nearly the whole span of options was found among the American states. Over time, the veto powers of governors increased, as the 2010 map confirms visually.

While governors retain this institutional potential, they are ultimately subject to rules that bind the scope of their abilities to influence the budget. Most importantly, these budgetary powers occur in a decision-making environment in which issues and information overwhelm executives' attentive capacity. Thus, while governors' preferences *can* influence the budget, the job of being governor may overwhelm their ability to act on these preferences.

5.2 GUBERNATORIAL RESPONSIVENESS

As we show in Chapter 4, governors' challenges are not just institutional. Interest groups shape opportunities for governors to use their powers. Interest groups offer a window into understanding political costs as well as attention to specific issues. We suggest that governors enter office with relatively stable preferences, but find that their ability to express these preferences is a function of attention and institutional design.

Interest groups determine attention to political issues, and this relationship is complicated by the concentration of groups in an issue area (see Chapter 4). Interest groups seek to control attention, which typically means attracting very little of it; the primary way this is achieved is through something akin to Culpepper's (2011) "quiet politics" in which groups are less interested in noisy conflicts with other groups or shouting their demands to legislatures. For other issues, interest groups have learned to live in a noisy environment and are accustomed to high levels of attention to their issues. Attention generation is context-dependent. When policies trend toward a quiet coalition, relative silence reigns. Even quiet groups can become loud, however, when their interests are threatened.

Interest groups need to capture enough of a governor's attention to achieve their desires, all the while defending against significant policy changes that threaten their positions. As previously noted, interest groups want to control the options available to governors in policy areas; such control typically amounts to defending the status quo. From a budgetary perspective, a defense of the status quo often includes fighting any cuts and supporting increases. Naturally, governors are rarely interested in simply defending the status quo – we have yet to see a campaign slogan that advocates for change, $\pm$ 3 percent. Governors have a series of preferences they activate when offered the opportunity for change. At the same time, a governor's agenda is not entirely of their own choosing, given the role of events, entrepreneurs, and interest groups.

A governor's attention limits are both advantageous and disadvantageous to programs and the interest groups that defend them. Gubernatorial attention limits can be advantageous because most programs will be allowed to conduct business as they always have, which means they can control the options in front of the governor that suit the interests of their programs. The disadvantage, of course, is that attention instability can mean changes from the status quo.

Also in Chapter 4 we characterize the continuum of interest group competition is a function of equilibrium at two ends (*capture* and *deadlock*) and vacillation (*instability*) in the middle. These states of interest group competition have implications for gubernatorial attention to policy areas. Interest group competition clustered around deadlock depends on a wealth of attention, whereas groups in the capture scenario want less attention. These two ecosystems have evolved to coexist with a particular political climate of attention; interest groups are troubled to adapt to shifts in that attention. Governors are eager to pursue their spending preferences but are forced institutionally to attend, in some small part, to all categories because of their role in governing the whole.

5.3 PREFERENCES

Thus far, we may have underemphasized the fact that governors have distinct preferences. After all, governors run for office because they have goals to accomplish in state government, even if those goals are being elected to the federal government. Governors are no different from other political actors in that they have relatively fixed preferences and use institutional tools to advance them (Hallerberg et al., 2009; von Hagen and Harden, 1995). At the same time, also like other policymakers, governors have far more distinct preferences than there is agenda space to express them (Jones, 1994, 2001). Thus, governors must prioritize preference expression based on political opportunities, some of which they create and the remainder of which are enabled by the political environment. When attention shifts to specific issue areas, policymakers have an opportunity to express preferences; stronger governors are better able to both shift attention to *their* issues and insert *their* preferences into opportunistic political discussions.

The budget offers a unique opportunity to express multiple preferences simultaneously; they also offer challenges for governors to prioritize their preferences. Budget politics are beguiling for governors attempting to show leadership because they traditionally fare well when negotiating with legislatures (Kousser and Phillips, 2012). While issues abound on which governors take positions, the literature on gubernatorial power and legislative effectiveness suggests that governors are more effective when they pursue their preference via the budget rather than other legislative means (Ryu, 2011).

At this point, readers may ask: What about parties? We recognize the importance of parties in setting particular agendas subject to both national and state political forces. Generally speaking, the literature on parties and expenditures addresses three broad expectations – two centrifugal (Democrats and Republicans have particular items they want to spend money on) and one centripetal (divided governments force compromise).

The first centrifugal force is that Democrats want to spend more than Republicans, both in general and in specific areas of the budget (Alt and Lowry, 2000; Blais et al., 1993; Cusack, 1999). Insofar as Democratic and Republican governors share similarities to the national parties in how they view the role of government, one might generally expect Democrats to view government as a potential solution to problems and Republicans to view governments as a problem to solve. Obviously, this assertion is an oversimplification of partisan politics and the politics of fifty different states (but see Epp et al. (2014)). There are plenty of examples of Republicans signing budgets with significant increases in spending and Democrats signing budgets that cut services to the bone. For example, during the 1990 recession, Democratic Governor L. Douglas Wilder of Virginia slashed agency budgets between 10 percent and 25 percent to compensate for a spending shortfall. The Governor further created a rainy day fund, but did not allow the legislature to use it to offset the 15 percent budget hole facing the state during the 1990 budget cycle. On the Republican side, in 2006, California Governor Arnold Schwarzenegger called for an 8.4 percent increase ($7.7 billion) in expenditures, which, interestingly, outstripped projected tax revenues (the state would use a previously unexpected tax windfall to make up the remainder). But, broadly, the general notion of observers of state politics is that Democrats want to spend more than Republicans.

Another way to consider the role of parties in accounting for patterns of expenditures is to consider what "expenditure" actually means. Tax expenditures have been shown to represent significant chunks of the federal budget, but are not commonly thought of in the same terms as normal outlays (Faricy, 2015, 2016). Subsidizing mortgage rates, while expensive, occupies a different space in the average citizens' political consciousness than supplemental income assistance programs (Mettler, 2010). Importantly, such programs are subject to different political coalitions and forces (Faricy and Ellis, 2014; Mettler, 2011). Some readers might rightly protest that Republicans spend as much as Democrats; they simply choose to allocate large portions of the budget to tax cuts. Indeed, this observation is true and hard to capture using outlays (which we do here).

Given that we have framed our analysis around how governments spend money, we posit that Democratic governors are more likely top-off budgets while Republican governors are more likely to bottom-out budgets. Put another way, in treating budgets holistically, Republican and Democratic governors are disposed to make different compositional budget decisions as a function of their party's view toward the functions of government. When faced with budget shortfalls, Democrats are prone to spread out the cuts across categories in a desire to maintain equal government services. Republicans are likely to use these opportunities to make specific cuts to programs that might otherwise be protected. Cuts to specific programs are important credit-claiming devices for both parties, but particularly for small-government-minded Republicans. Conversely, Democrats are inclined to use the funding of government programs as mechanisms to achieve political goals in general.

Second, Democrats spend more than Republicans on some budget items, but the inverse is also true (Barrilleaux et al., 2002; Kiewiet and McCubbins, 1988). The types of programs that governors of different parties choose to top-off and bottom-out are probably not a random assortment. We examine specific, though broad, categories of expenditure likely to fit within general preferences of Democratic or Republican governors. One might generally expect Democrats to favor increased expenditures in areas such as education, welfare, and parks, while Republicans might favor increased expenditures in areas related to police, prisons, natural resources, or transportation (Adolph et al., 2018). Conversely, we might expect Republican candidates to target Democratic preferences for cuts to pay for preferred increases and the same to be true of Democratic administrations. Thus, partisan preferences may expand some categories and reign in others. Therefore, centrifugal forces may arise from partisan preferences as much as from institutional powers.

Scholars have voiced doubt about these traditional expectations regarding the relationship between partisanship and particularistic spending (see Grossmann, 2019 for a comprehensive rebuttal to the argument that parties have a more important role in expenditures than other factors). We have argued (Breunig and Koski, 2006, 2009) and argue again in a few pages that gubernatorial power is the key to understanding extreme changes, distributions of change, and the long-term growth of budgets. The mechanisms of this argument are not as simple as saying a strong governor can do more of what they want. Rather, gubernatorial power exacerbates a series of features specific to institutional decision-making to produce particular patterns of policy change.

Casual and scholarly readers of state politics may need some time to accept this argument, especially as most of the literature about governors – either in policymaking or in budgeting – is interested in understanding changes in particular kinds of spending. Do Democrats actually increase welfare spending? Do Republicans actually increase police funds? Budgets, after all, are about who wants what and state expenditures can tell important stories about the direction of national political issues (Grumbach, 2018). In most instances, these preferences largely correspond to left–right ideological positionings: Often, scholarly focus is on the relative strength of political parties in terms of size or cohesion as critical explanations for the shape of final appropriations.

While it is true that governors advance particular agendas within budget politics, peculiar features of budget politics can create challenging left–right characterizations of budget discussions. Democrats and Republicans can have diverging preferences within a category such as education, but each party might choose to maintain or even increase expenditures within that category. For example, a Republican governor could desire to increase education expenditures when a Democratic governor may not wish to do so. This scenario may not be tightly coupled with specific preferences for both candidates – returning to our perfect budgeting world with no constraints, we might envision the Democrat spending more – but that none of these choices occur in isolation. There are, ultimately, trade-offs in budgeting, and these trade-offs may not be easily explainable by partisanship alone. Adolph et al. (2018) find partisan differences in trade-offs associated with expenditure at the state level: Republicans cut welfare spending and increase highway spending, while Democrats add to welfare spending and cut prisons. Such partisan priorities make sense. Curiously, Adolph et al. also find that Republicans are more inclined to increase higher education spending, but that there is no difference between governors of different parties in K-12 education spending preferences. Following the authors' argument, this finding might occur because partisan governors not only increase some items, but also strategically target spending items of the opposition party for cuts.

While parties are central to setting the partisan agenda, budgets require compromises not only between parties but also within parties as they are compositional documents. Budgets are preference-driven (centrifugal) and managerial (centripetal) which requires compromises that can sometimes conform to extant political logics, but can also be less straightforward. The good news for governors is that budgets generally – except perhaps in times of economic crisis – are constantly growing, so there is an opportunity to serve extant commitments of states, to serve multiple constituencies, and to still pursue their own interests. Stronger governors are able to expand the budget further to include their spending priorities, either through making incremental increases in other categories even smaller, in spreading small cuts across categories, or in taking large portions out of one category to serve the needs of others. Insofar as categories represent interests, these are all hard fights, but stronger governors are positioned to win more of them simply because governors are managers of the whole pie.

Third, divided governments force compromise and constrain extreme spending. Most of the early literature linking political science and public policy to public budgeting outcomes focused on the role of divided governments in influencing expenditure outcomes. Alt and Lowry (1994, 2000) find that divided governments are less adaptable to varying revenue streams. Policy theory tells us that divided governments are more liable to engage in partisan mutual adjustment (Lindblom, 1975), which ought to lead to a more consistent updating of budgets to adhere to a broad range of preferences. Put another way, if parties have specific preferences that lead to the expansion of budgetary categories, then it also follows that parties in power will be expected to realize their categorical goals.

At the same time, classic political science theory studying federal-level policymaking suggests that divided governments are responsible for landmark legislation (Mayhew, 1991). The result of this legislation could be major programmatic change that overhauls expenditures in a particular spending category, or it could be that the legislation comprises omnibus legislation affecting multiple categories. From the perspective of centripetal versus centrifugal budgeting, we are inclined to believe that divided government, in general, contributes to a more even distribution of expenditures across categories because of negotiations intended to offset expenditures across different sets of preferences.

5.4 GOVERNORS AND BUDGETS: TOPPING-OFF AND BOTTOMING-OUT

Thus far, we have painted a picture of governors that places the job somewhere between managerial accountant, messianic martyr, or parent to quintuplets. Governors have all these things they want to do, but have trouble prioritizing given the budget constraints they face. Governors must grapple with problems they might not care about, but do so because of an obligation they feel toward a statewide constituency. Even when governors are able to focus attention on problems that match solutions they would like to offer as policy, they become sidetracked by conflicts between different interest groups.

We argue that the intersection of attention, institutional strength, and preferences create a scenario in which all governors face similar limitations in processing information and attending to new issues, but that not all governors are created equally in the powers given to them to insert their preferences into budgets. Governors vary in their ability to draw attention to issues and vary in their ability to negotiate with legislatures. Issues that receive little attention are likely to change little. Most changes at the state level will be relatively small – in part, because of interest group environments that favor the status quo, but also because of the limited attention span of governors. For issues that are in the legislative spotlight, stronger governors can negotiate a position closer to their own in the attention-limited policy space of nonincremental change.

We expect two outcomes that result from this logic. The first is our overarching argument in this chapter: Stronger governors make large budgetary changes larger. This logic stems from both a desire to use programmatic spending within the budget to maximize multiple gubernatorial preferences, but also an ability to fashion the composition of the budget to accommodate such an increase. Budgets are relatively fixed pies; topping-off a category requires that governors necessarily do not spend that money in other categories. The practical implications for this decision-making might be that other categories see smaller increases in already incremental spending, or that categories that are already under the knife are cut deeper. In both cases, gubernatorial strength is needed to exert centrifugal forces on preferred categories and centripetal forces on the budget as a whole.

A corollary to this argument is that stronger governors are more likely to make large positive changes than large negative changes. While we have presented evidence that the party of the governor may dictate preferences for cuts versus increases as a means of preference expression in the budget, we suggest that all else equal, governors are more likely to add to big increases than to make large decreases deeper. There are many reasons for this difference, but generally speaking, governors can better serve the interests of groups and constituents by augmenting programs rather than subtracting from them. Risk-averse governors can distribute the costs of their increases across several programs rather than risk angering a particular constituency. Practically speaking, many budget categories have a fixed level of expenditure because of federal or state mandates; therefore, large cuts may be less feasible legally.

Second, we also expect that public budgets are more punctuated because of topping-off and bottoming-out. A major consequence of topping-off and bottoming-out governors is an exacerbation of the mechanisms that form punctuated budgets. Thus, in places where we find stronger governors, we should find more punctuated budgets. This is a technical point, to be sure, but still worth testing.

5.5 INVESTIGATING TOPPING-OFF AND BOTTOMING-OUT

Our task is to determine not just whether gubernatorial strength influences changes in budgets, but whether and how gubernatorial strength influences a range of changes. Methodologically speaking, this challenges standard techniques of analytically describing causal relationships, specifically ordinary least squares (OLS) regression. The standard approach to understanding changes in budgets might be to think of what, on average, causes changes to the mean value of the budget. In other words, OLS expects for the effect of a factor (say, gubernatorial strength) to be the same for changes at the low end of the distribution (say, −50 percent), the middle of the distribution (say, 3 percent), and the high end (say, 125 percent). For most studies of budgets, this approach is a fine way of understanding how political, institutional, or demographic characteristics might generally affect changes in expenditures. However, our expectations are that variations in gubernatorial strength likely account for changes in the low and high end, but are probably not that useful in understanding the middle. That is, it is more likely that both weak and strong governors make incremental changes in a budget. Weak and strong governors should vary in how they contribute to changes at the tails of distributions.

One way to solve the problem of disproportionate influence of explanatory variables over the range of a dependent variable is to simply record values of the dependent variable into categories (e.g., low, medium, and high) (Robinson et al., 2007), regress a series of factors on each categorical value, and then determine if there is variation in effect for each of these regressions. Essentially, an analytical technique is equivalent to multinomial logistic regression. While such a scaling technique might move us closer to understanding variations in effects along the range of values in the dependent variable, we would inevitably make well-informed but imperfect cutoffs in the data.

5.5.1 Quantile Regression

Moving beyond linear regression methods enables us to assess important relationships across the whole response distribution. We can probe the effects of political variables on budget cuts and expansion, as well as the typical "mean" changes in a state budget. Quantile regression enables us to analyze the distribution of budget changes at any point of the conditional density function of the response variable. Quantile regression (Breunig and Jones, 2011; Koenker, 2005; Koenker and Bassett, 1978) estimates models for conditional quantile functions by using a least absolute deviation estimator (for recent empirical quantile regression work in political science, see Breunig (2011); Krause (2006); Stasavage (2002)).

Quantile estimation offers three advantages for our inquiry. First, quantile regression allows for modeling heterogeneous variance without specifying the relationship between variance and mean or specifying a particular exponential family of distributions. Second, quantile regression is robust to outliers and does not rely on normality assumptions of classical techniques. The nonnormality of budget distributions provides us with a good reason for not using OLS regression. Third, and most importantly, our theoretical predictions suggest that distinct processes drive budget cuts, incremental change, and expansions. Using quantile regression enables us directly to condition on all parts of the response distribution, which is an improvement over cutting the response distribution in various segments and then using classical techniques (e.g., Robinson et al. (2007)). Quantile regression also may allow us to discover the effects of variables that have been nonsignificant based on estimates that only condition on the mean.

5.5.2 Specification and Presentation

Our individual estimations start at the 4th and end at the 96th percentile of budget changes (i.e., $0.04 \leq \tau \leq 0.96$) in steps of two percentiles. At the τth quantile for each programmatic budget change y_{kit} in budget category k, state i, and year t, we specify an equation regressing y_{kit} on a vector of contemporaneous political variables $\mathbf{x}_{it}$, a vector of lagged economic variables $\mathbf{z}_{i,t-1}$, and a set of dummies for budget function, $\mathbf{w}_{kit}$, and region $\mathbf{r}_{it}$. The full estimation can be summarized as:

$$y_{kit} = \beta_{0\tau} + \mathbf{x}_{it}\boldsymbol{\beta}_\tau + \mathbf{z}_{i,t-1}\boldsymbol{\gamma}_\tau + \sum_{k=1}^{K}\delta_{k\tau}\mathbf{w}_{kit} + \sum_{r=1}^{3}\zeta_{r\tau}\mathbf{r}_{it} + u_{kit\tau} \qquad (5.1)$$

For our model specification, we regress the functional budget changes on six political variables – governor power, budget stringency, supermajority requirement, democratic governor, divided government, and legislative professionalism – and three economic variables – unemployment rate, income per capita, and federal funding. We also control for the state's region and budget function. Several alternative covariates are considered in a separate model, including budget power interacting with two forms of partisan preferences (governor party and partisan control of the legislature). As each state's budget is divided into ten budget categories, our working sample encompasses 9,800 cases.[1]

We display the forty-seven regression estimates graphically. It is impractical and unreadable to tabulate the regression results for all covariates from the 4th to the 96th percentile. Instead, we plot the results of forty-seven distinct quantile regression estimates for τs ranging from 0.04 to 0.96 as the dots on a scatter plot. For each of these coefficients, the point estimates can be interpreted as the impact of a one-unit change of the covariate on budget change, holding other covariates fixed. Each of the plots display the quantile τ on the horizontal axis, and the vertical scale indicates the covariate's effect. The gray shaded area illustrates the 5 percent confidence region on either side of the estimate for each τ in the quantile regression. When the confidence band is not "touching" the x-axis, we can reject the null hypothesis with the typical 95 percent confidence. The confidence bands are based on a kernel estimate of the sandwich.

5.5.3 Operationalizing the Budgeting Space and the Covariates

We conduct our analysis of topping-off and bottoming-out in the context of the budget data we have used throughout the book. Again, we examine categorical spending across the states from 1985 to 2010. We compute annual budgetary changes for each of the ten functions in a state's budget. We described these data in detail in Chapter 3. In Figure 5.2, we plot all annual changes per year and add the several quantiles for interest, including the 50th quantile, also known as the median budget change. The figure serves as a reminder that large increases and cuts in budgets occur quite frequently, and that we can condition our regression model on these variegated changes.

Gubernatorial Power. Our main independent variable of interest for this chapter is this general concept of gubernatorial power. As we conceive of it, gubernatorial power means stronger governors are those that have the power

---

[1] Omitting Alaska because of a peculiar revenue structure based on oil extraction and Nebraska because of its unicameral legislature does not alter the results substantively.

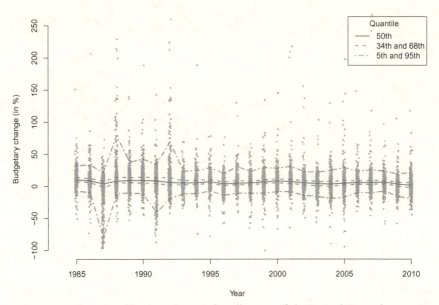

FIGURE 5.2 Functional budget changes for all states of the United States from 1985 to 2010. The scatter plot shows all categorical state budget changes over time and adds the 5th, 34th, 50th, 68th, and 95th quantile of the data for each year.

to both set the budgetary agenda and veto legislation. We consider each of these as having distinct influences over a governor's ability to top-off and bottom-out budget items; specifically, that veto powers might generally be used more for cuts than for increases. The literature on budget negotiation suggests that both powers can be used to increase as well as decrease budget items (Brown, 2012; Carter and Schap, 1987, 1990; McGrath et al., 2018). Quantitatively, we use Beyle's index of gubernatorial power to characterize the agenda-setting power of governors and their veto power (Beyle, 1996, 2003). For agenda-setting, stronger governors maintain a greater degree of autonomy over the budget process. Weaker governors compile the budget with members of the legislature or other actors, not necessarily of their choosing (e.g., elected officials). Stronger governors construct the budget as they see fit, with other officials of their choosing. Stronger governors also submit budgets to legislatures that are constitutionally limited in how much they can modify budgets.

For veto strength, we consider governors who are able to item-veto with a supermajority requirement for overrides to be stronger than governors who must veto the entire budget. In between these strong and weak poles are governors who can item-veto, but can be overridden by a smaller margin in the legislature. At the bottom are some governors who can veto an entire package, but can be overridden by a simple majority of the legislature. These veto powers have practical implications for specific expenditures. Each of these

TABLE 5.1 *Descriptive statistics for quantile regression on budgetary change.*

Statistic	Min	Pctl(25)	Median	Pctl(75)	Max
Budgetary change	−1.00	0.003	0.06	0.12	10.13
Governor power	3	7.7	8	9	10
Agenda-setting power	1	3	3	4.3	5
Veto power	0	4.8	5	5	5
Budget stringency	0	6	10	10	10
Supermajority req.	0	0	0	0	1
Democratic governor	0	0	1	1	2
Divided government	0.00	0.00	1.00	1.00	1.00
Democratic gov preferences	0	0	0	0	2
Legislative professionalism	0.06	0.16	0.24	0.32	0.90
Unemployment rate	2.30	4.30	5.30	6.60	17.40
Income per capita	9.83	18.91	24.96	32.36	56.96
Federal funds	0.001	0.01	0.02	0.04	0.35

items is scored from 0 to 5 on Beyle's scale. While a rough approximation of gubernatorial power, this quantitative characterization fits with our theoretical expectations of gubernatorial behavior. We expect governors scoring higher on both of these scales to make large changes larger.

While we are primarily interested in gubernatorial abilities to top-off and bottom-out legislation, other features of budgeting may contribute to centrifugal (pushing out categorical expenditures) and centripetal forces (reigning in categorical expenditures) in budgeting. We examine the power of governors in the context of partisanship, budget rules, legislative professionalism, and economic features of states. Descriptive statistics of all variables are summarized in Table 5.1.

Partisanship. Partisanship can affect budgetary decisions in three different ways. First, we consider the influence of the governor's party on topping-off and bottoming-out. As we indicated previously, the literature might expect that Democratic governors are more inclined to top-off budgets than Republican governors, and that Republican governors could be the inverse. Second, partisanship can influence specific categories of spending. Governors have preferences regarding which categories they might benefit with budget increases and which categories they might burden with budget cuts. Specifically, Democratic governors could philosophically support increased productivity of labor and capital through redistribution and an expansion of the public sector. Republican governors also want economic expansion, but might prioritize investment in infrastructure to achieve this. As a rough approximation of these preferences, we identify Democratic gubernatorial partisanship as spending on education, public welfare, and health categories. For our third partisanship variable, we test for the influence of divided government from the perspective of the governor. Ours is a simple measure of divided government in which the party of the governor differs from at least one branch of the legislature.

Budget Rules. While governors are institutionally able to fiddle with budgets and parties would very much like to expand areas of their liking at the expense of areas they care less about, budget institutions exist to reign in both these desires (Primo, 2006, 2007; Wildavsky, 1986). As with previous models, we identify two types of legislative rules that may influence the extent to which budgets are topped off or bottomed out (see Chapter 4). First, rules require states to have supermajorities to pass budgets. During our study period, five states required some kind of supermajority to pass a budget: California (changed to a simple majority in 2010), Nebraska, Arkansas, Louisiana, and Rhode Island (a supermajority in Illinois is required if a budget does not pass by June 1). We expect that supermajorities act as a centripetal force on budgets, given the need to incorporate a broader range of preferences in a final budget bill. Second, while nearly all states have some kind of balanced budget amendment, there is considerable variability in the extent to which states can deficit spend using other techniques. We include the ACIR score that measures how strictly states follow their balanced budget amendments. We expect that states with stricter deficit spending rules are likely to have more balanced budgets because policymakers will be bound by available revenues.

Legislative Professionalism. As Kousser and Phillips (2012) and others (King, 2000; Ryu, 2011; Squire, 2012) have demonstrated, professionalized legislatures are better able to attend to a variety of issues, engage independently with interest groups, coordinate across legislative bodies to achieve a common purpose, and outlast governors on policy issues given their more consistence presence in state capitols throughout the year. Professionalized legislatures can outmaneuver governors in achieving their own goals, and those goals are likely to represent a broader range of preferences held by members across the legislative body. Thus, we expect that professionalized legislatures are likely to exert centripetal forces on the budget.

Economic Forces. Finally, we acknowledge that state budgets are subject to key economic forces that shape both the demands for services and the supply of revenue. We focus on three forces: unemployment, personal income, and federal fund transfers to states. Unemployment rates represent a demand on budgets: During times of high unemployment, governments contend with less revenue but also face a greater need for government spending to both assist individual citizens and stimulate state economies (Hoover and Pecorino, 2005). National governments often react to this scenario by deficit-spending; however, state and local governments do not have this option. A period of high unemployment forces governments to make tough choices, not just about whether to cut budgets, but where to cut them deeper. All services will probably receive budget cuts, some deeper than others.

States are generally heavily dependent upon sales taxes, income taxes, or both for revenue. Shifts in personal income represent shifts in the supply of revenues for states, but also in citizens' demands for government services. While increases in unemployment should force governments to make tough, uneven decisions about where to make cuts, increases in personal income should allow states to fund categories beyond those deemed to be "necessary." In other words, we expect increasing personal income to enable the states to spread the wealth across categories, resulting in more moderate changes in state budget categories.

A third piece of the state revenue puzzle is the transfer of federal funds to states, which represent varying proportions of state budgets (Elis et al., 2009). States are tasked with implementing a variety of federal programs and receive a significant sum of revenue transfers from the federal government. While states cannot deficit spend, the federal government can. Thus, if states' revenue targets are inaccurate because of economic downturns, federal funds can better weather fiscal storms (which is not to say that the federal government does not adjust its funds downward during times of revenue shortfalls). Federal funds provide a relatively consistent source of revenue for a variety of budget categories; therefore, we expect these funds to generally moderate budget changes, particularly negative budget changes.

5.6 QUANTILLION RESULTS

Interpreting quantile regression results across over forty models is challenging. In essence, there are three quantities of interest that are common to most statistical analyses: (1) whether there is a relationship between a variable and a given quantile, (2) the direction and magnitude of that relationship, and (3) whether the relationship is statistically distinguishable from zero. Figure 5.3 shows a series of plots of the aggregation of estimates from forty-seven distinct regressions, where the estimates are conditioned on different magnitudes of the outcome variable: budgetary change. The y-axes chart the estimated effects of the variable in the title of the scatter plot; the x-axes specify the quantile τ of the conditional budget distribution. The dot represents the point estimates. The gray shading around the dots represents confidence intervals around the estimates – the result resembles a gray watercolor streak painted over a two-axis chart. Where the brush strokes are above or below zero (i.e., the horizontal line), there is a statistically significant difference in an effect; where our brushstroke crosses zero, we are less certain. Brushstrokes above zero on the left side of the chart indicate that a variable has a moderating effect on budget cuts; brush strokes below zero on the left side of the chart indicate that a variable exacerbates large decreases. Brushstrokes above zero on the right are indicative of variables that increase already large increases, while those below zero on the right indicate a moderating effect on budget increases.

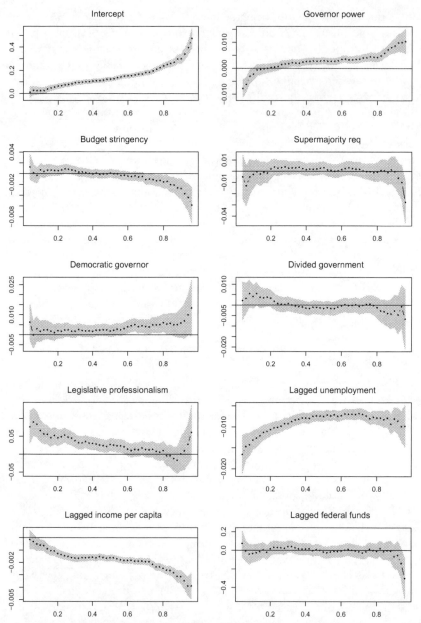

FIGURE 5.3 Quantile regression for functional budget changes. The x-axis represents the quantile of each estimate, and the y-axis indicates the estimate of the variable stated in the title of each plot. The black dots are point estimates, and the gray band is the 90 percent confidence band. The regression is based on annual programmatic changes in budgets for the US states, 1985–2010.

The figure makes it immediately apparent that the relationship between features of state institutions, parties, rules, professionalism, and economic forces varies within the range of budget changes. In short, the same features responsible for cuts in a budget may not be responsible for increases. In technical terms, the slope estimates for each estimated value are not necessarily the same. The analysis of the data tells a complex story that fits the budgeting environment facing governors.

Consistent with our expectations, the analysis in Figure 5.3 shows that gubernatorial power has a distinct influence over a range of changes, with noticeable influences over large cuts and large increases. This finding is visible by the negative estimated effect at low τs and the positive estimates for high τ. Statistically significant from zero is a large range of estimates where the gray band does not touch the horizontal line. For bottoming-out, the governor's options are generally narrower – only for the deepest cuts do we see any gubernatorial influence with a magnitude much less than for increases. But it is in increases, particularly substantial increases, that we see governors flex their political muscle to top-off already large budget changes.

In order to assess whether veto or agenda-setting powers drive this process, we separated both measures and reestimated the model. This model is displayed in Figure 5.4. The two plots for each power show that veto power and budget power independently affect budget changes in the same way, in enabling governors to top-off and bottom-out. Subtle but important differences are noticeable. Agenda-setting powers nearly always have an estimated positive and statistically significant effect, suggesting that governors with strong agenda-setting powers prevent cuts and abet budget increases. Veto powers are used in tandem with agenda-setting; they enable governors to deepen potential large cuts and, curiously, have a positive effect on budget increases. In short, we see consistent evidence that gubernatorial strength contributes to the stretching of individual budget categories to meet the governor's attention and preferences.

While the power of institution matters in achieving preferences, our partisanship data show that the composition of these preferences (again, insofar as partisan identification is indicative of distinct preferences between Republicans and Democrats) does not appear to have a noticeable impact. The quantile regression in the base model of Figure 5.3 shows that the brush of "the confidence band" typically touches the zero line, occasionally missing the line for values at the upper end of the distribution. Democrats – if we squint – are responsible for *some* categorical increases, but the magnitude of these increases is small (though in line with expectations). A focus on Democratic spending preferences is tested and displayed in Figure 5.5. Again, we generally do not find a relationship between Democrats' preferred spending categories and larger changes. All point estimates are positive, but most touch the horizontal line. The only area where Democratic spending preferences have some

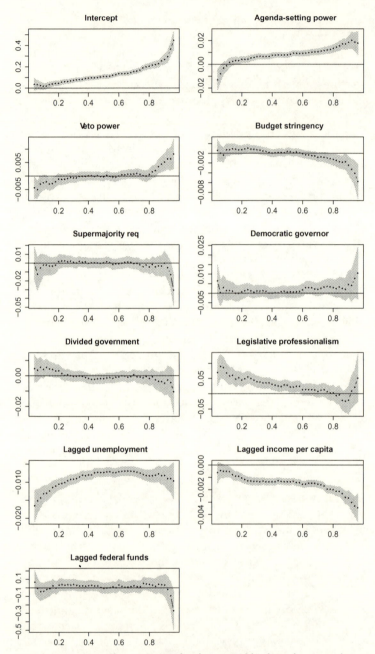

FIGURE 5.4 Quantile regression for functional budget changes when separating governor powers. The x-axis represents the quantile of each estimate, and the y-axis indicates the estimate of the variable stated in the title of each plot. The black dots are point estimates, and the gray band is the 90 percent confidence band. The regression is based on annual programmatic changes in budgets for the US states, 1985–2010.

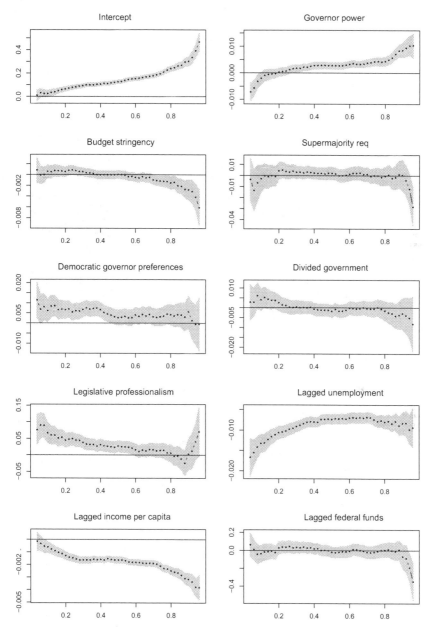

FIGURE 5.5 Quantile regression for functional budget changes when specifying democratic governor preferences. The x-axis represents the quantile of each estimate, and the y-axis indicates the estimate of the variable stated in the title of each plot. The black dots are point estimates, and the gray band is the 90 percent confidence band. The regression is based on annual programmatic changes in budgets for the US states, 1985–2010.

traction is for conditional cuts, where Democratic governors appear to prevent cutbacks at the margins.

We also see relatively little influence on categorical changes in states with divided governments, though the trend of the estimates across the three models is suggestive of a moderating force on budgets. We find that states with divided governments are likely to see large cuts moderated. As we argued previously, we expect divided governments to produce more moderate results. Empirically, this manifests as fewer large cuts, but no real changes in increases (large or small). While American politics scholars posit that divided governments come together to produce major or significant legislation, our data show that partisan division does not result in extreme budgets. Perhaps this is what citizens expect from legislatures in the first place – foster the status quo – and why citizens create the conditions for divided government in the first place.

While divided governments tend to prevent very large categorical cuts, budget rules prevent large categorical increases. Across the three models in Figures 5.3 to 5.5, there is a persistent, negative, and statistically significant estimated effect of budget stringency at the upper end of the budget distribution. In line with theoretical expectations, policymakers find it challenging to pass fattened budgets in states with stricter balanced budget requirements and carryover restrictions. Interestingly, the supermajority requirement for budget changes has only a slight impact (the gray confidence bands hover around zero) save for only the most extreme values in all of our models.

The review of the relevant literature on state politics also suggests we should expect professionalized legislatures to exert a similar centripetal influence over budget changes in a divided government scenario. More specifically, state politics scholars expect professionalized legislatures will not just maximize legislative preferences, but will also constrain the ability of governors to express their own. The results in Figure 5.3 show that legislative professionalism has a similar, but stronger influence over categorical budget expenditures than divided government. Legislative professionalism moderates small cuts. These findings suggest legislatures are better able to defend preferred programs from gubernatorial cuts than they are able to constrain gubernatorial increases. Thus, the strategies governors may employ to pay for their large increases might change depending on the professionalism of the legislature.

Budget policymaking takes place in the context of changes in the economy. We have identified gubernatorial powers as centrifugal forces on the budget and other structures in the states as centripetal. Figure 5.3 also shows the impact of changes in economic conditions related to unemployment and income. In general, unemployment represents a drag on expenditures. The findings across the distribution of changes are uniformly negative: When unemployment is high, large increases are smaller, and large decreases are larger. The effect is somewhat uneven across the distribution of budget changes, suggesting that unemployment affects budget cuts differently than budget increases.

Some government programs are hard to cut because of policy-based commitments and/or ties to federal programs. Other programs are easier to cut in times of crises, such as parks or other capital expenditure heavy programs like hospitals. While we cannot read too much into the unemployment findings, it is apparent that governors make decisions about where to cut programs rather than where to increase them. States with strong governors during times of high unemployment are likely to see deep cuts in some categories.

The effects of income are challenging to parse. As incomes rise, categorical changes decrease. In some cases, this means that some moderate cuts become a bit deeper, some incremental increases become a bit smaller, and large increases become comparatively much smaller. While different states have different ways of capturing a share of personal income as revenue, it is likely that states with higher personal incomes have the capacity to invest public monies in a variety of programs. Additionally, poverty-fighting programs may be simply less necessary in states where incomes are better; thus, it may be less necessary for governors and legislatures to top-out many public welfare programs. Interestingly, we do not see much influence from federal transfers to states, which is to say that federal monies appear to be neither responsible for moderating nor exacerbating categorical budget cuts.

5.6.1 Comparing the Quantile Method with OLS

Ordinary least squares regression analysis is an econometric method that intends for the relationship between independent and dependent variables to be conditioned on the expected mean value. Quantile analysis conditions the relationship between an independent variable and a dependent variable at different percentiles of the distribution. Instead of conditioning only on the mean, quantile regression can be conditioned at any number of percentiles of our choosing. In the graphical form of Figure 5.3, we have chosen forty-seven different conditional percentiles spaced two percentiles apart. These plots visually confirm that variation in slopes across the conditional distribution occurs; we can also statistically verify whether these slope differences are, indeed, different from one another. We use an ANOVA test of equality of distinct slopes in Table 5.2 to show variation in influence between the 5th, 50th, and 95th percentiles of the distribution of categorical budget changes.

We choose these percentiles as examples of conditional deep cuts (5th percentile), large increases (95th percentile), and incremental changes (50th percentile). Admittedly, the ANOVA test does not indicate which slopes are different from which slopes; it only indicates that between these three percentiles of the distribution there is a statistically significant difference. That said, Table 5.2 shows that slopes for gubernatorial power, balanced budget rules, supermajority requirements for budget bills, unemployment, and personal income differ in a statistically meaningful way between large cuts, large

TABLE 5.2 *ANOVA tests of equality of distinct slopes for $\tau = 0.05, 0.5, 0.95$ for quantile regression displayed in Figure 5.3.*[†]

Covariates	Df	F-value	$Pr(> F)$
Governor power	2	11.69	0.00***
Budget stringency	2	2.34	0.09˙
Supermajority req	2	5.13	0.01***
Democratic governor	2	0.28	0.75
Divided government	2	1.51	0.22
Legislative professionalism	2	1.33	0.26
Unemployment	2	7.25	0.00***
Income	2	16.41	0.00***
Federal funds	2	2.19	0.11

Note: *p <0.1; **p <0.05; ***p <0.01
[†] Functional and regional fixed effects are not shown.

increases, and changes in the middle. This finding is not only methodologically important, but also theoretically so.

Another way of understanding centripetal and centrifugal forces of public budgeting is to directly compare the quantile results with an ordinary least squares analysis of the data. In Table 5.3, we conduct an OLS regression and compare this with regressions conditioned at the 5th, 34th, 50th, 68th, and 95th percentiles of the distribution of budget changes. The comparison across the findings is most important for our main variable of interest: governors. While the OLS estimate is suggestive of a positive relationship between gubernatorial power and budgetary change, the variation in slope across the conditional percentiles is significant (see Table 5.2 again), and the OLS coefficient would really mischaracterize the shifting relationship between gubernatorial power and *types* of policy change. The OLS estimate would overestimate the power of governors to influence budget increases for much of the distribution, but greatly underestimate this power for the largest increases. If we dive deeper into the data and condition the distribution at the fourth or second percentile (where the deepest cuts lie), we see that the OLS coefficient would incorrectly indicate directionality of the relationship between gubernatorial power and budget changes. Thus, OLS would tell us that gubernatorial power is associated, on average, with increases in categorical budgets, and we would be, well, wrong.

Other findings from the quantile analysis would be missed if we used OLS. According to the results in Table 5.3, both balanced budget rules and supermajority requirements are not statistically significant in the OLS model. However, as we see in Figure 5.3, Table 5.3 shows that these variables are actually

TABLE 5.3 *Ordinary least squares and quantile regressions for functional budget changes.*[†]

Covariates	OLS	0.05	0.34	0.50	0.68	0.95
Intercept	18.47	1.00	9.90	12.53	16.99	42.91
	(2.21)	(2.47)	(1.08)	(1.04)	(1.14)	(3.89)
Governor power	0.34	−0.59	0.20	0.29	0.35	1.04
	(0.17)	(0.20)	(0.08)	(0.08)	(0.08)	(0.24)
Budget stringency	−0.12	0.01	0.03	0.01	−0.05	−0.42
	(0.10)	(0.12)	(0.05)	(0.05)	(0.05)	(0.17)
Supermajority req	−0.25	−0.98	0.30	0.31	0.19	−2.37
	(0.83)	(1.19)	(0.34)	(0.34)	(0.38)	(0.93)
Democratic	0.43	0.12	0.22	0.19	0.45	0.76
governor	(0.42)	(0.47)	(0.18)	(0.18)	(0.20)	(0.67)
Divided government	0.20	0.80	−0.04	−0.16	0.02	−0.45
	(0.44)	(0.51)	(0.20)	(0.19)	(0.21)	(0.70)
Legislative	6.11	7.34	3.17	2.71	1.79	5.85
professionalism	(2.37)	(2.60)	(1.09)	(1.06)	(1.19)	(3.78)
Lagged	−1.25	−1.61	−0.83	−0.75	−0.70	−1.01
unemployment	(0.15)	(0.24)	(0.08)	(0.07)	(0.08)	(0.26)
Lagged income per	−0.21	0.00	−0.16	−0.16	−0.19	−0.41
capita	(0.03)	(0.04)	(0.02)	(0.01)	(0.02)	(0.05)
Lagged federal funds	−9.09	2.02	2.76	−1.80	−0.75	−21.71
	(8.56)	(7.48)	(3.76)	(3.69)	(4.11)	(10.64)
N	13,500	13,500	13,500	13,500	13,500	13,500
AIC	111,809	112,395	99,173	98,931	101,717	122,171

[†] OLS regression with heteroskedasticity-consistent standard errors. Quantile regression at five percentiles (0.05, 0.34, 0.5, 0.68, 0.95) with kernel estimate of the sandwich. Standard errors are in parentheses. Function and regional fixed effects are not shown.

significant for extreme increases. Our economic context variables are estimated less poorly by the OLS model. Unemployment does not suffer from an egregious misinterpretation in the OLS version of the model, and indeed, the ANOVA results that investigate differences in slope across conditional percentiles in Table 5.2 bear this out. Ordinary least squares estimation also captures the essence of the relationship between income and categorical budget changes, but it would miss the tapering strength of this relationship at the lowest percentiles.

5.7 GOVERNORS AND PUNCTUATED BUDGETS

We have shown that governors use their institutional strength to top-off and bottom-out budgets. Public budgeting occurs in a compositional context in which these categorical shifts have consequences for changes in other – in some cases, seemingly unrelated – categories. The preceding analysis indicates that governors can expand large increases and cuts to budget categories. The aggregate impact of these individual extremes finds their expression in on the overall distribution of policy change at the state level.

Because budgets are compositional in nature, we envision a few possible state governmental responses to topping-off and bottoming-out of budget categories. The acts of topping-off and bottoming-out are decisions on the part of executives that are abstractly independent of other considerations, though, in reality, they are interconnected with multiple disparate decisions in composing the budget. When budget categories are expanded or contracted, they create several other challenges/opportunities for budget-makers in composing the rest of the budget. In many cases, governors are responding to their own decisions within a current budget, the ramifications of decisions they have made previously, or to decisions made by previous administrations.

Governors have options in how they "equilibrate" budgets. Governors might top-off and bottom-out one category and then respond to other categories in varying degrees as a function of changing problem conditions. This is a close-to-rational (CTR) scenario in which governors maximize their preferences and are also able to adjust other expenditures in line with available information. Another scenario, called overcorrection (OC), might find governors simply expanding budget categories one year only to severely cut them the following year while most other categories remain unchanged.

Though CTR appears to be an ideal case for politicians, a deep literature in decision-making indicates that these kinds of rational choices are possible mostly in theory. Politicians may wish to make choices that match problem characteristics, but the realities of information processing confound even the most righteous politicians. In the OC scenario, we expect budgetary drama accompanied by volatility and large change amid this volatility. Our expectation is that gubernatorial behavior results in a combination of these scenarios; that governors make big changes bigger and, in doing so, attend less to other policy change opportunities. Some substantial changes may linger rather than force a fiscal overcorrection. Programs created by an increase in categorical funding might be challenging to dissolve and, thus, may require maintenance on the part of state governments.

Our understanding of interest group competition and the argument we advance offers some guidance regarding the pattern of decision-making we expect for centrifugal and centripetal budgets. The budget literature broadly suggests that budget decisions, like most other policymaking decisions, will follow a pattern corresponding to a punctuated distribution. We offer an extensive review of this literature in Chapter 2, but suffice to say that governments are troubled to attend to all the problems that beset them. When governments finally address a problem, they often overcorrect and make large changes, all the while continuing to make smaller changes in other areas. Our argument builds on this foundation and suggests that governors are no different from governments in general; that consolidating power in the hands of the governor exacerbates the bottleneck of decision-making that affects other governmental decision-making processes; and that governors face their own attention limitations conditioned by the interest group environment that forms around different issues.

Thus, the culmination of centrifugal and centripetal budget forces exacerbates the patterns of budget change we come to expect from disproportionate information-processing theory. All governors have attention limitations and, therefore, will place most issues on autopilot to address preferred issues. In other words, gubernatorial attention is relatively fixed, while gubernatorial capacity to shape policy is not. As we show previously in this chapter, when governors make decisions, stronger governors will make more consequential choices. Stronger governors should make already punctuated budgets *more* punctuated.

We illustrate the influence of governors' centrifugal and centripetal forces on the extent to which budgets are punctuated. Budget punctuations are based on annual L-kurtosis scores of a state's budget for the twenty-five years of data. Figure 5.6 plots the expected relationship between budget punctuations and governor power. The box plot on the top left simply distinguishes between institutionally weak (governor powers below the median value) and strong (powers above the average). The difference in the mean L-kurtosis scores is about 0.06. A simple t-test suggests that both groups are statistically different. Budgets in states with strong governors are more punctuated.

The remaining two scatter plots in Figure 5.6 further probe the source of these differences. We pry open our budget measure to distinguish between the agenda-setting and veto powers of governors. Just as we found in the quantile regression, agenda-setting powers drive large-scale changes. The top right plot indicates that increasing agenda-setting powers of a governor is related to increases in budget punctuation as measured by L-kurtosis. In contrast, the line estimate for the relationship between veto power and budget punctuation is essentially flat. The low correlation suggests that veto powers of governors do not contribute a great deal to budget punctuation.

All in all, institutionally strong governors can top up as well as bottom out spending domains. By doing so, governors with strong agenda-setting and veto powers produce more punctuated budgets compared to governors who must engage with the legislature on more equal footing when making and passing a budget. In the late 1980s, New York and Pennsylvania governors, who are institutionally very powerful, produced some of the largest budget punctuations in the sample. These extremes can be contrasted with tranquility in Maine, where an institutionally weak governor contributed to some of the least punctuated budgets during the early 2000s.

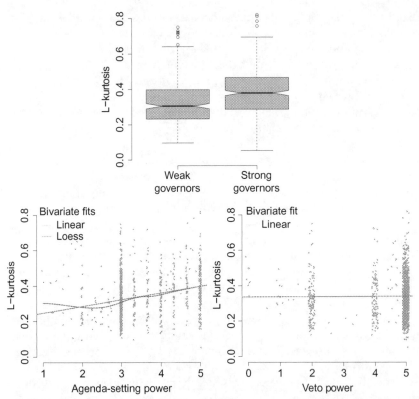

FIGURE 5.6 Governor powers and budget punctuations. The three plots relate governor powers to budget punctuations (L-kurtosis). The top boxplots distinguish between governors above (strong) and below (weak) the median value of governor power. The bottom plots distinguish between agenda-setting (left) and veto powers (right) of governors.

5.8 CONCLUSION: GOVERNORS RESHAPE STATE BUDGETS

In Chapter 4, we show how interest groups can create opportunities for change as a function of dynamics of competition, collusion, or instability. In this chapter, we turned our attention to executives in American states who are not without agency in crafting arguably the most important recurring piece of public policy in a state. We have taken a multifaceted look at how governors can influence the budget in the context of party preferences, institutional structures related to budgeting, and the economic context in which budgeting occurs. We draw conclusions that speak specifically to the role of governors in public budgeting and to the broader argument we advance in the book.

First, governors can accomplish their goals when they attend to particular policy issues. Their choices have consequences, even for items to which they do not attend. The budget offers governors opportunities to pursue and achieve multiple signature policies, with stronger governors in a particular position of advantage. Previous research has long focused on the ability of governors to reign in budget expenditures (Barrilleaux and Berkman, 2003; Clarke, 1998; Dearden and Husted, 1993); we paint a more detailed picture at the level of spending domains. Strong governors contribute to topping-off and bottoming-out, and we show that this power leads to greater punctuations. An old public policy chestnut is that governments make slow and/or poor decisions because authority is dispersed across several different actors. The solution to this problem (or, rather, the solution for which this problem is identified) is that a centralization of authority streamlines decision-making and creates more adaptive institutions. Our findings suggest the opposite is probably true. Centralization simply reduces the attention of governments to a smaller group – a small group which is less able to attend to a broad range of information (see also Koski and Workman, 2018). Less attention means more incremental changes that do not match actual changes in problem characteristics. Attention-deficit democracy manifests itself in wild swings in public policy as a function of changes information processing exacerbated by gubernatorial strength.

Governors capable of asserting their dominance in the budgeting process are able to cut and expand budget items to their liking. Low intra-branch decision-making costs and a clear ability to claim credit and the power to override legislative tampering by the House result in more control over policy outputs. Hence, governors with stronger institutional powers are able to change spending on an annual basis.

Second, if we examine the combined effects of economic variables and gubernatorial strength, we also show that strong governors could counteract or exacerbate the economic conditions they face. That is, while unemployment might reduce the magnitude of large increases, governors who wish to prioritize specific programs could use their power to mitigate unemployment-induced reductions. Or, strong governors could use high levels of unemployment as an opportunity to make large programmatic cuts even larger.

Third, budget rules work as centripetal forces. Some budget institutions can keep extreme changes from happening, which suggests they are working. Institutions that enable greater numbers of decision-makers and preferences constrain large budget changes. The long-term effect of these institutions is a more even-handed approach to policy change. An even-handed approach is certainly desired by groups seeking stable policy outputs, though perhaps not welcomed by governors wishing to top-off budget categories. Governors must navigate rules and strong legislatures to obtain the budget they desire, which makes the opportunities interest groups provide them all the more important. Our conclusion is somewhat tenuous given the relative weakness of the quantitative showings here, which could be seen as the result of relatively weak enforcement of budget rules (Primo, 2007; Von Hagen, 2002).

Taking a step back, we see that strong executives can serve both the interests of the state and their interests when they have the opportunity to make changes. We may consider punctuated distributions as a negative outcome in a normative sense, but governors' topping-off and bottoming-out can also represent executive "leadership." That is, politicians are rarely remembered for staying the course; they are more likely to be remembered for shaking things up. For ambitious politicians, a stronger governorship is a better opportunity than a weak one. From a policy perspective, though, an increase in large changes can also represent how political systems overcorrect based on shifts in attention and a finite capacity to process information. We argue attention is driven, in part, by the opportunities interest groups create for governors. Insofar as governors can seize upon those opportunities, stronger governors can more forcefully mold budgets. Therefore, governors can top-off or bottom-out budgets, though this process is still subject to the attention-driven disproportionate information-processing models that suggest outcomes that correspond to volatility-induced punctuated equilibrium.

The findings presented in this chapter and in Chapter 4 suggest that both interest groups and governors are important to explaining the politics of state budgets. Quantitative analyses we have presented in this book provide a grand view of the relationship between interest groups, gubernatorial powers, and budgets. Qualitative case studies offer a more fine-grained method of exploring this relationship, which we investigate in Chapter 6.

6

How Interests and Executives Set Public Policy
in Four States
with Nat Rubin

Our argument sets up a clash of the titans of state policymaking (governors) and agenda-setting (interest groups). We make distinct claims regarding interest groups' power to create opportunities for policy change or to dissuade policymakers from taking action. We then show that governors, while perhaps constrained in their choices by interest groups, are key players in determining the shape, form, and growth of budgets given their institutional means to make policy. In this chapter, we bring these two forces of state politics and policymaking together to understand how governors' motives are manifest in public budgets. Our wide-lens statistical modeling shows that interest groups and governors are both important in shaping public budgets, but how does this relationship work on the ground?

6.1 INTRODUCTION: TELLING (LESS THAN ONE MILLION) BUDGET STORIES

Let us recapitulate the empirical findings thus far. While we know that budgets are punctuated, we want to know more about the source of these punctuations, the politics that lead to them, and how they relate to the long-run fortunes of policy domains. We argue that this punctuated pattern of budget changes is a function of the institutional means of the executive branch, motives presented in budgets, and opportunities presented to governors by interest groups. We illustrated four important insights about budgetary change that emerge from this conflagration of institutional and political forces.

First, the politics within policy domains influences the size of budget punctuations rather than variation across political settings. From this, we infer that motives to engage with issues, rather than larger philosophical claims about the size of government, are the driving force of significant changes in public budgets. For example, we show that government and hospital spending is more punctuated than welfare and education spending. Second, these functional features have long-term consequences. Long-term growth occurs in policy domains with little punctuations, while punctuations are likely to happen in domains with little long-term growth. Long-term growth and punctuations do not happen in the same policy domain, especially when the size of this domain is also large.

Third, the means of executives matter for growth and punctuations. If the executive holds agenda-setting and veto power, then policy changes will be larger in the long run, and budgets will be more punctuated. This joint occurrence is due to strong governors' ability to top-off budget increases. A governor's focus on a particular budget item, their ability to legislate their preferences for change, and block alternative solutions, leads to long-term growth and punctuation. A strong governor must decide whether to cater to political interests occupying policy domains (either in a capture or deadlock scenario) or to follow the eruption of a volatile policy domain with a modest number of often changing interest groups. Fourth, opportunities to exercise these means are a function of interest group dynamics occurring within policy domains. Variations in interest group concentrations provide different kinds of opportunities to contribute to long-term trends or make short-term deviations. If the executive engages in policy domains that are captured by a few interest groups or that are openly contested by many groups, long-term growth is likely. In domains with a volatile interest group population, policy change will be a see-saw affair, providing short-term changes but lower long-term growth. These domains are occasionally punctuated (or perhaps we can think about this as "rejuvenated") by large-scale changes, though.

While our quantitative data analysis tells an omnibus story, one that offers insights into general patterns of change associated with interest group competition and gubernatorial power, these data are less helpful in identifying actual relationships as they exist "on the ground." This "ground" is expansive: The data we use span a vast political geography over two decades. Although we can measure budgetary commitment, interest group concentration, and other general political characteristics to show this variation, states also have particular interests, different political agenda sizes, experience unique problems, and have a unique cast of institutional characters inhabiting political institutions. These very same features that make state politics interesting and exciting – plenty of variation in political institutions and policy responses – make generalizations about state politics challenging. Take the example of the Beaver State.

The evolution of welfare spending in Oregon illustrates how executive powers, interest groups, and policymaking work together. Oregon's governors are institutionally strong, with extensive agenda-setting and veto power they can use to influence the budgeting process. The welfare policy domain in Oregon is, on average, populated by 134 interest groups, representing 27 percent of all interest groups in the state. The share of welfare groups as a percentage of all groups changes little over time: Their share grew by 9 percent between 1990 and 1997. Consequently, spending on welfare is an important issue in every budget cycle. In this environment, the executive is unable and, we theorize, unwilling to shift policy dramatically; instead, welfare spending grows slightly above budget almost every year. The share of welfare spending in the Oregon budget more than doubled between 1984 and 2010; perhaps unsurprisingly, the long-term growth of welfare is greater than any other budget category for Oregon.

While examining the budget politics of each state individually over the twenty-six-year period would likely yield the best understanding of the mechanisms behind the phenomena that we model, we opt for a more practical and insightful approach. We choose four states as cases to examine variations in issues and institutions across the states. We choose states based on variation in state gubernatorial power to test expectations between strong and weak governors. We choose budget categories marked by interest group competition consistent with the categories we identify in Chapter 2: capture, instability, and deadlock. The logic of this case selection would produce two states and three budget functions; however, the budgeting environment of large versus small states is different. Large states on average have more issues to which to attend, a greater capacity to attend to them, and more complexity. Larger states also *generally* have more professionalized legislatures, with a greater capacity to seek and sort information related to policy. Simply put, larger budgets have more money to spend, more things to spend it on, and more people asking for it.

Table 6.1 displays our general approach to case selection. In this base model, we choose four different states and three different functions for each state. The functions are chosen based on interest group competition found in each area; thus, the functions may or may not be the same across states depending on each interest group environment.

Finding different interest group dynamics that fit each of the cases is straightforward as all states contain capture, instability, and deadlock scenarios for interest groups. Matching governors with state size is more challenging, however. Small states have both strong and weak governors, so we choose Vermont (weak governor) and West Virginia (strong governor). Both have similarly professional legislatures and relatively small economies and populations (though West Virginia is larger in both these areas). America's largest states tend to have strong governors, but the same cannot be said for weak governors. Thus, we make a conscious trade between direct comparability in size for contrast in governorship. We choose New York, with a large economy, large population, and strong governor; we choose North Carolina with a relatively large population and a relatively large (though much smaller) economy and, importantly, one of the weakest governors in the data set (with particularly weak veto power).

TABLE 6.1 *Case selection criteria.*

	Interest group environment		
	Capture	Instability	Deadlock
Strong governor	Large state 1	Large state 1	Large state 1
	Function 1	Function 2	Function 3
	Small state 1	Small state 2	Small state 1
	Function 1	Function 1	Function 3
Weak governor	Large state 2	Large state 2	Large state 2
	Function 1	Function 2	Function 3
	Small state 2	Small state 2	Small state 2
	Function 1	Function 2	Function 3

TABLE 6.2 *States of budgetary change I.*

	Interest group environment		
	Capture	Instability	Deadlock
Strong governor	NY corrections	NY hospitals	NY welfare
	[IG: 2.5 percent]	[IG: 17 percent]	[IG: 28 percent]
	2008: 0.2 percent	2008: 6.5 percent	2008: −4.0 percent
	2009: −1.6 percent	2009: 20 percent	2009: 1.1 percent
	2010: 5.9 percent	2010: −2.3 percent	2010: 9.6 percent
Weak governor	NC corrections	NC hospitals	NC welfare
	[IG: 3 percent]	[IG: 15 percent]	[IG: 32 percent]
	2002: −1.5 1.8 percent	2002: 2 percent	2002: 10 percent
	2003: 2 percent	2003: −19 percent	2003: 14 percent
	2004: 5.9 percent	2004: 5.1 percent	2004: 12.6 percent
	2008: 4.1 percent	2008: 6.5 percent	2008: 6.2 percent
	2009: 2.2 percent	2009: 2.7 percent	2009: −3.7 percent
	2010: 6.1 percent	2010: 1.9 percent	2010: 1.8 percent

Tables 6.2 and 6.3 place states in the matrix we offer in Table 6.1. Each cell in Tables 6.2 and 6.3 contains the following information: (1) the spending category (e.g., welfare), (2) interest group density of the category expressed as a percentage of all interest groups (labeled "IG") in the state, (3) the years we investigate the politics of each budget function, and (4) the annual percent change in that category in a budget during each year. We control for temporal variation across cases, while also offering varying responses to different time spans.

We follow established methods in using quantitative methods in combination with qualitative case studies (Lieberman, 2005; Seawright and Gerring,

TABLE 6.3 *States of budgetary change II.*

	Interest group environment		
	Capture	Instability	Deadlock
Strong governor	WV corrections	WV hospitals	WV welfare
	[IG: 2.1 percent]	[IG: 14 percent]	[IG: 31 percent]
	2002: −5.3 percent	2002: 14 percent	2002: 11 percent
	2003: 6.9 percent	2003: 3.4 percent	2003: 4.4 percent
	2004: 0.5 percent	2004: −31 percent	2004: 3.1 percent
Weak governor	VT corrections	VT hospitals	VT welfare
	[IG: 3.5 percent]	[IG: 14 percent]	[IG: 25 percent]
	2002: 11 percent	2002: 2.8 percent	2002: 0.3 percent
	2003: 2.5 percent	2003: 38 percent	2003: 19 percent
	2004: 15 percent	2004: 12 percent	2004: 11 percent

2008). This nested design delivers additional evidence of the books' framework, probes into the causal mechanisms, and confirms these insights with potentially influential cases. A closer look at the data in Tables 6.2 and 6.3 suggests that we choose cases that both control for and offer variation in time, space, and category. Within all cases, we matched the same time span within each state to replicate the compositional nature of budget decision-making. Governors' decisions in one category will influence decisions in other categories, though the exact form of the trade-off is dependent upon increases (or cuts) to the overall size of the budget. Across cases, we examine state periods that are distinct from one another. We chose particular moments in American political history that correspond with different sets of budgetary challenges. Next, we provide an overview of the four cases and the rationale for the selected time periods.

6.2 FOUR STATES OF BUDGETING

Other than sharing a time zone, New York, North Carolina, Vermont, and West Virginia are different from one another along a number of characteristics. New York is the third-largest state in the union with nearly 20 million people; it also has a robust service-based economy, is the capital of the American financial sector, and is home to the largest city in America. While New York City is the quintessence of cultural diversity, upstate New York is whiter and more likely to resemble the Rust Belt. Notwithstanding the more sparsely populated upstate, New York is one of the most urbanized states in America (roughly 11 percent rural according to the 2010 Census of Population and Housing). New York's budget is quite large, the legislature quite professionalized, and the distribution of government services is vast and varied. Though North Carolina is not as large (a little over 10 million people), it has a growing financial sector, a significant agricultural sector, and an economy driven by innovations from the "research triangle." Rural North Carolina is both white and black and is significantly poorer than urban North Carolina. The state has a much smaller government than New York and a much larger rural population than states of comparable size (about 31 percent).

Although New York and North Carolina have relatively diverse and strong economies, the same cannot be said for Vermont and West Virginia. Vermont is one of the smallest states by population – smaller than a borough in New York City – and one of the most rural (over 70 percent). Vermont's economy is driven by agriculture, tourism, and a large medical center at the University of Vermont. Vermont's government is small, but the state is no stranger to taxes and regulation. Vermont is also over 90 percent white. West Virginia is also one of the most rural states in America (over 50 percent) with a small population (like Vermont, also over 90 percent white) that is generally much poorer than other states. The state economy relies on coal production, chemical manufacturing, and federal spending.

These brief snapshots are not intended to tell complete stories of the four states, but rather to emphasize what readers already know: American states are very different from each other. These differences might drive governments to favor or regulate particular sectors of the economy, and for interests to emerge to defend or attack those regulations. Therefore, we expect the share of resources at the state level to be related, in part, to the interests that defend the unique economies of each state. While these interests may shape the density of groups around particular spending categories (we find that this matters less than expected), we argue that interest group concentration determines opportunities to shift budget shares, rather than particular features of interest groups.

While the states are different, there are common themes between these and the other 46 states faced with creating a budget every year. State governmental agendas involve the same basic problem-solving issues that Adler and Wilkerson (2013) research in their study of Congress. States must continually administer and update their own programs and the programs they jointly implement with the federal government. Our four states also exhibit some similarities in their budget processes. In general, the process begins in the summer or early fall of the year prior to the passage of the budget, when the governor's office communicates budget priorities and limitations to agency heads. The agencies then spend the fall preparing budgets and submitting them to the governor. In early winter, the governor takes the agency proposals into account when crafting their own budget, which is then presented to the legislature at the beginning of the budget year. The legislature can then alter the budget according to their constitutional powers before returning it to the governor for a final signature (New York Division of the Budget, 2018; North Carolina Office of Budget and Management, 2018; Vermont Department of Finance and Management, 2018; West Virginia State Budget Office, 2022).

While West Virginia, Vermont, and New York go through this full process every year, North Carolina crafts a biennial budget on the odd years and has a shorter budget process on the even years to adjust for any necessary changes.

We chose two distinct time periods for our case comparisons, which occur in particular periods in US economic history that might influence the supply of problems and revenues states face. The first period is 2002–2004, which saw states beginning to climb out of a brief recession from March 2001 to November 2001. In the run-up to the 2001 recession, the United States had seen an incredible economic expansion felt across income categories. The US federal budget famously produced budget surpluses from 1999 to 2001. The period saw an increase in tax rates on higher-income earners, a relative draw-down of defense in the aftermath of the Cold War, and long-term budget deals beginning with George H.W. Bush as factors leading to the federal surplus. The federal government also cut domestic spending during this period, particularly social welfare policy. The Clinton Administration and the Gingrich Congress replaced a good deal of direct spending with tax expenditures (Faricy, 2016) and offloaded social programs onto states. The 1996 Personal Responsibility and Work Opportunity Reconciliation Act (known as "welfare reform") is a classic example; this legislation eliminated the federal welfare entitlement (Aid to Families with Dependent Children) and created welfare spending block grants (Temporary Assistance to Needy Families, or TANF). The block grant form enabled states to become even more independent in their administration of welfare and changed benefits available to recipients. In nearly all cases, this meant lower benefits.

Welfare is just one of the million stories in the federal budget that influences the environment of states; this example shows that states had exited an economic boom during which the impacts of devolved social spending were absorbed by healthy revenues and a decrease in demand for such programs given the state of the economy.[1] The period of 2002–2004 begins as a challenge for states as they dealt with decreased revenues, expensive problems demanding their attention, and less help from the federal government. The federal government solved its revenue shortfall by borrowing[2]; however, states do not have this luxury. Thus, 2002 starts with states trying to manage a new fiscal reality, but, by 2004, the economy had "recovered," but crucially without large

---

[1] In the specific case of welfare, demand for expenditures was also reduced by public policy.

[2] Some of the revenue shortfall was directly the government's doing. Readers will recall the $300 tax surplus rebate from the George W Bush administration in 2001 as part of a major tax overhaul, undoing much of the tax policy of not just the Clinton Administration but of the George H.W. Bush administration. That the economy simultaneously plunged was not lost on some Americans; the tax cut and resulting budget deficits served as the foundation for a *Futurama* episode "Three Hundred Big Boys" in which the head of Richard Nixon, serving as President of Earth in the year 3000, promises $300 to each person on earth from the spoils from a war against an alien race – the Spiderians. After the checks are distributed, but before the spoils of war are actually sold, they are burned in a fire, thus resulting in a huge deficit.

gains in employment – what the Democratic Party referred to as a "jobless recovery" – meaning that the problems of a recession persisted.

The second period we chose extends from 2008 to 2010, which covers the "Great Recession." Though it is challenging to encapsulate the impact of what the Minneapolis Federal Reserve Bank referred to as a "Macroeconomic Earthquake," the brief version is that the US government experienced a free fall in financial markets, credit markets froze, business investment stopped, consumer spending dried up, Americans lost whatever wealth they had accumulated in the stock market or their home and, eventually, lost their jobs. The resulting revenue shock affected both the federal government and state governments. While some energy-exporting states, such as Texas and North Dakota, experienced a delayed onset of the economic impacts of the financial crisis because of extremely high energy prices, no state could escape the massive layoffs that occurred as a result of a collapse of a financial system built on a shaky foundation of a hyper-inflated housing market. Similar to the 2001 recession, the federal government could deficit spend to compensate for losses; however, states had nowhere to turn, other than to ask the federal government to pass along some of the money it could borrow. The federal government stepped in to stop the worst of the revenue hemorrhage via direct funds to states as part of the American Recovery and Reinvestment Act (ARRA) in 2009.

This short-term relief was ultimately incommensurate with the twin challenges that states confront in any recession: less revenue and more demand for social assistance. States were also heavily involved in implementing the so-called shovel-ready projects associated with other ARRA programs (e.g., infrastructure) given the extant state-federal relationship in service delivery (e.g., transportation and energy). Thus, the 2008–2010 period was a turbulent time for states in determining their budgets: Revenue projections were challenging, the demand for services surged, and, at the same time, states had to manage a large influx of stimulus cash. Stimulus notwithstanding, states were forced to consider rearranging budget priorities at a fundamental level. Education cuts, even typically well-shielded K-12 education, were up for debate in the face of cratering state revenues. The 2008–2010 economic climate created real opportunities for raw budget volatility, and also created a budget-making environment which enabled significant shifts in the budget *share* of particular items.

As these macroeconomic events unfold, states still have funding commitments to put cops on the street, house prisoners, engage in basic road maintenance, and so on. There exists particular inertia for states to maintain expenditures on federally supported programs such as transportation, Medicaid, and welfare. Though many federal programs' matching grants help offset implementation costs, states lose those monies if they choose not to implement these programs.[3] Multiple states were concerned that a 90 percent

---

[3] For example, debates over cost-sharing were central to the Medicaid expansion of the Patient Protection and Affordable Care Act.

cost-share would essentially make the entire state budget dependent upon Medicaid implementation. This inertia builds in a commitment from states to create both centripetal forces (maintaining the budget as a whole) and to continue particular kinds of centrifugal forces (ensuring a particular share of the budget for specific programs). This inertia is a factor in molding budgets in times of economic recovery (2002–2004) and in economic decline (2008–2010).

For comparison purposes, we examine two states during the recovery period of 2002–2004 (Vermont and West Virginia), one state during the decline of 2008–2010 (New York), and one state across both periods (North Carolina). We examine three spending categories for each state. As our analysis in Chapter 3 shows, punctuations exist everywhere, but policy issues rather than states drive this variation in the end. Interest group concentrations around these policy issues create opportunities for spending interventions, as we find in Chapter 4. When faced with these opportunities, governors use their institutional powers to make large changes even larger (Chapter 5).

The motives of interest groups, governors, and legislators are a critical component of budgetary outcomes. Throughout the book, we assume the policymakers follow their overriding motives. These analyses have been largely devoid of the actual political context of budgetary decision-making. For our case studies, our task is to identify similar budget categories across states that also have similar *relative* interest group densities for the purpose of assessing the combined effect of gubernatorial power and interest group density. As indicated in Tables 6.2 and 6.3, we choose corrections as the setting of a *capture* scenario, hospitals as *instability* and welfare as *deadlock*. Next, we provide an overview of these categories in states over the chosen years. Then, we relate these cases back to our underlying theoretical concepts. We end the chapter with lessons drawn from these cases related to motives, means, and opportunities in public budgeting.

6.3 MOTIVES AND OPPORTUNITIES IN THE FOUR STATES: SETTING BUDGETS FOR CORRECTIONS, HOSPITALS, AND WELFARE

We have described budget categories elsewhere in the book as providing motives for governors and interest groups to intervene in the policy process (see Chapter 3). In this section, we explicate the broad problem context in which particular categorical spending occurs beyond a mechanistic description of expenditure types. In all spending categories, states spend monies as directed by their participation in federal programs, in addition to their own distinct programs. State corrections, hospitals, and welfare spending compete with each other and other programs in the policy milieu that forms a state budget. State-specific idiosyncratic factors cause variation, but, there are general themes that span states for each of these categories.

Capture and Corrections. The United States has the highest incarceration rate of any country in the world, the vast majority of whom are incarcerated for violating state laws and, therefore, reside in state prisons or local jails. Such a large number of imprisoned individuals creates a series of problems for states. From a financial perspective, corrections illustrate how policy decisions not viewed as direct expenditures have a significant impact on budgets. Since the 1980s, policies like the "war on drugs," mandatory minimum sentences, and a decrease in the use of parole led prison populations to explode and a subsequent increase in prison expenditures as a share of state budgets (The Sentencing Project, 2022). Legislatures may not have realized that the consequences of their "tough on crime" policies would also be "tough on the budget."

From 1985 to 2010, the number of people incarcerated at the state level nearly tripled (Bureau of Justice Statistics, 1987b, 2011). The growth in incarceration at the state level has entrenched racial inequities, with Black and Hispanic men having far greater rates of lifetime incarceration (Bureau of Justice Statistics, 1987a; Guerino et al., 2012; The Sentencing Project, 2017). As tougher sentencing increased the supply of prisoners, the demand for both prisons and prison staff also increased significantly. The number of state prison employees grew from 140,959 in 1984 to 389,882 in 2005, while the number of state facilities more than doubled (Bureau of Justice Statistics, 1987a, 2008). State spending on prisons rose from $6.7 billion in 1985 to $51.4 billion in 2010 (The Sentencing Project, 2017).

The stakeholders in prison budgeting tend to be relatively few, making this category well-suited for the capture designation in our interest group analysis scheme. Relevant groups of organized individuals include prison employees, prison towns, prisoners, and criminal justice reform groups. Interestingly, most groups involved in attempting to influence corrections policy want the state to spend more on prisons. Prison guards want more money, prison towns want more employees, prisoners want better facilities, and criminal justice reform groups want fewer prisoners, though they ultimately want them to have access to services while in prison. Most of these budget desires are not orthogonal, and certainly all point toward increasing budgets.

Conversely, groups that are likely to oppose increases in prison spending are likely to oppose spending in general and, perhaps ironically, are likely to prefer an increased supply of prisoners. Prisons are generally not a highly salient part of budgets (though there are exceptions to this, such as California). The small clutch of organizations wedded to the corrections budget, coupled with a steady stream of prisoners, ensures a relatively stable share of the budget. Correction budgets provide opportunities for governors to solve budget problems in the form of facility closures, pay cuts, and programs designed to reduce the number of incarcerated individuals (e.g., early release, parole); and similar opportunities to reward established interests in new prison construction, prison expansion, corrections employee pay increases, and programs to better serve incarcerated individuals. The reality of mass incarceration led many states we studied to simultaneously open and close prisons, caught in between budget pressures and growing inmate populations.

Instability and Hospitals. We choose the hospitals category for our discussion of instability in American state budgeting because of variation in state support, constituent service, and interest group commitment. The hospitals category includes investment in specific public hospitals and clinics run by states, counties, and other local governments. Our graphs in Chapter 3 indicate that the pulse of hospital expenditures is marked by severe palpitations, no doubt a function of state-level financial anxiety.

Public hospitals vary widely in size and mission: from Los Angeles County Hospital to the Marias Medical Center in Shelby, Montana to the University of Washington Medical Center. These facilities rely to varying degrees on state funding because of their broad service missions. The hospitals budget category excludes public health expenditures, such as Medicaid *directly*, though public facilities are particularly dependent on federal funds as primary care facilities for lower-income citizens who are most likely receiving public support. The hospitals sector provides substantial opportunities for governors given the wide range of disparate, often unconnected, interests. As hospitals vary in their missions, they also vary in constituencies and relationships to the state. Private hospitals tend to serve more affluent patients and rely more on private insurance than state dollars. University hospitals serve not only as a medical facility, but as an educational facility as well. They often rely on the state for capital projects and may have a constituency that expands beyond medical professionals and patients to researchers and academics. Generally, though, most hospital-based budget talks focus on capital improvements or Medicaid reimbursements. Capital projects, particularly for university hospitals, may involve hundreds of millions of dollars, but attract little attention due to the narrow constituency they serve. Hospital and clinic budget negotiations can be idiosyncratic, particularly in smaller states. Similar to corrections, local communities tend to organize in defense of particular facilities rather than taking a position on state hospital funding broadly: Lobbying for funding is place-based as well as issue-based.

In contrast to the politics of capital expenditure, hospitals are one of many players in negotiations over health care funding. It is in the interest of all hospitals, but particularly so for public hospitals, not simply to advocate for more funding for health care but more funding for *their provision* of health care. All hospitals have a stake in publicly funded health care reimbursement rates, eligible services, and increased insurance availability (notably Medicaid at the state level) – for example. However, this partial stake that hospitals have in public funding contrast with the direct stake that groups have in delivering public health services (in the form of eligibility and access) directly to constituents. Thus, groups with stable direct interests in hospitals are few, while, at the same time, interests affiliated with other budget categories occasional or indirect interests in hospital expenditures are potentially many. This interest group environment is a prime example of instability.

Deadlock and Welfare. The welfare category provides significant motivation for governors to pursue policy initiatives in shaping major policies (e.g., expanding health care or trimming cash payments to the poor), but the extensive, long-term, and competitive interest group environment provides limited opportunities for major change. At the state level, the welfare category is a large part of the budget and one that has been growing more quickly than other kinds of state spending due to increases in health care costs and the hollowing out of federal contributions to the welfare state (The Urban Institute, 2017). Large welfare programs like Medicaid, the Children's Health Insurance Program, and Temporary Assistance for Needy Families (TANF) are all administered by states, and budgeted by states, backed by federal grants. Because welfare is a large budget category, it can be a tempting place to cut in times of budget distress.

When governors or legislators look to cut welfare, they know they are walking into a political firestorm. Programs in the welfare budget category have much wider constituencies than prisons or hospitals, leading them to draw more public attention and interest groups. Groups who advocate for the poor, young, or disabled are often actively engaged in the budget process, trying to maintain or increase welfare budgets. Welfare is also closely watched by conservative or business groups who advocate for less government spending and regulation. Further, the structure of welfare funding from the federal government varies by program. Temporary Assistance for Needy Families is a block grant, while Medicaid is not. The block grant structure of TANF gives states wide latitude in determining where federal dollars go, with only about 20 percent of TANF funds going to what we would commonly call welfare (i.e., basic assistance). In addition to specific programmatic goals associated with social welfare programs, the politics of policies in the welfare category is the vanguard of fundamental conflict over redistribution in the United States. Lots of money, lots of interests, and lots of obligations from states. We now investigate these categories across our four chosen states, beginning with Vermont.

6.4 MANAGING THE GREEN MOUNTAIN IN VERMONT

From 2002 to 2004, Vermont saw two very different personalities in the governor's office. Governors in Vermont serve two-year terms, and 2002 was the final year of Democrat Howard Dean's tenure. Dean, a former physician, was a loud and confrontational aspiring presidential candidate unafraid to speak his mind. Previously a state representative and lieutenant governor, Dean became governor in 1991 due to the death of his predecessor, Richard Snelling. He then was elected for five consecutive terms, comfortably defeating his opponent each time. He was also gearing up for a 2004 presidential run, hoping to take his brand of fiscally moderate progressivism to the national stage. In his final year as governor, Dean's political motivations focused on his signature health-care programs – specifically an expansion of Medicaid – well as environmental protection (Dean, 2002).

Following Dean was Jim Douglas, a Republican chosen by the state legislature after all candidates failed to receive a majority in the 2002 general election (FairVote.org, 2015). Douglas was much more reserved, and staked his governorship on a dedication to bipartisanship, which he called "The Vermont Way." His agenda during his first two years as governor mainly concerned holding the line on state spending while implementing a flagship jobs program. He sought to maintain the health-care advances that occurred under Dean, while seeking cuts in all state departments (Douglas, 2003, 2004b). Both governors faced divided government. From 2002 to 2004, the Vermont Senate was held by the Democrats while the House was held by Republicans. In addition, Vermont was somewhat affected by the general economic downturn in the early 2000s. Unemployment reached a high of 4.4 percent in the first half of 2003, before dropping to 3.5 percent by December 2004 (Vermont Department of Labor, Economic & Labor Market Information, 2020). Both Dean and Douglas acknowledged the economic trouble and tailored their priorities with it in mind. Dean called on, "old-fashioned New England frugality," while Douglas called the situation, "the worst budget crisis since World War II" (Dean, 2002; Douglas, 2003). The budget was indeed dire. The state faced a $100 million drop in revenues in 2002 (Occaso, 2002). In this political environment, both governors considered closing correctional facilities in Springfield and Woodstock; hospital construction at the University of Vermont and the state psychiatric hospital; and cutting back the Medicaid budget.

6.4.1 Prisons in Vermont

In 2002, a lack of revenues had opened a large budget hole in Vermont. In response, Governor Dean recommended a $8.5 million cut to the Department of Corrections (DOC) (Sneyd, 2001b). The most obvious target for cuts within the department was the Woodstock prison, an aging facility that cost the state more per prisoner than other state facilities. The closure was supported by the DOC but opposed by local politicians, the area's state representatives, local law enforcement, prison employees, the state employees association, and high-ranking legislators (Mace, 2002g; Moxley, 2001a,b; Smallheer, 2001). Part of the uproar stemmed from the prison's planned closure far ahead of the 2004 opening of the new Springfield prison. However, Dean maintained that Woodstock's closure was simply a budgetary necessity (Curtis, 2002). He claimed that if the prison's supporters could fund it without "flimflam money," he would agree to keep it open, but no such money was ever found (Schmaler, 2002c). The issue was contentious in the legislature, nearly delaying the passage of the year's budget (Mace, 2002e). Though some in the Senate tried to keep the facility open for another year, none were successful and the prison closed (Sneyd, 2002d).

More budget issues arose in 2003, leading Governor Douglas to include only one growth item in his budget: $10 million to open the Springfield prison on time (Smallheer, 2002). He included the prison in his budget address as well. Douglas and the Senate voiced their opposition to the House budget because it delayed opening the prison until July 2004 (Schmaler, 2003b; Smithwick, 2003b). As the budget season reached crunch time, the town of Springfield lobbied both the legislature and Douglas to advocate for a timely opening. They sent a lobbyist to the capitol, sent Douglas a letter about the prison's economic benefits, and gave the governor a tour of the facility (Smithwick, 2003a). Douglas then revised his budget to include an additional $700,000 to open the prison, while a top Democrat called it a "key agenda [item] for the Douglas administration" (Schmaler, 2003e,g). With the support of the governor and the state senate, the final budget funded the prison to open on time in October 2003 (Schmaler, 2003a).

Douglas's 2004 budget was centered on restraint and balance. In his State of the State address, he recommended few changes to the general budget, but included more general funding to the Department of Corrections to help remedy what he called "shameful neglect" (Douglas, 2004b). Though the prison system was excoriated in a state auditor's review of prisoner treatment, the head of the department outlined a plan to fix the issues, and corrections subsequently received a large increase in its budget without much debate (Marx, 2004a,b).

6.4.2 Hospitals in Vermont

The fluctuations in Vermont's comparatively tiny hospital budget can largely be attributed to the Fletcher Allen Renaissance project scandal. The Renaissance project was a $173 million construction project intended to expand the hospital. The state granted Fletcher Allen a permit on their $173 million project in 2001. That same year, two smaller hospital projects were rejected by the same committee (The Associated Press, 2001). In both cases, Governor Dean was either publicly or privately opposed to the smaller plans, and seemed to have influence over the decisions made by the Department of Banking, Insurance, Securities and Health Care Administration (Mace, 2002d; Malek, 2001).

By late 2001, opposition to the Renaissance project had risen on two fronts. First, mental health advocates opposed the relocation of Fletcher Allen's psychiatric care unit in order to make room for new construction (Mace, 2002d; Sneyd, 2001a). Additionally, some lawmakers and competing health-care groups noted that Fletcher Allen was constructing a $55 million parking garage, which had not been included in their permit (Mace, 2002c). Despite the controversy and without obtaining the permit, the company constructing the hospital broke ground on the parking garage. There was a petition to have public hearings about the garage permit, but Dean had the permit approved in exchange for around $300,000 in fines (The Associated Press, 2002a). By mid-2002, questions arose about whether the hospital's leadership had intentionally misled regulators about the parking garage. As Dean was leaving office, Fletcher Allen revealed that the true cost of the project would be $356 million and that they would need to apply for a new permit (Mace, 2003h). Dean called the leadership at Fletcher Allen "crooks," and said he hoped for criminal prosecution of hospital officials (Mace, 2002b).

When Douglas became governor, he blamed the fiasco on both the Dean administration and the hospital's board (Rutland Herald (VT), 2002a). He made no comments about prosecution but showed support for legislative action to reform the permitting process (Mace, 2003h). After Douglas called for leadership changes, eight members of Fletcher Allen's board resigned (Mace, 2003e). Later, in 2003, the legislature passed a bill reforming the hospital permitting process, and an investigation found that Fletcher Allen had deliberately lied about the real cost of the project (Mace, 2003g). Douglas, "said the state should do all it can to support the hospital," and Fletcher Allen's second permit was approved without additional fines (Mace, 2003g,k). In response to the permit being granted, Douglas's spokesperson said he was "satisfied" (Mace, 2003f).

Budget discussions also included the fate of the Vermont State Hospital, a public psychiatric hospital. In 2003, reports emerged that the hospital had failed state and federal inspections. The mental health advocacy group Vermont Protection and Advocacy had been critical of the hospital and its treatment of patients prior to the inspections, but had failed to gain much traction politically (The Associated Press, 2003a). In response to the inspections, the hospital was threatened with the loss of federal funding (Gram, 2003b). Douglas also hired new staff at the hospital, growing its budget by 21 percent, but this did little to stop tragedies at the hospital, including two suicides and an attack on a doctor (Gram, 2003c; Larson, 2003; Mace, 2003d). The hospital's failure to meet federal standards led it to lose its federal funding, up to $700,000 a year (Larson, 2003). In response, Vermont Protection and Advocacy suggested closing the facility and moving the hospital to a new, better-equipped location (Mace, 2003a,i). Meanwhile, the head of the Department of Developmental and Mental Health Services met with the Douglas administration, who permitted the hospital to make several new hires before the legislature made mid-year budget adjustments (Mace, 2003l). Before the start of the 2004 budget session, Douglas announced that the hospital would lose $2.4 million in Medicaid reimbursements, over three times the original projection. He asked for a total of $3.7 million in additional funding for the hospital as part of the mid-year adjustment, including only $47,000 in additional funding (Allen, 2003). A legislative panel recommended closing the hospital instead, but Douglas pushed back, arguing that closing the hospital would not be possible until the patients could be rehoused (Gram, 2003a). Douglas included calls to fund the hospital in both his State of the State and Budget addresses (Douglas, 2004a; Rutland Herald (VT), 2004). Without much debate, the legislature included $2.7 million for the hospital in the 2004 budget.

The Vermont hospital sector represents the volatility of a budget category which has few stable interests, multiple interests that have temporary interests in the benefits provided by the sector, and varying degrees of executive attention. There are few publicly funded hospitals in Vermont, but, there is a significant ecosystem of actors who are affected by certain funding decisions directed at those facilities. Sometimes actors such as patients, physicians, and other social welfare groups are heavily invested in hospital decisions, but only ephemerally. The governor is a key player in these negotiations, in this case relative to the scale of the fight. It may be strange to some to think that a sitting governor would devote such interest to the minutiae of hospital construction, but, for Dean and a lesser extent Douglas, the interest group environment provided opportunities to make real and visible changes.

6.4.3 Welfare in Vermont

The Dean-Douglas years in Vermont marked multiple attempts to intervene in the Medicaid budget, all of which were hampered by interest group activities directly engaged with the executive and legislature. In 2002, Dean proposed a budget cut of $16.5 million from Medicaid (Mace, 2002f); though this cut was somewhat disingenuous, as his true goal was to demonstrate the kind of cuts that would be necessary if the legislature did not pass a cigarette tax (Schmaler, 2002d). Still, advocates for the poor and elderly wrote op-eds and rallied against the cuts (Graff, 2002; Mace, 2002a) which helped to pressure the House to pass a 36-cent cigarette tax increase, while the Senate passed Dean's preferred 67-cent increase. Accordingly, the House avoided some of Dean's cuts, while the Senate restored almost all of them (Sneyd, 2002b,c). However, the politics of the moment were not simply related to the budget cuts themselves, but also other policy proposals related to Medicaid, which were part of the budget package. Dean threatened to veto the budget if the Senate's version prevailed, calling them spineless for removing some rate increases he viewed as legitimately necessary (Sneyd, 2002a). Meanwhile, groups ranging from the Community of Vermont Elders and the Vermont Low-Income Advocacy Council to the Vermont Business Roundtable supported plans that raised the cigarette tax and restored the cuts (Rutland Herald (VT), 2002b; Sneyd, 2002c). The two houses eventually agreed on a 75-cent increase over two years, while conceding to some $4.5 million in cuts (Schmaler, 2002a,e). The expected tax money enabled the legislature to restore some cuts while also creating a fund for future years, almost entirely in line with Dean's original Medicaid funding plan (Schmaler, 2002b).

In 2003, Douglas planned to reduce Medicaid spending by creating a system of deductibles, in addition to requiring higher co-pays for those with higher incomes still receiving Medicaid through the Vermont Health Access Program from the Dean years (Graff, 2003) – amounting to $7.4 million in cuts to funding (Schmaler, 2003d). The same groups active in the 2002 Medicaid budget battles, in addition to the state AARP and the Vermont Coalition for Disability Rights, objected to the plan claiming some people would lose coverage or be forced to sell assets to maintain coverage (Lang, 2003; Schmaler, 2003c,f). As the House and Senate also sought savings, they planned to restructure nontraditional Medicaid like VHAP using a premium system. However, Douglas opposed the plan, claiming it did not cut enough (Mace, 2003b). The legislative plan was included in the final budget, though the changes were not to be implemented until January 1, 2004 (Mace, 2003c,j).

Governor Douglas prioritized health care in his 2004 budget address, outlining a program to partner with small businesses to provide state health care, create health savings accounts, and increase Medicaid reimbursements to providers (Douglas, 2004b). The plan's estimated cost was $17 million, but was supported by the conservative Ethan Allen Institute because it would increase competition (Allen, 2004b; McClaughry, 2004). However, Douglas' plan failed to win favor in the legislature, and was not included in the budget (Barlow, 2004). The legislature took the rare step to fully fund the Medicaid trust fund, which was facing an expected $250 million deficit (Allen, 2004a). The back and forth between the legislature and the executive in Medicaid spending represents the limits to gubernatorial intervention in such an entrenched area of policy. Even a change in partisanship in the executive does not fundamentally alter the path of Medicaid spending despite changes in preferences and, presumably, political capital.

6.4.4 Conclusions about Vermont

The Vermont case displays the motivations of governors from two parties in shaping budget categories. However, the Vermont case also shows Dean and Douglas's limited formal means when confronted with interest group conflict found in the capture, instability, and deadlock scenarios. Dean and Douglas generally get what they want, but are challenged to make major cuts – even in economically challenging times – to programs with particular patterns of interest group competition.

In the capture case, local stakeholders, including town officials, prison employees, and state representatives, all worked to support the prisons in their area, and no interest groups opposed them. Local communities' investment made it difficult to close Woodstock and prevented the delay of Springfield opening. Noticeably, local communities only became involved when their prison was at stake; Vermont had no interest groups invested in the prison budget from year to year. Douglas made prisons a high priority in his budgets, and kept the number of prisons operating in Vermont stable across the time period examined.

In contrast to the long-term stability of the prison budget, the hospital budget was plagued by uncertainty and unexpected costs. Fletcher Allen dominates hospital funding attention in Vermont, but faced some opposition from rival health care providers and health-care activists. Despite Dean and Douglas' statements condemning Fletcher Allen's deception, their administrations both continued to issue hospital permits and fund the Renaissance Project's overruns. As a large university hospital in a small state, Fletcher Allen was nearly able to set their own budget for renovations and strong-arm the state into supporting them. In the deadlock case, a variety of unions and advocacy groups for the elderly, poor, and disabled were involved in discussions involving Medicaid. In budget talks, lawmakers focused on sources of funding and the Medicaid deficit. Changes in spending were relatively stable and grew year to year. Dean and Douglas proposed strong visions for health-care, but only Dean was able to use his agenda-setting ability to get the changes he wanted, threatening lawmakers with his proposed budget cuts. The modesty of these accomplishments across each issue leads us to suspect that it is the relative weakness of the institution of the governor in Vermont and not the weakness of Dean or Douglas personally as executives.

6.5 ALMOST HEAVENLY BUDGETING IN WEST VIRGINIA

Our West Virginia case follows the actions of an institutionally strong governor in a small state attempting to navigate similar interest group environments as in Vermont. From 2002 to 2004, West Virginia was governed by former state representative Bob Wise, a one-term governor who chose not to seek reelection after reports of his extramarital affair (Vanden Brook, 2003). During his term, West Virginia was mired in the same recession and budgetary issues plaguing the rest of the country: Rising unemployment and a growing budget deficit estimated between $120 million and $250 million by 2004. Wise made it a priority to recommend hundreds of millions in spending and tax cuts to appeal to businesses and while also working to improve education. Wise, a Democrat, oversaw a unified government, with Democratic majorities in both the House of Delegates and Senate.

Like governors Dean and Douglas in Vermont, Wise faced a tumultuous budgetary environment with similar political decisions regarding jail closures, state hospital construction, and increasing welfare costs. However, unlike Dean and Douglas, Wise had much stronger institutional powers to individually influence the budget. We describe the interaction of the interest group environment and Wise's budgetary proposals during a time of declining revenues in Section 6.5.1.

6.5.1 Corrections in West Virginia

Between 2002 and 2004, as was the case in many states, the share of West Virginia's budget devoted to corrections looked to expand in large part because of a growing population of prisoners – a 10 percent increase (West Virginia Division of Corrections, 2005). This trend occurred despite little population growth in the previous decade. As a result, West Virginia faced an acute prison-bed shortage that Wise had to balance with shrinking revenues and increasing expenditures in other budget categories, such as Medicaid. While some activists suggested reform of the parole process to reduce the prison population, Wise instead responded by proposing $15.7 million in new prison operating costs, pay raises for correctional officers, and 190 new positions at correctional facilities in 2002 (Kabler, 2002a; Tranum, 2002). In addition, the West Virginia Regional Jail Authority (within the state department of corrections) ordered the construction of two new juvenile facilities at a combined cost of $19 million (Messer, 2002).

In his 2003 proposed budget, facing a then-estimated $250 million budget hole, Wise asked agencies across the government to look for ways to cut personnel. Wise even went as far as suggesting that workers might switch jobs to other departments funded with nongeneral fund revenues, such as federal grants (Wrenn, 2003b). Importantly, Wise noted that the corrections department would be exempt from these severe budget measures (Wallace, 2003). Prison interests, notably prison guards, saw the budget as acceptable, but still pushed for a greater share. These interests found themselves represented in two, ultimately doomed, pieces of legislation: West Virginia State Senate Bill 140 proposed a $4,000 increase for prison guards and Senate Bill 174 which would have guaranteed that corrections workers would receive double any normal pay raise that state employees received (Wrenn, 2003a). Prisoner advocates pushed for early release programs, sentencing reform, and treatment instead of more prison construction (Fraser, 2003). In comparison to other states, few inmates in West Virginia were granted parole, thereby inflating the prison population (Castelle, 2003). Some members of the courts, including a state supreme court justice, advocated for investments in community corrections, which they argued would relieve overcrowding and would save money (Kabler, 2003; Starcher, 2003).

In his 2004 State of the State, Wise announced that his budget exempted the corrections department from 9 percent across-the-board cuts to state agencies and gave the department an extra $7.2 million (Kabler, 2004f; Wise, 2004). The Senate budget wanted to close three prisons, but the effort failed, and the facilities remained open. The final legislative budget cut the extra $7.2 million that Wise had proposed be given to the department (The Herald Dispatch Staff, 2004). During the following special session, the head of the West Virginia Regional Jail Authority began lobbying Wise and the legislature to include $600,000 to fund the beginnings of a community corrections program

(Kabler, 2004e). The legislature approved $800,000 in funding late in the year (Tomblin, 2004).

Despite the activities of a few actors, the overall salience of corrections was low from 2002 to 2004, with little visibility in budget discussions and a lack of passionate engagement from interest groups. While Wise was successful in maintaining the corrections budget in the face of budget declines (including avoiding prison closures), his efforts to increase the budget fell flat in the legislature. The result of the political machinations of these three years was a relatively stable corrections budget, with some minor changes that emerged from a dominant interest (the new community corrections program from the regional jail authority) – something we would expect to see in our capture scenario.

6.5.2 Hospitals in West Virginia

The politics of hospitals in West Virginia during the 2002–2004 time period appear, at least in some form, an exercise in contradictions. On the one hand, the state was experiencing an incredibly slow-growing population, increasing unemployment, and more specifically increasing rates of uninsured West Virginians. The majority of West Virginia's patients access medical care via nonprofit or state-owned facilities. The state's largely rural population depended on small state and county hospitals for basic medical care, much of it either insured through Medicaid or uninsured care. Rural hospitals have relatively few beds and poor patients which makes for precarious finances – be they state-owned, nonprofit, or private. Rural hospitals nationally have been closing as rural populations decline and the price of health care increases.[4]

Because of declining revenues at state-owned hospitals and affiliates, the government of West Virginia was making hard choices about keeping rural hospital doors open. At the same time, the West Virginia Health Care Authority (the state's regulatory agency) was also faced with a number of requests for hospital consolidation and hospital expansions ($650 million in expansions in 2003 alone, which dwarfed the state's hospitals budget that year). Consolidation and expansion threaten to further accelerate the two worrying trends of rural hospital closure and increasing health-care costs (either through increased rates to support hospital construction or declining competition). Hospital spending in West Virginia, as in Vermont, is a very small percentage of the overall state budget (in most years, less than 2 percent). Also, similar to Vermont, the most visible recipient of state hospitals dollars is the state medical school's hospital: Ruby Memorial Hospital at West Virginia University.

---

[4] In 1997, the federal government passed a law to stem the tide rural hospital closures via the critical access hospitals (CAH) program which allows for increased Medicare reimbursement rates for hospitals that meet certain rural criteria.

The accounts of West Virginia hospital finances are dire during this period. The West Virginia Hospital Association (WVHA) declared that 2002 was the year they would persuade the legislature to fix the "financial instability" of the state's hospitals, as 48 out of 64 operated at a deficit (Gorczyca, 2001). While the WVHA's state was true, the actual budget politics of West Virginia hospitals – at least from the state perspective – during this time are fairly mild in part because they were driven by the largely well-regarded, stable, and largely self-sufficient Ruby Memorial Hospital.

Much of the politics of state public hospitals expenditure, thus, is largely the province of subsystems where decisions are opaque. In contrast with Vermont's Fletcher Allen hospital, there is no real scandal that draws the governor into hospitals spending during this time. West Virginia University had a $75 million hospital project approved in 2003,[5] but the process was handled by the Health Care Authority rather than the governor or legislature (Smith Cox, 2003). Wise's 2003 state of the state address, however, posited a more controversial budgetary decision: a new tobacco tax or $300 million in cuts to health care (The Associated Press, 2003b). While health-care groups and hospitals lobbied Wise in opposition to the cuts, Wise brought health-care and hospital groups to the capitol to lobby legislators on the taxes (Finn, 2004; Heys and Finn, 2004; The Associated Press, 2003c). In the end, legislators rejected the tax but kept Wise's recommended level of funding for Medicaid, avoiding cuts using ad-hoc funding (Searls, 2004; The Associated Press, 2004d). Governor Wise pushed to exempt nurses from overtime rules (essentially, allowing nurses to take more overtime), which might have increased the hospitals budget more were it not for the fact that many state hospitals employees were already subject to collective bargaining agreements which were exempt from such compensation policy changes. WVU Hospitals also quietly began another project in 2004: a much smaller $26 million office space project (Charleston Daily Mail (WV), 2004).

In the West Virginia hospitals case, we see a relatively minor budget item with a number of potentially interested parties (e.g., rural communities, university systems, community hospitals) that have trouble collectively organizing for the sake of particular budget items. Some stronger players, such as WVU, can operate with relatively low-conflict insofar as they avoid scandal as we see in the Fletcher Allen case. We also show hospitals funding and groups swept up into the relatively high-conflict arena of health care funding in Wise's efforts to expand a tobacco tax. Here, the governor acts as an organizer of groups for his own purposes with some partial success because of the lack strongly organized groups in the hospitals sector. While perhaps occasionally intervening in the hospitals budget category during these three years, Wise is highly engaged in the politics of welfare which we turn to next.

---

[5] Much of this funding did not come from the state.

6.5.3 Welfare in West Virginia

Welfare spending in West Virginia involves a much larger share of the budget than corrections or hospitals as well as more vested interests. Despite a worsening financial situation in the state, the welfare budget steadily grew at an incremental rate as we would predict given the high concentration of affiliated groups. The specific stories that we focus on here are the overall initiative that Governor Wise offers to trim social welfare programs, with a particular focus on children's programs and cash grants in the form on the temporary assistance to needy families (TANF) program administered by the state. While it would strain credulity to refer to anti-poverty groups as powerful, this case shows how large numbers of groups representing a diverse coalition of stakeholders are able to guide the governor's budget knife, but not dull it completely.

In late 2001, Wise appointed the Temporary Assistance to Needy Families Advisory Council to seek out solutions to the growing expense that cash payments to the poor represented to the West Virginia budget framed as mismanagement by the governor. The previous administration had used a temporary TANF surplus as a result of the Personal Responsibility and Work Opportunity Act to fund welfare checks. The TANF Advisory Council ultimately recommended $90 million in cuts to welfare and welfare-to-work programs in late 2001 to take effect in July of 2002 (Miller, 2001). Both the council and the head of the Department of Health and Human Resources (DHHR) hoped the legislature would reconsider $20 million of the cuts (Kabler, 2002b). In his 2002 State of the State, Wise announced his budget would, in fact, reconsider the $20 million, and that he hoped these funds would go to bolstering foster care services (Wise, 2002). Social workers and children's advocacy groups, such as the Coalition for Children West Virginia, opposed the cuts, especially the possibility of cutting cash assistance (Miller, 2002a; Pratt, 2001). Shelters and other welfare centers warned the cuts would force them to close their doors (Miller, 2002b). The final budget cut the $90 million from cash assistance programs, but gave the DHHR the $20 million they and Wise had requested (Keith, 2002).

In his 2003 State of the State, Wise proposed a merger of the Cabinet on Children and Families, an independent state organization concerned with children's and family welfare that received $2.9 million annually in state funding, with the Department of Health and Human Resources (Miller, 2003a; Wise, 2003). The Cabinet on Children and Families was intended to be an organization chaired by the governor to specifically highlight eponymous issues separate from the much larger DHHR. While advocates and detractors agreed that the Cabinet was working rather poorly (e.g., the legislature removed its ability to direct revenue and the committee and the committee had a hard time even convening), there was no agreement on the solution. The merger between the Cabinet on Children and Families and the DHHR was opposed by some former members of the cabinet and the Coalition for West Virginia's Children, who asked the legislature to pass a bill to study how to continue the cabinet's work (Miller, 2003b,f). The program even received out-of-state support from the national group Family Support America (Miller, 2003c).

At the same time, current and former members of the legislature, including the health advocate who originally co-wrote the bill creating the Cabinet on Children and Families in the first place, supported Wise's plan (Miller, 2003d). The DHHR eventually stated that the merger would only save the state $700,000, though the coalition, along with the Family Resource Network Association and the National Association of Social Workers, claimed it would actually cost the state money (Miller, 2003e). Wise's effort to merge the cabinet into the DHHR failed, as the legislature passed the advocates' preferred bill and funded the cabinet in the 2003 budget (The Associated Press, 2003d).

Following the end of the budget session in 2004, more concerns about welfare funding arose. Governor Wise reconvened the Temporary Assistance to Needy Families Advisory Council (hitherto dormant since their 2001 recommendation to cut $90 million in TANF grants), which asked the DHHR to cut an additional 25 percent from TANF recipients' checks (The Associated Press, 2004c). Twenty separate child advocacy groups joined forces and re-branded themselves as the Legislative Action Team on Families and Children, who then presented their own plan for welfare. They recommended a 5 percent cut to cash assistance, using the state budget surplus as a way to compensate for declining assistance (The Associated Press, 2004b). Wise criticized the Team's plan, saying it relied on temporary funding, but the head of DHHR said he would show the plan to the legislature (Kabler, 2004b,c). The legislature gave the DHHR $ 5 million, enough to fully fund TANF for the fiscal year, but not enough to implement the Team's plan into the future (Kabler, 2004g). The Legislative Action Team had hundreds of welfare recipients call DHHR to complain, and a larger coalition of 96 groups asked Wise to limit cuts to 5 percent a year, while the legislature was working on the budget (Bundy, 2004; Kabler, 2004d; The Associated Press, 2004a). Despite the groups' efforts, the DHHR made $37 million in cuts to everything except childcare programs funded through TANF (Kabler, 2004a).

6.5.4 Conclusions about West Virginia

West Virginia's budget story illustrates how a state attempted to cope with economic challenges even before a national economic crisis created fiscal headwinds. In each of the three spending categories, the governor was broadly motivated by an overarching goal to balance the budget. While Wise's individual issue preferences are important, the governor seemed to lack particular policy motivations when enacting change; rather, he tried to work with what he was given by the interest group environment he faced. In contrast to Governors

Dean and Douglas in Vermont, Governor Wise was better able to enact spending preferences, which included cuts and increases. That said, interest group competition provided different opportunities for gubernatorial intervention, resulting in relative stability in the budget for corrections and welfare while sacrificing some dollars for hospitals.

Ultimately, Wise possessed powers that many American governors might envy: a strong agenda-setting position relative to the legislature and veto powers that would be difficult to override. Further, Wise enjoyed unified government, as well as tight connections with the state's Democratic delegations in Congress. Theoretically, Wise should have his way in the budgetary environment that characterized the 2002–2004 period – one of shrinking revenues and increases in demands for government services. Indeed, Wise was able to successfully increase some parts of the corrections budget despite early budgetary headwinds; however, his attempts to restructure and trim welfare programs were largely rebuffed by coalitions of interest groups. Hospital funding, relative to other categories, found itself a decreasing share of the overall budget given the multiplicity of interests (community health, state hospitals, mental health facilities) and lack of consistent interest group advocacy for state resources (the WVHA represented multiple private hospitals in a time of consolidation). Despite a fundamentally different economy, culture, and financial context; the governor of New York, who possesses similar means, encountered similar choices in 2008 which yielded strikingly similar results.

6.6 POLITICAL AND FINANCIAL CRISES IN THE EMPIRE STATE

In 2008, hitherto lieutenant governor, David Paterson, unexpectedly became the 55th governor of New York after Eliot Spitzer was forced to resign. Spitzer quit less than one year into his first term as a result of revelations that he had patronized a high-priced escort service over multiple-years. As governor, Paterson inherited New York's finance-heavy economy on the eve of the Great Recession, which plunged the state's budget into chaos (Kaplan, 2014). In addition to this financial crisis, Paterson struggled to overcome the perception (and reality) of widespread corruption in Albany. Paterson's tenure was challenged further by his own scandals. In February 2010, facing a 26 percent approval rating and an investigation for covering up an aide's domestic abuse, Paterson announced he would not run for reelection (Poll, 2010; Scherer, 2010).

Though both Democrats, Spitzer and Paterson, focused their efforts on fairly bipartisan issues: ethics in government, children's health care, infrastructure, property taxes, and business taxes. In addition, Paterson spearheaded a renewable energy program called "45 by 15," which aimed to have 45 percent of the state's energy supplied "through improved energy efficiency and clean renewable energy" (Paterson, 2009). The New York State Assembly is reliably Democrat-controlled, and the Senate Republican-controlled. However, Paterson became the only New York governor with unified party rule in recent memory when the Senate flipped toward the Democrats in 2008. While unified on paper, the Democrats' 32–30 majority in the Senate proved fragile. At a point of high tension in 2009, two Democratic senators defected to the Republican side for a month before returning (Hakim and Peters, 2009; Richburg, 2009).

Like governors Dean (D-VT), Douglas (R-VT), and Wise (D-WV); Paterson faced trade-offs in budgeting with regard to prison closures, hospital funding, and social welfare funding. Like Wise, Douglas, and Dean, Paterson was a first term governor. Similar to Dean and Wise, Paterson did not seek reelection for political (rather than institutional) reasons. Paterson, like Dean and Wise, "enjoyed" a political sympathetic legislature, and, yet, like all governors discussed thus far, was ultimately guided by the opportunities given to him by the interest group environment of each budget category.

6.6.1 Corrections in New York

New York Democratic governors' prison reforms have long been motivated by major scandals in places such as Riker's Island. Prior to his ignominious departure in 2008, Governor Spitzer created a commission to study possibly closing four prisons (Confessore, 2007). The prison population had decreased, and many low- and medium-security prisons had unfilled beds. The decade-long movement within the Department of Corrections to close underpopulated prisons pre-dated Spitzer's governorship, but an alliance of Republicans in the state legislature and the prison guard union, the Correctional Officers & Police Benevolent Association (COPBA), had successfully blocked any closures (Lee and Kaufman, 2008). The COPBA held rallies throughout the budgeting process, including some with appearances by top Republican lawmakers (Conner, 2008c). Soon after his inauguration, Paterson worked to amend the corrections portion of the budget bill. Against the recommendations of the Department of Corrections, Paterson worked with interest groups to create a revised budget, which kept the four prisons open at an estimated cost of $33 million to $70 million (Dwyer, 2008; The Post-Star Editorial Board, 2008). The president of the COPBA praised Paterson after budget talks concluded (Flanagan Jr., 2008).

Paterson's 2009 budget proposed closing the underpopulated McGregor, Pharsalia, and Gabriel minimum-security prison camps that were nearly closed in 2008. Like Spitzer, he kept his plan to close the prisons out of his State of the State address, perhaps hoping to keep them out of the headlines. The COPBA said Paterson's budget proposal was "shortsighted," and "put ... the public at risk" (Coleman, 2008). The union went to work with their traditional allies in the state legislature to prevent the cuts, but with much less energy and drama than in 2008. They failed to prevent the closures being included in the budget, and by mid-year, COPBA's president conceded the camps would close (Karlin, 2009). The three prison camps were closed in July (Nelson, 2009).

The 2010 budget cycle began with Governor Paterson announcing the intended closure of four more prisons (Samuels, 2010). Upstate legislators, including Democrats, immediately began to fight the closures. The corrections officer's union began a television, radio, and mail advertising campaign, telling Paterson to cut Department of Corrections' administrative costs instead of closing prisons. Union president Donn Rowe testified at the legislature, arguing that prison closures would be "absolutely devastating," to small towns that relied on them for jobs (The Ogdensburg Journal, 2010).

Within a few months, all Senate Republicans and a few Senate Democrats, along with the union, pressured the governor and the Democrats in the legislature to change the budget. In particular, the closure of Ogdensburg prison was heavily protested by the COPBA and the area's representatives in the legislature. The area's Democratic senator, Darrel J. Aubertine, promised to vote against the budget if it included Ogdensburg, a move that would prevent the whole budget from passing (Reagan, 2010). In the final budget, Ogdensburg and one other facility, Moriah Shock, avoided closure, while Lyon Mountain and Butler did not (New York States Department of Corrections and Community Supervision, 2011). In sum, after three years of various budget conflicts over corrections budgets, much of which focused on prison closures, Governor Paterson was unable to achieve major changes, but, was able to get at least some of the correctional facility closures he wanted.

6.6.2 Hospitals in New York

Regardless of the state, hospital interest group environments are notoriously complex given the mix of federal and direct spending to maintain public services. As in West Virginia and Vermont, the hospitals portion of the state budget funds myriad facilities represented by myriad, often difficult to organize, interests. Spitzer's and Paterson's plans to mitigate declining revenues involved targeting the hospital sector, where intervention opportunities *seemed* to be present given the lack of organized interest group competition. However, interest groups banded together to form coalitions in this space, which created a political opportunity for the Paterson administration to successfully propose a major budget increase during a time of financial challenge.

Part of Spitzer's 2008 budget plan included in his State of the State address, was to reduce Medicaid reimbursements for hospital procedures. While the year's main budget did not include reimbursement cuts, Paterson asked for a 7 percent ($ 62.1 million) reduction as part of an emergency session in August (Solomont, 2008; State of New York Division of the Budget, 2008). The Greater New York Hospital Association (GNYHA), a hospital lobbying group with 199 member hospitals, responded by running radio ads against the cuts. GNYHA president Kenneth Raske declared that Paterson's plan would lead to fatalities (Byrne, 2008). In a special session, the legislature eventually eliminated that year's inflation adjustment and capped the annual inflationary growth of Medicaid reimbursements at 2.3 percent, effectively cutting $130 million from reimbursements (New York State Division of the Budget, 2008).

In 2009, Paterson tackled New York's deficit by calling for cuts across the board, including changes to Medicaid reimbursements in an attempt to reduce the use of emergency care in hospitals. Paterson's plan would have reduced hospital reimbursements for emergency care and increased reimbursements for preventive care. Total cuts to hospitals were estimated at $699.7 million (Bomyea, 2008). Early in the budget season, the Service Employees International Union (SEIU), GNYHA, and 152 religious leaders published an open letter opposing Paterson's plan, asserting it would cause hospitals to reduce staffing and services, and possibly result in hospital closures (Jay Liu, 2008). GNYHA and the SEIU delivered 5,000 anti-cut "Valentines" to the New York Senate Majority Leader, and also created a website so New Yorkers to see estimated cuts to their local hospitals (Harris, 2009; Madden, 2008). They also began a multimillion-dollar television ad campaign against the plan, in which a blind man in a wheelchair asked Paterson (himself visually impaired), "Why are you doing this to me?" (New York Times Editorial Board, 2009). Paterson challenged the leader of GNYHA to a debate with the New York Health Commissioner, an offer that he declined (The New York Post Editorial Board, 2009). Throughout the budget process, Paterson ridiculed the hospital groups while remaining defiant about his Medicaid reform plan. When budget legislation was introduced, around 70 percent of the planned cuts to hospitals were restored, but over $300 million in cuts to acute care and graduate education remained in the bill (Davis, 2009). However, the final bill eliminated the cuts, with around $1 billion restored to hospitals (Stachowski, 2009). Ultimately, interest groups prevailed in not only rebuffing Paterson's cuts, but in securing additional funds for hospitals.

The interest group environment provided different opportunities for the Paterson administration in 2010 with new players and coalitions. With support from the Rockefeller Institute (Barnes et al., 2010), a nonpartisan think tank, Paterson proposed two major budget cuts that enraged hospital groups: (1) depeg Medicaid reimbursements from inflation, saving $98 million, and (2) cut $187 million in funds for hospitals to provide charity care. The planned cuts were again opposed by the GNYHA and the SEIU who had formally formed the "The Healthcare Education Project," which ran ads against the governor's plan. In solidarity, the Healthcare Association of New York State (HANYS) ran YouTube ads particularly hostile to the proposed budget measure calling Paterson "Cutzilla" (Benson, 2010; Solnik, 2010b). HANYS also sponsored a lobbying day and rally, bringing hundreds of hospital representatives to Albany to protest the cuts to inflation adjustments and indigent care (Mrozek, 2010a). In March, GNYHA, the SEIU, and HANYS issued a statement saying the proposed Senate budget addressed most of their concerns, except the charity care cuts (Madden, 2010; Solnik, 2010a).

Unfortunately, budget negotiations dragged on into the summer, past the budget deadline. In New York, once the previous year's budget period ends, the governor can propose weekly extensions until a new legislative budget is passed. In one of these extensions, Paterson proposed a $72 million cut in charity care (Karlin, 2010). Though the move outraged HANYS and individual hospitals, the legislature had to approve it to prevent a government shutdown (Thompson, 2010). The legislature finally passed a budget in August that increased funding for charity care while converting the reimbursement scheme from one that gave each hospital its own rate to one that established rates based on region. This was met with some opposition by hospitals that stood to lose under the new scheme, but otherwise there was little debate over the final budget (Mrozek, 2010b). In contrast to the previous year when hospitals experienced a large growth in the overall share of the budget by creating an environment that provided fewer opportunities for the governor to intervene, by 2010 the dynamics had changed and Paterson was able to execute some of his priorities in the face of interest group opposition.

6.6.3 Welfare in New York

In addition to Medicaid funding challenges that had direct impacts on hospital expenditures, the budgetary environment of 2008–2010 found the liberal Governor Patterson in a position of responding to increased demand for social services in the wake of the recession couched in a political environment created by his predecessor. Like other states, New York social assistance programs include food stamps, housing subsidies, and a basic grant for families in need. In 2008, a coalition of welfare families, interest groups, newspaper editorial boards, and church leaders pressured then-governor Spitzer to include an increase to the basic TANF grant – which had not increased for eighteen years – in the budget. Foremost among the groups was the Hunger Action Network (HAN), who spent most of early 2008 writing op-eds, organizing rallies, and informing the public of the implications of not raising the grant. Alongside New York's National Organization for Women (NOW), HAN was involved in advocating a grant increase in the "People's State of the State," delivered the day before the governor's State of the State Address (Bandhold, 2008). In one op-ed, HAN executive director Mark Dunlea documented his attempts to live on the grant, which failed even to cover his expenses for food, rent, or utilities (Dunlea, 2008). Members of HAN also demonstrated at Spitzer's office and in the Senate, sometimes in concert with other anti-poverty or religious groups (Conner, 2008b; Karlin, 2008). Governor Spitzer said little about the grant, leaving it out of his State of the State, but Democrats in the legislature seemed interested in raising it. Spitzer did, however, plan to have counties pay 52 percent of welfare benefits, compared to 50 percent previously (Conner, 2008a). This move drew the ire of the New York Association of Counties, who officially opposed it at their annual conference (Gormley, 2008). Under pressure from the counties, newly installed governor Paterson eventually backed off the cost shift. The legislature also rejected an increase in the welfare grant.

In 2009, Paterson veered sharply from Spitzer's agenda and proposed a 30 percent welfare grant increase, providing for a 10 percent increase each year for the next three years. In a press release, he called it "a much needed (sic) investment to help assist vulnerable New Yorkers who are suffering as a result of the current economic crisis, far too many of whom are children" (State of New York Division of the Budget, 2008). The estimated yearly cost of $109 million was a difficult sell in the face of a $15 billion deficit (Jay Liu, 2008). That year, the grant increase itself was opposed by the counties, as they would be required to pay $76 million annually if it passed (Jay Liu, 2008; The Associated Press, 2008). The business group, Unshackle Upstate, also opposed the increased grant; however, Paterson's plan was lauded by a similar coalition of groups that supported the grant raise in 2008. Mark Dunlea of HAN called it, "a unique opportunity for New York to strengthen its safety net" (Dunlea, 2009). HAN organized a press conference with religious groups and a rally outside the capitol during the final weeks of budget negotiation (Daily Messenger, 2009; Seiler, 2009). The budget passed in April, including the 30 percent raise.

Paterson's budget plan in 2010 was focused on cutting spending to fix the $7.3 billion state deficit (The Times Union Editorial Board, 2010), including a delay to the welfare grant increase he proposed just the preceding year, only raising it by 5 percent per year, through 2013. Though HAN, United Way, and the Agency Executive Association opposed the delays, they were much less vocal about the grant than in 2009 (O'Brien and Weiner, 2010; The Post-Standard Editorial Board, 2010). Mark Dunlea and HAN had shifted their focus to general social services cuts at the state and federal level. Dunlea said Paterson's budget speech ignored, "the plight of average New Yorkers," and pushed for a plan that included job creation (Dunlea, 2010; Goldberg, 2010). The budgeting process extended into August, with HAN criticizing the deeper welfare cuts negotiated by the administration (The Record, 2010). Despite the lack of attention from advocacy groups, Paterson's plan to delay the grant increase failed, and the budget kept the annual 10 percent raise intact. The diverse array of interest groups responsible for providing the opportunity for Paterson's proposed increase in welfare grant funding in 2009 provided little opportunity for change in 2010. Paterson may have had the means through veto authority to cut benefits associated with welfare and was certainly motivated to do so; he did not have the right opportunity.

6.6.4 Conclusions about New York

Interest group mobilization is a crucial part in understanding the three years in which Paterson attempted to find opportunities for budget cuts and increases. It is true that Paterson's transition from Lt. Governor to Governor required taking on some Spitzer administration policy commitments, but that did not stop Paterson from trying to play his own budget game. It is also true that Paterson may not have been the most *politically* powerful governor given his sudden ascension to the governor's office, he nonetheless had access to powerful institutional tools to give him the means to shape budgetary policy.

In large part, interest group coalitions provided him few opportunities to shape the budget, despite his very public desires to do so. The corrections category witnessed interest groups preventing closure of most facilities under years-long consideration for closure (capture); the welfare categories both saw established interest group as strong allies when in successfully convincing Paterson to deliver significant budget gains and equally successful enemies prevent the governor from paring back those benefits in the time of budget crisis (deadlock); and, in the hospitals category, rapid mobilizations of a broad coalition of groups changed the opportunity structure (instability) for Paterson to move from doubling down on cuts to a significant (20 percent) increase in the hospitals budget in 2009.

6.7 BUDGETING IN NORTH CAROLINA

We chose two time periods for the North Carolina analysis to offer a triangulated comparison between the small states we chose and New York. Though North Carolina has a weak governor, the governor in our case spanned (most of) both time periods, so we can understand how a state makes categorical choices in digging out of one recession and is buried by another. Even though the economic context changes in each of these periods, the interest group environment exerts an even influence on the opportunities governors have to make decisions regarding the use of public funds.

The North Carolina governor has limited agenda-setting and veto powers, which means several other policy actors participate considerably in budgeting. This lack of power reduces the governor's ability to top-off and bottom-out budget changes. In this environment, as we previously argue, continuous budget wins are harder to achieve; therefore, interest groups fiercely compete for attention, especially in a domain such as hospitals.

As governor from 2001 to 2009, Mike Easley was regarded as an even-keeled leader who dedicated much of his tenure to improving North Carolina's education system. His successor, Bev Perdue (governor from 2009 to 2013), also prioritized education while trying to guide the state through the Great Recession. Both 2001 to 2004 and 2008 to 2010 were periods of unified government under the Democrats. However, both were also periods of economic turmoil in the state and nationwide. In 2001, North Carolina's financial state was so desperate that Governor Easley declared a budget emergency (Kirkpatrick, 2001). Similarly to Vermont and West Virginia during this period, both the governor and lawmakers looked for cuts in state spending. Easley spent the recession trying to shield his education programs from cuts while avoiding tax increases and protecting the state's AAA bond rating (Easley, 2003). By 2004, the state had recovered with a revenue surplus (Gardner, 2004), though this was short-lived given the start of the 2008 recession, when the state's GDP fell by over $15 billion (Bureau of Economic Analysis, 2018). When Perdue became governor in 2009, the budget shortfall totaled $3 billion (Perdue, 2009). Like Paterson in New York, Perdue cut her budget to work within the state's strained finances.

North Carolinian governors ultimately entered the budget-making arena with fewer formal powers to top-off or bottom-out budgets, which led to comparatively moderate changes in the categories of corrections, hospitals, and welfare. Indeed, North Carolina governors were faced with very similar issues as their counterparts in Vermont, West Virginia, and New York: prison closures, increased health-care expenses, and oversubscribed welfare programs relative to financial capacity. In addition, North Carolinian governors faced financial challenges in the states' mental health system which weighed on hospitals budgets as well as experimented with early childhood development programs in the welfare sector. In each of the sections that follow, the institutionally weaker North Carolinian governors offer programmatic changes to shape the budget, but are more likely to engage in overt trade-offs between interests than to top-off or bottom-out budgets. We see this on display in the parallel efforts to close and open prisons in Section 6.7.1.

6.7.1 Corrections in North Carolina

Corrections spending in all states represents the financial cost of decisions regarding crime and punishment, though political fights from a budgetary perspective are often less focused on reform that might result in more equitable (and perhaps less expensive) justice and more focused on the bill that must be paid now. As with the states we investigate in this chapter, North Carolina was wrestling with decisions to close failing prisons; however, unlike the remainder of the cases, North Carolina was also wrestling with solutions to a burgeoning prison population – dominant among them, paradoxically, prison construction. The politics of prisons in North Carolina and the general interest group environment, is similar to other states – criminal justice advocates seeking less carceral solutions, prison employees in favor of prisons, and localities dependent upon prisons as economic development. The two periods (2002–2004 and 2008–2010) represent volatile budgetary contexts for states (including small deficits, large deficits, and even a surplus), but the growth of prisoners in North Carolina remained steady throughout both periods as did the interest groups that shaped the policy image of corrections. Consequently, as a share of the budget, corrections spending also remained remarkably stable. We begin with the 2002–2004 story.

North Carolina Corrections 2002–2004 In 2001, the North Carolina legislature decided to close several prisons. The House wanted to close Scotland and Union prisons, while the Senate put Alamance and Blue Ridge prisons on the chopping block (Eisley et al., 2001). The final budget closed Scotland and Alamance, saving $10.2 million (North Carolina Department of Correction, 2002). That same year, without much input from Governor Easley or interest groups, the legislature passed a bill authorizing the construction of three new prisons (Cimino et al., 2001). While preparing his 2002 budget, Easley announced plans to cut hundreds of correctional positions, mostly by closing three correctional facilities (Rawlins and Gardner, 2002a). This was opposed by the State Employees Association of North Carolina and the conservative John Locke Foundation (Hood, 2002a; Mooneyham, 2002a). Easley's budget eventually included the closure of two prisons and two boot camps (Bickley, 2002). The legislature then eliminated two more prisons, bringing the job cuts to 366 (Durhams and Griffin, 2002). However, in his 2003 budget, Easley included funds to build three new prisons (Durhams, 2003a). Both the state House and state Senate supported the new prisons, funding them in the final budget (Durhams, 2003b). The Department of Corrections also secured $6 million in new funding (Collins, 2003).

Prior to the start of the 2004 budget process, the North Carolina Sentencing and Policy Advisory Commission reported that, despite the recently approved prisons, the state would still need thousands of new beds to meet projections for the prison population (Kane, 2003b). Lawmakers were faced with the choice of approving an estimated $100 million for more prison construction or reforming sentencing to reduce overcrowding (Gulley, 2004). Most refused the possibility of shorter sentences for fear of appearing soft on crime (Wright, 2004). A few groups such as the Z. Smith Reynolds Foundation, Families Against Mandatory Minimums, and the NAACP supported sentencing reform, particularly efforts to remove statutes that increased sentences for those identified as habitual felons (Barksdale, 2004; Dalesio, 2004; Kane, 2004b; Ross, 2004). Further into the budget session, another advisory panel recommended building thirteen new juvenile correctional facilities, at a cost of $79.7 million (Hartsoe, 2004). In the final budget, the legislature funneled over $30 million toward juvenile facilities while failing to take action on the adult overcrowding problem (Durhams, 2004). The Department of Correction rather unceremoniously received a $11 million budget cut (Crawford, 2004).

North Carolina Corrections 2008–2010 Beginning our second time period, in the 2008 session that immediately preceded the "Great Recession," state reports showed that the prison population was growing and called for more prison construction as at least part of the solution (Kane, 2008d). Governor Easley responded with over $170 million in prison construction (The Salisbury Post, 2008). Though State Senator Ellie Kinnaird, along with the North Carolina Justice Policy Center, advocated sentencing reform over new construction, the idea was literally laughed at by legislators in the budget committee (Kane, 2008a). The final budget included projects at all the prisons Easley had included in his budget, with a total of over $100 million for 1,500 new beds (Kane, 2008c).

In 2009, North Carolina faced a $2 billion budget shortfall, and newly inaugurated Governor Perdue ordered every department to recommend cuts (Charlotte Observer (NC), 2009). The Department of Corrections recommended closing seven prisons to save $24 million (Charlotte Observer (NC), 2009); however, reports also showed that $150 million in new prison space would be needed to house North Carolina's still-expanding prison population (The News & Observer Editorial Board, 2009). The North Carolina Justice Center and Kinnaird again recommended incarcerating fewer people in the first place (Kane, 2009; Woolverton, 2009). Perdue, on the other hand, hoped for major savings by proposing the closure of the seven prisons recommended by the Department of Correction and double-bunking new inmates in existing prisons (Niolet and Johnson, 2009). Though the Senate first only wanted to cut four prisons, the final budget closed all seven of the proposed facilities (Charlotte Observer, 2009a,b). The only prison closure that faced much resistance was Union Correctional Facility, where town officials, businesses involved in a prison employment program, and even local churches all advocated for the facility's survival (Niolet and Christensen, 2009a).

In 2010, Perdue planned to cut $45.5 million from the prison system, including $20.5 million that would be saved by standardizing the cost of medical care inside prisons (Niolet et al., 2010a,b). The House budget cut $45.9 million (Niolet, 2010a). The public sector employees union did protest personnel cuts, but their outcry focused on public employees overall and not just prisons (Biesecker, 2010b). The final budget cut $41.2 million from the Department of Corrections in general, but also included funding a $24 million prison education program, which was never mentioned previously (Niolet, 2010b). The corrections sector during this time period witnesses quite a bit of cost-shifting *within* corrections-related programs – for example new facilities closing and opening – but the overall *share* of the budget that corrections spending occupies incrementally increases throughout this period. The losses that carceral interests might have otherwise felt were offset by gains allowing for otherwise steady returns in keeping with our expectations of a capture category. A similar story emerges in the multiple efforts to address mental health facilities in hospital spending.

6.7.2 Hospital Spending in North Carolina

Debates regarding funding for North Carolina's hospital sector will feel somewhat familiar to the reader by this point, with sticking points on Medicaid reimbursements and university hospital grants occupying a large proportion of the discourse between governors, interest groups, and the legislature. The interest groups involved may feel familiar, too, with state hospital associations and patient advocacy groups leading the (largely successful) charge against proposed cuts to Medicaid reimbursements. In addition, much of the funding discourse in the hospitals category centered on funding the state's psychiatric hospitals. Funding for hospitals to reserve beds for psychiatric emergencies and the fate of 150-year-old Dorothea Dix Hospital were also at issue from 2001 through 2010.

Here the interests are quite varied–specific doctor's associations, groups representing individuals experiencing mental illness, and the wide range of alternate facilities that would be called upon to fill in the coverage gap should the state close one of its mental health institutions. Governor Easley tried multiple times to close Dix with little success. Paradoxically, at times this resulted in *more* funding for the hospital rather than less. Governor Perdue was ultimately successful in closing the facility in 2010 after two more years of trying. In the paragraphs that follow, we detail some of these negotiations, but the upshot is that this category is generally more stable than the hospitals categories in the other three states we examined in part because the institutional strength of North Carolina governors is comparatively weak.

North Carolina Hospital Spending, 2002–2004 In 2001, North Carolina health agencies considered cuts to hospitals' Medicaid reimbursements, a move supported by the conservative John Locke Foundation (Mooneyham, 2001a; Washington, 2001). The North Carolina Hospital Association opposed the change, claiming that hospitals could not sustain these cuts. Preliminary budgets de-pegged reimbursements from inflation but faced opposition by the NCHA, the North Carolina Health Access Coalition (NCHAC), and the N.C. Health Care Facilities Association (Bonner and Rawlins, 2001; Damico, 2001; Rice, 2001b). This provision was cut from the final budget (Gardner, 2001a).

In 2002, the Department of Health and Human Services included a $21 million cut to Medicaid reimbursements to hospitals as part of their budget recommendation to Easley (Gardner, 2002b). NCHA and NCHAC both opposed the Medicaid cuts, citing precarious hospital finances, but the president of the John Locke Foundation claimed the cuts were overstated by hospital groups (Hood, 2002b; Rice, 2002; The Associated Press, 2002b). Easley's budget did not include the cut (Easley, 2002). The final budget cut $2.9 million from mental hospitals, but followed Easley's recommendation and not include reimbursement cuts to hospitals (Dyer, 2002a; Gardner, 2002a). In a stimulus bill later that year, lawmakers wanted $175 million for hospital projects at UNC and NC State. Though they were opposed by groups across the spectrum, including the John Locke Foundation and AARP, provisions for planning the projects were included in the stimulus (Griffin and Durhams, 2002; Serres, 2002).

In 2003, Easley wanted to reduce Medicaid costs by not adjusting hospital reimbursements for inflation. NCHA and NCHAC opposed this move, pointing to what they claimed were dismal hospital profits (Kane and Barrett, 2003; Rice, 2003). Hospitals testified against the measure in the Senate, and the final bill included the inflation adjustment (Gardner and Kane, 2003; Kane and Bonner, 2003a). There was also debate about funding the cancer center at the University of North Carolina, with the Senate budgeting $180 million to build it and the House budgeting $2.5 million to merely plan it (Durhams, 2003c). The two chambers could not agree: the Senate pushed for full funding, which lead to the House voting against all funding (Hunter, 2003).

In 2004, however, the legislature eventually agreed to build the UNC cancer center they had considered in the 2003 session and another $60 million cardiovascular center at East Carolina University (Rawlins and Bonner, 2004). The two facilities, both of which had been previously proposed, were part of a $463 million spending plan, which exceeded the $310 million debt cap that Easley had stated was his limit (Rawlins, 2004a). Ultimately, Easily relented, signing the bill and visiting the sites of the newly funded centers (Gardner et al., 2004).

Hospital budgeting discussions during both periods (2002–2004 & 2008–2010) considered the possible closing of Dorothea Dix psychiatric hospital. A 2001 Senate bill set a date for closure, but, after protests by advocates for the mentally ill, the final budget included no closure date (Damico, 2001; Rawlins, 2001; Robertson, 2001). In 2002, Department of Health and Human Services officials announced their intention to close Dorothea Dix and Umstead mental hospitals and replace them with a new hospital that would require about half the number of employees (Assis and Graybeal, 2002). Opposition came from hospital workers and supportive unions, as well as county officials who wanted to retain the economic presence of the hospitals in their districts (Lewis, 2002a,b; The News & Observer Editorial Board, 2002). Though an alternative site for displaced Dix and Umstead patients was selected and the process of transferring patients out of Dix and Umstead begun, the legislature failed to fund the construction of a new mental hospital (Lewis, 2002c). Finally, in 2003, the legislature voted to fund the new psychiatric hospital (Jacobs, 2003).

North Carolina Hospital Spending 2008–2010 In 2001, North Carolina lawmakers passed a program that attempted to deinstitutionalize the mentally ill by integrating them into local communities. By 2008, it was clear that the plan had failed. The system had become privatized by wasteful companies (Stith and Raynor, 2008). The deinstitutionalization process was eventually opposed by mental health advocates, like members of the state National Alliance on Mental Illness (NAMI), the NC Psychiatric Association, and the Mental Health Association (Alexander, 2008; The News & Observer, 2008). Easley also spoke out against the failed deinstitutionalization, blaming the legislature (The News & Observer Editorial Board, 2008). Easley's budget that year included $65 million for mental health, which included money for hiring at mental hospitals, and opening an overflow unit at Dorothea Dix mental hospital, which had still not been closed (NBC17 Staff, 2008). The president of the N.C. Psychiatric Association called it "a good-faith effort to improve things," while the head of the Public Service Workers Union wanted pay raises included as well (Bonner, 2008). Outside DHHS office in Raleigh, nurses also held weekly protests against the closing of Dix hospital (Biesecker, 2008). While the Senate budget included Easely's recommended mental health funding, the final budget included only $21 million for the Division of Mental Health (Wilmington StarNews, 2008). Part of those funds went to Dix to fund the overflow unit.

Bev Perdue's first budget focused on cutting the budget wherever possible, and Dix might have been seen as an extra expense the state could do without. While, Perdue included $6 million in DHHS recommended cuts (Niolet and Christensen, 2009b) from mental hospitals in her own budget, she also added $3 million for beds at Dix hospital and $12 million to pay for beds at local hospitals for mental health patients (Bonner, 2009b; Office of the Governor, 2009). The state NAMI praised the budget for avoiding deep cuts during the middle of the recession (Bonner, 2009b). Perhaps this was due in part to increased media attention on the poor state of mental health care in North Carolina. Previous years' cuts to hospital beds were critiqued by such different groups as NAMI, NC Policy Watch, and the John Locke Foundation (Calhoun, 2009; Fitzsimon, 2009; Hood, 2009). An investigation by Disability Rights North Carolina exposed reports of mentally ill patients forced to wait days in the ER before securing a room in a psychiatric facility (Ahearn, 2009). Despite this appropriation, there was little to no coverage of the mental hospital budget while the legislature was debating it. The final 2009 budget included $12.9 million in staff cuts at state mental hospitals, but included Perdue's $12 million for mental health beds at local hospitals and a $6 million one-time appropriation to keep Dix open for the year (Biesecker, 2009a,b; Bonner, 2009a).

In 2010, a number of interests including state and local chapters of NAMI, local law enforcement, and NC Mental Hope remained vocal about the need for more beds in the state's mental health system (Bethea, 2010; Cornwell, 2010; McBrayer, 2010). Perdue's budget included another $12 million for 50 local psychiatric beds (Niolet et al., 2010a). Additional bills appeared in the legislature to add between $10 million and $32 million for local hospital beds; in the end, the final budget settled on $29 million (Alexander, 2010; Brock, 2010a).

The year 2010 also saw the culmination of the fight over closing Dix hospital. The state budget included no funding for the hospital, which prompted a letter of protest signed by Wake County NAMI and the Public Service Workers Union (Biesecker, 2010c; Brock, 2010c). According to Perdue, the state's fiscal situation required the hospital to close (Rocky Mount Telegram, 2010). Wake County NAMI was extremely active in the movement to save the hospital, giving a presentation to the legislature, commenting in news stories, and planning rallies (Brock, 2010b; Charlotte Observer Editorial Staff, 2010; Rocky Mount Telegram, 2010). The hospital's closure was also publicly opposed by some doctors, lawmakers, and the state NAACP (Biesecker, 2010d; The News & Observer, 2010). Ultimately, the funding that was removed from the budget stayed out and Dix was forced to close, saving the state $30 million in annual operating costs (Biesecker, 2010a). Despite this closure, hospital spending in North Carolina remained relatively steady–in part because the Dix hospital closure (similar the corrections budget in North Carolina) was counterbalanced by increased spending in other parts of the hospital space. North Carolinian governors' repeated attempts to close Dix were met by repeated counter-mobilizations of interest groups that delayed the closure long enough to increased funding to other areas of the hospitals budget.

6.7.3 Welfare in North Carolina

While it is likely that neither Easley or Perdue intended to build legacies on closing prisons and state mental health facilities, in welfare politics both governors had specific, very public, policy agendas. Here, too, though, governors manifest more as partners in a negotiation engaging in more explicit trade-offs with legislators and interest groups. Despite the churn of interest groups and the vast sums of money at stake in welfare politics, this deadlock category exhibits a similar level of stability as the much smaller corrections category – vastly different interest group concentrations produce a similar outcome. The pattern of negotiation is perhaps most prominently displayed in the effort to create the "More at Four" program.

North Carolina Welfare Spending 2002–2004 In 2001, Governor Easley began his efforts to implement "More at Four," a free preschool program that became one of his signature issues. His budget recommended $40 million a year for two years to begin the program, funded in part by cutting $23.5 million from Smart Start, a public-private subsidized daycare program (Gardner and Rawlins, 2001). The North Carolina Partnership for Children and its local chapters, who administered Smart Start across the state, expressed support for More at Four, as long as it did not affect Smart Start (Gardner, 2001e; Mooneyham, 2001b). Also expressing support for Smart Start were the Covenant with North Carolina's Children, the North Carolina Child Advocacy Institute, and the N.C. Budget and Tax Center (Gardner, 2001d,f; Johnson, 2001a). In fact, when Easley gave a talk to Covenant with North Carolina's Children early in the budget season, they gifted him with a small glass piggy bank meant to remind him of the need to fund the program (Gardner et al., 2001).

As the budget moved into the legislature, proposed cuts to Smart Start grew to between $30 and $40 million (Gardner, 2001c; Johnson, 2001c). Easley reaffirmed his support for the program, and legislators claimed to be inundated with calls and emails opposing the cuts (Bonner and Christensen, 2001; Dyer, 2001; Gardner, 2001b). The John Locke Foundation supported cuts to Smart

Start to save money by targeting children who needed it most (Hood, 2001). As possible cuts to Smart Start grew to $58 million in the proposed House budget, Smart Start advocates held a rally at the legislature and delivered a petition with over 3,000 signatures (Jarvis, 2001; Rice, 2001a). Perhaps the outcry worked, as the final budget reduced Smart Start cuts to $10 million, and gave $6.5 million to More at Four (Johnson, 2001b).

In anticipation of more Smart Start cuts in 2002, the North Carolina Partnership for Children, along with the Child Care Services Association released a study showing the program's benefits (Wilson, 2002). Their fears were confirmed when the agency responsible for the program presented a possible cut of $15 million to Easley (Rawlins and Gardner, 2002a). County partnerships wrote op-eds opposed to the cuts, while the John Locke Foundation and the anti-tax Citizens for a Sound Economy expressed support for cuts at a public event (Bryan, 2002; Howard, 2002; Leskanic, 2002). Easley's budget recommended $17 million in cuts to Smart Start (Gardner and Simmons, 2002). The state and local partnerships, the Covenant, Common Sense Foundation, and daycare workers all opposed the cuts. Multiple interest groups held rallies, a children's author spoke on the Senate floor, and one local partnership even sent 18 kids enrolled in Smart Start to the state capitol to lobby (Offen, 2002; Rawlins and Gardner, 2002b; The Fayetteville Observer, 2002; The Observer Editorial Board, 2002; Wheless, 2002). That same day, Citizens for a Sound Economy rallied at the capitol to advocate cuts in state programs (Mooneyham, 2002b). The legislature followed with a proposal to cut $10 million more than Easley did from Smart Start (Rawlins et al., 2002). Easley's aides convinced the Senate to drop a $1.1 million cut to More at Four, but the Smart Start cut remained intact (Dyer, 2002b). The John Locke Foundation endorsed the legislature's cuts in an op-ed (Franklin, 2002). After drawn-out budget negotiations, the Smart Start cuts totaled $ 20 million, while funding for More at Four grew by $28 million (Rawlins, 2002).

Easley's 2003 offered a continuation of the funding trade-off from Smart Start – cutting $7.7 million – to More at Four – adding $8.6 million (Woolverton, 2003). More at Four had become a "nonnegotiable" priority for Easley (at least in the sense that it would receive some funds, even of those came at the expense of other programs via negotiation) (Gardner, 2003), while Smart Start, was attacked by Republican lawmakers and the John Locke Foundation for its reported inefficiency (Gardner, 2003; The Charlotte Observer Editorial Board, 2003). The cuts to Smart Start worried the Partnership for Children and former governor Jim Hunt, who had made Smart Start his marquee program (Gardner, 2003; Wilson, 2003c). Hunt lobbied lawmakers and contacted newspapers to oppose the Smart Start cuts. The House proposed a $9 million decrease, while the Senate stayed closer to Easley's recommendation with a $7.3 million cut (Gardner and Barrett, 2003; Wilson, 2003a). The Senate version found support from the Partnership for Children, who brought hundreds of children to rally at the capitol in support of Smart Start

(Gardner and Barrett, 2003) and the return of four-year-olds lobbying their representatives to prevent cuts (Abbott, 2003). While the legislature debated, Easley was focused on doubling the number of children in More at Four; he became very involved in the budget process with a hope of increased funding (Kane and Bonner, 2003b; Wilson, 2003b). The final budget included Easley's exact recommended amounts: $8.6 million for More at Four and $7.7 million cut from Smart Start (Dyer, 2003; Kane, 2003a).

Easley's efforts to fund More at Four could largely be viewed as a success after three years of budget negotiations across multiple interest groups creating clear winners and losers (at least in terms of the budget). By 2004 the program had begun to receive negative audits which made legislators more hesitant to fund the governor's full recommendation – $9 million more in 2004 – than in years past (Kane, 2004c; Kane and Stancill, 2004). As negotiations continued, the House agreed with Easley's funding proposal, while the Senate wanted to cut the growth in half (Bonner, 2004; Kane, 2004a). The final budget fully funded More at Four at Easley's recommended level (Rawlins, 2004b). For the first time in his efforts to pay for the More at Four program, Easley also recommended retaining Smart Start funding at the same level as 2003. Pro-Smart Start organizations, such as the North Carolina Partnership for Children, advocated for an extra $17 million to claw back some of the losses the program had seen at the expense of the expansion of More at Four (Martinez, 2004). Despite these efforts, no additional Smart Start funding was included in the 2004 budget (Crawford, 2004).

The budgeting period between 2001 and 2004 in North Carolina was characterized by generally increasing revenues, but the same could not be said for the other two states we examine during this time period – Vermont and West Virginia. While governors Dean (D-VT), Douglas (R-VT), and Wise (R-WV) looked for ways to distribute cuts to social welfare programs (at least as a share of the budget), Easley pursued an expansion of programs related to children. But, to do so, he had to make cuts to other programs – notably Smart Start – that were already devoted to child welfare. Like the institutionally weaker governors of Vermont, Easley had more limited powers to influence spending in the welfare budget without making major concessions. Wise, too, faced interest group opposition, but was able to get the budget outcomes he wanted. In the second period of our North Carolina analysis (2008–2010), Easley and Purdue found themselves dealing with a similar issue–this time, children's health–in a much less certain fiscal environment.

North Carolina Welfare Spending 2008–2010 After years of economic good times with no real sense of the financial catastrophe that would engulf the country looming, Governor Easley proudly announced that his 2008 budget would include $10.4 million for North Carolina Health Choice (NCHC), which administered the state's Children's Health Insurance Program (CHIP) (Kane, 2008b). The expansion, enabled by federal matching funds, would have allowed over 10,000 new children to be enrolled in the program. Easley's budget received a warm reception by Action for Children North Carolina (Niolet, 2008). While the House funded Health Choice to Easley's recommendation, the Senate planned to freeze the program until 2009 (Kane, 2008e). The senior vice president at Action for Children called the Senate's decision "cruel to children" (Kane, 2008e). In general, Health Choice had low media presence and was quietly reconciled in the joint budget, which provided funding to add 7,300 new children to the program (Dickson, 2008).

The financial picture for North Carolina darkened in 2009 and, thus, it appeared that large cuts to social welfare programs for all ages were imminent – including the NCHC. The state chapter of the National Association of Social Workers' fears of NCHC cuts were realized when the House announced that the program, including CHIP, would not receive inflationary increases (Observer, 2009; Reese, 2009). The House eventually proposed a new budget to raise taxes and allow Health Choice to expand by $17 million (Niolet, 2009). The funding made it into the final budget without significant debate, which could be seen as a victory of sorts were it not for the significantly increased demand for child health services that resulted from the Great Recession.

An Action for Children North Carolina (a nonprofit advocacy organization) op-ed from early 2010 praised the recent expansions of Health Choice, but expressed disappointment with the number of children who were still uninsured (Ableidinger, 2010). They wanted to resurrect NCHC's Kid's Care, a program that would expand eligibility to families whose income was greater than the cutoff NCHC. The program had been passed in 2007, but no progress had been made toward implementation. As part of her campaign to become governor, Perdue supported implementing Kid's Care and expanding NCHC outreach (Niolet, 2010c). In a turn of events, once in office, she claimed she could not implement Kid's Care given the state of the economy (Niolet, 2010c). Perdue's budget included $8.5 million in funding to add 10,000 more children to Health Choice, while cutting inflationary increases (Niolet et al., 2010a). Later in the budget season, a member of North Carolina chapter of MomsRising asked the legislature in an op-ed to fully fund Health Choice to cover the 100,000 uninsured but eligible children in the state (Messersmith, 2010). The legislature, however, chose to give an additional $6 million to Health Choice in the 2010 appropriations bill, a decision that failed to attract much media coverage.

Welfare in North Carolina, our deadlock category, exhibited greater stability than even the corrections, our capture case – this despite significant intra-categorical trade-offs. The state budget funded More at Four while cutting Smart Start every year from 2001 to 2003, creating limited but consistent growth. Despite budgetary uncertainty, Health Choice also grew consistently in the time period studied. With children's groups supporting welfare growth and fiscal conservatives opposing it, any action on the welfare budget was controversial and high profile. Its incremental growth contrasts with Paterson's more punctuated story in New York where the institutionally stronger governor made a significant commitment to increasing welfare and then was unsuccessful because of interest group opposition to make it smaller.

6.7.4 Conclusions about North Carolina

The contexts in which Easley and Perdue found themselves as governors varied significantly. At the turn of the century, North Carolina was in good financial shape and the budgetary landscape presented options to policymakers to expand existing programs or create new ones. By the time Governor Perdue took office, the economy was in free fall and policymakers were looking for any ways to cut – not just trim – the budget. Governors bring their preferences to each scenario, such as Easley's desire to create a new (or perhaps, different) pre-K program and Perdue's desire to expand health care for children. However, their ability to see changes manifest is influenced by their relative institutional power and the options interest groups present them.

What we see in the North Carolina budget stories are governors that are engaging in years-long drawn-out negotiations over changes to programs, financial shifts within categories, and trade-offs that are responsive to interest group mobilization. Corrections, welfare, and even hospitals budget categories, in general, see much steadier outputs when compared with other states that have stronger governors (e.g., WV and NY) – in times of affluence and penury. Perhaps the best example of this is the decade-long effort to close Dorothea Dix mental hospital. Facility closure of any kind would offer an opportunity to move a large amount of funds to other within-category programs or across categories. The slow process involved steadily shifting resources over time to other facilities so that, by the time Dix did eventually close, the shock was minimized.

The More at Four program offers a similar trajectory. Easley opened negotiations in year one with a large increase for his new pre-K initiative and a large cut for Smart Start (a mature program); after interest group pressure, the trade-off was chipped away in a process that repeated over years. During this time the politics of More at Four itself matured from a novel program to a program with a mixed record, which lead to less enthusiasm for the revenue shift from Smart Start. Like with Dix, the result was a more attenuated budgeting process over the long-term, as we would expect. It is possible that a stronger governor with more formal control over the budgetary agenda or line-item veto strength may have closed Dix sooner or started More at Four with greater haste, but governors of North Carolina are less able to make these massive changes.

6.8 DRAWING LESSONS FROM THE CASES

The case studies we investigate provide a richer context for the theory that we advance in Chapter 2 and the empirical analysis we engage in Chapters 3–5. Specifically, the analysis in this chapter suggests a pattern of relationships between governors and interest groups that largely affirm the theoretical claims we make throughout this book. Overall, we find support for the underlying political contexts created by the interest group dynamics we hypothesize: Interest groups are more consistently present and focused in the capture and deadlock cases than in the instability case. While differing in scope (e.g., prisons are a much smaller category than welfare), these categories have relatively predictable players. The hospitals category finds some players (such as individual hospitals, university hospitals, and associations of clinics) who do not have the benefit of a similarly organized labor force across facilities (as in prisons), who have a highly variable constituency (people who go to hospitals), and find other larger groups who occasionally intervene in related policy of which hospitals are but one part (as in Medicaid).

Despite large variations in prison populations and the politics of criminal justice, the interest group dynamic in this area across these states is similar. In all states, prison guards and prison towns are pitted against governors who want to save money in the budget: concentrated interests attempt to maintain their share of the budget in the face of governors who attempt to reduce costs.[6] These contests are ultimately decided by compromise, where closures are typically offset by the opening of new facilities, such as was the case in North Carolinian prisons in 2002 and 2003. In cases of prison openings and closings, the governor does not really move the needle much on categorical spending (good for existing groups) to claim credit for affecting policy change in corrections (good for the governor). Even still, credit claiming is perhaps not as critical an issue for governors given that most prison closure issues are not highly salient to the state at large, but are more in line with traditional distributive politics. Interest groups and individual members of the legislature from prison districts tend to fight for resources in ways that are similar to Gamm and Kousser's (2010) findings regarding other distributive politics in states.

On the other side of the distribution of interest group attention, debates over welfare spending draw the governor into political conflict. This political conflict occurs in both good times and in bad, and in small and large states. The governor must address these issues not only as the CFO of the state given welfare's share of the budget, but also as a policy leader. Despite the number of very interested groups, powerful and weak governors result in relatively stable policy outputs. For example, West Virginia Governor Wise's efforts to fundamentally change the structure of welfare policy resulted in the governor expending great effort to change the existing structure of welfare service delivery (placing the DHHR with the Cabinet to reduce its independence), even though his plans never came to fruition. In all cases, we find that interest groups dominate the structure of the welfare policy debate; governors must

---

[6] There is some cognitive dissonance here given that, in many cases, governors often advocate for policies that increase the supply of prisoners for facilities that they struggle to pay for.

tangle with these groups, but often on terms that are set by previous policy commitments which interest groups have risen to defend. Paterson's attempt to reduced promised increases to welfare illustrate this dynamic: even in a time of severe budgetary crisis, the institutionally strong governor was unable to reduce welfare expenditures due to opposition from well-organized groups. Paterson's power as governor also results in a punctuated output: He made a large change to a budget category in line with opportunities given to him by interest groups, but interest group power prevents him from using his power to attenuate spending.

In the middle of the distribution, instability categories show issues that rise and fall with some regularity. Here, governors are able to intervene more freely and interest group competition is variable by issue. In the New York hospitals case, some groups advocated indirectly for hospitals' interests – such as the Healthcare Association of New York State (HANYS) – through Medicaid reimbursement rates. In addition, hospital networks acted as individuals in advocating for direct needs – such as the Greater New York Hospital Association. This interest group dynamic includes groups that are powerful but not entirely focused on the issue, as well as lesser-known groups advocating for group interests in a field where individual hospitals are often in danger of closure or could benefit from renovation. The political environment is structured such that governors have opportunities to occasionally close some hospitals or build new ones. This process is particularly pronounced in smaller states (Vermont and West Virginia), where university hospitals are a large portion of the hospitals budget (Fletcher Allen in Vermont and West Virginia University). In Vermont, for example, the structure of interest group competition provided the opportunity for Governor Dean to intervene in the Fletcher Allen scandal. Though Dean's institutional weakness prevented him from ultimately achieving the cuts he wanted, governors need not be successful to be coaxed into attempts to remake policy in the instability category.

The legislature is a key player in these discussions, though not one of our explicit focus. Legislative approval is needed for all budgets, and legislators respond to interest groups, just as governors do. Importantly, the role of legislatures is varied across state institutional contexts. Our cases find legislatures as having particular influences over budgeting processes where governors are weaker. The interaction between the governor and legislature on issues (such as corrections, hospitals, and welfare) varies by institutional strength – in weak governor cases, the legislature is more likely to resist the governor in all types of policy. Take North Carolina's prison debate: Governor Easley initially planned prison closures, but the legislature went further in asking for more.

Throughout these four states, interest groups were incredibly active in specific cases within specific categories. From attempts to close county jails in Vermont, to welfare cuts in West Virginia, to welfare increases in New York, and to the long saga of the Dorothy Dix hospital in North Carolina, our cases show governors are motivated to address budgets holistically and policy issues individually. Interest groups are active in lobbying the budgeting process, and directly active in lobbying the governor. Examples abound from our cases. The town of Springfield, Vermont, sent a letter and a lobbyist to the governor on jail closures; the Governor Wise organized with hospital groups to influence the legislature in West Virginia; Covenant with North Carolina's Children presented Governor Easley with a glass piggy bank; Governor Paterson even challenged the Greater New York Hospital Association to a debate! This kind of executive lobbying demonstrates the power of interest groups to provide the policymaking environment for governors to shape budgets using the means provided by their institutional powers.

The dynamic between the political opportunities interest groups provide and the institutional means that governors have to act on these opportunities is manifest in our cases and has consequences for the distributional patterns of expenditures as well as the long-term growth of budget categories. Vermonter and North Carolinian governors are important players in budget negotiations, to be sure, but they ultimately have to compromise with legislatures. Interest groups, thus, are less reliant upon governors to get their way, which reduces the opportunity structure for governors to intervene. The result is that weaker governors can still make big proposals (e.g., "More at Four" in NC or major Medicaid cuts in VT), but these proposals are less likely to be major shifts in spending. Stronger governors are better able to get what they want from legislatures, which increases opportunities for them to intervene in the budgeting process, given the need for interest groups to lobby them more directly. West Virginian and New Yorker governors have more meaningful, direct interactions with interest groups and can make larger annual changes in budgets if they so desire.

We articulate the consequence of this interaction in Chapter 3: steadier budget changes in states with weaker governors and greater long-term growth in budgets. Beyond these empirical findings, our cases describe a fundamental trade-off in governing philosophies manifest in state-level institutional design between responsiveness and stability. Strong governors can react quickly and sharply, but in so doing can over-correct. Weak governors may shift the budget more moderately through compromise, but their decisions can be viewed as part of a long-term series rather than a reification of a reaction to a particular event.

PART III

PUBLIC POLICY AND BUDGETING IN THE AMERICAN STATES

7

Conclusion

Public Government of Public Monies

Budgets can be times of political thanksgiving for organized interests, where groups stake claims to their traditional pieces of the budget pie. Government delivers pieces of the pie to its citizens, but chooses the size and recipients based on preexisting political arrangements. Some groups are accustomed to the same sliver they largely eat themselves, while others are used to a large piece they have to share, and still others are uncertain what they will receive from year to year. Hence, the politics of budgeting is about the politics within and across policy domains. These policy domains are related to particular issues and serve distinct groups in society. Budget functions are the manifestations of public policy and the location of political conflict.

In this book, we examined annual budget battles knowing that it matters where, by whom, and how fights over the distribution of individual pieces of the budget pie transpire to understand spending of public monies overall. Our inquiry addresses fundamental questions about the relationship between interests, institutions, and public policy. To what extent are interest groups able to influence public policy? Is government – particularly a governor – serving these interest groups? How do governors get the policies they want?

This final chapter considers the broader implications of our argument about politics and policy. We develop policy recommendations about how governments might spend their monies more efficiently and how institutional designs might support the public in achieving that goal. Finally, we place the book's argument in the context of American governance to address two questions: What is the role of the federal government in state spending? Does federal budgeting also follow our logic and, if so, how can American presidents influence spending? Before we can answer these questions, we first synthesize our theoretical and empirical findings.

7.1 HOW PUBLIC GOVERNMENTS SPEND PUBLIC MONEY

In Chapter 3, we delve into how states spend their monies empirically. Equipped by punctuated equilibrium theory's expectations about rapid policy change, we amass budget data from all fifty states from 1984 to 2010. The data split each of these 1,350 budgets into 10 budget functions, ranging from social welfare and education to spending on corrections and the environment. These 13,000 observations tell us four stories. First, state budgets are punctuated. In a typical state budget, most functions change very little. When a change in a particular domain occurs, it is massive. For every year in our data, at least one state changes a particular budget function by at least 30 percent. Large shifts in budget fortunes are real and consequential. The general empirical law of budgeting (Jones et al., 2009) also applies to the American states. Apolitical updating based on incremental decision-making does not happen. Not in Albany, Annapolis, or Atlanta. Not in Tallahassee, Topeka, or Trenton.

Second, punctuated budgets exist regardless of the particular political and institutional environment of any given state. While all states manifest punctuated budgets, not all budget functions are affected equally. Spending on welfare, education, and highways lack the frequent and massive budget changes that occur regularly in the domains of hospitals, parks, and government. Punctuations in spending on health, police, and corrections lie somewhere in the middle. By the same token, differences at the functional level, and not at the state level, alter budgetary growth over time. These descriptive insights are a simple first indication that massive changes in budgets and their long-term consequences must have something to do with how politics plays out in particular policy domains.

Third, spending in the American states has increased substantively over long periods of time. Over the twenty-six years we examine, the average budget item is more than tripled. Yet, individual fortunes fluctuate considerably around these averages and display different growth trajectories. Punctuated budget items grow more slowly in the long run compared to those that display more smooth adjustments. In other words, sudden overreactions to previous underadjustments in a budget item are not enough to catch up to spending in more incremental domains. This empirical regularity signifies the two motives for policy change: large short-term transformations or incremental long-term gains.

The final empirical takeaway from our budget data exploration is that the degree of punctuation clusters together with a budget's long-term development. Spending on items, such as hospitals and government affairs, can be described as low growth–high punctuation. Welfare and health spending predominately evolves incrementally with substantial long-term changes. Finally, spending on highways, natural resources, and police exhibit low long-term growth and rather incremental year-on-year changes. The various empirical findings raise questions about how contestation and competition occur for individual budget functions. How are these constituencies organized to ensure a small but steady increase in funds? How does politics play out in domains where budgets fluctuate, and occasionally dramatic changes transpire? Which political processes can influence budget change, and in what ways? Finally, what is the role of state government – especially governors responsible for submitting a whole budget – in these variegated fortunes across policy domains?

7.2 THERE AND BACK AGAIN: OUR BUDGET STORY

We have stylized policymaking as similar to establishing guilt in a criminal proceeding: a function of means, motive, and opportunity. Existing literature on state politics does consider the means (power of governors and legislatures) and the establishment of motive (variation in constituent demands based on state and district characteristics) but tends to overlook opportunity. Conversely, the policy process literature suggests that means and motive are secondary to the political opportunities presented to policymakers. Understanding the emergence of political opportunities is tantamount to understanding policy change. Against conventional wisdom, our findings in Chapter 3 lay the foundation for an approach that considers differences in institutional strength as one feature of budget analysis, but one that must consider the political dynamics of issues. With their narrow focus on specific budget items, interest group politics are budget function politics. Thus, in a world where the functional level of budgets serves as the stage for political theater, interest groups are the political actors. We argue and find that group contestation shapes the political environment that affects how states spend money in particular issue areas. By itself, this finding is not particularly interesting – interest groups affect public policy; otherwise, why are they there? But our analysis reveals a curvilinear relationship between interest group concentration and volatility in budgeting and policymaking. We show that spending items are affected by interest group concentration, but certain interest group constellations make some policy domains more volatile than others.

Budgets are bundles of policy domains. While interest groups are useful in understanding individual functional behavior, the governor is responsible for budgeting the whole. Means, motives, and opportunities emerge out of the engagement of interest groups with governors in the annual budget process. The interest group environment creates distinct choice opportunities for governors: (1) *capture* in which an interest group dominates in a policy domain; (2) *deadlock* in which many powerful groups offer consistent competition over policy outputs; and (3) *instability* in which interest group competition is transient. While the political environments for capture and deadlock are distinct, the outcomes are similar. Governors are able to assess the rewards for following a small, exclusive group of interests (capture) or choosing a side in a major battle (deadlock). However, governors struggle with an instability scenario because it is challenging to identify relevant interest groups and resulting payoffs. Every year, governors seek out opportunities and then make budget choices based on their assessment of these three budget environments. The interaction of these two entities – governors and interest groups – produces a particular political dynamic that explains the change, volatility, and long-term growth of a budget.

Governors' ability, their means, to influence spending comes in the form of topping-off budget categories. In this way, they contribute to more volatile or punctuated patterns insofar as they top off a punctuating category. Governors are not the primary source of categorical budget punctuations, but they can make a category *more* punctuated if they are institutionally powerful. Similarly, governors may make a budget punctuated by bottoming-out cuts (i.e., making cuts deeper) that emerge through interest group policymaking, though this relationship is less apparent than topping-off (i.e., making increases larger). The converse is, in terms of executive power, not true. Weak governors are associated with neither extreme cuts nor extreme increases, but rather with a moderating effect on a budget. Our cases in Chapter 6 illustrate this claim: Institutionally weak, yet popular governors of Vermont were less able to wring concessions from their legislatures than the institutionally strong, yet scandal-laden, governor of West Virginia. Institutionally weak governors of North Carolina pursued a consensus-oriented budget strategy, while the strong, abruptly installed, governor of New York engaged in more unitary budget-making.

These counterintuitive findings suggest an important symbiotic relationship between interest groups and executives. The literature on executives, particularly state executives, suggests that strong governors also ought to be responsible for making tough decisions during budgetary crises. Strong governors do employ institutional tools at their disposal, but also have a stronger tendency to encourage the profligate fiscal behavior of particular interest groups. In this way, executives are *part* of the cascade of attention associated with issue expansion, but we show that executives – even strong ones – are less likely to mobilize and more likely to be mobilized.

Interest groups influence policy punctuations in three ways. First, groups may expand conflict beyond the capture scenario, or rival groups in the deadlock scenario might become weakened. In each case, the dominant pattern of interest group interaction is significantly changed, and the interaction moves to a instability scenario in which, for a time, the interest group environment attempts to return to equilibrium. However, some interest group environments remain in the instability scenario – a volatile equilibrium in which rents associated with a policy are insufficiently strong to attract a consistent range of groups and where attention is sufficiently ephemeral to disallow for group conflict equilibria to form. In the long run, policy domains associated with instable interest group environments end up in budgetary purgatory (and hope to move into limbo).

Second, in pursuing their own goals, groups affect the capacity of other groups to garner policymaker attention: Groups indirectly influence other groups such that cascades of mobilization in one sphere may absorb available agenda spaces for others. Even marginal increases in attention to policy domains with numerous groups can have significant consequences for less-populated domains. Groups in capture domains, specifically dominant groups, exist in niches that depend upon a low level of attention in any case. These groups consistently receive their policy gains because they remain largely unnoticed by the broader policymaking community – thus, the more attention other groups get, the better. Groups in unstable domains are most dependent upon shifts in attention for shifts in budget categories; yet, this curses groups in constant volatility to ride the waves of attention that spill over from deadlock domain groups in years where attention is stable or low to deadlock issues. This movement is rare, by definition, since deadlock domains are defined by sustained attention resulting from consistent political conflict.

Third, patterns of interaction between interest groups influence the attractiveness of a policy domain for executive intervention. Weak governors ride waves of attention spreading through communities of interest; in some ways, this produces a less-punctuated budget than strong governors who add to large positive changes or cut negative changes further. There is a certain irony in the finding that weak governors are most likely to be faithful to their charge of producing a stable, fiscally sound budget.

7.3 IMPLICATIONS

Our theory draws on three vast and important literatures in political science – policy process theory, interest groups, and executive politics, and we empirically tested this theory in the context of two other vast and important literatures – state politics and the politics of public budgeting. We distill three implications from our theoretical argument in this empirical context and offer two insights for public policy. We begin with our theoretical implications. First, our theory brings interest groups back into the spotlight of policy process theory, particularly punctuated equilibrium theory. Second, our work speaks to the decades-long somewhat ironic shift in fiscal federalism in which states have more autonomy over federal dollars, but political discourse is more nationalized. Third, our work offers insight into and raises future research questions about the role of the executive in the budget process, specifically regarding comparisons between governors and presidents.

7.3.1 Policy Process Theory

The primary policy process theory on which we draw borrows a metaphor from the biological sciences: punctuated equilibrium theory (Prindle, 2012). Physics (via poet Allen Ginsberg) offers another metaphor for understanding the challenges political systems face in addressing the deluge of problems at any given moment: three laws of thermodynamics. First, "You can't win." Institutions have a finite capacity to deal with finite + X issues; thus, institutions will always be challenged to keep up with information processing demands. Second, "You can't break even." Institutions cannot reproduce the actual distribution of preferences that exist in the mass public; thus, a growing asymmetry always exists between existing policy outputs and mass preferences. Third, "You can't get out of the game." Institutions are hard to change, and even if they do change, they will still suffer from problems in the first and second "laws." Therefore, even if institutions do change, the political dynamics of information flows and asymmetric problem definitions will persist.

Our findings regarding the volatility of policy across interest group concentrations are suggestive of the dynamics of issue expansion as manifest by interest groups. We show that captured policy domains maintain stability through little interest group competition, deadlocked categories maintain stability through high competition, and the instable groups struggle with the right mix of groups to either capture or compete to produce consistent policy outputs. In addition to identifying the influence of interest group competition in structuring gubernatorial influence in budgeting, our findings also reveal how issue expansion or contraction can affect the number of groups that attempt to influence the policy process. One reason why domains beset with instable interest group competition are the place where budget volatility occurs could be that such domains represent transition phases between capture and deadlock for particular issues. The data suggest that these transition phases can take a long while, especially since we measure the concentration of groups as a relative concept within states. However, it is not unreasonable to suggest that captured categories undergoing a period of issue expansion shift to instability categories, that is, that the ephemeral nature of interest group competition in instability categories may conform to Baumgartner and Jones' (1993) discussion of issue mobilization. Further, we could envision deadlocked categories as experiencing major change when some of the dominant groups fade in influence – even if briefly so – thus creating instability-like conditions.

Though we may have implied that our stylized types of interest group competition are fairly static, we can also see the transition from capture to instability and back again to capture as a classic example of positive and negative feedback. This possibility does not imply the absence of categories for which consistent mobilization is challenging, but rather that our model's results speak to the mechanisms of mobilization in theories of agenda-setting. During transition phases, policy monopolies are forced to compete with alternative problem definitions, meaning that governors have a rare opportunity to engage in policy choices that differ from year to year. Once a problem definition is settled upon – via monopoly or competition – the certainty of gains and losses from attempting to change the status quo becomes clearer for governors, thereby reinforcing long-term equilibrium.

7.3.2 Federalism

State governments receive a significant amount of their funding and funding priorities from the federal government in the form of intergovernmental transfers. The federal government both enables and depends on states to pro-vide government services reflected in the budget priorities of a state. Thus, federal policy and federal politics can have a significant effect on state budgets. As federal budgets are volatile and punctuated, so might be the trickle-down effect to state governments.

Indeed, the Republican Party has been lauded for playing the "long game" in American politics by starting with flipping statehouses and governor's man-sions from a long period of Democratic control. The more visible end of the long game is a redistricting strategy that creates favorable House districts and a deep bench of statewide candidates who can move from state government to the Senate. The Republican long-game strategy is more than just an effort to place Republicans in positions of power at the federal level, but is also designed to fundamentally alter the size of government and the direction of governmen-tal priorities at the state level. A starting point for this strategy was to cut government spending by issuing tax cuts, thereby leveraging state-balanced budget requirements to produce cuts in government services.

Welfare reform demonstrates this ploy: a dramatic shift in the share of state expenditures from multiple categories to compensate for a growing share of welfare costs borne by the state. The share of welfare costs is concomitant with an increase in welfare expenditure – this is the entire point of welfare reform. Shifts in the budget (see Chapter 3) reflect losses in share of parks funding, natural resources, administrative costs of government, and even education to compensate for the gains in welfare.

While federal policies and politics can exacerbate changes within state budgets, they can also intervene to prevent significant downturns. A per-haps obvious example of the federal government intervening in state budgets to prevent bottoming-out is the 2009 American Recovery and Reinvestment Act (ARRA), more commonly known as the stimulus package. Most read-ers will recall that the ARRA was a massive expenditure package that used the deficit spending ability of the federal government to, among many other things, enable states to balance their budgets without rendering government services obsolete through the $48.6 billion State Fiscal Stabilization Fund. More monies came to states in the form of COVID aid from the Coronavirus Aid, Relief, and Economic Security (CARES) Act and the American Rescue Plan (ARP). In contrast to the ARRA which was tightly negotiated under what some might call an arbitrary ceiling of $1 trillion for the entire stimulus bill, CARES and ARP combined to dole out half a trillion dollars to states – roughly ten times the amount distributed in the ARRA. Our empirical findings from Chapter 5 show that, in general, federal funds to states have a moderating effect on state budgets: Federal expenditures to states reduce the magnitude of large cuts to state budgets.

Our argument contributes to the scholarship on fiscal federalism and offers implications for understanding the future of the politics of state spending. As the federal government continues to give states more discretion over federal programmatic expenditures with fewer resources, the battle over scarce resources will be fought by governors and interest groups. The changing financial mosaic of fiscal federalism may shift the resources available to interest groups, regardless of their efforts to lobby at the state level. It is challenging for us to predict the impact of changes in federal financial resources on the distribution of budget changes as a function of the governor–interest group interaction. On the one hand, changes in spending will increase the scarcity or abundance of resources, thereby influencing the number and specificity of competing groups in a state. Changing federal revenue streams might challenge the patterns of interaction between interest groups and governors, such as the transition of Medicaid to a block grant having a profound impact on interest group ecology at the state level. These changes might shift interest group dynamics between capture, instability, and deadlock. On the other hand, extant group dynamics might shape the method by which states spend federal dollars. That is, groups will still shape the opportunities for governors to change expenditures as a function of influxes of federal dollars. In this scenario, we expect group dynamics to mediate the impact of intergovernmental transfers rather than vice versa.

7.3.3 Presidents versus Governors

States are often considered laboratories of democracy; but there are certainly different budgeting rules and resources for the federal government compared to states. Presidents and governors have distinct – and by distinct, we mean different – roles in the budgeting process. Part of this division emerges because the American government can borrow (relatively) easily. The president finds themselves in a different position than state governors when proposing to spend public monies. Presidential budgets' aspirations can be limitless – they can include significant increases in expenditures on programs without including revenue sources for those expenditures. While presidents typically offer budgets paid for as the result of trade-offs for preferred cuts and increases, the sky is the limit for presidential budget aspirations (or, a more apt metaphor may be an ever-increasing ceiling).

Federal executives may have fewer fiscal constraints than executives at the state level, but the budgeting process favors state governors, who essentially write the budget story for the legislature. Presidential budgets are aspirational not only in terms of the seemingly limitless opportunities to spend money, but also in terms of their actual likelihood of adoption in a form that resembles these aspirations. Federal budgeting is as much a creature of Congress as it is the president.

The power differentials between presidents and governors manifest in particular interest group strategies to influence policy outcomes. Ultimately, governors have more control over the shape of budgets than presidents do; hence, lobbying is largely focused on Congress rather than presidents. Legislatures are certainly key players in state budgets, but governors are more directly engaged in budget battles than presidents if for no other reason than governors are responsible for ensuring that the budget not only is constructed but that the budget is within the bounds of incoming revenue.

The model's implications are that if presidents were given more power – such as the line-item veto – we should expect that federal budgets would be even more punctuated than they have been historically (Jones et al., 2003). On the one hand, the information processing literature tells us that the concentration of decision-making simply tightens a bottleneck and exacerbates the decision-making outcomes related to a serial information processing environment. We could theorize this implication without the empirical results we present in Chapters 3–6. However, the concentration of authority in the hands of the executive should encourage interest groups to shift their focus from the legislative branch (in this case, Congress) to the executive. The strengthened executive is also incentivized to attend to the interest group environment in identifying relevant opportunities to wield their advanced powers.

Our findings also have implications beyond gubernatorial strength. Future work in federal budgeting could examine the interest group environment of subsystems in Congress as a way to trace presidents' influence over the budgetary process. While the state budgeting process is distinct, the politics of avoiding captured or competitive subsystems is logical to any executive.

7.4 INSIGHTS FOR POLITICS AND POLICY

Throughout this book, we argue that budgets are not only important in and of themselves, but have broad implications for understanding public policy. Budgets also help determine the answers to fundamental questions of politics: Who gets what and why? Our analysis offers counterintuitive insights regarding the institutional structure to which states might aspire: increase interest group competition and weaken governors to produce more stable policy outcomes. The consequence of this stability is the long-term growth of a policy domain.

7.4.1 Shaping Interest Group Conflict

At first blush, the act of fostering interest group competition seems both challenging and perhaps out of bounds for democratic governments. After all, idyllic American pluralism suggests that interests will simply arise to compete over problems offering alternatives in line with the range of preferences broadly held by the public. This, of course, is not true, as we detail the asymmetry of interest group power between preferences and resources in Chapter 2. In addition, contrasting with theories of interest group formation, some policy areas struggle to find "publics" other than narrow groups of (often in government) experts (May, 1991).

Public policies provide not only niches (Gray and Lowery, 1996, 2000), but also entirely new habitats for federal, state, and local interest groups. The project of modifying policy for the purpose of modifying groups has a long history in American politics (Anzia and Moe, 2016). The GI Bill, while designed to achieve positive educational outcomes associated with veterans, created a large constituency of actors with not only military service in common but also an interest in maintaining veterans' benefits (Mettler, 2005). The same could be said for the creation of lifetime veterans' health-care benefits. These policies predate the placement of Veterans Affairs as a cabinet-level position in government.

We find other examples of policies that more purposefully create constituent consciousness. The initial creation of the Environmental Protection Agency (EPA) was, in part, designed to provide a location for environmental groups to specifically lobby for environmental protection, which had hitherto been scattered across a disparate range of policy subsystems (May, 2003). Further environmental protection acts (such as the Clean Air Act of 1970 and the Clean Water Act of 1972) created explicit opportunities for citizen enforcement of federal environmental law (Naysnerski and Tietenberg, 1992). While these structures and statutes may not have overtly contained organizing documents for the interest groups that followed or the expansion strategy for existing groups, these policies were clearly a gift to environmental organizations.

In another example, several governance organizations to tackle issues related to state and local food systems have emerged over the past twenty years. Food systems are notoriously challenging to coordinate – eaters are everywhere. Food policy councils have been a tool to provide new habitats for interest groups to both expand and form (Koski et al., 2018; Siddiki et al., 2015). The motivating documents for these council creations explicitly give access to groups otherwise excluded from the policymaking process (Koski et al., 2018).

In addition to the use of policy to mobilize interest groups, political actors have used the policy process to weaken the power of opposition groups. At the federal level, for example, a distinct response to the Deepwater Horizon disaster was an effort to break up interest group dominance in hydrocarbon exploration policy (Kurtz, 2013). The agency in charge of regulation, the Minerals Management Service, was split into three distinct agencies in an attempt to alter the landscape of interest groups influencing permits for, among other things, offshore drilling.

In public budgeting, we see a version of intentional demobilization in the "starve the beast" strategy pioneered by anti-tax crusaders such as Grover Norquist. In advocating for reduced government spending, conservative organizations reduce the rents that progressive interest groups can provide constituents via public policy. Curtailing taxation dovetails with a desire to curtail public expenditure in order to empower private interests over public goods. Balanced budget amendments at the state level are broad (and variable, as we note in our empirical analysis) attempts to make the costs of government transparent. In so doing, government decisions in particular policy areas inherently must grapple with trade-offs from other constituencies as we note throughout the book as well as a broad constituency of citizens asked to pay for spending increases. Thus, stricter balanced budget amendments make it harder for *all* interest groups to extract rents from governments and, therefore, make it harder for *all* groups to take shape.

The long-standing strategy to weaken the power of unions illustrates how policy reform can be used to change interest group dynamics. Union membership in the United States has steadily declined for decades; much of this decline is a function of right-to-work legislation explicitly promulgated to reduce union membership by allowing nonmembers to receive the benefits of members. In 2011, the Scott Walker administration passed Assembly Bill 10 in Wisconsin despite significant protest from Democrats and public-sector unions. The bill reduced public sector employees' collective bargaining capacity, required greater contributions from members for benefits, and did not allow employers to collect union dues from members.[1] Battles over public-sector unions in Wisconsin vividly demonstrate explicit efforts to demobilize political opponents in the long term. Governor Walker was not just interested in weakening unions, but also in weakening the education lobby that stood in the way of other initiatives he championed.

In 2018, the Supreme Court ruled in *Janus v. AFSCME* that public-sector unions could not require membership of employees in order to receive benefits resulting from collective bargaining. Right-to-work laws at the state level and the *Janus* case nationally are explicit attempts to weaken the power of an interest group. The Janus case, in particular, is part of a broader effort to weaken the power of employees who might advocate for government services in general (Hartney, 2022). Thus, while policies certainly produce interest groups, policies can also (at least attempt to) reduce interest groups.

Governments can explicitly empower groups indirectly through government programs such as the Clean Air Act or climate action plans, but can also explicitly structure representation for underrepresented groups, as in the case of food policy councils. Underrepresentation can take many forms dependent upon policy domains, but underrepresentation also cuts across policy domains in terms of race, gender, sexual orientation, and so on. For example, we know that women may be underrepresented in the policy domain of welfare, but we also know that women's interests are underrepresented across all policy domains. Government can also reduce established groups' power through specific programmatic strategies, as in the case with unions or broad political campaigns against the size of state budgets in general.

These examples show how policies provide habitats for interest groups. Most of the time, policies are not explicit about group creation; however, a

---

[1] Firefighters' and police officers' unions were exempt.

time-honored adage in political science is "policy produces politics" (Lowi, 1964). We argue that policymakers can embrace Lowi's inevitability and be more thoughtful about the way they structure policies to allow for diversity – by which we mean more groups with alternative definitions of the problems polices intend to solve – in representation. Policymakers should think about the long-term impacts that policies have not just on the citizens or industries that are targeted, but also on the mobilization of interests that will affect politics in a narrow issue area as well as democratic participation broadly (Mettler, 2005; Schneider and Ingram, 1997).

Restructuring of interest group competition is easier said than done, but opportunities for alternative preferences to intervene in policy decisions ought to produce more stable policy outcomes for all parties in the long run. It is true, though, that dominant groups – particularly those in our capture scenario – will be loath to share the distribution of what tends to be relatively scarce resources. At the same time, however, structured competition maximizes another goal of most interest groups: certainty in policy competition and outputs. Groups may dominate for long periods, though the policy literature suggests that groups will lose control at some point.

7.4.2 Tinkering with Gubernatorial Strength

Governors remain the single most important player in creating state budgets. Governors are responsible for budgeting for the whole in the face of interest groups and legislators interested in budgeting for the few. This situation is also complicated by governors' desire to benefit narrower groups than the whole – some that may be similar to those advocated by interest groups and legislators. Governors have to thread several needles to weave the budget together,[2] be it meeting requirements for federal grants, state-balanced budget requirements, serving or opposing interest groups, and negotiating with the legislature.

Governors have several institutional and political advantages to assist them in assembling a coalition of interests and legislators to get what they want out of a budget, as well as powers to resist the preferences of others (Beyle, 1996, 2003; Dometrius and Wright, 2010; Ferguson, 2003; Ferguson and Bowling, 2008; Kousser and Phillips, 2009, 2012). Institutionally, governors have the power to both set the budgetary agenda and veto changes that legislatures might make to their budgets. Politically, governors are active even when legislatures are not in session. While legislators also interact with interest groups and governors outside of session, the formal process of attending to budgetary issues is a priority of the governor's day-to-day tasks. The same is not true for legislators, particularly those in states with less professionalized legislatures. Interest groups, too, are active when legislatures are not: in informing bureaucratic decisions, interacting with implementation, and in mobilizing members

---

[2] We take this metaphor too far in other work; see Breunig et al. (2016).

to pressure the statehouse. Thus, the governor enjoys a privileged position mediated by interest groups in processes associated with budgeting, particularly in most states where legislatures are absent for at least some portion (in some cases a significant portion) of the entire budget cycle.

Interest group theories suggest that these interactions are the point of forming groups in the first place; groups will advocate on behalf of members outside formal methods of participation, such as voting. However, good-government advocates who believe elected officials should service *constituents* rather than members may be uncomfortable with interest groups structuring gubernatorial intervention in public budgeting processes. Further, we show that interest groups contribute to both the politics of equilibrium and the "politics of disequilibrium."[3] Rather than moderating the policy responses of government to these demands, strong governors exacerbate the effects of an interest group-structured dynamic that maintains stability through competition and capture at the expense of volatility in budget areas that simply acquire fewer specific interests.

We previously offered ideas about how to address issues related to interest groups' influence over public budgeting; we now confront the central feature of state budgeting: the role of governors. A discussion of the appropriate power and role of governors in the United States not only contrasts the philosophies of Governor Christie and Governor Moonbeam, but of Hamilton versus Jefferson. How much power do we vest in the executive, and under which conditions?

A common response to information processing and decision-making problems in government is to double-down on the "centralization thesis," wherein unitary actors with greater powers are viewed as the solution to a system that produces supposedly suboptimal policy outputs as a function of collective action problems. The collective action lens supports a notion of solving budgetary gridlock by empowering the governor to lower transaction costs; however, transaction costs in the classic sense are not the primary causes of stickiness in budgetary decision-making. Rather, stability (or gridlock) stems from an inherent lack of government attention – which impedes a full information search for all existing problems – coupled with cognitive limits to sort information. Thus, embracing the "centralization thesis" may result in swifter decision-making, but swift decision-making is even further subject to shifts in macro-political attention. A swift decision-making political system often results in overcorrection (Jones et al., 2014b), laying the groundwork for future policy volatility.

Let us consider the dilemma between centralization and delegation in another way. Delegation of decision-making authority can be thought of as a delegation of attention. Subgovernments (e.g., committees) are also subject to

---

[3] Thanks to Frank Baumgartner and Bryan Jones for this term, which served as the original title of their now canonical book: *Agendas and Instability*.

cognitive constraints and attention limitations, but their purpose is narrower and, thus, they are better able to seek and sort information relevant to one slice of problems facing governments. Further, subgovernments enable governments to process information in parallel, even if they ultimately make decisions in serial. To further consolidate decision-making power into one actor may solve the speed with which the government can make serial choices, but does nothing to solve the essential problem of government: information. If higher transaction costs lead to governments unable to address the range of issues with which they are faced, then stronger governors might theoretically be better able to adapt governments to problem conditions – but they do not. Our evidence shows that stronger executives make big changes bigger while, at the same time, maintaining a pattern of incremental changes.

Budgetary institutions could become more responsive or adaptable (Koski and Workman, 2018) by vesting more authority in alternative budget structures outside the direct control of the governor, but not necessarily vested in the legislature. The problem of volatile budgets, as we identify it, results from competing stabilizing forces intended to balance the budget *and* destabilizing forces emerging from political opportunism. Opportunism can be a reflection of political responsiveness to the range of needs of citizens. However, the political opportunism that emerges from the nexus of gubernatorial power and interest group competition is perhaps better described as governors taking what they can get when they can get it. One could argue that interest groups provide a concentration of preferences for citizens, but there is ample evidence to stop that discussion before it starts (Schlozman et al., 2012).

We suggested previously that fostering more interest group competition might create more defenders of policies that have ephemeral interests. A complementary suggestion is to broaden the decision-making process by reducing the governor's power relative to another entity ultimately responsible for the budget. Policy process theory tells us it is simply very difficult to structure governments that avoid large shifts between equilibrium and disequilibrium. Nevertheless, we find that policy concentration produces punctuated policymaking that overcorrects policy outputs and ultimately provides suboptimal output for citizens, even while providing policymakers with opportunities to make political gains.

Both the solutions we offer – enhancing interest group competition where it is ephemeral and weakening gubernatorial budget authority – have obvious downsides and are not likely to be implemented in isolation. Policy reform often results in political paradoxes that spawn new theoretical solutions (Patashnik, 2014). Relying on interest groups, absent executives, might lead to a government with little attention to overall state fiscal health. Further, there are several policies (e.g., disaster policy) for which there are few "publics" and for whom experts, not interest groups, are the primary advocates (May, 1991; May et al., 2016). In addition, strong and weak governors are politically motivated and held responsible for statewide problems. Research suggests governors are actually rewarded for fiscal health (Cummins and Holyoke, 2018). Reducing gubernatorial power may not necessarily reduce gubernatorial responsibility in the eyes of voters. Strong and weak governors alike must weave together narratives that justify the expenditure of public monies in the constantly evolving canon of budgetary stories.

7.4.3 What's Next?

In this book, we provided a simple framework for how public policy comes about. Policies, in our case budgets, are the motive of political actions while interest groups signal political opportunities that governors holding the institutional means try to seize. Across Chapters 3–6, we marshalled empirical evidence from the American states. Each of our three themes raise important questions for future inquiry. On motives, we postulated that policy domains are fixed over time and display distinct trade-offs. At the moment, domains are set by the state budget categories. A more open approach would incorporate the idea that political competition and societal change encourage the creation of new policy domains. Would the emergence of new domains, one might, for example, think of digitalization or the environment, change how interest groups and governors interact? Would these new domains be attractive for long-term returns, or rely on short bursts of policy change? We also claimed that welfare provides long-term, small but steady returns, whereas in a domain such as hospitals policy change transpires in short bursts. But we need to know more about how these differences in motives across domains emerge, and if political actors would detect changing motives in a domain?

For opportunities, our study of interest groups is ultimately limited by the data that exist. While closer to understanding the role that interest groups play in the policymaking systems, our work scratches the surface of the role that the interest group *environment* has on structuring choice opportunities for policymakers. Future research could ask deeper questions about the form and function of interest group environment, questions such as how groups interact, how groups form in or move to a policy domain, and, importantly, how politicians perceive this interaction.

Finally, for means, we have a sense of the specific tools that governors have with regard to budgetary and policy processes; however, it is less clear *when* governors actually use them to what effect. Further investigation of gubernatorial budget powers might specifically consider the electoral implications of a tortoise or hare approach to budgeting. Does the ultimate arbiter of these incidents – the voter – prefer decisive action of strong governors over incremental changes by the weak?

Answering these questions well informs societal solutions to the governance challenge of our time: balancing interest group involvement, politicians' desires, and most importantly, the issues citizens care about. The American political system developed institutional advantages around the status quo.

While policy stability is not inherently a bad thing, artificial stability distinct from the preferences of the governed contributes to a lack of faith in the political system and becomes corrosive to the tenets of democracy. Active participation in politics, especially outside of elections, presents an antidote to these beliefs. As such, interest group politics could provide a positive path for more continued engagement, so long as groups exist to represent the interests of the many or at least many interests. More representative interest groups provide better opportunities for elected officials to make good public policy.

References

Abbott, Kelly. 2003. Smart Starters find friends, not funds. *The Daily Dispatch*, May 20.

Ableidinger, Mandy. 2010. Insuring more of our children. *The News & Observer*, Feb. 19, 13A.

Abney, Glenn, and Lauth, Thomas P. 1983. The governor as chief administrator. *Public Administrative Review*, 43(1), 40–49.

Adler, E. Scott, and Wilkerson, John D. 2013. *Congress and the Politics of Problem Solving*. New York, NY: Cambridge University Press.

Adolph, Christopher, Breunig, Christian, and Koski, Chris. 2018. The political economy of budget trade-offs. *Journal of Public Policy*, 40(1), 1–26.

Ahearn, Lorraine. 2009. Mentally ill may face longer stays in the ER. *News & Record*, May 31, A1.

Ahlquist, John S., and Breunig, Christian. 2012. Model-based clustering and typologies in the social sciences. *Political Analysis*, 20(1), 92–112.

Ahlquist, John S., and Levi, Margaret. 2013. *In the Interest of Others: Organizations and Social Activism*. Princeton, NJ: Princeton University Press.

Aldrich, John H. 1995. *Why Parties?: The Origin and Transformation of Political Parties in America*. Chicago: University of Chicago Press.

Alesina, Alberto, and Perotti, Roberto. 1996. Fiscal discipline and the budget process. *American Economic Review*, 86(2), 401–407.

Alexander, Ames. 2010. Officials: Mental hospital needs aid. *The Charlotte Observer*, June 20, 1A.

Alexander, Lex. 2008. Funds urged for mental-health care. *The News & Record*, Mar. 26, B1.

Allen, Darren M. 2003. State hospital much costlier to state than expected. *Rutland Herald* (VT), Dec. 16.

Allen, Darren M. 2004a. Deficit in state's Medicaid fund looming, officials say. *Rutland Herald* (VT), June 30.

Allen, Darren M. 2004b. Douglas boosts the environment and health care. *Rutland Herald* (VT), Jan. 21.

Alt, James E., and Lowry, Robert C. 1994. Divided government, fiscal institutions, and budget deficits: Evidence from the states. *American Political Science Review*, 88(4), 811–828.

Alt, James E., and Lowry, Robert C. 2000. A dynamic model of state budget outcomes under divided partisan government. *The Journal of Politics*, 62(4), 1035–1069.

Alt, James E., and Lowry, Robert C. 2003. Party differences in state budget outcomes are there after all: Response to 'Reexamining the dynamic model of divided partisan government'. *Journal of Politics*, 65(1), 491–497.

Alt, James E., and Lowry, Robert C. 2010. Transparency and accountability: Empirical results for US states. *Journal of Theoretical Politics*, 22(4), 379–406.

Alt, James E., Lassen, David Dreyer, and Skilling, David. 2002. Fiscal transparency, gubernatorial approval, and the scale of government: Evidence from the states. *State Politics & Policy Quarterly*, 2(3), 230–250.

Alt, James E., Lassen, Dreyer, David, and Rose, Shanna. 2006. The causes of fiscal transparency: Evidence from the US states. *IMF Staff Papers*, 53(1), 30–57.

Alvarez, R. Michael, Garrett, Geoffrey, and Lange, Peter. 1991. Government partisanship, labor organization, and macroeconomic performance. *American Political Science Review*, 85(2), 539–556.

Ansolabehere, Stephen, and Snyder, James M. 2006. Party control of state government and the distribution of public expenditures. *Scandinavian Journal of Economics*, 108(4), 547–569.

Ansolabehere, Stephen, and Snyder, James M. 2008. *The End of Inequality: One Person, One Vote and the Transformation of American Politics*. New York: W. W. Norton.

Anzia, Sarah F. 2019. Looking for influence in all the wrong places: How studying subnational policy can revive research on interest groups. *The Journal of Politics*, 81(1), 343–351.

Anzia, Sarah F., and Moe, Terry M. 2016. Do politicians use policy to make politics? The case of public-sector labor laws. *American Political Science Review*, 110(4), 763–777.

Assis, Claudia, and Graybeal, Geoffrey. 2002. Umstead closing plan a surprise for many. *The Herald-Sun*, Mar. 21, A1.

Austen-Smith, David. 1993. Information and influence: Lobbying for agendas and votes. *American Journal of Political Science*, 37(3), 799–833.

Axelrod, Robert. 1967. Conflict of interest: An axiomatic approach. *Journal of Conflict Resolution*, 11(1), 87–99.

Bandhold, Stacy. 2008. The people's state of the state. *Record, The* (Troy, NY), Jan. 9.

Banfield, Jeffrey D., and Raftery, Adrian E. 1993. Model-based Gaussian and non-Gaussian clustering. *Biometrics*, 49(3), 803–821.

Bardhan, Pranab K., and Mookherjee, Dilip. 2000. Capture and governance at local and national levels. *American Economic Review*, 90(2), 135–139.

Barksdale, Titan. 2004. Group protests N.C.'s habitual-felon law. *Winston-Salem Journal*, Feb. 18, 1.

Barlow, Daniel. 2004. Rising health costs mulled. *Brattleboro Reformer* (VT), May 28.

Barnes, Steve, Crowley, Cathleen, Odato, James, Nearing, Brian, Waldman, Scott, Churchill, Chris, and O'Brien, Tim. 2010. Budget plan spreads pain. *Times Union, The* (Albany, NY), Jan. 20, A3.

Baron, David P. 1991. Majoritarian incentives, pork barrel programs, and procedural control. *American Journal of Political Science*, 35(1), 57–90.

Barrilleaux, Charles. 2000. Party strength, party change and policy-making in the American states. *Party Politics*, 6(1): 61–73.

Barrilleaux, Charles, Holbrook, Thomas, and Langer, Laura. 2002. Electoral competition, legislative balance, and American welfare state policy. *American Journal of Political Science*, 46(2), 415–427.

Barrilleaux, Charles J., and Berkman, Michael. 2003. Do governors matter? Budget rules and the politics of state policymaking. *Political Research Quarterly*, 56(4), 409–417.

Barrilleaux, Charles J., and Miller, Mark E. 1988. The political economy of state Medicaid policy. *The American Political Science Review*, 82(4), 1089–1107.

Bartels, Larry M. 2016. *Unequal Democracy: The Political Economy of the New Gilded Age*. 2nd ed. Princeton NJ: Princeton University Press.

Battista, James Coleman. 2012. State legislative committees and economic connections: Expertise and industry service. *State Politics & Policy Quarterly*, 12(3), 284–302.

Baumgartner, Frank, and Jones, Bryan D. 2015. *The Politics of Information Problem Definition and the Course of Public Policy in America*. Chicago: University Of Chicago Press.

Baumgartner, Frank R., and Jones, Bryan D. 1993. *Agendas and Instability in American Politics*. Chicago: University of Chicago.

Baumgartner, Frank R., and Leech, Beth L. 1998. *Basic Interests*. Princeton NJ: Princeton University Press.

Baumgartner, Frank R., and Leech, Beth L. 2001. Interest niches and policy bandwagons: Patterns of interest group involvement in national politics. *The Journal of Politics*, 63(4), 1191–1213.

Baumgartner, Frank R., Green-Pedersen, Christoffer, and Jones, Bryan D. 2006a. Comparative studies of policy agendas. *Journal of European Public Policy*, 13(7), 959–974.

Baumgartner, Frank R., Foucault, Martial, and Francois, Abel. 2006b. Punctuated equilibrium in the French budgeting process. *Journal of European Public Policy*, 13(7), 1086–1103.

Baumgartner, Frank R., Berry, Jeffrey M., Hojnacki, Marie, Leech, Beth L., and Kimball, David C. 2009a. *Lobbying and Policy Change: Who Wins, Who Loses, and Why*. Chicago: University of Chicago Press.

Baumgartner, Frank R., Foucault, Martial, and François, Abel. 2009b. Public budgeting in the French Fifth Republic: The end of *La République Des Partis*? *West European Politics*, 32(2), 404–422.

Baumgartner, Frank R., Breunig, Christian, Green-Pedersen, Christoffer, Jones, Bryan D., Mortensen, Peter B., Nuytemans, Michiel, and Walgrave, Stefaan. 2009c. Punctuated equilibrium in comparative perspective. *American Journal of Political Science*, 53, 603–620.

Baumgartner, Frank R., Carammia, Marcello, Epp, Derek A., Noble, Ben, Rey, Beatriz, and Yildirim, Tevfik Murat. 2017. Budgetary change in authoritarian and democratic regimes. *Journal of European Public Policy*, 24(6), 792–808.

Beck, Nathaniel, and Jackman, Simon. 1998. Beyond linearity by default: Generalized additive models. *American Journal of Political Science*, 42(2), 596–627.

Béland, Daniel, Rocco, Philip, and Waddan, Alex. 2016. *Obamacare Wars: Federalism, State Politics, and the Affordable Care Act*. Lawrence: University Press of Kansas.

Beland, Louis-Philippe, and Oloomi, Sara. 2017. Party affiliation and public spending: Evidence from U.S. governors. *Economic Inquiry*, 55(2), 982–995.

Benson, Barbara. 2010. Health care lobby prepares to fight calls for big cutbacks – Unions and hospital groups are hoping to use revenue raised in soda tax as offset; weighing Ravitch role. *Crain's New York Business*, Mar. 1, 0022.

Bernick, E. Lee. 2016. Studying governors over five decades: What we know and where we need to go? *State and Local Government Review*, 48(2), 132–146.

Berry, William D., and Lowery, David. 1990. An alternative approach to understanding budgetary trade-offs. *American Journal of Political Science*, 34(3), 671–705.

Besley, Timothy, and Case, Anne. 2003. Political institutions and policy choices: Evidence from the United States. *Journal of Economic Literature*, 41(1), 7–73.

Bethea, April. 2010. More psychiatric beds sought as demand jumps. *The Charlotte Observer*, Apr. 4, 7A.

Beyle, Thad. 1996. Governors: The middleman and women in our political system. Pages 207–252 of: Gray, Virginia, and Jacob, Herbert (eds), *Politics in the American States: A Comparative Analysis*, 6th ed. Boston: Little Brown.

Beyle, Thad. 2003 (April). *Gubernatorial Power: The Institutional Power Ratings for the 50 Governors of the United States*. www.unc.edu/beyle/G-PartyControl-501.doc.

Beyle, Thad L. 1968. The governor's formal powers: A view from the governor's chair. *Public Administration Review*, 28(6), 540–545.

Bickley, Rah. 2002. Workers confront job loss – State offers counseling, services to laid-off workers. *The News & Observer*, May 26, B1.

Biesecker, Michael. 2008. Another attack at Dix rekindles concerns. *The News & Observer*, June 21, B1.

Biesecker, Michael. 2009a. Budget forces mental hospitals to slash jobs. *The Charlotte Observer*, Aug. 20, 2B.

Biesecker, Michael. 2009b. Dix will remain open. *The News & Observer*, Aug. 28, A1.

Biesecker, Michael. 2010a. After 154 years, end at hand for Dix. *The News & Observer*, Nov. 30, 1A.

Biesecker, Michael. 2010b. Defenders of state workers unite to stop the budget ax. *The News & Observer*, June 9, 1B.

Biesecker, Michael. 2010c. Groups demand that Dix Hospital stays open. *The News & Observer*, Sept. 29.

Biesecker, Michael. 2010d. NAACP joins the Dix debate. *The News & Observer*, Nov. 4.

Blais, André, Blake, Donald, and Dion, Stéphane. 1993. Do parties make a difference – parties and the size of government in liberal democracies. *American Journal of Political Science*, 37(1), 40–62.

Boehmke, Frederick J, Gailmard, Sean, and Patty, John W. 2013. Business as usual: Interest group access and representation across policy-making venues. *Journal of Public Policy*, 33(1), 3–33.

Bomyea, Laura. 2008. How big are hospital cuts? This will hurt a bit ... Or more, say area hospital chiefs. *Daily Courier-Observer (Massena, NY)*, Dec. 17, 1.

Bonner, Lynn. 2004. Senate, House juggle figures. *The News & Observer*, June 26, B5.

Bonner, Lynn. 2008. Funds for mental health in governor's plan. *The News & Observer*, May 13, A8.

Bonner, Lynn. 2009a. Mental health funds cut. *The Charlotte Observer*, Aug. 6, 1B.

Bonner, Lynn. 2009b. Perdue budget cuts mental health system. *The Charlotte Observer*, Mar. 19, 3B.

Bonner, Lynn, and Christensen, Rob. 2001. Childhood program defended. *The News & Observer*, May 10, A3.

Bonner, Lynn, and Rawlins, Wade. 2001. Budget confounds negotiators. *The News & Observer*, Aug. 10, A3.

Bowling, Cynthia J, and Ferguson, Margaret R. 2001. Divided government, interest representation, and policy differences: Competing explanations of gridlock in the fifty states. *Journal of Politics*, 63(1), 182–206.

Bowman, Ann O'M., Woods, Neal D., and Stark, Milton R. 2010. Governors turn pro: Separation of powers and the institutionalization of the American governorship. *Political Research Quarterly*, 63(2), 304–315.

Bräuninger, Thomas. 2005. A partisan model of government expenditure. *Public Choice*, 125(3), 409–429.

Breunig, Christian. 2006. The more things change, the more things stay the same: A comparative analysis of budget punctuations. *Journal of European Public Policy*, 13(7), 1069–1085.

Breunig, Christian. 2011. Reduction, stasis, and expansion of budgets in advanced democracies. *Comparative Political Studies*, 44(8), 1060–1088.

Breunig, Christian, and Busemeyer, Marius R. 2012. Fiscal austerity and the trade-off between public investment and social spending. *Journal of European Public Policy*, 19(6), 921–938.

Breunig, Christian, and Jones, Bryan D. 2011. Stochastic process methods with an application to budgetary data. *Political Analysis*, 19(1), 103–117.

Breunig, Christian, and Koski, Chris. 2006. Punctuated equilibria in the American states. *Policy Studies Journal*, 34(3), 363–379.

Breunig, Christian, and Koski, Chris. 2009. Punctuated budgets and governors' institutional powers. *American Politics Research*, 37(6), 1116–1138.

Breunig, Christian, and Koski, Chris. 2012. The tortoise or the hare? Incrementalism, punctuations, and their consequences. *Policy Studies Journal*, 40(1), 45–68.

Breunig, Christian, and Koski, Chris. 2018. Interest groups and policy volatility. *Governance*, 31(2), 279–297.

Breunig, Christian, Koski, Chris, and Mortensen, Peter B. 2009. Les dynamiques budgétaires dans une perspective comparée. *Revue internationale de politique comparée*, 16(3), 441–464.

Breunig, Christian, Koski, Chris, and Mortensen, Peter B. 2010. Stability and punctuations in public spending: A comparative study of budget functions. *Journal of Public Administration Research and Theory*, 20(3), 703–722.

Breunig, Christian, Koski, Chris, and Workman, Samuel. 2016. Knot policy theory. *Policy Studies Journal*, 44(S1), S123–S132.

Brock, Martha. 2010a. Mental health services won't improve until N.C. funding does. *The Charlotte Observer*, June 17, 12A.

Brock, Martha. 2010b. NAMI Wake County plans rally Thursday to save Dorothea Dix Hospital in Raleigh. *The Raleigh Examiner*, Oct. 27.

Brock, Martha. 2010c. Wake Commissioner Gurley says NAMI Wake's report reveals a "double standard" in services. *The Raleigh Examiner*, Aug. 10.

Brouard, Sylvain, Wilkerson, John, Baumgartner, Frank R., Timmermans, Arco, Bevan, Shaun, Breeman, Gerard, Breunig, Christian, Chaqués, Laura, Green-Pedersen, Christopher, Jennings, Will, John, Peter, Jones, Bryan D., and Lowery, David. 2009.

Comparer les productions législatives : enjeux et méthodes. *Revue internationale de politique comparée*, **16**(3), 381–404.

Brown, Adam R. 2012. The item veto's sting. *State Politics & Policy Quarterly*, **12**(2), 183–203.

Brown, Robert D. 1995. Party cleavages and welfare effort in the American states. *American Political Science Review*, **89**(1), 23–33.

Brownback, Sam. 2011 (Jan. 12). *State of the State Address 2011*.

Bryan, Jay. 2002. Budget cuts will cost dearly later on. *The News & Observer*, Apr. 24, A4.

Bundy, Jennifer. 2004. Welfare changes at issue advocates ask Wise to reverse cut in cash assistance. *Charleston Gazette (WV)*, July 24, P1A.

Bureau of Economic Analysis. 2018. *GDP by State*.

Bureau of Justice Statistics. 1987a (Aug. 1). *1984 Census of State Adult Correctional Facilities*. Tech. rept. US Department of Justice.

Bureau of Justice Statistics. 1987b (Dec. 1). *Correctional Populations in the United States, 1985*. Tech. rept. US Department of Justice.

Bureau of Justice Statistics. 2008 (Oct. 1). *Census of State and Federal Correctional Facilities, 2005*. Tech. rept. US Department of Justice.

Bureau of Justice Statistics. 2011 (Dec. 15). *Correctional Populations in the United States, 2010*. Tech. rept. US Department of Justice.

Burstein, Paul, and Linton, April. 2002. The impact of political parties, interest groups, and social movement organizations on public policy: Some recent evidence and theoretical concerns. *Social Forces*, **81**(2), 380–408.

Byrne, Kathleen. 2008. Should the state budget cut more deeply into the sick or the young? *New York Examiner (NY)*, Nov. 20.

Calhoun, Jennifer. 2009. Group gives state poor grades on care. *The Fayetteville Observer*, Mar. 24.

Carter, John R., and Schap, David. 1987. Executive veto, legislative override, and structure-induced equilibrium. *Public Choice*, **52**(3), 227–244.

Carter, John R, and Schap, David. 1990. Line-item veto: Where is thy sting? *The Journal of Economic Perspectives*, **4**(2), 103–118.

Cashore, Benjamin, and Howlett, Michael. 2007. Punctuating which equilibrium? Understanding thermostatic policy dynamics in Pacific northwest forestry. *American Journal of Political Science*, **51**(3), 532–551.

Castelle, George. 2003. Prison paradox overcrowding could be stopped with moderate parole rate. *Charleston Gazette (WV)*, Feb. 10, P5A.

Charleston Daily Mail (WV). 2004. WVU to start building new medical complex. http://infoweb.newsbank.com/resources/doc/nb/news/103AB37970F6E5F1?p= AWNB, July 2, P10A.

Charlotte Observer. 2009a. Differing proposals. *The Charlotte Observer*, Apr. 10.

Charlotte Observer. 2009b. N.C. budget breakdown. http://infoweb.newsbank.com/ resources/doc/nb/news/129E6E526FEDF560?p=AWNB, Aug. 5, 5A.

Charlotte Observer Editorial Staff. 2010. State hasn't come to grips with mental health woes. *The Charlotte Observer*, Oct. 15, 14A.

Charlotte Observer (NC). 2009. Proposed N.C. cuts: From road repairs to libraries. http://infoweb.newsbank.com/resources/doc/nb/news/1262700B748CCA10 ?p=AWNB, Feb. 3, 3B.

Chatfield, Sara, and Rocco, Philip. 2014. Is federalism a political safety valve? Evidence from congressional decision making, 1960–2005. *Publius: The Journal of Federalism*, 44(1), 1–23.

Cimino, Karen, Beshears, Erica, Mitchell, Hannah, Howard, Heather, and Soper, Aileen. 2001. Briefs. *Charlotte Observer (NC)*, July 28, 2B.

Clark, Benjamin Y., and Whitford, Andrew B. 2011. Does more federal environmental funding increase or decrease states' efforts? *Journal of Policy Analysis and Management*, 30(1), 136–152.

Clarke, Wes. 1998. Divided government and budget conflict in the U.S. states. *Legislative Studies Quarterly*, 23(1), 5–22.

Cline, Kurt. 2008. Working relationships in the national superfund program: The state administrators' perspective. *Journal of Public Administration Research and Theory*, 20(1), 117–135.

Cobb, Roger William. 1983. *Participation in American Politics: The Dynamics of Agenda-Building*. Johns Hopkins University Press.

Cohen, Marty, Karol, David, Noel, Hans, and Zaller, John. 2009. *The Party Decides: Presidential Nominations before and after Reform*. University of Chicago Press.

Cohen, Michael D, and March, James G. 1974. *Leadership and Ambiguity: The American College President*. New York: McGraw Hill.

Cohen, Michael D., March, James G., and Olsen, Johan P. 1972. A garbage can model of organizational choice. *Administrative Science Quarterly*, 17(1), 1–25.

Coleman, Lee. 2008. Prison camp slated for closure. *Daily Gazette, The (Schenectady, NY)*, Dec. 17, A1.

Collier, David, LaPorte, Jody, and Seawright, Jason. 2012. Putting typologies to work: Concept formation, measurement, and analytic rigor. *Political Research Quarterly*, 65(1), 217–232.

Collins, Jeffrey. 2003. After years of big cuts, prisons get more money. *The Charlotte Observer*, June 8, 2Y.

Confessore, Nicholas. 2007. Spitzer seeks panel to study prison closings. *The New York Times*, Feb. 5.

Conlan, Timothy. 2017. Intergovernmental relations in a compound republic: The journey from cooperative to polarized federalism. *Publius: The Journal of Federalism*, 47(2), 171–187.

Conner, Bob. 2008a. Counties won't face welfare hike. *Daily Gazette, The (Schenectady, NY)*, Apr. 5, A1.

Conner, Bob. 2008b. Critics decry block of tax on wealthy. *Daily Gazette, The (Schenectady, NY)*, Apr. 4, A4.

Conner, Bob. 2008c. Prisons slated for closure spared by budget agreement. *Daily Gazette, The (Schenectady, NY)*, Apr. 1, A1.

Constantelos, John. 2010. Playing the field: Federalism and the politics of venue shopping in the United States and Canada. *Publius: The Journal of Federalism*, 40(3), 460–483.

Cornwell, David. 2010. About compassion. *The News & Observer*, June 18.

Crain, W. Mark. 2003. *Volatile States: Institutions, Policy, and the Performance of American State Economies*. University of Michigan Press.

Crain, W. Mark, and Miller, James. 1990. Budget process and spending growth. *William and Mary Law Review*.

Crawford. 2004 (July 20). *2004 Appropriations Act.*

Crone, Theodore M, and Clayton-Matthews, Alan. 2005. Consistent economic indexes for the 50 states. *Review of Economics and Statistics*, 87(4), 593–603.

Culpepper, Pepper D. 2011. *Quiet Politics and Business Power : Corporate Control in Europe and Japan.* New York: Cambridge University Press.

Cummins, Jeff, and Holyoke, Thomas T. 2018. Fiscal accountability in gubernatorial elections. *State Politics & Policy Quarterly*, 1532440018792260.

Curtis, Brent. 2002. Dean predicts taxing session. *Rutland Herald (VT)*, Jan. 8.

Cusack, Thomas R. 1999. Partisan politics and fiscal policy. *Comparative Political Studies*, 32(4), 464–486.

Daily Messenger. 2009. Albany: Protest for the poor. http://infoweb.newsbank.com/resources/doc/nb/news/12710110B75CDA00?p=WORLDNEWS, Mar. 18, 4B.

Dalesio, Emery P. 2004. Families press for sentencing reform. *The Charlotte Observer*, Apr. 14, 3B.

Damico, Dana. 2001. Proposal for the state's health budget would generate changes in Medicaid. *Winston-Salem Journal*, Aug. 9, 2.

Davenport, Paul. 2009a. Arizona has a budget but no end to money troubles. *Associated Press: Phoenix Metro Area (AZ)*, Sept. 9.

Davenport, Paul. 2009b. Brewer Deletes School Cuts from Ariz. Budget Plan. *Associated Press: Phoenix Metro Area (AZ)*, Sept. 4.

Davenport, Paul. 2009c. Report Puts Ariz. Shortfall at Nearly $1 billion. *Associated Press: Phoenix Metro Area (AZ)*, Sept. 8.

Davis, Henry L. 2009. Health care takes it on the chin in budget – Hospitals will lose millions in aid. *Buffalo News, The (NY)*, Apr. 5, C1.

Davis, Otto A., Dempster, M.A.H., and Wildavsky, Aaron. 1966. A theory of the budgetary process. *The American Political Science Review*, 60(3), 529–547.

Davis, Otto A., Dempster, M.A.H., and Wildavsky, Aaron. 1974. Towards a predictive theory of government expenditure: US domestic appropriations. *British Journal of Political Science*, 4(4), 419–452.

de Figueiredo, Rui J.P. 2003. Budget institutions and political insulation: Why states adopt the item veto. *Journal of Public Economics*, 87(12), 2677–2701.

Dean, Howard. 2002 (Jan. 8). *State of the State Address 2002.*

Dearden, James A., and Husted, Thomas A. 1990. Executive budget proposal, executive veto, legislative override, and uncertainty: A comparative analysis of the budgetary process. *Public Choice*, 65(1), 1–19.

Dearden, James A., and Husted, Thomas A. 1993. Do governors get what they want?: An alternative examination of the line-item veto. *Public Choice*, 77(4), 707–723.

DeCarlo, Lawrence T. 1997. On the meaning and use of kurtosis. *Psychological Methods*, 2(3), 292–307.

Dickson, Margaret. 2008. Session ends: Here are the results. *The Fayetteville Observer*, July 29.

Dilger, Robert Jay. 1998. TEA-21: Transportation policy, pork barrel politics, and American federalism. *Publius: The Journal of Federalism*, 28(1), 49–69.

DiStaso, John. 1993. Burns to seek compromise on budget. *New Hampshire Union Leader*, July 13, 4.

Dometrius, Nelson C. 1979. Measuring gubernatorial power. *The Journal of Politics*, 41(2), 589–610.

Dometrius, Nelson C., and Wright, Deil S. 2010. Governors, legislatures, and state budgets across time. *Political Research Quarterly*, 63(4), 783–795.

Douglas, James. 2003 (Jan. 23). *State of the State Address 2003*.

Douglas, James. 2004a. Governor Douglas' budget address. *Vermont Business Magazine (VT)*, Jan. 1.

Douglas, James. 2004b (Jan. 6). *State of the State Address 2004*.

Downs, Anthony. 1957. *An Economic Theory of Democracy*. New York: Harper.

Downs, Anthony. 1972. Up and down with ecology: The issue attention cycle. *Public Interest*, 28(1), 38–50.

Drutman, Lee. 2015. *The Business of America Is Lobbying: How Corporations Became Politicized and Politics Became More Corporate*. New York: Oxford University Press.

Dunlea, Mark. 2008. Could you live on a welfare grant? *Post-Standard, The (Syracuse, NY)*, Jan. 20, E1.

Dunlea, Mark. 2009. Government needs to help put people to work. *Citizen, The (Auburn, NY)*, Apr. 1.

Dunlea, Mark. 2010. There are currently more than 850,000 New Yorkers unemployed, with more than 300,000 jobs lost in the last 18 months. *Record, The (Troy, NY)*, Mar. 28, 15D.

Durhams, Sharif. 2003a. Easley balances budget with cuts. *Charlotte Observer (NC)*, Mar. 6, 1A.

Durhams, Sharif. 2003b. Easley signs 2-year budget. *The Charlotte Observer*, July 1, 1B.

Durhams, Sharif. 2003c. Legislators in conflict on cancer center. *The Charlotte Observer*, July 20, 1B.

Durhams, Sharif. 2004. Legislators will borrow for 5 university projects. *The Charlotte Observer*, July 15, 2B.

Durhams, Sharif, and Griffin, Anna. 2002. N.C. legislators OK lean-year budget. *The Charlotte Observer*, Sept. 20, 1A.

Dwyer, Jim. 2008. Less crime: No reason to shut prisons. *The New York Times*, Apr. 12, 1.

Dye, Thomas R. 1984. Party and policy in the states. *Journal of Politics*, 46(4), 1097–1116.

Dyer, Eric. 2001. Tough budget choices loom. *The News & Record*, May 20, B1.

Dyer, Eric. 2002a. House, Senate back $14.3 billion budget. *The News & Record*, Sept. 20, A1.

Dyer, Eric. 2002b. N.C. Senate could vote on budget today. *The News & Record*, June 19, B1.

Dyer, Eric. 2003. In change of heart, Easley signs budget. *The News & Record*, July 1, A1.

Easley, Michael. 2002 (May). *The North Carolina State Budget, 2002–2003 Recommended Adjustments*.

Easley, Michael. 2003 (Mar.). *State of the State Address 2003*.

Eisley, Matthew, Kane, Dan, Gardner, Amy, and Rawlins, Wade. 2001. Senate, House budgets must reconcile gaps. *The News & Observer*, June 23, A21.

Elis, Roy, Malhotra, Neil, and Meredith, Marc. 2009. Apportionment cycles as natural experiments. *Political Analysis*, 14(4): 358–376.

Elman, Colin. 2005. Explanatory typologies in qualitative studies of international politics. *International Organization*, 59(2), 293–326.

Epp, Derek A. 2018. *The Structure of Policy Change*. Chicago: University Of Chicago Press.

Epp, Derek A., and Baumgartner, Frank R. 2017. Complexity, capacity, and budget punctuations. *Policy Studies Journal*, 45(2), 247–264.

Epp, Derek A., Lovett, John, and Baumgartner, Frank R. 2014. Partisan priorities and public budgeting. *Political Research Quarterly*, 67(4), 864–878.

Esteve, Harry. 2013. GMO bill a political necessity, Oregon Gov. John Kitzhaber says. *The Oregonian*, September 25.

Fagan, E. J., Jones, Bryan D., and Wlezien, Christopher. 2017. Representative systems and policy punctuations. *Journal of European Public Policy*, 24(6), 809–831.

Fairlie, John A. 1917. The veto power of the state governor. *The American Political Science Review*, 11(3), 473–493.

FairVote.org. 2015. *Plurality in Gubernatorial Elections*.

Faricy, Christopher. 2016. The distributive politics of tax expenditures: How parties use policy tools to distribute federal money to the rich and the poor. *Politics, Groups, and Identities*, 4(1), 110–125.

Faricy, Christopher, and Ellis, Christopher. 2014. Public attitudes toward social spending in the United States: The differences between direct spending and tax expenditures. *Political Behavior*, 36(1), 53–76.

Faricy, Christopher G. 2015. *Welfare for the Wealthy: Parties, Social Spending, and Inequality in the United States*. Cambridge University Press.

Ferejohn, John, and Krehbiel, Keith. 1987. The budget process and the size of the budget. *American Journal of Political Science*, 31(2), 296–320.

Ferguson, Margaret R., and Bowling, Cynthia J. 2008. Executive orders and administrative control. *Public Administration Review*, 68, S20–S28.

Ferguson, Margaret Robertson. 2003. Chief executive success in the legislative arena. *State Politics & Policy Quarterly*, 3(2), 158–182.

Finn, Scott. 2004. Medicaid cuts will hurt all, pros say health-care groups lobby legislators to prevent loss of funds. *Charleston Gazette (WV)*, Feb. 12, P1A.

Fiorina, Morris P., Abrams, Samuel J., and Pope, Jeremy. 2010. *Culture War?: The Myth of a Polarized America*. 3rd ed. Chicago: Longman Publishing Group.

Fishkin, James S. 2011. *When the People Speak: Deliberative Democracy and Public Consultation*. Oxford University Press.

Fitzsimon, Chris. 2009. Budget like it's 2005? *The News & Observer*, May 21, A11.

Flanagan Jr., Larry. 2008. State's plan to close four correctional facilities was unfair, ill-conceived. *Times Union, The (Albany, NY)*, May 17, A6.

Flink, Carla M. 2017. Rethinking punctuated equilibrium theory: A public administration approach to budgetary changes. *Policy Studies Journal*, 45(1), 101–120.

Fraley, Chris, and Raftery, Adrian E. 1998. How many clusters? Which clustering method? Answers via model-based cluster analysis. *The Computer Journal*, 41(8), 578–588.

Fraley, Chris, and Raftery, Adrian E. 2002. Model-based clustering, discriminant analysis, and density estimation. *Journal of the American Statistical Association*, 97(458), 611–631.

Franklin, Jeremy. 2002. 12% cut not deep enough for critics. *The Daily Dispatch*, June 22.

Franzese, Robert J. 2010. The multiple effects of multiple policymakers: Veto actors bargaining in common pools. *Rivista italiana di scienza politica*, 40(3), 341–370.

Fraser, Ronald. 2003. Reducing prison costs can save W.Va. taxpayers millions. *Herald-Dispatch, The (Huntington, WV)*, Apr. 17, 8A.

Furlong, Scott R. 1997. Interest group influence on rule making. *Administration & Society*, 29(3), 325–347.

Furlong, Scott R, and Kerwin, Cornelius M. 2004. Interest group participation in rule making: A decade of change. *Journal of Public Administration Research and Theory*, 15(3), 353–370.

Gamm, Gerald, and Kousser, Thad. 2010. Broad bills or particularistic policy? Historical patterns in American state legislatures. *American Political Science Review*, 104(1), 151–170.

Garand, James C. 1985. Partisan change and shifting expenditure priorities in American states, 1945–1978. *American Politics Quarterly*, 13(3), 355–391.

Garand, James G., Ulrich, Justin, and Xu, Ping. 2014. Fiscal policy in the American states. Pages 611–642 of: Haider-Markel, Donald P. (ed), *The Oxford Handbook of State and Local Government*. Oxford: Oxford University Press.

Gardner, Amy. 2001a. Budget spares health, education programs. *The News & Observer*, Sept. 23, B1.

Gardner, Amy. 2001b. Easley suggests new guidelines for Smart Start. *The News & Observer*, May 9, A1.

Gardner, Amy. 2001c. Hunt skips Smart Start debate. *The News & Observer*, May 15, A3.

Gardner, Amy. 2001d. Key programs face deep cuts in budget plan. *The News & Observer*, May 8, A3.

Gardner, Amy. 2001e. Preschool funding at issue. *The News & Observer*, Feb. 14, A1.

Gardner, Amy. 2001f. Proposed cuts summon advocates to legislature. *The News & Observer*, May 24, A1.

Gardner, Amy. 2002a. Lobby takes its shot. *The News & Observer*, July 18, B5.

Gardner, Amy. 2002b. State ponders cutting Medicaid. *The News & Observer*, Apr. 2, A1.

Gardner, Amy. 2003. Smart Start eyed for cuts. *The News & Observer*, Mar. 27, B1.

Gardner, Amy. 2004. State projects revenue surplus. *News & Observer*, May 1, B1.

Gardner, Amy, and Barrett, Barbara. 2003. Senate favors taxes to avoid service cuts. *The News & Observer*, Apr. 30, A1.

Gardner, Amy, and Kane, Dan. 2003. Senate wrestling with budget. *The News & Observer*, June 11, B5.

Gardner, Amy, and Rawlins, Wade. 2001. Budget relies on lottery, other what-ifs. *The News & Observer*, Mar. 13, A1.

Gardner, Amy, and Simmons, Tim. 2002. Budget cuts are deep. *The News & Observer*, May 22, A1.

Gardner, Amy, Wagner, John, and Myers, Steve. 2001. Think tank gives Hunt a C. *The News & Observer*, Feb. 25, A3.

Gardner, Amy, Kane, Dan, and Christensen, Rob. 2004. Easley to sign university bonds bill. *The News & Observer*, Aug. 5, B5.

Gelman, Andrew, and Hill, Jennifer. 2006. *Data Analysis using Regression and Multilevel/Hierarchical Models*. Cambridge University Press.

Gerber, Elisabeth R., and Gibson, Clark C. 2009. Balancing regionalism and localism: How institutions and incentives shape American transportation policy. *American Journal of Political Science*, 53(3), 633–648.

Gilens, Martin. 2012. *Affluence and Influence: Economic Inequality and Political Power in America*. Princeton: Princeton University Press.

Gilens, Martin, and Page, Benjamin I. 2014. Testing theories of American politics: Elites, interest groups, and average citizens. *Perspectives on Politics*, 12(3), 564–581.

Gist, John R. 1977. 'Increment' and 'base' in the congressional appropriations process. *American Journal of Political Science*, 21(2), 341–352.

Gist, John R. 1978. Appropriations politics and expenditure control. *The Journal of Politics*, 40(1), 163–178.

Givel, Michael. 2006. Punctuated equilibrium in limbo: The tobacco lobby and US state policymaking from 1990 to 2003. *Policy Studies Journal*, 34(3), 405–418.

Goggin, Malcom, Bowman, Ann O'M., Lester, James P., and O'Toole, Laurence J., Jr. 1990. *Implementation Theory and Practice: Toward a Third Generation*. Glenview, IL: Scott Foresman/Little Brown.

Goldberg, Delen. 2010. Paterson speech seen as short on specifics. *Post-Standard, The (Syracuse, NY)*, Jan. 10, A11.

Goodman, Doug. 2008. Executive budget analysts and legislative budget analysts: State budgetary gatekeepers. *Journal of Public Budgeting, Accounting & Financial Management*, 20(3), 299–322.

Goodman, Doug, and Clynch, Edward J. 2004. Budgetary decision making by executive and legislative budget analysts: The impact of political cues and analytical information. *Public Budgeting & Finance*, 24(3), 20–37.

Gorczyca, Beth. 2001. W.Va.'s economic future is focus of 2002 legislature. *Herald-Dispatch, The (Huntington, WV)*, Dec. 9, 1A.

Gormley, Michael. 2008. Counties say Spitzer budget would raise taxes. *Evening Sun, The (Norwich, NY)*, Jan. 30, 008.

Gouras, Matt. 2011. 'VETO': Schweitzer fires up branding irons to veto bills. *Billings Gazette*, Apr.

Graff, Christopher. 2002. Balancing act. *Rutland Herald (VT)*, Jan. 26.

Graff, Christopher. 2003. The best job they'll ever love. *Rutland Herald (VT)*, Jan. 11.

Gram, David. 2003a. Douglas gets tough on permit reform. *Rutland Herald (VT)*, Dec. 19.

Gram, David. 2003b. Staffing shortages trigger failed inspections at VSH. *Rutland Herald (VT)*, Apr.16.

Gram, David. 2003c. Vt. State Hospital is ordered to treat patients who resist. *Times Argus, The (Barre-Montpelier VT)*, Sept. 4.

Gray, Virginia, and Lowery, David. 1993. Stability and change in state interest group systems, 1975–1990. *State & Local Government Review*, 87–96.

Gray, Virginia, and Lowery, David. 1996. A niche theory of interest representation. *The Journal of Politics*, 58(1), 91–111.

Gray, Virginia, and Lowery, David. 1998. To lobby alone or in a flock: Foraging behavior among organized interests. *American Politics Quarterly*, 26(1), 5–34.

Gray, Virginia, and Lowery, David. 2000. *The Population Ecology of Interest Representation: Lobbying Communities in the American States*. Ann Arbor: University of Michigan Press.

Gray, Virginia, and Lowery, David. 2001. The expression of density dependence in state communities of organized interests. *American Politics Research*, 29(4), 374–391.

Gray, Virginia, Lowery, David, Fellowes, Matthew, and McAtee, Andrea. 2004. Public opinion, public policy, and organized interests in the American states. *Political Research Quarterly*, 57(3), 411–420.

Gray, Virginia, Hanson, Russell L, and Kousser, Thad. 2017. *Politics in the American states: A Comparative Analysis*. 11th ed. New York: CQ Press.

Griffin, Anna, and Durhams, Sharif. 2002. House panel cuts recovery package. *Charlotte Observer (NC)*, Oct. 1, 1A.

Groneveld, Richard A. 1998. A class of quintile measures for kurtosis. *American Statistician*, 52(4), 325–329.

Grossmann, Matt. 2006. The organization of factions: Interest mobilization and the group theory of politics. *Public Organization Review*, 6(2), 107–124.

Grossmann, Matt. 2012. *The Not-So-Special Interests: Interest Groups, Public Representation, and American Governance*. Stanford University Press.

Grossmann, Matt. 2013. The variable politics of the policy process: Issue-area differences and comparative networks. *The Journal of Politics*, 75(1), 65–79.

Grossmann, Matt. 2019. *Red State Blues: How the Conservative Revolution Stalled in the States*. New York, NY: Cambridge University Press.

Grumbach, Jacob M. 2018. From backwaters to major policymakers: Policy polarization in the states, 1970–2014. *Perspectives on Politics*, 16(2), 416–435.

Guerino, Paul, Harrison, Paige M., and Sabol, William J. 2012 (Feb. 9). *Prisoners in 2010*. Tech. rept. US Department of Justice.

Gulley, Wib. 2004. Time to get 'smart on crime'. *Charlotte Observer (NC)*, Feb. 25, 18A.

Gunnison, Robert. 1999. Davis raises expectations for students, teachers – State of State address focuses on education. *San Francisco Chronicle (CA)*, Jan. 7, A1.

Haeder, Simon F., and Weimer, David L. 2013. You can't make me do it: State implementation of insurance exchanges under the affordable care act. *Public Administration Review*, 73(s1), S34–S47.

Haeder, Simon F., and Yackee, Susan Webb. 2015. Influence and the administrative process: Lobbying the U.S. president's office of management and budget. *American Political Science Review*, 109(3), 507–522.

Hakim, Danny, and Peters, Jeremy W. 2009. G.O.P. regains control of New York state senate. *The New York Times*, June 8.

Hale, George E. 2013. State budgets, governors, and their influence on "Big-Picture Issues": A case study of Delaware Governor Pete du Pont 1977-1985. *Administration & Society*, 45(2), 127–144.

Hall, Peter A., and Taylor, Rosemary C. 1996. Political science and the three new institutionalism. *Political Studies*, 44(5), 936–957.

Hallerberg, Mark. 2004. *Domestic Budgets in a United Europe: Fiscal Governance from the End of Bretton Woods to EMU*. Ithaca: Cornell University Press.

Hallerberg, Mark, Strauch, Rolf, and von Hagen, Jürgen. 2001. *The Use and Effectiveness of Budgetary Rules and Norms in EU Member States*. Report Prepared for the Dutch Ministry of Finance by the Institute of European Integration Studies in Bonn.

Hallerberg, Mark, Strauch, Rolf, and von Hagen, Jürgen. 2009. *Fiscal Governance in Europe*. Cambridge: Cambridge University Press.

Halpin, Darren. 2011. Explaining policy bandwagons: Organized interest mobilization and cascades of attention. *Governance*, 24(2), 205–230.

Hamm, Keith E., Hedlund, Ronald D., and Martorano, Nancy Martorano. 2006. Measuring state legislative committee power: Change and chamber differences in the 20th century. *State Politics & Policy Quarterly*, 6(1), 88–111.

Hamm, Keith E., Hedlund, Ronald D., and Miller, Nancy Martorano. 2014. State legislatures. Pages 293–318 of: Haider-Markel, Donald D. (ed), *The Oxford Handbook of State and Local Government*. Oxford University Press.

Hammond, Thomas H., and Miller, Gary J. 1987. The Core of the Constitution. *The American Political Science Review*, 81(4), 1155–1174.

Hanegraaff, Marcel, van der Ploeg, Jens, and Berkhout, Joost. 2019. Standing in a crowded room: Exploring the relation between interest group system density and access to policymakers. *Political Research Quarterly*, 73(1), 51–64.

Hansen, John Mark. 1991. *Gaining Access: Congress and the Farm Lobby, 1919-1981*. University of Chicago Press.

Harris, Michael A. 2009. 'Valentines' delivered to Albany in lobbying effort. *New York Examiner (NY)*, Feb. 14.

Hartney, Michael T. 2022. *How Policies Make Interest Groups: Governments, Unions, and American Education*. University of Chicago Press.

Hartsoe, Steve. 2004. State eyes keeping purse zipped up. *The Herald-Sun*, May 9, A1.

Haskins, Ron. 2007. *Work Over Welfare: The Inside Story of the 1996 Welfare Reform Law*. Brookings Institution Press.

Hastie, Trevor J. 2017. Generalized additive models. Pages 249–307 of: *Statistical models in S*. Routledge.

Heclo, Hugh, and Wildavsky, Aaron B. 1974. *The Private Government of Public Money: Community and Policy Inside British Politics*. London: Macmillan.

Hedge, David. 2018. *Governance and the Changing American States*. Routledge.

Hedge, David M. 1983. Fiscal dependency and the state budget process. *The Journal of Politics*, 45(1), 198–208.

Hegelich, Simon, Fraune, Cornelia, and Knollmann, David. 2015. Point predictions and the punctuated equilibrium theory: A data mining approach–U.S. nuclear policy as proof of concept. *Policy Studies Journal*, 43(2), 228–256.

Heinz, John P, Laumann, Edward O, Nelson, Robert L, and Salisbury, Robert H. 1993. *The Hollow Core: Private Interests in National Policy Making*. Harvard University Press.

Hendrick, Rebecca M., and Garand, James C. 1991. Expenditure tradeoffs in the US states: A pooled analysis. *Journal of Public Administration Research and Theory*, 1(3), 295–318.

Heys, John, and Finn, Scott. 2004. Cutting Medicaid, state lawmakers would have to target 1 of 5 big programs. *Charleston Gazette (WV)*, Feb. 15, P1A.

Hibbs, Douglas A. 1977. Political-parties and macroeconomic policy. *American Political Science Review*, 71(4), 1467–1487.

Hinchliffe, Kelsey L, and Lee, Frances E. 2016. Party competition and conflict in state legislatures. *State Politics & Policy Quarterly*, 16(2), 172–197.

Hojnacki, Marie, and Kimball, David C. 1998. Organized interests and the decision of whom to lobby in Congress. *American Political Science Review*, 92(4), 775–790.

Hojnacki, Marie, Kimball, David C., Baumgartner, Frank R., Berry, Jeffrey M., and Leech, Beth L. 2012. Studying organizational advocacy and influence: Reexamining interest group research. *Annual Review of Political Science*, 15, 379–399.

Holtz-Eakin, Douglas. 1988. The line item veto and public sector budgets: Evidence from the states. *Journal of Public Economics*, 36(3), 269–292.

Holyoke, Thomas T. 2003. Choosing battlegrounds: Interest group lobbying across multiple venues. *Political Research Quarterly*, 56(3), 325–336.

Holyoke, Thomas T. 2009. Interest group competition and coalition formation. *American Journal of Political Science*, 53(2), 360–375.

Holyoke, Thomas T. 2019. Dynamic state interest group systems: A new look with new data. *Interest Groups & Advocacy*, 8(4), 499–518.

Holyoke, Thomas T., and Brown, Heath. 2019. After the punctuation: Competition, uncertainty, and convergent state policy change. *State Politics & Policy Quarterly*, 19(1), 3–28.

Hood, John. 2001. Now's the time to reduce Tar Heel taxes. *The Herald-Sun*, May 25, A13.

Hood, John. 2002a. Mike Easley's 1 percent hyperbole. *The Herald-Sun*, Apr. 2, A9.

Hood, John. 2002b. Odom takes on entrenched interests. *The Herald-Sun*, Apr. 16, A10.

Hood, John. 2009. Cut something other than mental health. *The Daily Dispatch*, July 10, 8A.

Hoover, Gary A., and Pecorino, Paul. 2005. The political determinants of federal expenditure at the state level. *Public Choice*, 123(1), 95–113.

Hosking, Jonathan R. M. 1990. L-Moments: Analysis and estimation of distributions using linear combinations of order statistics. *Journal of the Royal Statistical Society. Series B.*, 52(1), 105–124.

Hosking, Jonathan R. M. 1998. L-moments. Pages 357–362 of: Kotz, S, Read, C., and Banks, D.L. (eds), *Encyclopedia of Statistical Sciences*, update ed., vol. 2. New York: Wiley.

Hou, Yilin, and Smith, Daniel L. 2006. A framework for understanding state balanced budget requirement systems: Reexamining distinctive features and an operational definition. *Public Budgeting & Finance*, 26(3), 22–45.

Hou, Yilin, and Smith, Daniel L. 2010. Do state balanced budget requirements matter? Testing two explanatory frameworks. *Public Choice*, 145(1-2), 57–79.

Howard, Carol. 2002. Smart Start's funding ensures kids' success. *The News & Record*, Apr. 18, A10.

Howlett, Michael, and Cashore, Benjamin. 2009. The dependent variable problem in the study of policy change: Understanding policy change as a methodological problem. *Journal of Comparative Policy Analysis*, 11(1), 33–46.

Humphrey, Tom. 2006a. House OKs $26B budget; Senate votes on plan today – Agreement reached to send surplus revenue to education at all levels. *Knoxville News Sentinel (TN)*, May 26, A1.

Humphrey, Tom. 2006b. Budget shrinks, but few still gain – Bredesen finds funds for education, raises, health care in plan. *Knoxville News Sentinel (TN)*, Feb. 8, A1.

Humphrey, Tom. 2006c. Final stretch ahead for state lawmakers. *Knoxville News Sentinel (TN)*, May 21, B1.

Humphrey, Tom. 2006d. Surplus money plans outlined – Higher ed, chronically ill, state workers all benefit from budget. *Knoxville News Sentinel (TN)*, May 9, A1.

Hunter, Kathleen. 2003. House fails to fund cancer center. *The News & Observer*, July 23, A1.

Jacobs, Michael. 2003. Politicians recount their victory in hospital battle. *The Daily Dispatch*, Aug. 19.

Jacoby, William G., and Schneider, Saundra K. 2001. Variability in state policy priorities: An empirical analysis. *Journal of Politics*, 63, 544–568.

Jacoby, William G, and Schneider, Saundra K. 2008. A new measure of policy spending priorities in the American states. *Political Analysis*, 17(1), 1–24.

Jarvis, Craig. 2001. Day-care centers plead for funding. *The News & Observer*, June 27, B1.

Jay Liu, Irene. 2008. Pain, gain in budget figures. *Times Union, The (Albany, NY)*, Dec. 15, A1.

Jennings, Will, Farrall, Stephen, Gray, Emily, and Hay, Colin. 2020. Moral panics and punctuated equilibrium in public policy: An analysis of the criminal justice policy agenda in Britain. *Policy Studies Journal*, 48(1), 207–234.

Jensen, Carsten. 2009. Policy punctuations in mature welfare states. *Journal of Public Policy*, 29(3), 287–303.

Jewell, Malcolm E. 1982. The neglected world of state politics. *The Journal of Politics*, 44(3), 638–657.

John, Peter, and Jennings, Will. 2010. Punctuations and turning points in British politics: The policy agenda of the queen's speech, 1940–2005. *British Journal of Political Science*, 40(3), 561–586.

John, Peter, and Margetts, Helen. 2003. Policy punctuations in the UK. *Public Administration*, 81(3), 411–432.

Johnson, Mark. 2001a. It's every program for itself as cuts begin. *The Charlotte Observer*, Feb. 25, 2B.

Johnson, Mark. 2001b. N.C. budget raises taxes by $1 billion. *The Charlotte Observer*, Sept. 21, 1B.

Johnson, Mark. 2001c. N.C. Senate presents no-lottery budget. *The Charlotte Observer*, May 25, 1A.

Jones, Bryan D. 1994. *Reconceiving Decision-Making in Democratic Politics: Attention, Choice, and Public Policy*. Chicago: University of Chicago Press.

Jones, Bryan D. 2001. *Politics and the Architecture of Choice: Bounded Rationality and Governance*. Chicago: University of Chicago Press.

Jones, Bryan D., and Baumgartner, Frank R. 2005. *The Politics of Attention: How the Government Prioritizes Problems*. Chicago: University of Chicago Press.

Jones, Bryan D., and Breunig, Christian. 2007. Noah and Joseph effects in government budgets: Analyzing long-term memory. *Policy Studies Journal*, 35(3), 329–348.

Jones, Bryan D., True, James L., and Baumgartner, Frank R. 1997. Does incrementalism stem from political consensus or institutional gridlock? *American Journal of Political Science*, 41, 1319–1339.

Jones, Bryan D., Baumgartner, Frank R., and True, James L. 1998. Policy punctuations: US budget authority, 1947-95. *Journal of Politics*, 60(1), 1–33.

Jones, Bryan D., Sulkin, Tracy, and Larsen, Heather A. 2003. Punctuations in political institutions. *American Political Science Review*, 97(1), 1–23.

Jones, Bryan D., Baumgartner, Frank R., Breunig, Christian, Wlezien, Christopher, Soroka, Stuart, Foucault, Martial, François, Abel, Green-Pedersen, Christoffer, Koski, Chris, John, Peter, Mortensen, Peter B., Varone, Frédéric, and Walgrave, Stefaan. 2009. A general empirical law of public budgets: A comparative analysis. *American Journal of Political Science*, 53(4), 855–873.

Jones, Bryan D., Zalányi, László, and Érdi, Péter. 2014a. An integrated theory of budgetary politics and some empirical tests: The U.S. national budget, 1791–2010. *American Journal of Political Science*, 58(3), 561–578.

Jones, Bryan D, Thomas III, Herschel F, and Wolfe, Michelle. 2014b. Policy bubbles. *Policy Studies Journal*, 42(1), 146–171.

Jordan, Meagan M. 2003. Punctuations and agendas. *Journal of Policy Analysis and Management*, 22(3), 345–360.

Kabler, Phil. 2002a. $2.93 billion budget includes raises reliance on lottery worries some. *Charleston Gazette (WV)*, Jan. 10, P7A.

Kabler, Phil. 2002b. Milder regular session expected lawmakers return on Wednesday. *Charleston Gazette (WV)*, Jan. 6, P01A.

Kabler, Phil. 2003. Community corrections saves money, court officer says. *Charleston Gazette (WV)*, Oct. 21, P10A.

Kabler, Phil. 2004a. Child care survives cutback, Agency OKs $37 million in welfare cuts. *Charleston Gazette (WV)*, July 7, P1A.

Kabler, Phil. 2004b. Cutting welfare funds studied Wise must decide whether to slash $42.3 million or not. *Charleston Gazette (WV)*, May 27, P1A.

Kabler, Phil. 2004c. Officials open to alternative welfare cuts funds insufficient to implement proposal from advocate groups, Nusbaum says. *Charleston Gazette (WV)*, May 28, P1C.

Kabler, Phil. 2004d. Recipients speak out on planned TANF cuts DHHR intends to slash $42M of welfare-to-work benefits effective Aug. 1. *Charleston Gazette (WV)*, June 11, P1A.

Kabler, Phil. 2004e. REGIONAL JAIL AUTHORITY Alternative sentencing funds sought. *Charleston Gazette (WV)*, June 2, P3A.

Kabler, Phil. 2004f. STATE OF THE STATE ADDRESS $3.078 billion budget introduced. *Charleston Gazette (WV)*, Jan. 15, P1A.

Kabler, Phil. 2004g. Welfare-to-work may retain some funding. *Charleston Gazette (WV)*, June 9, P1A.

Kahneman, Daniel, and Tversky, Amos. 1979. Prospect theory – Analysis of decision under risk. *Econometrica*, 47(2), 263–291.

Kamlet, Mark S., and Mowery, David C. 1980. The budgetary base in federal resource allocation. *American Journal of Political Science*, 24(4), 804–821.

Kane, Dan. 2003a. Budget facing veto Easley to veto budget. *The News & Observer*, June 29, A1.

Kane, Dan. 2003b. Prison crowding worsens. *The News & Observer*, Dec. 27, A1.

Kane, Dan. 2004a. Budget clears House hurdle. *The News & Observer*, June 8, B5.

Kane, Dan. 2004b. Habitual felon law could change. *The News & Observer*, Apr. 12, A1.

Kane, Dan. 2004c. House delays budget plan. *News & Observer, The (includes Chapel Hill News) (Raleigh, NC)*, May 28, B8.

Kane, Dan. 2008a. Few fixes for full prisons. *The News & Observer*, May 16, A1.

Kane, Dan. 2008b. Key numbers in Easley's budget. *The News & Observer*, May 13, A8.

Kane, Dan. 2008c. A look at N.C. budget plan. *The Charlotte Observer*, July 8, 2B.

Kane, Dan. 2008d. Rising inmate population puts state in a bind. *News & Observer, The (includes Chapel Hill News) (Raleigh, NC)*, Feb. 18, A10.

Kane, Dan. 2008e. Senate, House differ on state budget details. *The News & Observer*, June 17, A7.

Kane, Dan. 2009. Reduced sentences may ease crowding. *The Charlotte Observer*, Feb. 11, 2B.

Kane, Dan, and Barrett, Barbara. 2003. Budget allows no tax cuts. *The News & Observer*, Mar. 6, A1.

Kane, Dan, and Bonner, Lynn. 2003a. Budget given tentative approval. *The News & Observer*, June 30, A1.

Kane, Dan, and Bonner, Lynn. 2003b. Tobacco, alcohol taxes stay put. *The News & Observer*, June 27, A1.

Kane, Dan, and Stancill, Jane. 2004. Some proposed cuts raise eyebrows. *The News & Observer*, May 12, B5.

Kaplan, Thomas. 2014. Paterson is praised as portrait is unveiled. *The New York Times*, Mar. 2.

Karlin, Rick. 2008. Group wants welfare grant raised – Advocates say $291 monthly payment for family of 3 hasn't grown in 18 years; state cites other aid. *Times Union, The (Albany, NY)*, Feb. 6, A3.

Karlin, Rick. 2009. Camp McGregor up for closure. *Times Union, The (Albany, NY)*, May 1, A3.

Karlin, Rick. 2010. Forced vote on $385M in cuts. *Times Union, The (Albany, NY)*, June 5, A1.

Keele, Luke John. 2008. *Semiparametric Regression for the Social Sciences*. John Wiley & Sons.

Keith, Ryan. 2002. State budget ready for vote legislature to act on package today. *Charleston Gazette (WV)*, Mar. 17, P1A.

Kiewiet, D. Roderick, and McCubbins, Mathew D. 1988. Presidential influence on congressional appropriations decisions. *American Journal of Political Science*, 32(3), 713–736.

King, James D. 2000. Changes in professionalism in US state legislatures. *Legislative Studies Quarterly*, 25(2), 327–343.

Kingdon, John W. 1984. *Agendas, Alternatives, and Public Policies*. Boston: Little, Brown.

Kingdon, John W. 1995. *Agendas, Alternatives, and Public Policies*. New York: Harper-Collins College Publishers.

Kirkpatrick, Christopher. 2001. Easley declares fiscal emergency. *The Herald-Sun*, Feb. 9, A1.

Kittel, Bernhard, Obinger, Herbert, et al. 2003. Political parties, institutions, and the dynamics of social expenditure in times of austerity. *Journal of European Public Policy*, 10.

Klarner, Carl E., and Karch, Andrew. 2008. Why do governors issue vetoes? The impact of individual and institutional influences. *Political Research Quarterly*, 61(4), 574–584.

Koenker, Roger. 2005. *Quantile Regression*. Cambridge: Cambridge University Press.

Koenker, Roger, and Bassett, Gilbert. 1978. Regression quantiles. *Econometrica*, 46(1), 33–50.

Kollman, Ken. 1998. *Outside Lobbying: Public Opinion and Interest Group Strategies*. Princeton: Princeton University Press.

Koski, Chris. 2010. Greening America's skylines: The diffusion of low-salience policies. *Policy Studies Journal*, 38(1), 93–117.

Koski, Chris, and May, Peter J. 2006. Interests and implementation: Fostering voluntary regulatory actions. *Journal of Public Administration Research and Theory*, 16(3), 329–349.

Koski, Chris, and Workman, Samuel. 2018. Drawing practical lessons from punctuated equilibrium theory. *Policy & Politics*, 46(2), 293–308.

Koski, Chris, Siddiki, Saba, Sadiq, Abdul-Akeem, and Carboni, Julia. 2018. Representation in collaborative governance: A case study of a food policy council. *The American Review of Public Administration*, 48(4), 359–373.

Kousser, Professor Thad, and Phillips, Professor Justin H. 2012. *The Power of American Governors: Winning on Budgets and Losing on Policy*. New York: Cambridge University Press.

Kousser, Thad, and Phillips, Justin H. 2009. Who blinks first? Legislative patience and bargaining with governors. *Legislative Studies Quarterly*, 34(1), 55–86.

Krause, George A. 2006. Beyond the norm: Cognitive biases and the behavioral underpinnings of US federal agency macroeconomic forecasts. *Rationality and Society*, 18(2), 157–191.

Krause, George A., and Melusky, Benjamin F. 2012. Concentrated powers: Unilateral executive authority and fiscal policymaking in the American states. *The Journal of Politics*, 74(01), 98–112.

Krupnikov, Yanna, and Shipan, Charles. 2012. Measuring gubernatorial budgetary power: A new approach. *State Politics & Policy Quarterly*, 12(4), 438–455.

Kurtz, Rick S. 2013. Oil spill causation and the Deepwater Horizon spill. *Review of Policy Research*, 30(4), 366–380.

Lang, Nancy C. 2003. Keep promise to seniors. *Rutland Herald (VT)*, Feb. 26.

LaPira, Timothy M. 2015. Lobbying in the shadows: How private interests hide from public scrutiny, and why that matters. In: Cigler, Allan J., Loomis, Burdett A., and Nownes, Anthony J. (eds), *Interest Group Politics*. Washington: CQ Press.

LaPira, Timothy M, and Thomas, Herschel F. 2017. *Revolving Door Lobbying: Public Service, Private Influence, and the Unequal Representation of Interests*. Lawrence: University Press of Kansas.

Larson, Krista. 2003. State Hospital facing loss of federal funds. *Times Argus, The (Barre-Montpelier VT)*, Sept. 19.

Lasswell, Harold. 1936. *Politics: Who gets what, when, how*. New York: P. Smith.

Lee, Robert D. 1997. A quarter century of state budgeting practices. *Public Administration Review*, 57(2), 133–140.

Lee, Trymaine, and Kaufman, Leslie. 2008. Citing drop in inmate population, spitzer plans to close four prisons upstate. *The New York Times*, Jan. 12.

Lefler, Dion. 2010. Brownback: Tax cuts, less business rules. *The Wichita Eagle*, Aug.11, 1B.

Leifeld, Philip, and Schneider, Volker. 2012. Information exchange in policy networks. *American Journal of Political Science*, 56(3), 731–744.

Leskanic, Todd. 2002. Tax critics call for budget cutbacks. *The Fayetteville Observer*, Apr. 6.

Levendusky, Matthew. 2009. *The Partisan Sort: How Liberals Became Democrats and Conservatives Became Republicans*. Chicago: University of Chicago Press.

Lewis, Daniel C., Schneider, Saundra K., and Jacoby, William G. 2015. Institutional characteristics and state policy priorities: The impact of legislatures and governors. *State Politics & Policy Quarterly*, 15(4), 447–475.

Lewis, Hunter. 2002a. Hospital choice months away. *The Herald-Sun*, Apr. 1, B1.

Lewis, Hunter. 2002b. Mental health workers worry about patients. *The Herald-Sun*, May 5, C1.

Lewis, Hunter. 2002c. No funds this session for Butner hospital. *The Herald-Sun*, Oct. 4, A1.

Liang, Jiaqi, and Fiorino, Daniel J. 2013. The implications of policy stability for renewable energy innovation in the United States, 1974–2009. *Policy Studies Journal*, 41(1), 97–118.

Lieberman, Evan S. 2005. Nested analysis as a mixed-method strategy for comparative research. *American Political Science Review*, 99(3), 435–452.

Lieberman, Robert C. 2002. Ideas, institutions, and political order: Explaining political change. *American Political Science Review*, 96(4), 697–712.

Lindblom, Charles. 1959. The science of muddling through. *Public Administration Review*, 19(2), 79–88.

Lindblom, Charles. 1975. *The Policy-Making Process*. Englewood Cliffs: Prentice Hall.

Lindblom, Charles Edward. 1965. *The Intelligence of Democracy: Decision Making through Mutual Adjustment*. Free Press.

Lowery, David. 2013. Lobbying Influence: Meaning, measurement and missing. *Interest Groups & Advocacy*, 2(1), 1–26.

Lowery, David, and Gray, Virginia. 1995. The population ecology of Gucci Gulch, or the natural regulation of interest group numbers in the American states. *American Journal of Political Science*, 39(1), 1–29.

Lowery, David, Gray, Virginia, and Baumgartner, Frank R. 2010. Policy attention in state and nation: Is anyone listening to the laboratories of democracy? *Publius: The Journal of Federalism*, 41(2), 286–310.

Lowery, David, Gray, Virginia, and Cluverius, John. 2015. Temporal change in the density of state interest communities: 1980 to 2007. *State Politics & Policy Quarterly*, 15(2), 263–286.

Lowi, Theodore J. 1964. American business, public policy, case-studies, and political theory. *World Politics*, 16(4), 677–715.

Lowi, Theodore J. 1972. Four systems of policy, politics, and choice. *Public Administration Review*, 32(4), 298–310.

Lowry, Robert C., Alt, James E., and Ferree, Karen E. 1998. Fiscal policy outcomes and electoral accountability in American states. *The American Political Science Review*, 92(4), 759–774.

Mace, David. 2002a. Advocates urge legislators: Dip into state rainy day funds. *Rutland Herald (VT)*, Feb. 15.

Mace, David. 2002b. Dean: Fletcher Allen executives 'crooks'. *Rutland Herald (VT)*, Nov. 18.

Mace, David. 2002c. Fletcher Allen and regulators spar over garage. *Rutland Herald (VT)*, Feb. 11.

Mace, David. 2002d. Fletcher Allen officials have tough day before committee. *Rutland Herald (VT)*, Feb. 28.

Mace, David. 2002e. Jail closure could scuttle budget act. *Rutland Herald (VT)*, Feb. 19.

Mace, David. 2002f. Medicaid cuts to affect thousands. *Rutland Herald (VT)*, Jan. 22.

Mace, David. 2002g. Woodstock jail closure opposed. *Rutland Herald (VT)*, Jan. 10.

Mace, David. 2003a. Advocates consider closing state hospital. *Times Argus, The (Barre-Montpelier VT)*, Oct.

Mace, David. 2003b. Budget bill is advanced. *Rutland Herald (VT)*, Apr. 29.

Mace, David. 2003c. Budget bill is advanced. *Rutland Herald (VT)*, Apr. 29.

Mace, David. 2003d. Douglas appoints prison task force. *Times Argus, The (Barre-Montpelier VT)*, Nov. 15.

Mace, David. 2003e. Eight Fletcher Allen board members quit. *Rutland Herald (VT)*, Feb. 13.

Mace, David. 2003f. Fletcher Allen belatedly wins approval. *Times Argus, The (Barre-Montpelier VT)*, Nov. 21.

Mace, David. 2003g. Fletcher Allen probe may be near end. *Rutland Herald (VT)*, Aug. 6.

Mace, David. 2003h. Fletcher Allen seeks OK for project's true cost. *Rutland Herald (VT)*, Feb. 8.

Mace, David. 2003i. Legislators to target safety, oversight issues at state hospital. *Times Argus, The (Barre-Montpelier VT)*, Nov.

Mace, David. 2003j. Negotiators are snagged on Act 60. *Rutland Herald (VT)*, May 20.

Mace, David. 2003k. Panel recommends no more action against Fletcher Allen. *Rutland Herald (VT)*, Oct. 8.

Mace, David. 2003l. Vermont State Hospital can hire CEO, other staff. *Rutland Herald (VT)*, Nov. 6.

Madden, Rebecca. 2008. Web site is taking reaction to cuts – State's Hospitals: HANYS wants residents to tell lawmakers how they feel about plan. *Watertown Daily Times (NY)*, Dec. 24, B3.

Madden, Rebecca. 2010. North hospitals facing $1.8M in cuts – 'More challenging': State legislature's budget 'extender' includes reduction in indigent care funds'. *Watertown Daily Times (NY)*, June 10, B1.

Malek, George. 2001. The politics of medicine (viewpoint). *Times Argus, The (Barre-Montpelier VT)*, Nov. 15.

Manow, Philip, and Burkhart, Simone. 2007. Legislative self-restraint under divided government in Germany, 1976–2002. *Legislative Studies Quarterly*, 32(2), 167–191.

Marinucci, Carla. 1998. Public education: The defining issue for Davis, Lungren. *San Francisco Chronicle*, Aug. 11, A1.

Martin, Marie H., and Streams, Meg. 2015. Punctuated equilibrium theory: An empirical investigation of its relevance for global health expenditure. *Public Budgeting & Finance*, 35(1), 73–94.

Martinez, Amy. 2004. Group pushes child care subsidy. *The News & Observer*, June 17, D1.

Marx, Claude R. 2004a. Corrections may get considerably less than it's seeking. *Rutland Herald (VT)*, Apr. 21.

Marx, Claude R. 2004b. Senate panel curbs requested increases in state's programs. *Rutland Herald (VT)*, Apr. 23.

May, James R. 2003. Now more than ever: Trends in environmental citizen suits at 30 environmental citizen suits at thirty something: A Celebration & Summit: Part I. *Widener Law Review*, 10(1), 1–48.

May, Peter J. 1991. Reconsidering policy design: Policies and publics. *Journal of Public Policy*, 11(2), 187–206.

May, Peter J., and Jochim, Ashley E. 2013. Policy regime perspectives: Policies, politics, and governing. *Policy Studies Journal*, 41(3), 426–452.

May, Peter J., Jochim, Ashley E., and Sapotichne, Joshua. 2011. Constructing homeland security: An anemic policy regime. *Policy Studies Journal*, 39(2), 285–307.

May, Peter J., Koski, Chris, and Stramp, Nicholas. 2016. Issue expertise in policymaking. *Journal of Public Policy*, 36(2), 195–218.

Mayhew, David R. 1974. *Congress: The Electoral Connection*. Vol. 26. Yale University Press.

Mayhew, David R. 1991. *Divided We Govern*. Yale University New Haven.

McBrayer, Sharon. 2010. More money for mental health could ease strain. *The News Herald*, Apr. 29.

McCallum, Laura. 2005 (January 12). *MPR: Senate bill would restore MinnesotaCare cutbacks*. http://news.minnesota.publicradio.org/features/2005/01/13_mccalluml_mncare/. (Accessed on 03/01/2020).

McCarty, Nolan. 2000a. Proposal rights, veto rights, and political bargaining. *American Journal of Political Science*, 44(3), 506–522.

McCarty, Nolan M. 2000b. Presidential pork: Executive veto power and distributive politics. *American Political Science Review*, 94(1), 117–129.

McCarty, Nolan M., Poole, Keith T., and Rosenthal, Howard. 2006. *Polarized America: The Dance of Ideology and Unequal Riches*. Cambridge: MIT Press.

McClaughry, John. 2004. Competing health care visions. *Rutland Herald (VT)*, Jan. 28.

McFarland, Andrew S. 2004. *Neopluralism: The Evolution of Political Process Theory*. University Press of Kansas.

McGrath, Robert J., Rogowski, Jon C., and Ryan, Josh M. 2015. Gubernatorial veto powers and the size of legislative coalitions. *Legislative Studies Quarterly*, 40(4), 571–598.

McGrath, Robert J., Rogowski, Jon C., and Ryan, Josh M. 2016. Veto override requirements and executive success. *Political Science Research and Methods*, 1–27.

McGrath, Robert J., Rogowski, Jon C., and Ryan, Josh M. 2018. Veto override requirements and executive success. *Political Science Research and Methods*, 6(1), 153–179.

McKelvey, Richard D. 1976. Intransitivities in multidimensional voting models and some implications for agenda control. *Journal of Economic Theory*, 12(3), 472–482.

McNaughton, David, and King, Mike. 2007. OUR OPINIONS: Perdue's righteous ax – Maybe the governor was simply settling scores, but his vetoes killed some costly, useless projects. *The Atlanta Journal-Constitution*, June 1, A12.

Messer, Jacob. 2002. Making more space – New juvenile detention center will ease overcrowding. *Charleston Daily Mail (WV)*, June 4, 1A.

Messersmith, Beth. 2010. Budgeting for kids. *The News & Observer*, June 24, 8A.

Mettler, Suzanne. 2005. *Soldiers to Citizens: The GI Bill and the Making of the Greatest Generation*. Oxford University Press on Demand.

Mettler, Suzanne. 2010. Reconstituting the submerged state: The challenges of social policy reform in the Obama era. *Perspectives on Politics*, 8(3), 803–824.

Mettler, Suzanne. 2011. *The Submerged State: How Invisible Government Policies Undermine American Democracy*. University of Chicago Press.

Milburn, John. 2011. Budget proposals please regents. *The Wichita Eagle*, Jan.18, 3A.

Miller, Dawn. 2001. Wise to get welfare cut suggestions Panel recommends spending reduction of $86.87 million. *Charleston Gazette (WV)*, Dec. 7, P1A.

Miller, Dawn. 2002a. More funds sought for abused children, other social services. *Charleston Gazette (WV)*, Jan. 10, P6C.

Miller, Dawn. 2002b. Nonprofits that serve poor kids, families ask for public support. *Charleston Gazette (WV)*, Mar. 8, P1C.

Miller, Dawn. 2003a. Advocate 'dismayed' cabinet on children to be merged. *Charleston Gazette (WV)*, Jan. 9, P5A.

Miller, Dawn. 2003b. Advocates offer alternative to DHHR merger plan. *Charleston Gazette (WV)*, Jan. 15, P1C.

Miller, Dawn. 2003c. Children's cabinet called a 'model' for other states. *Charleston Gazette (WV)*, Mar. 5.

Miller, Dawn. 2003d. Kids' cabinet authors: Kill it 'Failed' experiment never lived up to potential, critics say. *Charleston Gazette (WV)*, Jan. 26, P1A.

Miller, Dawn. 2003e. Savings overestimated, cabinet advocates say. *Charleston Gazette (WV)*, Mar. 1.

Miller, Dawn. 2003f. Second former director urges keeping children's cabinet The CAPITOL REPORT. *Charleston Gazette (WV)*, Jan. 24, P6A.

Mintrom, Michael, and Norman, Phillipa. 2009. Policy entrepreneurship and policy change. *Policy Studies Journal*, 37(4), 649–667.

Mitchell, William C., and Munger, Michael C. 1991. Economic models of interest groups: An introductory survey. *American Journal of Political Science*, 35(2), 512–546.

Moe, Terry M. 1988. *The Organization of Interests: Incentives and the Internal Dynamics of Political Interest Groups*. University of Chicago Press.

Mooneyham, Scott. 2001a. Medicaid hurts N.C. budget. *The Star-News*, Mar. 15, 3B.

Mooneyham, Scott. 2001b. State budget writers scour programs for cuts. *The Herald-Sun*, May 8, A6.

Mooneyham, Scott. 2002a. Budget cuts may cost hundreds of state jobs – Governor and legislators are faced with the prospect of slashing $1.2B. *The Herald-Sun*, Mar. 28, A1.

Mooneyham, Scott. 2002b. Legislators pulled in both directions on taxes. *The Herald-Sun*, June 6, A8.

Morehouse, Sarah M, and Jewell, Malcolm E. 2004. States as laboratories: A reprise. *Annual Review of Political Science*, 7, 177–203.

Mortensen, Peter B. 2005. Policy punctuations in Danish local budgeting. *Public Administration*, 83(4), 931–950.

Mortensen, Peter B. 2006. *The Impact of Public Opinion on Public Policy*. Ph.D. thesis, Institut for Statskundskab, Aarhus Universitet, Aarhus.

Mortensen, Peter B. 2007. Stability and change in public policy: A longitudinal study of comparative subsystem dynamics. *Policy Studies Journal*, 35(3), 373–394.

Mortensen, Peter B. 2009. Political attention and public spending in the United States. *Policy Studies Journal*, 37(3), 435–455.

Moxley, Donna. 2001a. Lawmakers vow to fight to keep jail. *Rutland Herald (VT)*, Dec. 5.

Moxley, Donna. 2001b. Woodstock jail closing plan derided at forum. *Rutland Herald (VT)*, Dec. 4.

Mrozek, Paul. 2010a. Local hospital officials off to Albany. *Daily News, The (Batavia, NY)*, Mar. 3, 3A.

Mrozek, Paul. 2010b. State budget – Is a bitter pill – For hospitals – Health care group says – plan would be costly. *Daily News, The (Batavia, NY)*, July 23, 1A.

Mullany, Gerry. 2017. Chris Christie hits a closed state beach, and kicks up a fury. *N.Y. Times*, July 3.

Naysnerski, Wendy, and Tietenberg, Tom. 1992. Private enforcement of federal environmental law. *Land Economics*, 68(1), 28–48.

NBC17 Staff. 2008. Easley's $21.5 billion budget would increase cigarette, alcohol taxes. *CBS – 17 WNCN (Raleigh-Durham, NC)*, May 12.

Nelson, Paul. 2009. Camp McGregor becomes history. *Times Union, The (Albany, NY)*, July 1, A3.

New Hampshire Union Leader. 1993. Capital Plan Draws Veto From Merrill. Manchester Officials Split on Capital Budget Veto. Available at http://infoweb.newsbank .com/resources/doc/nb/news/0F54504191541A24?p=AWNB, July 8, 1.

New York Division of the Budget. 2018. *The Budget Process.*

New York State Division of the Budget. 2008 (Oct. 28). *Update to Annual Information Statement (AIS) State of New York.* AIS Update. New York State Division of the Budget.

New York States Department of Corrections and Community Supervision. 2011. *2011 Prison Closures Fact Sheet.*

New York Times Editorial Board. 2009. Why are you doing this? *The New York Times*, Feb. 2.

Niolet, Benjamin. 2008. First, the good news. *The News & Observer*, May 9, B1.

Niolet, Benjamin. 2009. As taxes rose, cuts shrank. *The News & Observer*, Aug. 6.

Niolet, Benjamin. 2010a. $18.9 billion House budget full of red ink. *The News & Observer*, June 3, 3B.

Niolet, Benjamin. 2010b. Highlights of the N.C. budget. *The Charlotte Observer*, July 1, 3B.

Niolet, Benjamin. 2010c. Perdue's scorecard so far. *The Charlotte Observer*, Mar. 28, 3B.

Niolet, Benjamin, and Christensen, Rob. 2009a. N.C. cuts needed, but prison survives. *The Charlotte Observer*, May 31, 1A.

Niolet, Benjamin, and Christensen, Rob. 2009b. Perdue orders agencies to try harder on cuts. *Charlotte Observer (NC)*, Jan. 29, 1A.

Niolet, Benjamin, and Johnson, Mark. 2009. Inside Perdue's budget. *The Charlotte Observer*, Mar. 18, 8A.

Niolet, Benjamin, Johnson, Mark, Bonner, Lynn, Chambers Jr., Stanley, Ferreri, Eric, Siceloff, Bruce, and Biesecker, Michael. 2010a. Highlights of proposed budget. *The Charlotte Observer*, Apr. 21, 4A.

Niolet, Benjamin, Bonner, Lynn, and Johnson, Mark. 2010b. Perdue proposes $19 billion budget. *The News & Observer*, Apr. 20.

Niskanen, William. 1971. *Bureaucracy and Representative Government.* Chicago: Aldine-Atherton.

North Carolina Department of Correction. 2002. *Annual Report Fiscal Year 2001– 2002.*

North Carolina Office of Budget and Management. 2018. *The Budget Process.*

Nownes, Anthony J, and Freeman, Patricia. 1998. Interest group activity in the states. *The Journal of Politics*, 60(1), 86–112.

O'Brien, Mark, and Weiner, Michael. 2010. Cuts in human services could exact a high cost later. *Buffalo News, The (NY)*, Apr. 25, G4.

Observer, The News &. 2009. Spending cuts in the preliminary house budget proposal. http://infoweb.newsbank.com/resources/doc/nb/news/1289FD9388B30530? p=AWNB, June 4, A6.

Occaso, Carla. 2002. Douglas sees dramatic drop in state revenues. *Caledonian-Record, The (VT)*, Dec. 4.

National Association of Budget Officers. 2015 (03). *Budget Processes in the States*. Tech. rept. National Association of Budget Officers.

Offen, Neil. 2002. Children make a stand – Parents, youngsters march down Franklin Street to back programs. *The Herald-Sun*, June 1, 1.

Office of the Governor. 2009. Governor Perdue announces 2009–2010 budget proposals. *CBS – 9 WNCT (Greenville, NC)*, Mar. 17.

Olson, Mancur. 1965. *The Logic of Collective Action: Public Goods and the Theory of Groups*. Harvard University Press.

Ostrom, Elinor. 1990. *Governing the Commons*. Cambridge England ; New York: Cambridge University Press.

Ostrom, Elinor. 2009. *Understanding Institutional Diversity*. Princeton University Press.

Padgett, John F. 1980. Bounded rationality in budgetary research. *American Political Science Review*, 74(2), 354–372.

Padgett, John F. 1981. Hierarchy and ecological control in federal budgetary decision making. *American Journal of Sociology*, 87(1), 75–129.

Page, Scott E. 2008. *The Difference: How the Power of Diversity Creates Better Groups, Firms, Schools, and Societies*. Princeton University Press.

Park, Angela YS, and Sapotichne, Joshua. 2020. Punctuated equilibrium and bureaucratic autonomy in American city governments. *Policy Studies Journal*, 48(4), 896–925.

Patashnik, Eric M. 2014. *Reforms at Risk: What Happens After Major Policy Changes Are Enacted*. Princeton University Press.

Paterson, David. 2009 (Jan. 7). *New York State of the State Address 2009*.

Perdue, Beverly. 2009 (Mar. 9). *State of the State Address 2009*.

Poll, Marist. 2010. *2/3: 26% Approval Rating for Paterson | Home of the Marist Poll*.

Poterba, James M. 1995. Balanced budget rules and fiscal policy: Evidence from the states. *National Tax Journal*, 48(3), 329–336.

Pralle, Sarah B. 2003. Venue shopping, political strategy, and policy change: The internationalization of Canadian forest advocacy. *Journal of Public Policy*, 23(3), 233–260.

Pralle, Sarah B. 2006a. *Branching Out, Digging In: Environmental Advocacy and Agenda Setting*. Washington DC: Georgetown University Press.

Pralle, Sarah B. 2006b. Timing and sequence in agenda-setting and policy change: A comparative study of lawn care pesticide politics in Canada and the US. *Journal of European Public Policy*, 13(7), 987–1005.

Pratt, Julee. 2001. Making a real difference TANF Council's report seen as a 'call to action'. *Charleston Gazette (WV)*, Dec. 15, P5A.

Primo, David M. 2006. Stop us before we spend again: Institutional constraints on government spending. *Economics and Politics*, 18(3), 269–312.

Primo, David M. 2007. *Rules and Restraint: Government Spending and the Design of National Institutions*. Chicago: The University of Chicago Press.

Prindle, David F. 2012. Importing concepts from biology into political science: The case of punctuated equilibrium. *Policy Studies Journal*, 40(1), 21–44.

Providence Journal Editorial Board. 1999. Good enough for now. *Providence Journal (RI)*, June 11, B–06.

Rawlins, Wade. 2001. Senate budget clears hurdle. *The News & Observer*, May 29, A1.

Rawlins, Wade. 2002. Differences resolved. *The News & Observer*, Sept. 20, a17.

Rawlins, Wade. 2004a. Projects face hurdle. *The News & Observer*, July 14, B5.

Rawlins, Wade. 2004b. Schools get more money. *The News & Observer*, July 18, A10.

Rawlins, Wade, and Bonner, Lynn. 2004. Deal would build UNC centers. *The News & Observer*, July 15, A1.

Rawlins, Wade, and Gardner, Amy. 2002a. Jobs, services targeted for cuts. *The News & Observer*, Mar. 28, A1.

Rawlins, Wade, and Gardner, Amy. 2002b. N.C. cupboard is bare. *The News & Observer*, May 26, A1.

Rawlins, Wade, Silberman, Todd, and Wilson, Trish. 2002. Senate budget avoids deep cuts. *The News & Observer*, June 12, A1.

Reagan, Jim. 2010. Aubertine: Keep OCF open, or lose my budget vote. *Daily Courier-Observer (Massena, NY)*, Jan. 20, 4.

Reese, Michelle. 2009. A step back from mental health. *The News & Observer*, June 4, A9.

Rhodes, R. A. W., Binder, Sarah A., and Rockman, Bert A. 2008. *The Oxford Handbook of Political Institutions*. Oxford: Oxford University Press.

Rice, David. 2001a. $14.4 billion budget gets initial OK. *The Winston-Salem Journal*, June 28, 1.

Rice, David. 2001b. State legislators deal a financial blow to rural hospitals. *Winston-Salem Journal*, Aug. 17, 1.

Rice, David. 2002. Medicaid cuts would end up deep. *The Winston-Salem Journal*, Apr. 2, 1.

Rice, David. 2003. Easley proposed $15 billion budget. *Winston-Salem Journal*, Mar. 6, 1.

Richburg, Keith B. 2009. Stalemate in N.Y. state Senate appears to be resolved as democrat rejoins caucus. *Washington Post*, July 10.

Richman, Jesse. 2008. Uncertainty and the prevalence of committee outliers. *Legislative Studies Quarterly*, 33(2), 323–347.

Robertson, Gary. 2001. House restores Senate cuts. *StarNews*, June 23, 1B.

Robinson, Robert R. 2016. Cultural change and policy images in policy subsystems. *Public Administration*, 94(4), 953–969.

Robinson, Scott E. 2004. Punctuated equilibrium, bureaucratization, and budgetary changes in schools. *Policy Studies Journal*, 32(1), 25–39.

Robinson, Scott E., Caver, Floun'say, Meier, Kenneth J., and Jr, Laurence J. O'Toole. 2007. Explaining policy punctuations: Bureaucratization and budget change. *American Journal of Political Science*, 51(1), 140–150.

Robinson, Scott E., Flink, Carla M., and King, Chad M. 2014. Organizational history and budgetary punctuation. *Journal of Public Administration Research and Theory*, 24(2), 459–471.

Rocky Mount Telegram. 2010. Money problems push psychiatric hospital's closure. http://infoweb.newsbank.com/resources/doc/nb/news/132F1D0E1BFA9CE8? p=AWNB, Oct. 17.

Romer, Thomas, and Rosenthal, Howard. 1978. Political resource-allocation, controlled agendas, and the status quo. *Public Choice*, 33(4), 27–43.

Rosenthal, Alan. 2001. *The Third House: Lobbyists and Lobbying in the States*. Sage.

Rosenthal, Alan. 2008. *Engines of Democracy: Politics and Policymaking in State Legislatures*. SAGE.

Ross, Tom. 2004. Right policies can make N.C. 'Smart on Crime'. *Winston-Salem Journal (NC)*, Apr. 12, 13.

Rowland, Christopher. 1999. Almond spreads the wealth in $2.1-billion spending plan. *Providence Journal (RI)*, Feb. 12, A-01.

Rudalevige, Andrew. 2002. *Managing the President's Program: Presidential Leadership and Legislative Policy Formulation*. Princeton: Princeton University Press.

Rutland Herald (VT). 2002a. Douglas faces first big test. http://infoweb.newsbank.com/ resources/doc/nb/news/10D8479587ADC260?p=AWNB, Nov. 23.

Rutland Herald (VT). 2002b. A timid step. Available at: http://infoweb.newsbank.com/ resources/doc/nb/news/10D84573A9BB8860?p=AWNB, Apr. 8.

Rutland Herald (VT). 2004. Gov. Douglas' State of the State address. http:// infoweb.newsbank.com/resources/doc/nb/news/10D84B8F67D981F0?p=AWNB, Jan. 6.

Ryu, Jay Eungha. 2009. Exploring the factors for budget stability and punctuations: A preliminary analysis of state government sub-functional expenditures. *Policy Studies Journal*, 37(3), 457–473.

Ryu, Jay Eungha. 2011. Legislative professionalism and budget punctuations in state government Sub-Functional expenditures. *Public Budgeting & Finance*, 31(2), 22–42.

Ryu, Jay Eungha. 2015. *The Public Budgeting and Finance Primer: Key Concepts in Fiscal Choice*. Routledge.

Ryu, Jay Eungha, Bowling, Cynthia J, Cho, Chung-Lae, and Wright, Deil S. 2007. Effects of administrators' aspirations, political principals' priorities, and interest groups' influence on state agency budget requests. *Public Budgeting & Finance*, 27(2), 22–49.

Sabatier, Paul A., and Jenkins-Smith, Hank C. 1993. *Policy Change and Learning: An Advocacy Coalition Approach*. Westview Press.

Sabatier, Paul A., and Weible, Christopher M. 2007. The advocacy coalition framework: Innovations and clarifications. Pages 189–222 of: Sabatier, Paul A. (ed), *Theories of the Policy Process*, 2nd ed. Boulder: Westview Press.

Saiegh, Sebastian M. 2011. *Ruling by Statute: How Uncertainty and Vote Buying Shape Lawmaking*. New York: Cambridge University Press.

Salisbury, Robert H. 1992. *Interests and Institutions: Substance and Structure in American Politics*. University of Pittsburgh Press.

Saltzman, Jonathan. 1999. Lawmakers refuse to speed release of URI arena. *Providence Journal (RI)*, Apr. 10, A-01.

Salzer, James. 2007. Decision day for state budget, laws – Governor expected to trim funding, veto bills in wake of today's deadline for his signature on this year's legislation. *The Atlanta Journal-Constitution*, May 30, B1.

Samuels, Michael H. 2010. New York Governor David Paterson budgets $1B in new taxes. *Long Island Business News (NY)*, Jan. 19.

San Francisco Chronicle Editorial Board. 1998. Gray Davis for Governor. *San Francisco Chronicle (CA)*, Oct. 25, 10.

Schattschneider, Elmer E. 1960. *The Semi-Sovereign People; a Realist's View of Democracy in America*. 1st ed. New York,: Holt Rinehart and Winston.

Scheck, Tom. 2005a (June 30). *MPR: Lawmakers fail to avert shutdown*. http:// news.minnesota.publicradio.org/features/2005/06/30_scheckt_court/. (Accessed on 03/01/2020).

Scheck, Tom. 2005b (July 13). *MPR: Legislature passes budget, cigarette fee before heading home*. http://news.minnesota.publicradio.org/features/2005/07/13 _mccalluml_hhsbill/. (Accessed on 03/01/2020).

Scheck, Tom. 2005c (January 25). *MPR: Pawlenty's budget hits health care*. http:// news.minnesota.publicradio.org/features/2005/01/25_scheckt_budgethealthcare/. (Accessed on 03/01/2020).

Scheck, Tom. 2005d (May 4). *MPR: Senate approves health bill with MinnesotaCare expansion*. http://news.minnesota.publicradio.org/features/2005/05/04_scheckt_hhs/. (Accessed on 03/01/2020).

Scherer, Ron. 2010. As scandal mounts, New York Governor David Paterson urged to step down. *Christian Science Monitor*, Mar. 3.

Schlesinger, Joseph A. 1965. The politics of the executive. Pages 210–37 of: Jacob, H, and Vines, KN (eds), *Politics in the American States: A Comparative Analysis*. Little, Brown.

Schlozman, Kay Lehman, Verba, Sidney, and Brady, Henry E. 2012. *The Unheavenly Chorus: Unequal Political Voice and the Broken Promise of American Democracy*. Princeton: Princeton University Press.

Schmaler, Tracy. 2002a. Adjournment imminent for session. *Times Argus, The (Barre-Montpelier VT)*, May 31.

Schmaler, Tracy. 2002b. Budget, smoking tax push session into June. *Rutland Herald (VT)*, June 1.

Schmaler, Tracy. 2002c. Extended life for jail wins panel's support. *Rutland Herald (VT)*, Jan. 24.

Schmaler, Tracy. 2002d. Legislature returns to tough slate of problems – Cutting the budget tops list of challenges for lawmakers. *Times Argus, The (Barre-Montpelier VT)*, Jan. 6.

Schmaler, Tracy. 2002e. State House negotiations continue; adjournment due this weekend? *Rutland Herald (VT)*, May 22.

Schmaler, Tracy. 2003a. Adjournment held up by budget impasse. *Rutland Herald (VT)*, May 28.

Schmaler, Tracy. 2003b. Douglas administration opposes House panel's budget proposal. *Rutland Herald (VT)*, Mar. 26.

Schmaler, Tracy. 2003c. Douglas' Medicaid proposal questioned. *Times Argus, The (Barre-Montpelier VT)*, Jan. 30.

Schmaler, Tracy. 2003d. Douglas outlines budget proposals. *Rutland Herald (VT)*, Jan. 23.

Schmaler, Tracy. 2003e. Douglas taking heat on trooper issue. *Rutland Herald (VT)*, Apr. 23.

Schmaler, Tracy. 2003f. Medicaid cutbacks protested. *Rutland Herald (VT)*, Feb. 18.

Schmaler, Tracy. 2003g. Senate Democrats, clash with Douglas on spending issues. *Rutland Herald (VT)*, Apr. 30.

Schneider, Anne, and Ingram, Helen. 1993. Social construction of target populations: Implications for politics and policy. *American Political Science Review*, 87(2), 334–347.

Schneider, Anne L, and Ingram, Helen M. 1997. *Policy Design for Democracy*. Lawrence: University Press of Kansas.

Schneider, Saundra K, and Jacoby, William G. 2006. Citizen influences on state policy priorities: The interplay of public opinion and interest groups. *Public Opinion in State Politics*, 183–208.

Schneider, Saundra K, Jacoby, William G, and Lewis, Daniel C. 2011. Public opinion toward intergovernmental policy responsibilities. *Publius: The Journal of Federalism*, 41(1), 1–30.

Schulman, Paul R. 1975. Nonincremental policy making: Notes toward an alternative paradigm. *The American Political Science Review*, 69(4), 1354–1370.

Searls, Tom. 2004. Step 7 money restored. Senators, delegates renew $33 million for schools funding. *Charleston Gazette (WV)*, Mar. 20, P1A.

Seawright, Jason, and Gerring, John. 2008. Case selection techniques in case study research: A menu of qualitative and quantitative options. *Political Research Quarterly*, 61(2), 294–308.

Sebók, Miklós, and Berki, Tamás. 2017. Incrementalism and punctuated equilibrium in Hungarian budgeting (1991–2013). *Journal of Public Budgeting, Accounting & Financial Management*.

Seiler, Casey. 2009. Welfare groups urge state to tap federal stimulus. *Times Union, The (Albany, NY)*, Mar. 6, A3.

Serhienko, Nikki Lane. 1999. Legislature wants more budget power; governor opposes lawmakers' proposal to gain planning control. *Bismarck Tribune (ND)*, April 13.

Serres, Chris. 2002. Senate OKs incentives; House a question mark. *The News & Observer*, Sept. 26, D1.

Sharkansky, Ira. 1967. Government expenditures and public services in the American states. *American Political Science Review*, 61(4).

Sharkansky, Ira. 1968. Agency requests, gubernatorial support and budget success in state legislatures. *American Political Science Review*, 62(4), 1220–1231.

Sheather, S. J., and Jones, M.C. 1991. A reliable data-based bandwidth selection method for kernel density estimation. *Journal of the Royal Statistical Society. Series B*, 53(3), 683–690.

Shepsle, Kenneth A., and Weingast, Barry R. 1981. Structure-induced equilibrium and legislative choice. *Public Choice*, 37(3), 503–519.

Shor, Boris. 2014. *July 2014 update: Aggregate data for ideological mapping of American legislatures*. http://dx.doi.org/10.7910/DVN/26799. (Accessed on 20/09/2017).

Shor, Boris, and McCarty, Nolan. 2011. The ideological mapping of American legislatures. *American Political Science Review*, 105(03), 530–551.

Siddiki, Saba N, Carboni, Julia L, Koski, Chris, and Sadiq, Abdul-Akeem. 2015. How policy rules shape the structure and performance of collaborative governance arrangements. *Public Administration Review*, 75(4), 536–547.

Simon, Herbert A. 1955. On a class of skew distribution functions. *Biometrika*, 42(3/4), 425–440.

Sinner, George, and Jansen, Bob. 2011. *Turning Point: A Memoir*. Washburn, North Dakota: Dakota Institute Press.

Smallheer, Susan. 2001. Woodstock prison need cited. *Rutland Herald (VT)*, Dec. 3.

Smallheer, Susan. 2002. Douglas says Springfield jail will open. *Rutland Herald (VT)*, Dec. 11.

Smith, Daniel L., and Hou, Yilin. 2013. Balanced budget requirements and state spending: A long–panel study. *Public Budgeting & Finance*, 33(2), 1–18.

Smith Cox, Therese. 2003. Hospital addition to get OK, state to approve $75 million project for WVU hospital. *Charleston Daily Mail (WV)*, Apr. 21, 1D.

Smithwick, Matt. 2003a. Douglas tours site of prison. *Rutland Herald (VT)*, Apr. 23.

Smithwick, Matt. 2003b. Senators want new prison open this year. *Rutland Herald (VT)*, Apr. 3.

Sneyd, Ross. 2001a. Regulators investigating Fletcher Allen expansion. *Rutland Herald (VT)*, Dec. 6.

Sneyd, Ross. 2001b. Woodstock jail may be closed. *Rutland Herald (VT)*, Nov. 16.

Sneyd, Ross. 2002a. Senate adds money to budget, angers Dean. *Rutland Herald (VT)*, May 8.

Sneyd, Ross. 2002b. Senate panel agrees on 2003 budget. *Rutland Herald (VT)*, May 4.

Sneyd, Ross. 2002c. Tax hikes for schools and Medicare find support in House. *Rutland Herald (VT)*, Apr. 6.

Sneyd, Ross. 2002d. Woodstock jail receives a stay. *Rutland Herald (VT)*, Feb. 21.

Solnik, Claude. 2010a. Hospitals mixed on N.Y. Senate budget. *Long Island Business News (NY)*, Mar. 23.

Solnik, Claude. 2010b. Lobby ad depicts N.Y. governor as monster. *Long Island Business News (NY)*, Mar. 10.

Solomont, E. B. 2008. City hospitals most affected under proposed Medicaid cuts. *New York Sun, The (NY)*, Aug. 14, 2.

Soroka, Stuart N., Wlezien, Christopher, and McLean, Iain. 2006. Public expenditure in the UK: How measures matter. *Journal of the Royal Statistical Society: Series A (Statistics in Society)*, 169(2), 255–271.

Squire, Peverill. 1992. Legislative professionalization and membership diversity in state legislatures. *Legislative Studies Quarterly*, 17(1), 69–79.

Squire, Peverill. 2007. Measuring state legislative professionalism: The squire index revisited. *State Politics & Policy Quarterly*, 7(2), 211–227.

Squire, Peverill. 2012. *The Evolution of American Legislatures: Colonies, Territories, and States, 1619–2009*. Ann Arbor: University of Michigan Press.

Squire, Peverill, and Moncrief, Gary. 2015. *State Legislatures Today: Politics under the Domes*. Rowman & Littlefield.

Stachowski, William. 2009. Maziarz's 'no' votes hurt Western New Yorkers. *Buffalo News, The (NY)*, Apr. 18, A6.

Starcher, Larry. 2003. Wasteful imprisonment state needs more alternative sentencing, drug programs. *Charleston Gazette (WV)*, Dec. 29, P5A.

Stasavage, David. 2002. Private investment and political institutions. *Economics and Politics*, 14, 41–63.

State of New York Division of the Budget. 2008 (Dec. 16). *Governor Paterson Proposes First Increase to Welfare Grant in 18 Years*.

Stein, Robert M. and Bickers, Kenneth N. 1997. Perpetuating the Pork Barrel: Policy Subsystems and American Democracy. Cambridge University Press.

Stith, Pat, and Raynor, David. 2008. Too much money, too little care. *Charlotte Observer*, Feb. 24, 1A.

Strickland, James. 2019. America's crowded statehouses: Measuring and explaining lobbying in the US states. *State Politics & Policy Quarterly*, 19(3), 351–374.

The Associated Press. 2001. HealthSouth files for state approval for surgery clinic. *Times Argus, The (Barre-Montpelier VT)*, Mar. 28.

The Associated Press. 2002a. Fletcher Allen wins state approval for new parking garage. *Rutland Herald (VT)*, July 16.

The Associated Press. 2002b. N.C. cuts would hit poor, elderly. *The Herald-Sun*, Apr. 3, C14.

The Associated Press. 2003a. Advocates say Waterbury state hospital is overcrowded. *Rutland Herald (VT)*, Mar. 14.

The Associated Press. 2003b. Gov. Wise outlines 'tough decisions'. *Charleston Gazette (WV)*, Jan. 9, P6A.

The Associated Press. 2003c. State urged not to cut Medicaid. *Charleston Gazette (WV)*, Dec. 27, P4C.

The Associated Press. 2003d. Status of major bills in the 2003 Legislature. *Charleston Gazette (WV)*, Mar. 10.

The Associated Press. 2004a. DHHR cuts bring 600 comments. *Charleston Gazette (WV)*, July 3, P7B.

The Associated Press. 2004b. Group will offer own welfare plan coalition seeking smaller cut in recipients' checks. *Charleston Daily Mail (WV)*, May 26, P6B.

The Associated Press. 2004c. Panel will meet to discuss welfare cutbacks. *Charleston Daily Mail (WV)*, May 5, P6D.

The Associated Press. 2004d. State budget headed toward Sunday vote. Plan contains more than $3 billion in general spending. *Charleston Daily Mail (WV)*, Mar. 20, P4C.

The Associated Press. 2008. Paterson plans tax hikes, increase in welfare grant. *Daily Messenger (Canandaigua, NY)*, Dec. 15, 4B.

The Charlotte Observer Editorial Board. 2003. Smart Start helps. *Charlotte Observer (NC)*, Mar. 6, 10A.

The Fayetteville Observer. 2002. Governor's Office slapshot fax goes wide. http://infoweb.newsbank.com/resources/doc/nb/news/0F54EF8FF5575E55?p=AWNB, June 10.

The Herald Dispatch Staff. 2004. Current budget pain destined to get much worse. *Herald-Dispatch, The (Huntington, WV)*, Mar. 23, 6A.

The New York Post Editorial Board. 2009. The cowardly bully. *New York Post (NY)*, Feb. 23, 024.

The News & Observer. 2008. Readers sound off about mental health care in N.C. http://infoweb.newsbank.com/resources/doc/nb/news/11F2A38D73DFE458?p=AWNB, Mar. 2, E3.

The News & Observer. 2010. Open door. *Charlotte Observer*, Oct. 31, 22A.

The News & Observer Editorial Board. 2002. An ailing system. *The News & Observer*, Mar. 24, a28.

The News & Observer Editorial Board. 2008. Blame to go around. *The News & Observer*, Feb. 27, A8.

The News & Observer Editorial Board. 2009. Locks or leeway. *The News & Observer*, Mar. 6, A12.

The Observer Editorial Board. 2002. The N.C. budget – Raising taxes is hard, but nobody said governing is easy. *The Charlotte Observer*, June 4, 12A.

The Ogdensburg Journal. 2010. COs Lobby Legislature, Oppose OCF Closing. http://infoweb.newsbank.com/resources/doc/nb/news/12DC45EF1E137A68?p=WORLDNEWS, Feb. 9, 14.

The Post-Standard Editorial Board. 2010. Halving welfare benefit hike breaks New York's promise to the poor. *Post-Standard, The: Blogs (Syracuse, NY)*, Jan. 29.

The Post-Star Editorial Board. 2008. Governor proposes bold steps on budget. *Post-Star, The (Glens Falls, NY)*, Apr. 24.

The Record. 2010. Paterson's emergency bill to cut $300M. http://infoweb.newsbank.com/resources/doc/nb/news/130F1900D1E9C120?p=WORLDNEWS, June 12, 4D.

The Salisbury Post. 2008. Gov. Easley works on final state budget. http://infoweb.newsbank.com/resources/doc/nb/news/125B35D50F8F42D8?p=AWNB, May 12.

The Sentencing Project. 2017 (June). *Trends in U.S. Corrections*.

The Sentencing Project. 2022. *Criminal Justice Facts*.

The Times Union Editorial Board. 2010. The cruelest cut. *Times Union, The (Albany, NY)*, Jan. 22, A12.

The Urban Institute. 2017 (Oct. 20). *Public Welfare Expenditures*.

Thompson, Maury. 2010. Local hospitals hit with state funding cuts. *Post-Star, The (Glens Falls, NY)*, June 8.

Thurmaier, Kurt M., and Willoughby, Katherine G. 2001. *Policy and Politics in State Budgeting*. London: M.E. Sharpe.

Tibbetts, Donn. 1993a. Capital budget deal heads off override vote. *New Hampshire Union Leader*, Sept. 14, 1.

Tibbetts, Donn. 1993b. Democrats offer budget cuts; would slice $10.7 million off capital construction plan. *New Hampshire Union Leader*, July 22, 6.

Tibbetts, Donn. 1993c. Lawmakers discuss odds for capital budget veto. *New Hampshire Union Leader*, Aug. 30, 4.

Tomblin, Earl Ray. 2004 (Dec. 6). *Making supplementary appropriations to various agencies*.

Tranum, Sam. 2002. Prison options weighed – Chief says new beds not only way to solve problem. *Charleston Daily Mail (WV)*, Feb. 2, 1A.

True, James L. 1999. Attention, inertia, and equity in the social security program. *Journal of Public Administration Research and Theory*, 9(4), 571–596.

Truman, David B. 1951. *The Governmental Process: Public Interests and Public Opinion*. New York: Alfred A Knopf.

Tsebelis, George. 1995. Decision making in political systems: Veto players in presidentialism, parliamentarism, multicameralism and multipartyism. *British Journal of Political Science*, 25(3), 289–325.

Tsebelis, George. 2002. *Veto Players: How Political Institutions Work*. Princeton, NJ: Princeton University Press.

Vanberg, Georg. 1998. Abstract judicial review, legislative bargaining, and policy compromise. *Journal of Theoretical Politics*, 10(3), 299–326.

Vanden Brook, Tom. 2003. More governors join exodus from statehouses. *USA Today*, Feb. 13.

Vermont Department of Finance and Management. 2018. *Budget FAQ*.

Vermont Department of Labor, Economic & Labor Market Information. 2020. *Vermont Labor Force & Unemployment.*

Von Hagen, Jürgen. 2002. Fiscal rules, fiscal institutions, and fiscal performance. *Economic and Social Review,* 33(3), 263–284.

von Hagen, Jürgen. 2008. Political economy of fiscal institutions. Pages 464–479 of: Weingast, Barry R., and Wittman, Donald (eds), *The Oxford Handbook of Political Economy,* vol. 1. Oxford: Oxford University Press.

von Hagen, Jürgen, and Harden, Ian J. 1995. Budget processes and commitment to fiscal discipline. *European Economic Review,* 39(3–4), 771–779.

Wallace, Jim. 2003. State budget will be the biggest ever – Cuts included in plan significant, Burdette says. *Charleston Daily Mail (WV),* Jan. 9, 5A.

Washington, Michelle. 2001. Budget woes threaten health care. *The Fayetteville Observer,* Apr. 21.

Weaver, R. Kent, and Rockman, Bert A. 1993. *Do Institutions Matter?: Government Capabilities in the United States and Abroad.* Washington, DC: Brookings Institution Press.

Webster, Gerald R. 2013. Reflections on current criteria to evaluate redistricting plans. *Political Geography,* 32, 3–14.

Wehner, Joachim. 2010. *Legislatures and the Budget Process.* New York: Palgrave.

Weingast, Barry R., Shepsle, Kenneth A., and Johnsen, Christopher. 1981. The political economy of benefits and costs: A neoclassical approach to distributive politics. *Journal of Political Economy,* 89(4), 642–664.

Weissert, Carol S. 1991. Policy entrepreneurs, policy opportunists, and legislative effectiveness. *American Politics Quarterly,* 19(2), 262–274.

Wells, Roger H. 1924. The item veto and state budget reform. *American Political Science Review,* 18(4), 782–791.

West Virginia Division of Corrections. 2005. FY 2004–2005 Annual Report: Corrections in West Virginia. www.wvdoc.com/wvdoc/Portals/0/documents/2005-Annual-Report.pdf, Dec.

West Virginia State Budget Office. 2022. *Budget Process Calendar (text).*

Wheless, Al. 2002. Children make case for Smart Start. *The Daily Dispatch,* June 6.

Wildavsky, Aaron. 1964. *The Politics of the Budgetary Process.* Boston: Little, Brown.

Wildavsky, Aaron. 1986. *Budgeting: A Comparative Theory of Budgetary Processes.* New Brunswick: Transaction Books.

Wilmington StarNews. 2008. Raleigh | Highlights of the $21.4 billion 2008–09 state spending plan given tentative Senate approval Wednesday. http://infoweb.newsbank.com/resources/doc/nb/news/131CAFBA8173D768?p=AWNB, June 19.

Wilson, James Q. 1974. *Political Organizations.* Princeton: Princeton University Press.

Wilson, James Q. 1989. *Bureaucracy: What Government Agencies Do and Why They Do It.* New York: Basic Books.

Wilson, Trish. 2002. Child care work still pays little. *The News & Observer,* Mar. 12, A1.

Wilson, Trish. 2003a. Auditor: Merge preschool programs. *The News & Observer,* Apr. 10, B1.

Wilson, Trish. 2003b. Easley's More at Four struggles to fill slots. *The News & Observer,* May 12, A1.

Wilson, Trish. 2003c. Hunt defends funding for Smart Start. *The News & Observer,* Apr. 4, B5.

Wise, Bob. 2002 (Jan. 10). *State of the State Address 2002.*

Wise, Bob. 2003 (Jan. 9). *State of the State Address 2003.*

Wise, Bob. 2004 (Jan. 14). *State of the State Address 2004.*

Wood, Simon N. 2011. Fast stable restricted maximum likelihood and marginal likelihood estimation of semiparametric generalized linear models. *Journal of the Royal Statistical Society: Series B (Statistical Methodology)*, 73(1), 3–36.

Woolverton, Paul. 2003. $800 million in cuts advocated. *The Fayetteville Observer*, Mar. 6.

Woolverton, Paul. 2009. Advocates: First priority is the poor. *The Fayetteville Observer*, Feb. 13.

Workman, Samuel. 2015. *The Dynamics of Bureaucracy in the US Government: How Congress and Federal Agencies Process Information and Solve Problems.* New York, NY: Cambridge University Press.

Wrenn, Deanna. 2003a. Financial woes don't stop salary bills – Kiss says pay raise measures aren't likely to pass. *Charleston Daily Mail (WV)*, Jan. 24, 7A.

Wrenn, Deanna. 2003b. Personnel budgets cut – Wise to leave task of cutting jobs with agency officials – BUDGET CRUNCH. *Charleston Daily Mail (WV)*, Jan. 6, 1A.

Wright, Gary. 2004. Carolinas face prison overflow. *The Charlotte Observer*, Feb. 16, 1A.

Wright, Gerald C., and Schaffner, Brian F. 2002. The influence of party: Evidence from the state legislatures. *American Political Science Review*, 96(2), 367–379.

Wu, Yonghong, and Williams, Dan. 2015. State legislative earmarks: Counterparts of congressional earmarks? *State and Local Government Review*, 47(2), 83–91.

Yackee, Susan Webb. 2006. Assessing inter-institutional attention to and influence on government regulations. *British Journal of Political Science*, 36(4), 723–744.

Yee, Chen May. 2009 (December 16). *New hospital debuts in Maple Grove; patients wanted – StarTribune.com.* www.startribune.com/new-hospital-debuts-in -maple-grove-patients-wanted/79275222/. (Accessed on 03/01/2020).

You, Hye Young. 2017. Ex post lobbying. *The Journal of Politics*, 79(4), 1162–1176.

Index

Printed in the United States
by Baker & Taylor Publisher Services